1974

GREENLAND

Jan Mayen

ICELAND

Lofoten Is.

Narvik

Wardhouse
(Vardö)

KOLA
PENINSULA

NORWAY

White
Sea

Archangel

Pechora R.

North West Passage

Trondheim

Rockall

Bergen

BALTIC SEA

NEWFOUNDLAND

DENMARK Copenhagen

Moscow (Muscovy)

Heligoland

Jutland

Lübeck

Louisburg

Halifax

Bremen

Hamburg

Dunkirk

Brest

Lorient

Quiberon Bay

La Rochelle

Ferrol

Oleron Is.

Constantinople

BLACK SEA

CASPIAN SEA

Cape Finisterre

Vigo

Corunna

Bordeaux

Azores

Lisbon

R. Tagus

Lagos

Cadiz

Cape St Vincent

Cape Trafalgar

Persian Gulf

Teneriffe

Canary Is.

Alexandria Suez Canal

Mecca

GUINEA

R. Niger

Gulf of Aden

Socotra

Equator

Zanzibar

BRASIL

Pernambuco

Camoro Is.

Bahia de Todos

BOLIVIA

St Helena

MADAGASCAR

Rio de Janeiro

R. Plate

Cape Corrientes

Cape Town

Cape of Good Hope

San Julian (Port Desire)

Magellan

Falkland Is.

ra del Fuego

ape Horn

see detailed map in text

Places mentioned in the text

SOVEREIGN OF THE SEAS: THE STORY OF BRITAIN AND THE SEA

BOOKS BY
DAVID HOWARTH

Sovereign of the Seas

THE STORY OF BRITAIN AND THE SEA

David Howarth

What was scattered in many volumes, and observed
at several times by eye-witnesses, with no cursory
pains I laid together, to save the reader a far longer
travail of wandering through so many desert authors.

> JOHN MILTON, preface of
> A Brief History of Muscovy,
> first published 1632

ATHENEUM

NEW YORK

1974

14.95+75+ox = $15.70.

CONTENTS

MAPS

DIAGRAMS

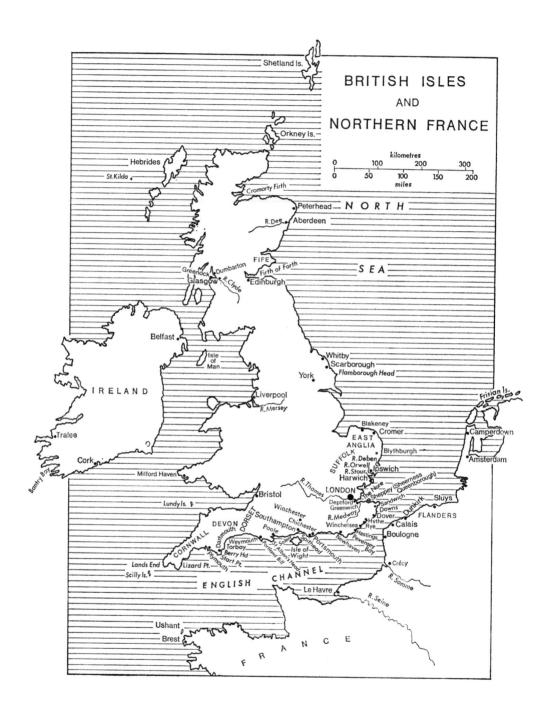

BRITISH ISLES
AND
NORTHERN FRANCE

kilometres
0   100   200   300
0   50   100   150   200
miles

Shetland Is.

Orkney Is.

Hebrides

St. Kilda

Cromarty Firth

NORTH

Peterhead

R. Dee   Aberdeen

FIFE

Greenock   Dumbarton   Firth of Forth
Glasgow   R. Clyde   Edinburgh

SEA

Belfast

Isle
of
Man

Whitby
Scarborough
Flamborough Head

York

IRELAND

Liverpool
R. Mersey

Tralee

Blakeney
Cromer

EAST
ANGLIA   Blythburgh

Camperdown

Frisian Is.

Amsterdam

SUFFOLK   R. Deben
R. Orwell   Ipswich
R. Stour
Harwich

Cork

Milford Haven

Bristol

R. Thames
LONDON   The Nore   Sheppey (Sheerness
Deptford   Queenborough)
Greenwich   Sandwich   Sluys
Downs
Winchester   R. Medway   Dover   Dunkirk   FLANDERS
Chichester   Winchelsea   Hythe
Rye   Calais
Hastings   Boulogne
Pevensey
Torbay   Newhaven   Bay
Berry Hd   Portland Bill   Isle of-
Lizard Pt.   Wight   Crécy

Lundy Is.

DEVON   DORSET   Southampton
Poole
CORNWALL   Dartmouth   Solent   Spithead
Weymouth   Alton's Head   Portsmouth
Start Pt.

Lands End

Scilly Is.

ENGLISH

CHANNEL

R. Somme

Le Havre

R. Seine

Ushant

Brest

FRANCE

ILLUSTRATIONS

Introduction

THIS book is about the growth of British skill and confidence at sea, from its obscure beginnings fifteen hundred years ago, up to its climax in the twentieth century when the British navy was twice as big as any other, and more than half the merchant shipping in the world was built and owned in Britain.

It is not only a naval history, because sovereignty of the sea is not only a matter of winning battles. In sea-power, merchant ships are just as important as fighting ships; and many other things are important too – shipbuilding, navigation, cartography and exploring, for example. So it is a big subject, and to fit it into a single book one has to be selective. I have tried to follow a trail of cause and effect, and to discover why the British became exceptionally good seamen, as they certainly did in the end. And in each stage of the story, I have chosen a few voyages to write about at length – the people who made them, and why and how they did it. Some of these voyages were successful, and some were disasters; some are well-known and some can only be found in ancient books. Anyone else might have made a different choice, but I hope nobody will quarrel very much with mine. I made it because each of these voyages seems to me to have carried the strength of Britain on the sea a little farther, so that it illustrates the theme. Even the disasters taught seamen what not to do.

The whole story divides itself into five parts, each with a character of its own, and perhaps it would be useful to sum them up. (1) The first king of England who claimed to be sovereign of the seas was King John: the phrase is as old as Magna Carta. But in those days it was not such a high ambition as it sounds. The seas he claimed were only what were called the Narrow Seas – the Straits of Dover and the neighbouring parts of the North Sea and the Channel. The claim was made again from time to time, but nobody acknowledged it, and in reality the British showed very little enterprise at sea in the Middle Ages, except in piracy. (2) Towards the end of the fifteenth century they began to awaken, and to search for trade routes of their own beyond the coasts of Europe, especially to the fabled country of Cathay; and in these searches, they tested their seamanship. (3) The fight against the Spaniards at San Juan de Ulloa in 1567 put a final end to their diffidence, and in Queen Elizabeth's time they found they could master the sea and anyone they met on it. (4) But after that great age, their mastery often faltered and always had to be fought for, against the rival powers of Holland, France or Spain, until the second half of the eighteenth century. (5) It was only then that the British won a dominance on the sea that everyone recognised. In the Napoleonic Wars, nobody ever doubted they would keep it. And in 1815 they found they possessed, in fact if not in name, the unchallenged sovereignty of all the seas of the world.

This world-wide dominance was not a privilege, or a burden, they had ever sought or even clearly imagined. The expansion of British trade was a constant process which began in the Middle Ages and never stopped. That was in the hands of city merchants. But the expansion of naval power was in the hands of kings and governments, and it was not a deliberate process at all. It was capricious and intermittent, and often a matter of chance. The British never tried to win naval supremacy at sea, except as a temporary means to other ends. Mainly they fought at sea to defend their own merchant ships, and either to prevent invasions of Britain, or to put armies ashore on foreign coasts to fight dynastic wars; and up to the nineteenth century, whenever they finished what they set out to do, they lost interest in the whole idea of naval power. After Queen Elizabeth's time, they were always proud of their seamanship, but they were never particularly proud of their navy until they had Nelson as a hero. Then suddenly, there was no foreign navy left to fight, and the only authority on the seas was Britain's. But even then, it was not because Britain had fought to gain that end, it was because Napoleon in his fall had dragged down with him all the possible rivals there might have been.

Luckily, when they found they possessed this unprecedented power, they did not lose interest again; they began to think of it as a trust, and they used it much more wisely than anyone might have expected. Their navy had won its battles so thoroughly, and it policed the seas so well, that there was no more war at sea for a century. In that peace, the British built up their Empire; but they also built up something else, of permanent and less argu-able use to all mankind – an unrivalled knowledge of the sea. They were always eager for discovery, not only in fighting and exploration but in surveying, navigation, astronomy, the sciences of the sea, and the design, construction and organisation of ships and their machinery and equipment; and they gave their discoveries with extraordinary freedom to other people. National pride is not an emotion that logic can justify, but perhaps the British may be allowed a touch of pride at this achievement; for nowadays, no ship of any nation goes to sea without some benefit of that age of British enterprise and ingenuity. Sea power has faded, and the power of Britain may be past; but still, the prime meridian runs through Greenwich.

*

To end this introduction, I want to add that writing a book like this would be far more difficult, almost impossible, without the London Library, and the kindness and efficiency of its staff. I also want to acknowledge my debt to the scholarship, past and present, of the Hakluyt Society, the Navy Records Society, and the Society for Nautical Research. And I am personally very grateful indeed for the erudition of Professor Christopher Lloyd, who has most kindly and patiently read my manuscript, corrected the worst of my faults, and given me many helpful ideas that were new to me – though I can hardly hope he agrees even now with every word I have written.

PART ONE

OBSCURITY

450–1418

In the Middle Ages,
the British are diffident at sea, and
are often invaded.
After the last invasion,
the kings and courts are more concerned
with chivalry than seafaring, but the
merchants begin to send their
ships abroad.

CHAPTER I

The Hermits of Ireland

ABOUT the end of the nineteenth century, when British imperial power was at its height, supremacy at sea was accepted as a right and a duty by the British people, as if they had always possessed it in the past and always would in the future:

> 'When Britain first, at heaven's command,
> Arose from out the azure main,
> This was the charter of the land,
> And guardian angels sung this strain:
> "Rule, Britannia, rule the waves;
> Britons never will be slaves." '

Perhaps nobody even then believed every word of their patriotic songs, but they sang them; and they certainly believed that in some special way the British had the sea in their blood. Hardly anyone foresaw that sea-power was not eternal, but might soon be subordinate to other kinds of martial power; and to judge by what they wrote, hardly anyone thought there had ever been a time when British seamen were not by nature better than any others.

But that was self-delusion. No race has the sea in its blood. On the contrary, any race will take to the sea if it has an incentive, which may be conquest, trade, defence, religion, greed, pure exploration, or the exploitation of the sea itself. Most of the other races of western Europe had times of supremacy at sea, in war or in trade or both, before the British started: Portugal, Spain, the Italian States of Genoa, Venice and Pisa; Germany in the Hanseatic League; Norway and Denmark, ancient Greece and Rome; and outside Europe, the Arabs and Phoenicians.

In fact, Britain was a late starter as a maritime power. The history of the British as a recognisable independent people goes back for 1500 years: an acceptable beginning is in the fifth century, at the end of the Roman occupation. But of those 1500 years there were 400 when the British had some power at sea, and 1100 years when they had none. For the first six of these centuries, from about 450 to 1066, Britain was always on the receiving end of seafaring expeditions, constantly being raided or invaded: first, after the Romans, by Anglo-Saxons, then by Vikings, and finally by Normans. The native Britons seem to have learned nothing from the Romans about the sea or ships – no more than the native American Indians learned from the English colonists. And each set of invaders, once established ashore, was slow to learn from the next. So, even after the Norman conquest, Britain remained poor-spirited on the sea, and may only have been saved from more invasions because, by that time, her neighbours across the North Sea and the Channel had lost the ability and the will to put to sea.

Yet all that time, seafaring knowledge must have been growing unrecorded among illiterate people, handed on from father to son in coastal villages. For in Elizabethan times, when all the arts of civilisation suddenly flowered, the British were ready in the humble art of seamanship; when the incentive came, they had the latent skill to carry them round the world and win a place on the sea in a single lifetime.

In history, therefore, the first eleven centuries can be seen as a preparation, a prelude to the centuries of power. They make a literary prelude too. After the coming of power, British sea history is full of adventurous voyages, well documented, and of extraordinary people, sea-captains, explorers, scientists, ship-builders, pirates, villains and heroes. Before that, in the period of the prelude, the records of voyages are sparse, and not many men were remembered for what they did at sea. But here and there, one finds an episode recorded in sudden contrasting clarity by an ancient chronicler. Trite though it may be, a sailor delving in that distant history thinks of the buoys and seamarks which loom up, distinct against an insubstantial background, when he is coasting in a misty dawn. And to take the simile as far as it will go, these episodes, like the seamarks, indicate what has been hidden by the mist.

*

The first episode of that kind was in Ireland, for the first authentic ocean voyages of the natives of the British Isles were made by Irish monks. Before the Vikings, these intrepid people certainly sailed to Iceland, probably to Greenland, and possibly to North America and the Caribbean.

The principal story of an Irish voyage is the *Navigation of St Brendan*.

It was written in Latin by an unknown scholar about the year 910: the oldest surviving manuscript of it is a copy made in the eleventh century which is in the British Museum. But the story was already an old tradition when it was written down, and the journey it told about was supposed to have happened nearly four centuries before.

St Brendan was a real person, a Benedictine Abbot who was born in Tralee about 484 and lived to be over ninety. In the year 539, according to the story, a visiting monk told him about an earthly paradise across the ocean, and he resolved to find it. He set sail from a creek in County Kerry with seventeen monks in a boat made of cowhide on a wooden frame, and it was seven years before he came home again.

The story is full of Celtic poetry and mythical adventures, some of which are also found in the myths of other races and in other Irish stories: there was a talking bird which gave him good advice, and a friendly whale which appeared each Easter and allowed the monks to celebrate on its back. But the strange thing about St Brendan's Navigation is that it seems to have a core of genuine exploration. The saint and his companions visited many islands, and the descriptions of all of them are convincing descriptions of real Atlantic islands.

The first was St Kilda, off the Hebrides. That was a likely start, because St Columba and his followers, in the same period, were founding the settlement of Iona and working up the coast of Scotland towards the Shetland Islands. Next was a pair of islands separated by a narrow sound, which are called in the story the Isle of Sheep and the Isle of Birds. These correspond very well with two of the islands in the Faeroe group. From them, after a voyage of several months, the travellers reached a verdant island which may be identified – though this time rather vaguely – with Madeira, where they found a settlement of Irish monks already established; and then an island with a spring of poisonous water, and a thick curdled sea not far beyond it – the mineral springs of the Azores, and the Sargasso Sea. Thence they sailed, rowed and drifted back to the Isle of Sheep.

Next year, St Brendan tried again to find the paradise, and sailed west for forty days from the Isle of Sheep; and he came to an island of stunted vegetation where there were whales, sea-cats and small dark fiends – possibly Greenland, with walruses and Eskimos. A long way south from there, he found a very flat island covered with flowers, and another, more mountainous, with trees which bore red fruit like grapes but as big as apples.

Hereabouts, the sea was so clear that the fish could be seen in flocks like sheep on the bottom. Such islands and seas could only have been among the Bahamas, or farther south in the Caribbean. Going north again, there was a huge column of crystal in the sea – an iceberg seen through the eyes of someone who had never heard of them. And there was an island covered with slag, where the sound could be heard of gigantic smiths working at their forges, and stinking fumes spread over the sea for miles. Still farther north, among mists and floating ice, they found an island with sheer black cliffs and a high mountain with smoke and flames coming out of the top. These were credible descriptions of the volcanoes of Iceland and Jan Mayen; and coming south again, they described the islet of Rockall, where they found a solitary hermit who told them St Patrick, on his deathbed, had instructed him to put to sea alone. Finally, at a third attempt, they reached the promised land, after sailing through a fog that surrounded it – the fog of the Newfoundland banks. It was a warm and fruitful country, and they walked inland for forty days without finding a farther sea, until they came to a river they could not cross. Unless the whole thing is totally untrue, this could only have been the mainland of North America.

This story has been held to prove that the Irish found North America, long before the Vikings or anyone else from Europe. But it cannot strictly be taken as history. There was much too long a gap between the voyage itself and the written record of it. It may be a collection of voyages, attributed by tradition to the saint.

What it does seem to prove is that an Irishman at the time when the story was written, early in the tenth century, knew of all the main Atlantic islands and the American continent, and very roughly of their relative positions. It is hard to believe the author invented them all and got them all right. He could have heard of some from classical sources, and others from the Vikings or from the long tradition of Ultima Thule, which went right back to the voyage of Pytheas the Greek three hundred years before Christ. But reading it, one has to believe that the author believed it: it seems a pious, earnest account of a Christian pilgrimage. Somebody must have seen these places and come back to tell about them. The question is, who?

The simplest answer remains the most likely: that the Irish, in the course of centuries, found them all. The Navigation does not make St Brendan the first or only explorer. On the contrary, he was told of the earthly paradise by another monk; and he found Irish monks already living in Madeira and the Faeroes, an Irish hermit on Rockall and another somewhat vaguer set of people, not specifically Irish, who sang hymns in the Bahamas, or somewhere in that direction.

And there is plenty of other evidence that the Irish went far afield. The remains of their groups of monastic cells, their churches and works of art, are found in Scotland, Orkney and Shetland. There are Celtic ruins and place-names in Faeroe, 450 miles from Ireland; and as for Iceland, 700 miles from home, there are positive reports that the strictest historians accept. In 825, fifty years before the Vikings came to Iceland, the Irish geographer named Dicuil completed his work *De Mensure Orbis Terrae*. Most of it was based on classical geography, but he also told about Irish monks who had been in Iceland thirty years before, and had come back with good descriptions of the midnight sun, and of the sea-ice farther north. And the Vikings themselves, in their Icelandic sagas, agreed that the Irish were established in the island before they came, but had disappeared. The *Landnamabok*, written in the twelfth century, has an evocative glimpse of a panic flight before the barbaric invasion: Irish books, bells and croziers were found abandoned when the first of the Vikings went ashore.

The sagas also tell of an Irish colony farther to the west. The Vikings did not know much about it; they simply took it for granted that it existed, and they called it either White Man's Land or Greater Ireland. About 1010, Thorfinn Karlsefni landed in Markland, which is supposed to be Newfoundland or southern Labrador; and there, his crew captured two of the people they called skraelings, who were usually Eskimos but might have been Indians. The skraelings told them of a land opposite their own, where there were strange people who wore white clothes, and carried poles before them with cloths attached, and shouted loudly. The Norsemen supposed without question that this was Greater Ireland, although it is most unlikely they had ever seen a procession of chanting monks with banners, or known that the Irish wore white habits. And there was a story of a man called Ari Marssen, who was driven to Ireland the Great by a gale. He could not escape, so he stayed and was baptised there; and his countrymen heard of his fate in Ireland itself – which, if one believes it at all, is proof that someone returned from the colony to the mother country.

From all the Celtic myth and the scraps of fact, one can faintly understand this early heroic era of seafaring from the British Isles; and St Brendan, however much or little he really did, can remain the archetype of the sailor monk.

None of it is impossible. People who could sail from Ireland to Iceland

and back, as the Irish undoubtedly did, could sail anywhere else in the Atlantic, given luck. It only needed a very strong incentive, strong enough to make them willing to put to sea with a very small chance of surviving. Their incentive was one that has seldom affected the British since those days: they felt compelled to be hermits.

The Irish lived in a primitive fashion, but there were scholars among them, well-read men who knew, among other things, that the earth was round. For centuries after the fall of the Roman Empire, they felt they were a remnant of Christian learning, hemmed in on the western edge of Europe by the advance of barbarians from the east. England, during those centuries, was overrun by the pagan Anglo-Saxons; its Celtic people were pressed into Cornwall and Wales. Ireland alone was free. For many generations, the Irish feared the barbarians would reach them too – as they did in the end, disastrously, when the Vikings landed in 832.

Looking out across the ocean from the rugged coast of western Ireland with that threat behind them, they had the strongest motive to take their faith beyond the heathens' reach – to build themselves a boat of skins and sail where God might guide them. And so they did, in small groups or some-times, perhaps, like the hermit of Rockall, alone. Three of them were blown ashore in Cornwall in 891 in a boat without any oars or sail, and the reason they gave for their plight was probably what any of them would have said. They had left home, they explained, 'because they wished for the love of God to be on pilgrimage, they cared not where.'

Nobody can have the slightest idea how many suffered this irresistible compulsion. A large proportion must surely have died at sea, accepting their fate as God's will; but some sailed farther and farther on, and at last saw another Atlantic shore; and sometimes, but very seldom, a few sailed home again, bringing the kind of stories the *Navigation of St Brendan* was founded on. Most were content if they found a place where they could end their lives in pious seclusion; and to judge by the ruins of their elementary huts, they preferred the smallest, most uncomfortable islands. But since most of them were celibate, their distant settlements lasted only a lifetime, and left only meagre remains.

Unluckily, the only lasting mark they made on maritime history was a very misleading myth. Although every island described in St Brendan's voyage had some resemblance to reality, a totally imaginary island named St Brendan's Isle was marked on globes and charts for well over a thousand years. At different times it was shown all over the Atlantic from the Canary

Islands to the West Indies, and from the equator to the latitude of Ireland. Columbus believed in it, and if the Bristol seamen of the 1480's had not wasted time in searching for it, they might have re-discovered America before him. Expeditions were still being sent to find it in the eighteenth century, thirteen hundred years after St Brendan set sail.

This island had really nothing to do with the saint or his chronicler. It was simply another version of the legends of Atlantis or Lyonesse. But when at last the island was proved to be mythical, people inclined to put the blame on the saint whose name it bore, and to give him a reputation he never deserved as a teller of tall stories.

CHAPTER 2

The Anglo-Saxons

In the lifetime of St Brendan, while the monks were fleeing from the west, the Anglo-Saxon migration had started to fall on the eastern coast of England, first fighting men to find or seize new land, then families to settle it. Throughout the fifth and sixth centuries, there must have been great activity at sea, from the coast of Kent northwards towards the Humber, and westwards along the Channel to Dorset. Whole tribes were brought across from Denmark and northern Germany. But of all their voyages, no sea story remains to compare with St Brendan's, only histories and heroic poems in which seafaring was an unimportant part. The Anglo-Saxons, however, did leave a relic of another kind: the first known seagoing British ship. This was the Sutton Hoo ship, which was buried, probably in the year 655, and found again in 1939. It was under a mound in the grounds of a house called Sutton Hoo, above the banks of the River Deben in Suffolk.

The pagan custom of burying kings in their ships was not maintained for very long in England, because the people who brought it from Scandinavia were converted to Christianity in a few generations. Only a few such ships have been found, and the ship at Sutton Hoo is much the biggest. To be precise, it was not a ship that was found, it was not much more than the imprint of a ship. The Anglo-Saxon and Viking ships which have been dug up intact in Scandinavia were preserved by clay or peaty soil, but the Sutton Hoo ship was buried in sand. Her timber had rotted away, leaving only a stain in the sand, and the rows of iron fastenings; but the sand itself showed her shape and structure. Before it disintegrated, the ship was measured and drawn, so that her lines are more exactly known than the lines of even the famous ships of the Tudor seamen.

She was clinker built, 85 feet long and 14 feet in beam, very shallow and double-ended, like all the early wooden ships of northern Europe. She had 9 planks a side; they were 15 inches broad amidships and fastened with iron clenches. She was steered by an oar on the starboard side. The stem and stern post were fastened by the same kind of scarph joint that is used in boat-building now. The frames had no iron fastenings, except at the top, and probably they were fixed to the planking by the method the Vikings used: lugs were left on the planks when they were adzed from the tree, and these were attached to the frames by thongs or supple tree-roots.

Amidships, a wooden roof had been built across the ship when she was buried, and underneath it was the most magnificent Anglo-Saxon treasure ever found in England. There were the insignia of a royal person, jewels and gold and silver ware of intricate design, a sword, a shield, helmet and coat of mail. And there was a purse with coins in it, which fixed the earliest possible date for the burial between 650 and 660. But there was no body, and no sign of a cremation: it was not a real burial, it was a very elaborate, costly symbolic burial, a cenotaph or memorial to a royal hero whose body was somewhere else.

The rulers of that part of England in the seventh century were a dynasty pleasantly called the Wuffings, after their first King Wuffa, who died about 577. In the 650's, three brothers, Wuffa's great-grandsons, were king in succession: two of them, named Anna and Aethelhere, died in battle within a year, Anna in 653 and Aethelhere in 654. It was probably one of these two who was given the splendid memorial, but nobody can be quite sure which.

At that time, conversion of the Wuffings to Christianity had begun, but was not complete. There was already a Bishop of East Anglia; and indeed, among the pagan grave-goods of Sutton Hoo were two silver spoons, in-scribed Paulos and Saulos, which seemed to be christening spoons. But there was still a pagan faction in the kingdom. Anna was mentioned in Bede's *Ecclesiastical History* as a good Christian, and he was given a Christian burial at Blythburgh, farther north in his kingdom. On the other hand, Aethel-here's Christianity was more dubious. He was killed in a battle far away in Northumbria – a battle fought across a flooded river in which many of the contestants were drowned. So for either brother, the elaborate burial with-out a body can be explained. It may have been a protest by the pagan faction against the Christian burial of Anna; or it may have been a memorial to Aethelhere, whose body perhaps was lost in the flood, and certainly was too far away to be carried home again. Whichever it was, the pagans among his people dragged his ship ashore for half a mile, and lowered it carefully into a hole in the sand, and then – in spite of what the Christians were saying – put his most precious possessions inside it and covered it all with a little hill of sand, to give him a worthy place to live in death.

One cannot be sure that this ship was built in England. She was not new when she was buried – she had been patched here and there with double rows of nails. But she cannot have been as old as the Wuffing migration, and since Wuffa is thought to have brought the whole of his tribe, he presumably brought his shipwrights. If her owner was a fourth generation Englishman, it seems fair enough to call her an English ship.

However, there was nothing peculiarly English in her design. It represented a stage in the evolution of shipbuilding in the Scandinavian and German homelands of the Anglo-Saxons. This evolution was quite independent of the long experience of Mediterranean seamen. In the Mediterranean, ships had been carvel built for centuries, but northern shipwrights until the fifteenth century had only mastered clinker building. Furthermore, they seem to have been building large ships for a very long time before they found a dependable way of joining their planks end to end; so they used enormous planks, hewn out of long straight trees, which ran in one piece the whole length of the ship. These primitive methods decided the kind of ships they built. Indeed, if a boatbuilder tried the same methods today, he would finish up – unless he tried hard to avoid it – with something like an early Anglo-Saxon ship: the shallow midship section, and the long curved overhanging stems.

In the course of time, scarphs for joining plank-ends were perfected – the Sutton Hoo ship had them – and later still, the shipwrights started to put together jointed planks with the sideways curve called an edge-set. Thereby, they were able to refine the ends of their ships, to make them more graceful and seaworthy, until they reached the final development of the Viking ships. But the well-known distinctive shape of all these northern ships was not fundamentally a matter of art or design, it grew from the limitations of clinker building with long straight planks. By a lucky chance, this primitive method can produce a ship that is fast and beautiful.

From a seaman's point of view, the strangest thing about the Sutton Hoo ship is that she had no place to step a mast. Instead of a keel, she had only a central plank laid horizontally, which could not have supported the thrust of a mast unless it was reinforced amidships; and there was no sign that it ever had been. So she cannot have been built to sail. She was simply a huge rowing boat. For rowing, she was well equipped, with tholes for nineteen pairs of oars. The oars were not buried with her, but in a ship with 14 feet of beam, there would have been plenty of room for two men on most of the oars; so she could have been rowed by a crew of anything from thirty-eight to sixty or seventy men.

Among the buried ships of Scandinavia, all until the seventh century have this same peculiarity: a horizontal keel-plank which could not have carried a mast. It is negative evidence, but it strongly suggests that the Anglo-Saxons in the migration period did not know how to sail – except perhaps in small boats and sheltered water. These people, among the principal ancestors of the nation, captured and settled a very large part of England, and did it all, so far as anyone can tell, in rowing boats. It is true they wrote about sailing here and there in their stories, and notably in the poem of Beowulf; but these were written in a later age when sailing had been re-discovered, and they seem to have given their ancient heroes a skill they did not possess. The Romans, of course, had sailed in northern seas, and so had the Phoenicians, the Irish and the people of the French Atlantic seaboard; but between the Roman and the Viking eras, it appears that the art was for-gotten in England.

It was a surprising lapse, but one can imagine reasons for it. The keel of a wooden sailing ship must be more or less T-shaped in cross section, and to hew it out of a log perhaps sixty feet long may have been beyond the skill of Anglo-Saxon shipwrights. Or perhaps, on the other hand, the Anglo-Saxon rulers simply did not want to sail. In the Baltic, or among the Danish sounds or Frisian islands, where distances were comparatively short, it may have been more practical for kings and chiefs to be rowed on their expeditions, rather than use the wind. Rowing may have acquired a social significance: to be rowed by a large and menial crew may have seemed – as it was in Tudor times – an enhancement of the dignity of a king. When at last they made the long voyage to England, the first of the migrants probably en-countered Roman sailing ships; but seamen all through history have been the most conservative of people, and certainly these adventurers went on using the kind of ships they knew.

At all events, whatever the reason, the Anglo-Saxons seem to have rowed to England. And that may be the explanation why they went no farther. For short sea crossings, to wait for calm weather and row might be the best way of reaching the other side; but it could never have been the best way of making an ocean voyage. Wuffa, for example, set forth from Jutland in Denmark, probably in a ship commanded by his father around the year 550. Rather than row straight across the North Sea, common sense would have sent them along the coast which now is Germany and Holland, putting ashore to shelter or rest; and then across to the coast of Kent, and past the estuary of the Thames, until they saw on the other side a stretch of sandy heathland rather like the home they had left in Denmark, which was sparsely inhabited by people they could easily defeat. Having laid claim to it, some of them would row the same way back to Denmark to bring their families and goods. Other similar parties, under other chiefs, went farther along the English coast in both directions before they found a place unoccupied. But rowing put a limit to the distance they wanted to go, and the west of England, Scotland and Ireland were spared from their invasion.

After a hundred years of occupation, when the ship was buried at Sutton Hoo, the kingdom of the Wuffings covered the whole of East Anglia. The remains of its settlements are mostly on the coasts and river banks, which suggests that the kings and their people travelled by water, rather than by the roads the Romans had left behind. Anna or Aethelhere, inspecting their domain, might have rowed from the River Deben up the coast, and inland by the Norfolk rivers; then farther by sea, along their northern shores, and up the Ouse and its tributaries to watch the defences of their western frontier. In the splendour of the royal regalia found at Sutton Hoo, rowed by their seventy oarsmen, appearing suddenly round the bends of the fenland rivers, they must have struck awe in the simple settlements. But their descendants were doomed to fight losing battles when the Norsemen, a few generations later, discovered how to hew a keel and step a mast on it.

*

The Vikings conquered because they could sail. Ashore, they had no new weapons, only a ferocity remarkable even in that ferocious age, and the stamina and discipline to march the whole way across Britain and back when their leaders gave the order. But through their mastery of sailing, they could always descend on the coast without warning wherever they wished; and the Anglo-Saxons could seldom assemble an army in time to stop their landings.

One cannot claim the Vikings' astonishing skill at sea as a part of British maritime history. Some of them settled in Britain, and all of them no doubt left half-bred offspring on their forays inland; and so they added their part to the mongrel origin of the British people. But most of them raided for profit in money or plunder, and when they had won what they could they went home again. Their seafaring prowess belonged to the countries they came from, Norway and Denmark. They maintained it in Iceland; but it faded away when they took up land and turned to farming in Britain, or in the other civilised countries they attacked. And the people of Britain, who suffered their depredations for over two hundred years, learned very little of their seamanship.

Their first recorded appearance in England shows the ubiquity of their landings: it was not in the north or east, but at Portland in the middle of the south coast, where three ships' companies came ashore about 790 and killed a local Anglo-Saxon official who had ridden down from Dorchester to ask them what they wanted. These, however, were Norwegian Vikings, a small fleet which had probably strayed up Channel from the west after sailing round Scotland and down the Irish Sea. Thirty years later, the first Danish Vikings landed in Sheppey, in the mouth of the Thames; and while the Norwegians founded colonies in the sparsely inhabited lands of the north and west – in Shetland, Orkney, the Hebrides, Scotland and ultimately Ireland – it was the Danes who landed, unpredictably, here and there all over the east and south of England, fought the Anglo-Saxons, and ravaged their settled communities until the people paid them to go away.

To intercept the raiders at sea was a matter of chance, but sometimes the Anglo-Saxons in their rowing boats achieved it, and the first sea-battles of British history were fought against the Danes. King Alfred, in 896, built ships for the purpose to his own design; and for this reason, some people have called him the father of the British navy. But this is a phrase, without much meaning, which is founded on very little. Alfred was a leader of genius and a scholar of distinction, the only Christian king who fairly fought the Vikings and drove them out of his kingdom; but his shipbuilding enterprise, so far as the records go, was not a great success. The story of it comes from the Anglo-Saxon Chronicle, the principal source of the history of that era; and freely translated, it reads as follows:

'This same year (896) the hosts of the Danes in East Anglia and Northumbria greatly harassed Wessex on the south coast with bands of raiders, using the warships they had built many years before. Then King Alfred ordered warships to be built to meet the Danish ships. They were almost twice as long as the others, some had sixty oars, some more; they were faster and steadier, and had more freeboard; they were not built after the Frisian or Danish designs, but in the way the King thought would be most effective. On one occasion the same year, six Danish ships came to the Isle of Wight and did much damage there, and in Devon and almost everywhere along the coast. Then the King ordered nine of the new ships to put to sea, and they blockaded the entrance (of a harbour) to stop the Danes coming out. The Danes sailed out with three of their ships; the other three were beached at the upper end of the harbour, and the crews had gone off inland. The English seized two of the three ships at the mouth of the estuary and slew their men, but the other one escaped; in her also all but five men were slain, and she escaped because the English ships ran aground. They were very awkwardly placed: three had gone aground on the side of the channel where the remaining Danish ships were beached, but all the others on the other side, so that they could not reach the Danes. But when the tide had ebbed many furlongs from the ships, the Danes came to the three ships stranded on their side, and there they fought. There were slain Lucumon, the King's reeve, and Wulfheard the Frisian, and Abbe the Frisian, and Aethelhere the Frisian, and Aethelfrith of the King's household, altogether sixty-two killed of English and Frisians, and a hundred and twenty Danes. But the tide came first to the Danish ships, before the Christians could push off their own, and so they rowed away to sea. They were so sorely crippled they could not row farther than Sussex, where the sea cast two of the ships ashore. The men were taken to the King at Winchester, and he had them hanged there.'

Poole Harbour seems the likeliest scene of this grim encounter, and Rome seems the likeliest source of King Alfred's inspiration. Oared galleys, armed with beaks or pointed prows to ram the enemy, were the classical fighting ships of Mediterranean navies; in battle, their sudden bursts of speed and quick manœuvres could overcome a ship that was under sail. King Alfred had been to Rome when he was a boy. Perhaps he had seen galleys there; and certainly, a man of his scholarship must have heard of them. The novel design of his sixty-oared ships, neither Danish nor Anglo-Saxon in origin, may well have been based on what he knew of galleys – altered, no doubt, to suit his shipwrights' skill, and clinker built instead of carvel. It is curious that his ships were partly manned by Frisians, who must have been imported mercenaries; it suggests that when he had built the ships, he had not enough Englishmen competent to put to sea in them. All in all, it was a bold experiment, which was not repeated for many hundred years, and never wholeheartedly. But if one must therefore regard King Alfred as the father of the British navy, one must also accept the embarrassing sequel: that in the first battle the British navy fought, it ran the whole of its fleet aground on a falling tide, the most ignominious error a seaman can make.

However, the Anglo-Saxon Chronicle has even earlier notes of battles at sea, among the numberless battles of that era which were fought on land. In 851, when Alfred was an infant, a minor king of Kent had a very successful fight at Sandwich. It is not quite clear whether he fought at sea or in the harbour: one manuscript of the Chronicle simply says that he 'destroyed a great host at Sandwich in Kent, captured nine ships and drove off the rest.' But another says he 'fought in ships,' as though this were a novelty. In 882, before he built his warships, King Alfred himself went to sea and defeated four Danish ships; and in 885, he sent a force in ships across the estuary of the Thames from the Medway towards East Anglia. In the mouth of the River Stour, where Harwich now stands, 'they met sixteen ships of pirates and fought against them, and captured all the ships and slew the crews. When they were on their way home with the booty, they met a great fleet of pirates, and fought against them the same day, and the Danes were victorious.' Perhaps that engagement, which was fought, as it happens, very close to Sutton Hoo, in waters well known to the Wuffings and to English seamen ever since, might justly be called the first fleet action of British history; and it seems to have ended suitably, with slaughter all round and honours on both sides.

It is hard to believe that by King Alfred's time, after a hundred years of defence against Vikings, the Anglo-Saxons had not learned to sail, if only because they had captured Viking ships. Yet there is still no positive reference to it in their chronicles, only in their epic stories of the past. Possibly some of them could do it, but seldom had the need or the opportunity. Sophisticated seamen rowed in battle and sailed on longer journeys; but the sea, to the Anglo-Saxons, had become a hostile place controlled by the enemy, and long journeys were better made by land. One has to go on for nearly another century to find the first historical hint of sailing by an Anglo-Saxon king. In the reign of the pious King Edgar, from 959 to 975, there was a lull in the Danish attacks; and a later medieval history says that his principal pastime was to make a royal progress every summer, sailing round the whole of his island kingdom, which was guarded by a navy of 4000 ships. Yet even in the history of King Edgar's time, the social significance of rowing and being rowed appears again. After his coronation, eight inferior British kings paid homage to him, and six of them rowed him in a boat on the River Dee in Cheshire while he held the steering oar. This may be a legendary story – it was not written down until Norman times – but whether it is strictly true or not, it clearly appealed to the English people as a symbol of submission: to be rowed was a mark of dignity; to be rowed by kings was the height of majesty.

The navy of 4000 ships should not be taken to mean that the King himself owned anything like that number. King Edgar, like King Alfred, probably owned a few ships and some of them may have been specially built for fighting; but in England all through the middle ages, the word navy had a different meaning. It did not mean only the King's ships, or only the fighting ships: it meant all the ships, of any kind, which belonged to loyal subjects and could be hired or mobilised by the King in times of crisis – the total seagoing resources of the realm. The most ancient maritime institution which still exists, at least in name, was created in Anglo-Saxon times, by King Edward the Confessor, to make sure that such a navy could be quickly mobilised. This was the Confederation of the Cinque Ports.

The original Cinque Ports were Hastings, Romney, Hythe, Dover and Sandwich. Winchelsea and Rye were added later, and other towns from Sussex to the Thames. Those towns undertook to provide the King with a fleet of ships for a specified period each year; in the later middle ages, the undertaking was for fifty-seven ships, free of charge for fifteen days a year, and at a fixed rate of charter for longer service. In return they were given exemption from tax, and many legal privileges. The original list of rights has the charm of a language which seems to be comprehensible but, for the most part, is not: it included the rights of sac and soc, of tol and team, of blodwit and fledwit, of pillory and tumbrel, infangentheof and outfangentheof, of mundbryce, waives and strays, and flotsam, jetsam and ligan. What it amounted to was a right within wide limits to make their own laws in their own parliament and administer them in their own courts. The towns played a central part in English maritime history until the fifteenth century, mainly in providing armed transport for the Kings' armies to cross the Channel. All their ports began to silt up before Tudor times, and the only one of the Cinque Ports which still has a harbour is Dover; their rights and their obligations vanished long ago; but the Lord Warden of the Cinque Ports still appears, as a picturesque if slightly preposterous figure, on state occasions. Among the recent Lords Warden were the Duke of Wellington, Lord Curzon and Sir Winston Churchill.

The Cinque Ports, on the narrowest part of the Channel reached their highest importance when the later medieval kings were fighting their interminable wars with France. By that time, the English were just beginning to think of the sea as a moat, a part of the island's defences which they could master; and so they have thought of it ever since. But when the Cinque Ports were founded, in the final years of the Anglo-Saxon period, the sea still had the opposite significance. Since the beginning of English history, enemies had come across it; and nobody who lived in England, not even the invaders who settled there, had ever tried to take the offensive, and put to sea, and win a lasting command of it for themselves. Their ideas of dominion stopped on the shores of Britain. The sea seemed not a protection but a threat – a road their enemies could travel but they could not. Far from being a maritime power in any sense, the English appear until then to have felt inferior on the sea, to have been afraid of it, or of the people they might meet on it. So once again, when the last invasion came, they could not stop its landing.

CHAPTER 3

Chivalry and Crusaders

THE Norman fleet left the mouth of the Somme at nightfall on 27th September, 1066, and began a new era in England. But as a fleet, it belonged to the past, not the future. The Normans had been landsmen ever since their Norwegian Viking ancestors came to the north of France. Like the Danes in England, they had turned away from the sea, and used their martial energy in rivalries ashore. When the Duke of Normandy, William the Conqueror, ordered ships to be assembled to take his army to England, the shipwrights and shipowners responded with a Viking fleet – not a fleet of the formidable Viking warships, but their transports. The ships in the Bayeux Tapestry are purely Norse in appearance: the square sails, the low freeboard, the steering oars, the upswept stems and stern-posts decorated with fearsome animals' heads – in shipbuilding nothing had changed, so far as the tapestry shows, in the past two hundred years. Some of the ships have ports for twelve pairs of oars, but none of them are being rowed; for the fleet in 1066 had waited six weeks for a southerly wind, and it crossed under sail.

During the night of the voyage the Duke set the course, with a lantern at his masthead that the fleet could follow. But his other ships were heavily laden, and he outsailed them. At dawn he was alone in the open sea.

Perhaps in that dawn he felt a little apprehensive, for the English also had a fleet in being at the time. Not much is known about it, but it was the same kind of fleet as his – ships of the Viking type, manned by seamen without the Viking flair. All summer, in face of the Norman threat, it had lain off the Isle of Wight, commanded in person by King Harold. But a fortnight before, the whole of it had sailed along the English coast and up the Thames to London. Historians of the invasion did not explain why this was done; but in 1940, at exactly the same time of year, the British relaxed their watch against Hitler's fleet because they thought the invasion season was over and nobody would try it in the winter. In 1940 they were right, but not in 1066. The Duke was left to wait unseen until his fleet came up with him, and then to land unopposed in Pevensey Bay.

In seafaring, the era begun by that landing lasted 350 years. On land in that period, Britain totally changed, in forms of government, social life, art, learning and language; it was a time of turbulent energy. But at sea, in contrast, the British were lethargic; there was nothing more than a slow evolution of ships, not always for the better – no great enterprise, few distant voyages. On land, the British fought battles which changed the direction of history: Hastings itself, Bannockburn, Crecy, Poitiers, Agincourt, were all within those centuries. But no important battle was fought at sea. In history, such an odd discrepancy demands a cause, and a portent of it can be seen in the ships of the Bayeux Tapestry: the horses which are depicted, peering incongruously over the gunwales of the transports. For the Normans brought mounted knights and the concept of chivalry, which before had scarcely penetrated England; and chivalry, one may fairly guess, was destructive of enterprise at sea.

Chivalry in those centuries after the Conquest pervaded the upper class of feudal society, not only in England but in France and Germany. Every court and castle was a school of it. It was a method of war, a basis of sport, and a system of morality; it influenced every part of the life of an aristocrat. And beneath all its ceremonial and religious trappings, it was essentially a matter of horsemanship. Knights were cavalry soldiers. But horsemanship and seamanship have always been incompatible: there is nothing more incongruous than a horseman in a boat, except perhaps a sailor on a horse. The upper classes of the age of chivalry, imbued from their childhood with this powerful mystique, had no reason to take an interest in ships. On the contrary, ships were alien to the things they valued most. They took ship with their horses and retainers when they could not avoid it, to reach a battlefield across the sea; but on board, they were unhorsed, undignified, and unable to fight in their monstrous suits of armour or use the skill they had practised. With distaste or even hostility among the ruling class, seafaring languished and became a menial trade.

Some naval historians have been surprised that galleys were seldom built in northern Europe; for the galley was an effective fighting ship. Frances Drake gave a blow to its reputation in his attack on Cadiz in 1586, but it was still in use in the Mediterranean in the eighteenth century. Some people have suggested that galleys could not stand the rougher northern seas, or that there was not a ready supply of slaves or serfs to row them. But it seems a likelier reason that nobody in the horse-minded aristocracy wanted to fight at sea, or cared about the technique of it: they only wanted to get ashore and fight as gentlemen should, on horseback. They could not have neglected it if there had been any hostile sea-power within reach, but there was not. The whole of civilised northern Europe, when the Viking age had faded, was similarly steeped in chivalry.

Thus British ships, after the Norman Conquest, began to evolve not for fighting, but humbly for trade. It was the merchants of England, not the crown or the nobles, who became the principal owners of ships – men with no standing in the feudal hierarchy, and none of the romantic ambitions of chivalry. And it is from this time that one can trace the evolution of sea-borne trade, which continued to grow ever after, quite independently of the whims of kings.

The merchants built ships to suit their own purposes, which mainly were fishing, the export of wool and the import of wine. In the course of time, they grew rich and formed a separate, powerful class. But the evolution of their ships was extremely slow. For at least two more centuries, ships remained Viking or Anglo-Saxon in style, and for even longer than that, they remained clinker-built. But for carrying cargo, the fine Viking lines began to vanish and the ships grew more broad in the beam. The length of the Sutton Hoo ship had been six times its breadth, and the Viking long-ships may have had a higher ratio still; but twelfth-century ships could be half as wide as they were long. They must have been slow and unhandy, and they are known with good reason as roundships. But life was unhurried, beyond the affairs of court, and ships could afford to wait for tide and wind.

All the kings after the Norman conquest are believed to have had some ships of their own, but none of them had nearly enough to match the size of their armies. When they needed to take their armies overseas, they chartered merchants' ships, first calling on the Cinque Ports and then on other coastal towns. Ships which joined the king's service were taken first to the Tower of London, or in later years to certain other ports. The words 'de la Toure', 'of the Tower', were added to their ordinary names, much as 'HMS' would be put before the name of a modern merchant ship in naval service. The King's carpenters built wooden castles on the ships to suit the army's wishes – forecastles and aftercastles; and finally the knights, their horses, retainers and equipment came aboard, and the bowmen and humbler ranks of a medieval army. The merchant crews continued to sail the ships, but under the orders of knights. That social distinction still has a relic today. The names of non-commissioned ranks, seaman, boatswain, coxswain, master, are Anglo-Saxon, the language of the people; but the officers', lieutenant, captain, admiral, are French, the language of the court.

A soldier's needs are often a sailor's nightmare, and in medieval pictures of ships, which mostly are on the seals of coastal towns, the castles perched on the bow and stern look absurdly unseamanlike. The crews, one may imagine, watched them built with the mocking despair which sailors still like to show when they have to take soldiers to sea. They have little battlements and Gothic windows, and even sometimes what seems to be brickwork painted on; they are like toy castles, as if they were built to make the knights feel rather more at home in awkward surroundings. They must have been lightly built, or the ships would have rolled over, and so they cannot have given much real protection against an enemy. No doubt, if enemy ships were encountered – which seldom happened – the castles, like real castles, gave the advantage of height in throwing missiles. But also, the windage of them must have made unhandy ships still worse – impossible to sail unless the wind was almost dead astern.

At first, the castles were only put on for the King's service, and taken off again when the service was ended. But merchant owners probably found them useful against the pirates who infested the North Sea and the Channel in the later middle ages: whatever their practical use, they would give the impression that soldiers were aboard. So in the course of time, they became a permanent part of every seagoing ship. The aftercastle developed another use, in providing a cabin for the master or for the merchant–owner himself, and a shelter for the helmsman; and so it lasted, renamed a poop, almost up to the age of steam. (Indeed, by the same tradition, naval officers' quarters were still in the stern until very recent times, although that position, over the propellers, had been for a century past the most uncomfortable part of the ship.) The forecastle must have been the more unseaworthy of the two It obscured the helmsman's view, and when ships were trying to sail to windward it blew their heads off the wind. It finally disappeared when John Hawkins, a practical seaman, became responsible for Queen Elizabeth's ships; but oddly enough, its name is still in use.

*

Almost always, the ships which were mobilised by the medieval kings were used to carry armies to France or Flanders. But by far the most ambitious British voyages of the middle ages were made in the ultimate cause of chivalry, the Crusades. Throughout the twelfth century, English pilgrims attempted the journey to the Holy Land, some going on foot or on horseback through Europe, and some in fleets of ships. Their enterprises stand alone, for no British fleet had ventured so far before, or did so again for another three hundred years. And yet, by coincidence, these pioneering voyages remind one of the backwardness of British seamanship. Their destinations were the ports of Acre or Tyre; and it was from Tyre that Phoenicians had constantly come with trading ships to England, sailing the same long route, a thousand years before.

The first of these fleets is recorded in the history of Jerusalem, but not of England. In 1107, it is said, only forty years after the Conquest, seven thousand Englishmen, with some Danes and Flemings, sailed into the harbour of Joppa. Their spokesmen told the King of Jerusalem they had sailed, by the help of God, through mighty and large seas from the far country of England to worship in the holy city. The King allowed them to go there, and in gratitude they joined his army and fought for him before they went home again. But who they were, or what part of England they came from, is unknown.

Another large party left England in 1147. This time, they had Flemings and Frisians with them, and perhaps on both occasions the foreigners had been enrolled as expert seamen. This fleet put in to Lisbon, and the men took service with the King of Portugal against the Moors. There, they found plenty of infidels to slaughter, and it is not clear from any account of their journey how many went on to the Holy Land, or how many felt they had done enough and so came home again.

But when King Richard Cœur de Lion set forth for his crusade, two purely English fleets put to sea, and some of the ships undoubtedly reached the Holy Land. In August 1189, a fleet left London on its own initiative, and in the spring of the following year the King dispatched his own fleet with orders to meet him at Messina in Sicily. To his crews, he gave the earliest British naval laws that have been preserved. They were simple, short and ruthless. For murder on shipboard, the offender was to be tied to the corpse and thrown into the sea; for murder on land, to be tied to the corpse and buried; for threatening with a knife, to lose his hand; for striking any person without the effusion of blood, to be plunged three times in the sea; and for reviling or cursing anyone, to pay an ounce of silver for each offence. Thieves or felons lawfully convicted were to have their heads shorn and boiling pitch and feathers poured on them.

The King himself, with his nobles, knights and squires, and his army, rode overland through Europe while the fleet sailed round the coast of

Spain and through the Strait of Gibraltar. Somewhere in Spanish waters, the ships were scattered by a storm; but the sailors prayed, and Thomas Becket, whose murder and canonisation were very recent memories, appeared to them in visions on three occasions and told them not to fear. Some crews put in to Lisbon and travelled by land to join the army at Marseilles. But others pressed on and reached Messina in safety before the King.

Probably not a single man in the fleet had been so far away from home before, and there is evidence that they behaved with the insular truculence that fleets are apt to show in foreign ports. The chronicler Geoffrey de Vinsauf, who went with the King, wrote that the men of Messina 'were excited by jealousy on account of their wives, to whom some of our men had talked, more for the purpose of irritating their husbands than with the intention of seducing them . . . These wicked people, hostile to our men, annoyed them by repeated insults, by pointing their fingers into their eyes, and calling them stinking dogs, and mocking them in many other ways, privately killing some of them, and throwing others into the sewers.' Ill-feeling grew until at last, on King Richard's orders, the English sacked the city and slaughtered or raped its more distinguished citizens; for the Crusaders were neither gentle nor holy men by any standards other than those of their time.

Perhaps the English sailors were made more churlish by feeling inferior. They had fitted out their ships as well as they could: one carried three spare steering oars, thirteen anchors, thirty oars, two sails, three sets of ropes of all kinds, and a duplicate set of everything else except the mast and the ship's boat. But when they saw Mediterranean ships, they must have felt their own were small, old-fashioned and outlandish. These voyages were made before even castles had been added to the simple northern ships, and they still had nothing but a single mast and a square sail. Now, for the first time, they saw ships far bigger than anything in the north, carvel built, with two or three masts, lateen sails, straight stems and more complicated rigging. When the King saw them, he must have understood that his fleet would be helpless if it met a Mediterranean enemy; and he bought or chartered a fleet of Mediterranean ships to supplement his own. He manned them with English crews. So Englishmen, for the final part of the voyage, were rowing in fighting galleys and sailing unfamiliar ships called busses and dromons. These names, like most of the names of early ships, were used for different kinds of ships at different times; but on this occasion a buss was described as a merchant ship much bigger than those that had made the voyage from

39

England, and a dromon as a ship that was heavy, slow and safe. The King chose a dromon to carry his sister Joanna and Princess Berengaria, daughter of the King of Navarre, whom he married when they all reached Cyprus.

The King and his army and navy wintered in Sicily, and in April 1191 the whole mixed fleet of English and foreign ships set sail again, now carrying the King and the knights, and their horses and equipment. In the company, there were 24 busses, 39 galleys and 156 ships of other kinds, including some if not all of those that had come from England. They sailed in columns, each ship within hailing distance of the next, and each column within the sound of a trumpet. The King, still showing the ancient preference for being rowed, brought up the rear with the galleys, and in his own galley he hoisted a lantern by night.

For the first two days and nights they had favourable breezes, or calms in which the fleet was obliged to anchor; but on Good Friday a storm blew up from the south and threw them into confusion. It only lasted a day, but it must have been a new and unpleasant experience for the knights and soldiery. Geoffrey de Vinsauf wrote a landsman's description of it: the boiling sea, the furious roar of the waves, the creaking of the ships and the terror of the passengers – some were so seasick that they were almost insensible of the danger. The ships, he said, were unmanageable; no helmsman could steer a course. Again the fleet was scattered. But that evening the wind abated and the ships assembled again round the King's lantern. Five days later, they sighted the island of Crete, and put in there to rest; but twenty-five of the ships were found to be missing. Another storm drove the King and some of the ships as far as Rhodes, and cast others ashore on the coast of Cyprus. Some weeks were spent in subduing the Emperor of Cyprus; but at last, towards the end of May, the shore of the Holy Land was sighted – and off shore, an immense ship which had three tall masts and towering sides, decorated with streaks of red and yellow.

The King sent a galley to ask who commanded this monstrous vessel. Its crew replied that it was a ship of the King of France. The King, in his own galley, hastened towards it, for the King of France was his ally in the Crusade. But seeing it close at hand, he began to be doubtful: it did not look like a French ship, and it flew no Christian standard. A second galley was sent to ask again, and this time the crew said they were Genoese, and bound for Tyre. Suspicion grew, and one of the King's galleymen insisted the ship was a Saracen. As a test, the King sent a galley to row past it without giving any salute, and at that the crew abandoned their pretences and began to throw

Modern curraghs in Co. Kerry:
not much changed since the time of St. Brendan

Ships of the Viking type in the Bayeux Tapestry:
horses peer above the gunwales

Ships of the time of Agincourt carved
on the end of pews from the church of
St. Nicholas, Kings Lynn

The last page of a 15th century book
of sailing directions for the coast of England

darts and shoot arrows at the galley. So began one of the strangest of battles fought at sea.

The English had rowed their galleys all the way from Sicily, but most of them, it seems, had not been told how a galley was meant to fight. Their only thought was to grapple and board the enemy, for that was the only way sea battles had ever been fought in northern waters. They rowed round and round the ship, but could not find any way to get aboard: its sides were too high and too solid, and they were defended by warriors who kept throwing darts at the galleys from their superior height. Annoyed by the darts, the English began to lose heart. But the King cried shame on them, called them cowards and threatened severest punishment. His anger was well-known, and under its spur some sailors jumped into the sea, swam under the ship and bound its rudder with ropes to stop it sailing. Others climbed up its cables. A series of bloodthirsty battles was fought on the bulwarks and deck. Heads, arms and hands were chopped off the boarders as they came, and the survivors were beaten back into the sea.

Again and again, they rowed round the ship, trying to find a solution to the problem. But it was not until scores of men had been killed in attempting to board that anyone thought of ramming. The galleys had iron-tipped beaks, which were their principal, indeed their only weapon; they were built, and had been built since earliest classical times, for no other purpose than to ram their enemies. At last, the King thought of this, or somebody pointed it out to him. He gave the order; the galleys drew back, turned, and rowed full speed at the ship, the beaks pierced through its planking and it instantly started to sink. They may have wondered why nobody had thought of it before, but any regret they felt was forgotten in victory; for it was indeed a Saracen ship, on its way to relieve the siege of Acre. It was said to have been manned, among others, by seven admirals, and to have had on board a hundred camel-loads of slings, bows, darts and arrows, a large quantity of Greek fire in bottles, which was a kind of self-igniting oil, and two hundred most deadly serpents for the destruction of the Christians. With this achievement to his credit, King Richard joined the King of France outside the walls of the beleaguered city, and began a year of ferocious fighting ashore.

*

English people continued for many years to go crusading, or at least to say they were going. Twenty years after King Richard's expedition, it was said that sixty thousand Englishmen, besides old men and women, had 'taken the Cross', which meant they had put their names on a register of pilgrims. 'On Mid-Somer night,' the historian Matthew Paris wrote, 'the Lord appeared in the Firmament, in crucified forme and bloudy, to show how acceptable this devotion was to him. This was seene neare Uxbridge, by a Fishmonger.'

CHAPTER 4

Ships, Laws and Navigation

ONE might have thought that experience of Mediterranean ships would have had some permanent influence on ship design and seamanship in Britain, but it did not – except that perhaps it was this that gave the knights the idea of building castles. King Richard's seamen remained uninfluential people. Nobody recorded what happened to them in the end – whether they brought their ships home again, or whether they ever saw home again at all. And influential people remained preoccupied with horses.

There have always been men who like the sea and ships, and men who hate them, and in that era the progress of shipping depended to some degree on whether the king was a man who liked the sea; for the king, at the very top of the feudal structure, was the only aristocrat who was likely to detach himself from the bonds and hopes of chivalry. And in so far as a love of the sea depends very much on whether one is seasick, progress may have depended on the trivial chance of whether the king was sick. Kings cannot appear ridiculous, and even then, seasickness was thought to be very funny by people who were immune to it; one of the earliest British sea-ballads has a comic description of the suffering of pilgrims who could only eat salted toast although they had paid for their dinner. Richard is said to have been seasick, and he remained a soldier and only took ship when he had to. King John, who succeeded him in 1199, was probably not, for he had a positive interest in ships: he possessed a good many himself, and it was he who hopefully proclaimed himself the Sovereign of the Seas. But on his death the ships were sold, and under Henry III, who reigned for over half a century, aristocratic interest lapsed again.

With only this capricious encouragement, the merchant owners continued to persevere; but they were still slow with innovations. It was a hundred years from King Richard's crusade before they began to build a radically different kind of ship. This was the cog. It was not a native invention, nor was it a Mediterranean type; it was copied from the ships of the

43

German ports of the Hanseatic League, which dominated the sea-borne trade of northern Europe.

Cog was another name which had sometimes been used for different kinds of ships, but at this time, about the year 1300, it meant a ship with a straight stem and sternpost, slightly raked, instead of the old Scandinavian curves. This cog was a stocky, sturdy ship with none of the ancient elegance of line. It still had only a single mast and a square sail, but its hull was deeper, and even in the rough contemporary drawings it looks as if it would sail better on a beam wind. It also brought about a revolution in steering – the rudder. Probably some builders before this time had tried to hang a rudder on the old curved sternpost: there is a well-known picture of one, dated about 1180, on the font in Winchester Cathedral, although it is thought not to be English. But the straight sternpost of the cog made it very much easier and the steering oar went quickly out of use, leaving only its name for the starboard side of the ship, the side it had always been hung on.

With improvements in sailing and steering, the cog was the first northern ship designed entirely for sail. It had no provision for oars. So it could be built with more freeboard, and decked overall; and the higher deck, with the greater depth of hull, gave it much more capacity for cargo. Very slowly, from one generation to another, people ventured to build their cogs a little larger. But they were still clinker-built, and that put a limit to their size.*

Through the thirteenth and fourteenth centuries, ships such as these continued to creep round the coasts of Britain and northern Europe. Their

---

* Perhaps this important point needs a full explanation. Clinker-built ships have overlapping planks, and the planks are fastened to each other by through nails, riveted over small discs called roves on the inside. The strength of this joint depends on the resistance of the planks to splitting along their grain; they tend to split along the lines of nails. The frames of this kind of ship either have to be shaped to the irregular inner surface of the planking, or else only touch each plank at one point. The latter leaves a gap which can never be painted or tarred, and it does not support the planking properly. But by the former method, the ship has first to be planked over some kind of mould, and the frames then fitted to the planking, which is a long, painstaking and expensive job.

In a carvel built ship, the planks are laid edge-to-edge; they are not fastened to each other, but only to the frames. There is no tendency to split; once they are put in the water and swell, they are always in compression. The frames are made and set up first, and the planking is fitted straight on to them and caulked. But on the other hand, you cannot caulk a very thin plank, and therefore carvel building is seldom attempted for very small boats. Clinker building is the thing for small boats, carvel building for large ones.

It is hard to say how large a clinker-built ship could be, but the larger it is, the more its relative cost, and the more its inherent weakness, its tendency to split its planks. Northern Europeans in the Middle Ages, not having mastered carvel building, were straining to make clinker-built ships as large as they could, and larger than can either have been safe or economical.

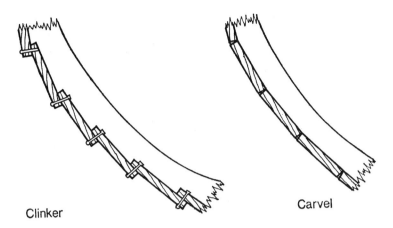

Clinker Carvel

longest regular voyages were down through the Bay of Biscay to Bordeaux.
The trade in the wine of Bordeaux, which was carried in British ships from
a very early time, brought two innovations to northern waters. One was
the system of measuring ships by tonnage, to the confusion of landsmen and
a good many seamen ever since. The original tun, of course, had nothing to
do with a ton in weight: it was a wine barrel, and a ship's tunnage was simply
the number of barrels she could carry. And the other innovation was the
code of sea laws called the Judgments of Oléron.

Oléron is an island north of the mouth of the Gironde. It provided a
landfall and a shelter for the wine ships, and its name had been given to
twenty-four very ancient judgments of maritime problems. The origin of
these judgments is lost in antiquity; they resemble an even older set of laws
propounded in Rhodes. Tradition is that Richard Cœur de Lion heard of
them during his crusade, and introduced them in England; so they became
the first basis of British maritime law. More rules and ordinances were
added to them as time went on, and they were all put together during the
fourteenth century in a bound volume called the Black Book of the Admiralty The Black Book was kept in the Admiralty Court, and for several
centuries it was the principal guide to behaviour at sea. It was lost in about
1820, but found again fifty years later at the bottom of a chest in which the
Registrar of the Court, who had recently died, had kept his private papers.

The original twenty-four laws showed a rough kind of equity and a
shrewd understanding of human weakness: they were much wiser than the
crude list of crimes and merciless punishments Richard had given his fleet
before it sailed. They concerned the relations between the owners, masters

45

and crews of ships, and the merchants who owned their cargoes. The master, for example, was protected against excessive claims by merchants if he had to jettison cargo in a storm, or cut away his mast to save his ship, or if he was wrecked – provided he and his crew had done all they could to save the cargo. He had to look after his crew if they were ill, but not if they were hurt in drunken brawls. The crew was not allowed ashore until the ship was safely anchored with two or three cables. When the master ran short of money in a foreign port, he ought not to sell the ship, but he could sell some of her gear if the crew agreed. And the master was obliged to consult the crew about the weather before he sailed: if he sailed in spite of a majority opinion and the ship was wrecked, he had to pay for it, if he could afford it. In sixteenth-century English, this curious clause ran as follows: 'The mayster ought take councell with his felowes and saye, Mates howe lyke ye this wether? Some will saye, it is not good, lete it over passe. Other will saye, the wether is good and fayre. The mayster ought to agre to the most, or els if the shyp perysh he is bound to restore the value as it is praysed, yf he have wherewith. This is the judgement.'

The later laws which were added in the fourteenth century were similar common-sense provisions; but conspicuous among them is one example of medieval justice. If a pilot undertook to take a ship into port and through his fault the ship was lost, the crew, if they pleased, might take him to the windlass and cut off his head, without being bound to answer before any judge.

When printing began, these simple laws, already ancient, were included in many books about seafaring matters. Before that, no doubt, a score of generations of good professional seamen had known them by heart, for they were the only guide to their rights and duties.

*

Guides to navigation were also simple: masters found their way by landmarks, memory, the compass and the lead. The lead was the oldest of navigational aids – it is mentioned in the voyages of St Paul – and the compass had come into use in Europe in the twelfth century. Possibly some of King Richard's ships had a compass on board, for an English philosopher named Alexander Neckham wrote about it less than a generation later. But by his description, it was only used in his time as a last resort in foggy weather. Ships carried a lodestone, a piece of magnetic iron ore. When fog came down, or a night was overcast and the Pole Star could not be seen, the master rubbed a needle with the stone, then stuck the needle in a cork or a straw and floated it in a bowl of water. Pivoted needles were invented some time in the fourteenth century, and the needles had been mounted on cards by the time of Chaucer, who mentioned them obliquely in a treatise of 1391.

But the compass, like every other nautical invention, was slow to find favour from practical seamen, who have always preferred to do things the way their fathers did them. In 1258, Roger Bacon in Oxford showed a compass to Brunetto Latini, who was the tutor of Dante but had not heard of compasses before; he judged it would one day be very useful to seamen, but that no master at that time would dare to use it for fear of being thought a magician, under the influence of an infernal spirit. But meanwhile, the magnetism of the lodestone was held to be useful for other purposes: among them, to cure the gout, and to influence wives to confess their adulteries.

No doubt a good many masters, in their old age, wrote down what they had learned about the coast and handed it on to their sons or apprentices. Such sailing directions had existed for the Mediterranean coasts since the time of the ancient Greeks. In England, they were known for several hundred years as Rutters, from the French word routier. Before printing, documents which were used at sea were unlikely to survive: the few copies would be worn out with use, or soaked with salt water, or lost in some kind of disaster. But one English Rutter was copied by a professional scribe between 1461 and 1481, and happened to be bound with some tracts on chivalry which belonged to the library of a knight. So it was preserved, and is now in the British Museum. A second copy of it, which was illustrated, has disappeared within the last seventy years; but it was photographed before it was lost.

This unique little treatise, full of erratic spelling and punctuation, has more of a flavour of medieval seamanship than any modern writing. There are only five pages of it, but it covers the coasts of England, Wales and Ireland, gives courses for crossing the Channel, and extends down the Bay of Biscay to Spain and Portugal. It has an air of having been written or dictated by one man: on some parts of the coast there are soundings, and notes on the nature of the sea bottom, but on other parts there are none. It gives compass courses from point to point, the direction of tidal streams, and occasional warnings of dangers, but it gives no distances. Reading it now, one is impressed not by the usefulness of the information, but by its sparse-ness; this, one reflects, is all a master had to guide him, even in the later middle ages. Seamen in earlier times, of course, had managed their pilotage without any guide at all, and so did the explorers of later generations. But this work reminds one that a medieval master, even if he only coasted round the shores of England, was venturing into seas that were more mysterious, hiding more unsuspected dangers, than any in the whole of the world today. Here, for example, in more modern English and in the original, is the whole of its directions – omitting some of the cross-Channel courses – for the 200 miles of coast from the Isle of Wight to Lands End: its successor, the modern Admiralty Pilot, describes the same stretch of coast in 160 pages.

'From St Helens to Chichester is half tide, and a south moon maketh high water within Wight. The Needles and the Four Rock (Brittany) lie SW and by W, NE and by E, the Needles and Cornwall E and W. At the Needles it floweth SE and by S. From the Needles to Portland the course is WSW and ENE. At Poole in the harbour it floweth NW and SE, and in the fairway SSE and NNW, at Weymouth within the harbour E and W, at Portland Bill SSE and NNW. Portland and Berry Head is E and by N, W and by S, Berry Head and the Start WSW and ENE. Between Portland and the Start every haven has tide E and W. Between Berry Head and the Land's End of England there is half tide. In the fairway between the Start and Lizard the course is E and W. And beware of the hidden rocks. All the havens be full at a WSW moon between the Start and Lizard. The Lands End and Lizard lie ESE and WNW. At Lands End lieth the Runnel Stone. A little berth of but 12 fathoms shall lead you well outside him. And SSE of Lands End lieth the Gulf.'

This is the original:

'And from Seint Elenes to Chakkeshorde is half tide and a south moone makith high watir within Wiet the nedlis and the forne lieth south west, and by west north est and by est the nedlis and Corneland est and west. At the nedlis it flowith south est and by south fro the nedles to Portlonde the course is west south west and est north est at the Polketh in haven it flowith northwest and southest, and in the fairway south southest and north north-west. At Waymouth within havyn Est and West at the Bill at Portlonde south south est and north northwest. Portlande and bery land is est and by north west and by south. bery laund and the Start west south west and Est northest, betwene Portlande and the Stert ever havyn is tide est and west betwene Bery londe and the Londis ende of Englonde there is half tide. In the fairway betwene the Start and Lisart the cours is est and west. And beware of the hidre stonys. All the havens be full at a west south west moone betwene the Start and Lisart, the Londis ende and Lisard lieth est southest and west northe west. At the Londis ende lieth Raynoldis stone. A litill birth of but xij. fadom shall lede you all be owten hym and south south est of the Landes ende lieth the gulf.'

CHAPTER 5

Battles and Pirates

PATIENTLY waiting for winds and tides, away from their homes for un-predictable periods, seamen pursued a calling both dangerous and dull. Their voyages, and whatever disasters they met, went unrecorded. Their lowly lives were only interrupted by the sudden demands of kings, and those were the only events which dragged them into history. A host of ships, for example, was caught up without any warning in one such event in June 1340.

This was a moment in the Hundred Years War against France when the King of England, Edward III, was in alliance with the rulers of Flanders, and also deeply in debt to them. He came home from Flanders in February 1340 to ask Parliament for money for further campaigns, and for paying the debts; and while he was away, the King of France sent a huge fleet up the Channel to stop him coming back. Among the French ships were those of a notorious Flemish pirate called Lanisius Spoudevisch, and some galleys commanded by a Genoese sea-rover or mercenary called Barbaveria. This fleet put into the Flanders harbour of Sluys. Sluys at that time was one of the principal ports of northern Europe, but it silted up long ago and now the town is miles away from the sea.

The Archbishop of Canterbury and other advisers told the King the return crossing was too dangerous to attempt, but he angrily rejected that advice. He had promised his Flemish creditors he would be back in the summer; he had pledged his golden crown, among other things, and had also left his wife Philippa, perhaps as a hostage, in Flanders with two small babies. So at the end of May he rode to Ipswich, where his own few ships were lying in the River Orwell, and he sent out a summons to all the ship-ping in nearby ports to assemble with crews, provisions, archers and men-at-arms. Within a fortnight, his fleet could be numbered in hundreds – a fleet of miscellaneous merchant ships of all sizes, taken straight from their peaceful trading. 20,000 men were said to be aboard. If they built castles on the ships, they must have done it quickly, for early in the morning of 22nd June the King embarked, with four earls and a bishop, in a cog called *Thomas*, and ordered the fleet to sea. A fortnight later, he wrote a letter in French to his son Edward, the Black Prince, who was left in England as regent. 15th June had been the Prince's tenth birthday.

'My dearest son, We are sure you will want to hear good news of us, and all that has happened since we left England. So we must tell you that on Thursday, after we left the port of Orwell, we sailed all day and all the following night, and on Friday about noon we reached the coast of Flanders off Blankenberghe, where we sighted our enemy's fleet all packed together in the harbour of Sluys, and because we had missed the tide we anchored off for the night. On Saturday, St John's day, soon after noon on the tide, in the name of God and trusting in our just cause, we sailed into the harbour upon our enemies, who had drawn up their ships in a very strong array and offered a noble defence all that day and the night after; but God, through His miraculous power, gave us victory, for which we devoutly thank Him. And we must tell you that the ships, galleys and great barges of the enemy numbered 910, all of which were taken except 24; and the number of gentlemen-at-arms and other armed men amounted to 35 thousand, of whom only five thousand escaped, and we have heard from some who were taken alive that the bodies are scattered all over the coast of Flanders . . . Dearest son, may God be your guardian.'

The King's figures are incredible, but other eye-witnesses filled in the details of this unique and bloody fight. It was the only battle of such consequence in the Middle Ages which was fought in ships. But it can hardly be called a sea battle, because the ships were in harbour, and because it was fought on both sides with the same weapons they used on land, and so far as possible with the same tactics. The French drew up their ships like an army in three ranks across the harbour. The first rank was chained together, in the hope of stopping the English, and consequently the ships were unable to move. Barbaveria the Genoese adventurer, whose profession was fighting in ships, withdrew his galleys angrily in protest at this landlubberly disposition, saying that the French commander knew more about book-keeping than battles; and the twenty-four ships which escaped the ensuing slaughter were those of the pirate Spoudevisch, who also knew what he was doing.

King Edward, in the cog *Thomas*, led his ships in a headlong attack which resembled a cavalry charge. He had posted his men-at-arms in every third ship, bearing their usual weapons, the sword and lance. Two ships out of three were full of archers. In this age, just after the probable lifetime of Robin Hood, English skill with the longbow had reached perfection; and by luck, or, as the English would have said, by the grace of God, the last of the flood tide had come at a time of day when the French archers, who used the crossbow, had the sun in their eyes. Long before the ships collided, English archery had made a massacre of the French; unable to retreat or manœuvre, their men were jumping overboard. When the hulls touched, the men-at-arms went to work in hand-to-hand encounters on the decks. And the local Flemings, who had lined the harbour banks to watch what happened, finished off the French who swam ashore.

When it was all over, the English joined the King in thanking God for this ghastly affair, and an abbot was quoted as saying with unholy humour that if the Lord had given speech to fishes, they would have had to speak French after all the bodies they had eaten. The episode showed bravery and discipline among the merchant seamen, who did the King's bidding and sailed their ships to attack. But it reflected no credit on the seamanship, imagination or ingenuity of either side, except the pirates. It showed that France and England, although they delighted in fighting, were equally far from any conception of how to fight at sea.

*

One reason why medieval fleets so seldom met at sea – although they often crossed the Channel – must have been that in practice they could only sail down wind. The master of a single cog might have put to sea in a beam wind, especially to coast in an off-shore breeze. But nobody commanding a miscellaneous fleet would have tried to take it across the Channel until the wind was settled astern of it. So whenever a fleet could cross from north to south, a fleet on the other side would be stuck in harbour.

Another reason was still that nobody on either side who was trained in chivalry was looking for fights at sea, which by their nature would be dangerous, unpleasant and inconclusive. There was still no weapon that could damage a ship at a distance: engines for throwing missiles were commonly used on land, but there is no record that any were ever mounted in ships for use at sea. Ships had to grapple before they could fight, and even then the fighting was man-to-man, and nothing much could be done to hurt the opposing ship. There were several secret recipes for Greek fire, learned from the Saracens; the stuff could be thrown on board the enemy, but at a risk that both ships would catch on fire. And large rocks and bars of iron were sometimes thrown or dropped from the tops of castles; with luck, they smashed through the enemy's deck and out through the bottom. But that was all. And of anti-personnel weapons, the only one invented specifically for use at sea seems more like a classic practical joke. Soft soap was poured on the enemy's deck, together with triangular iron spikes called triboli, which fell with one point sticking up: the enemy slipped on the soap and sat down on the spikes, and was discomfited.

However, in 1350, Edward III did meet and fight a Spanish fleet at sea. It was coming down Channel before a north-easterly wind, and he was waiting in Dover. The Spanish ships were larger and faster than his, and could have avoided battle. But they altered course towards him, and the fleets converged downwind until they met off Winchelsea.

The name of that fight conveys its unusual nature; it was not called by the name of the place where it was fought, but was known afterwards as the battle of Les Espagnols sur Mer. The King had no galleys, but he gave the order to ram a Spanish ship: the account of the battle, in French, uses the same word for 'ram' that was used for 'tilt' in tournaments on horseback. It was a brave and desperate thing to do, and the only way to bring a faster ship to battle; but a clinker-built cog was not designed for tilting. The Spaniard's mast went overboard, with the men in the fighting top; but the King's cog was split by the impact, and even his knights had to bail to keep her afloat. The Black Prince, in another ship, copied his father with even more dire results: he rammed a Spaniard and his own ship sank. But he and his men succeeded in getting aboard their opponent and throwing her crew into the sea. In British sea history, this was the first time an ordinary man, who was neither a lord nor a knight, was remembered by name for a personal deed of daring. He was called Halking, and he was a servant of the captain of a ship: when the ship was about to be captured, he jumped aboard the enemy all alone and cut the sheets and halyards with his sword, so that her sail fell on to the deck and she was taken.

*

Between these two battles, one other Englishman made a voyage which was notable because his motive for putting to sea was neither war nor trade: it was love. His name was Robert Macham, and he eloped with a girl called Anne d'Arfet and chartered or bought a ship in Bristol. What happened to them was remembered in Spain and Portugal, and two hundred years later the Portuguese historian Antonio Galvano included the tragic story among his *Discoveries of the World*. It was translated late in the sixteenth century:

'About this time also the island of Madera was discovered (in 32 degrees) by an English man called Macham: who sailing out of England into Spaine, with a woman of his, was driven out of his direct course by a tempest, and arrived in that island, and cast his anker in that haven, which now is called Machico, after the name of Macham. And bicause his lover was then sea-sicke, he there went on land with some of his companie, and in the meane time his ship weyed and put to sea, leaving him there: whereupon his lover for thought died. Macham, which greatly loved her, built in the island a chappell or hermitage to burie her in, calling it by the name of Jesus Chappell: and wrote or graved upon the stone of her tombe his name and hers, and the occasion whereupon they arrived there. After this he made himselfe a boate all of a tree, the trees being there of a great compasse about, and went to sea in it with those men of his companie that were left with him, and fell with the coast of Africke without saile or oare, and the Moores among whom he came took it for a miracle, and presented him unto the king of that countrey: and that king also admiring the accident, sent him and his companie unto the king of Castile.'

*

When fleet encounters were so rare, piracy had an added historical import-ance. In later ages, organised naval warfare gave seamen and shipbuilders an interest in squeezing the last fraction of a knot out of their ships on any point of wind; but in the Middle Ages, the same incentive was given only by piracy. A pirate in any age must be a better seaman than his opponents, or his life is short; and though piracy in the Middle Ages disrupted trade, it may have done more than anything else to improve the quality of British seamanship.

Piracy had always existed since anyone went to sea, and it continued until the world-wide dominion of the British navy put an end to it, at least in its organised forms, about 1860. In the middle Ages, this was one kind of seafaring in which the British were second to none: in the words of a fifteenth-century poet, they were 'the greatest rovers and the greatest theevis, that have bene in the sea many one yeere'. There may not have been many professional British pirates, but there were not many British seamen who missed a chance of piracy if they saw it. The English were well placed for it, close to the Channel which was a trading route for every northern nation, but the Irish, Scots and Welsh took a hand in it too. At that time, it was not a disreputable trade; on the contrary, it was more like a popular sport, the poor seaman's equivalent of the jousting and adventuring of knights. As a sport, it had all the essentials: a test of skill against opponents who had an equal chance, a taste of danger, the excitement of a chase, and a gambler's hope of winning money, balanced by the risk of losing it. Generally, it was not even against the law. All maritime nations had their own codes of law at sea, but there was no accepted international standard, except when rulers made specific treaties. Anyone on the high seas took his chance, and piracy was as much an accepted fact as any other danger. Chaucer's pilgrims took it for granted. The Merchant traded to Flanders over the same sea-route that King Edward had used ('Upon his head a Flaundrissh bevere hat'), and he wanted the sea kept clear:

> 'He wolde the see were kept for any thing
> Bitwixe Middleburgh and Orewell.'

On the other hand, the Shipman was as typical a master as the writer of the sailing directions:

> 'He knew alle the havenes as they were
> Fro Gootland to the Cape of Finistere,
> And every cryke in Britaigne and in Spaine.'

He was a trader and a pirate too:

> 'Of nice conscience took he no keepe.
> If that he faught and hadde the hier hond,
> By water he sente him hoom to every lond.'

In other words, if he won his fights he threw his opponents overboard, whatever country they came from, and Chaucer could make an ironic joke of it. But piracy was not essentially murderous. Pirates in every age had one advantage: that merchant ships and their cargoes did not belong to their crews, and therefore the crews were seldom willing to defend them with their lives. When they were caught they surrendered; and most pirates preferred to take them prisoner, because they could hold them to ransom.

About Chaucer's time, piracy came to one of its periodical peaks. In 1388 the Master General of Prussia sent ambassadors to Richard II to complain of English piracy during the past ten years, and the two rulers started a correspondence about it which lasted until both of them died and bequeathed the insoluble problem to their heirs. The letters were friendly, as if both rulers understood the lure of piracy and knew they could not stop it, but had to make a gesture to satisfy their merchants. They sent each other lists of scores of piratical acts, with demands for compensation down to the last penny. On the whole, the King seemed to be on the defensive, which suggests that English pirates were more successful than Prussians; when the King put in a claim, the Prussians could always reply with a larger counter-claim. And the Master General did not only ask for cash: he also requested the King to pray for the souls of Prussian seamen drowned by the English. At last, after twenty years of haggling, King Henry IV agreed to pay over £16,000, and his letter ended: 'After we shall be by your letters advertized of the number, state, and condition of the sayd parties drowned, we will cause suffrages of prayers and divers other holesome remedies profitable for the soules of the deceased and acceptable to God and men, religiously to be ordained and provided: upon condition, that for the soules of our drowned countrey men there be the like remedie provided by you.' But he probably never paid the money or said the prayers, for the argument continued.

It extended too to the towns of the Hanseatic League. Here the English had more justice on their side. In 1405, the King complained to the towns of Lubeck, Hamburg and Bremen of thirty-seven separate acts of piracy by their citizens, who had seized English ships and cargoes all over the North Sea and even, on one occasion, off the coast of Devon. Some of the victims had learned the names of the men who attacked them, and some of the names occurred again and again, especially those of Clays Sheld, Godekin Michael and a man called Storbiken, or Stertebeker. The goods they took make a thoroughly medieval list: woollen cloth, oil, wax, red wine, bow staves, meal, fishes, butter, masts, spars, boards, salt, salmon, harness and furs. There were also cargoes of osmundes, which were a kind of Swedish pig-iron, and of questingstones, which may have been lodestones under another name.

The Hanseatic League was a trading organisation, and had always been opposed to piracy. What had happened was that its citizens who had a piratical bent had been forced to band together to evade their own laws. They were putting to sea in fleets, so powerful that the Hansa towns themselves had to declare a kind of war on them. Stertebeker was the most flamboyant of their captains: a disgraced knight who took to the sea to retrieve his fortune or escape his creditors. The various forms of his nick-name meant big beaker or a beaker at a gulp, his crest was two wine-goblets with bottoms up, and his whim was to try his victims by drinking-contests.

In 1422, a Hansa fleet caught up with him off Heligoland and fought him in a three-day battle. He lost, and was beheaded in Hamburg with eighty of his men. It was said that people searched his ship in vain for booty until they found that the mast was hollow and full of gold – enough to pay for the war and compensate his victims, and to make a golden cross for the spire of a Hamburg church.

In England too, when the King at the merchants' urging became too hard on pirates, the pirates had to form syndicates and fleets to protect themselves, and piracy tended to change, from individual crews who tried their luck, towards an organised business. In 1409, Henry IV laid fines on all the inhabitants of Scarborough, Blakeney, Cromer, Plymouth and Dartmouth, who had sent fleets to sea under local pirate captains. Cromer's captain was called John Jolly – a name, or a nom-de-guerre, which expressed the English attitude. Plymouth's was Harry Paye; like Drake, he was a self-appointed scourge of the Spaniards, and he was known all along the northern shores of Spain as Arripay. From Dartmouth, John Hawley chartered the whole of the local shipping from time to time for enterprises in Normandy and Brittany. The Cinque Ports were supposed to be on the side of law and order, and to keep down the pirates in the Strait of Dover; but they turned their duties into a protection racket, and the member of Parliament for Winchelsea was under arrest at one time for leading a hundred of his electorate to sea on illegitimate business. One of the principal cargoes that came up the Channel was wine, and among the joys of the sport were the staggering parties which followed a lucky capture. In 1399, John Hawley brought 1500 tuns of claret into Dartmouth, and it was said the streets ran red with it. A few years later, when Harry Paye came into Plymouth with 300 tuns, the celebrations went on for three months, and the King's Vice-admiral himself, Sir William de Ethingham, was accused of making off with the lion's share of the booty. Paye also put into Poole with port and brandy, and reports came out of the town that not a man was sober.

All these adventures were an open secret. No doubt the captains were ruffians, but some were also respected citizens and popular heroes, and a good many held offices under the crown. Harry Paye fought for the King when he was asked to, with conspicuous success, and John Hawley became a very rich man and a deputy admiral. Officials of every rank were involved in the irresistible game, or were paid to keep their eyes shut. As it grew in complexity, rich influential men who enjoyed a gamble took part in financing and organising it, and disposing of the spoils. And above all, the brains behind it were the landed gentry of the south west of England.

This gave it a double importance. Piracy trained the English in seamanship. And it was not trade, but the gamble of piracy, which first gave some of the English aristocracy and gentry an interest in the sea, and lured them away from the old pursuits of chivalry. In the south-east of England, close to London, the influence of courtly life was strong, and no man of substance could risk his position in activities the King was certain to condemn. But down in the south-west, farther away, the gentry were more independent. On the coasts of Dorset, Devon and Cornwall, people of every walk of life from Lords Lieutenant to the humblest seamen became involved together in a sporting conspiracy. Although their aims were nefarious, a pride in adventure and seamanship grew among them. This was the birth – in piracy, not in trade – of the pride that conquered the seas in Queen Elizabeth's time; these west country gentlemen and seamen were ancestors of the Tudor privateers.

CHAPTER 6

The Great Ships of
Agincourt

At long last, in the early fifteenth century, English shipwrights suddenly broke free of their ancient conservatism, and built a few ships four times as big as any they had ever built before. In 1340, the King's cog *Thomas* had been only 200 tons, and the biggest ship in his fleet at the Battle of Sluys was 250. In 1360, a gold coin, the noble, was minted with a picture of a ship on it that does not look any bigger. But fifty years later, between 1410 and 1418, shipyards at Winchelsea and Southampton built ships for King Henry V up to 1400 tons – almost 200 feet in overall length and 50 in beam, ships of nearly the size of Nelson's *Victory*. And then, after only eight years of this great endeavour, they stopped; and no other ship of anything like this size was built in England for another hundred years.*

No doubt the Kings of England had coveted bigger ships for a long time, as a mark of prestige, if not as a practical need. And in the preparations for the campaign of Agincourt, in 1415, a scene must have occurred which emphasised that envy. Henry V, in the manner of his predecessors, assembled a fleet to transport his army to France. The army was under fifty thousand men, but it needed no less than 1500 ships. Even making allowance for horses, artillery and equipment, the ships must therefore have been small. The assembly port was Southampton, and during that summer the multitude of little ships, each with its single mast and sail, must have filled a good part of Southampton Water. And yet, sailing up from Spithead and towering over them, came Mediterranean carracks from Genoa, two- and three-masted, large, elegant and far more sophisticated. They were bringing regular cargoes by then of wine, oil, figs and dates, soap, cotton, paper, cloth of gold and silk; and they loaded English wool from the Wool House which

---

* Figures of tonnage should not be taken too seriously. The ways of measuring it have often changed – from the original medieval idea of the number of tuns of wine that would go in the hold, up to the modern methods of displacement, gross registered and net registered tonnage. So the figures can only be used for comparing the sizes of ships within a limited period.

still stands by the modern docks. Also in Southampton at the time was the King's principal shipyard, under a master carpenter named Huggekyns. Neither Huggekyns nor the King could have failed to see the contrast between the puny English ships and the powerful carracks, a challenge and a reproach to them both. And in the next few months, Huggekyns laid the keel of a ship which may have been the biggest in the world.

Unluckily, not a single picture is known of any of Henry V's big ships, nothing more than a wood carving from the end of a pew in a chapel at King's Lynn, which may be a representation of one of them. But among the Exchequer Accounts in the Public Record Office in London there are still some inventories made by the Clerks of the King's Ships under Henry IV and V. They are only lists of ships' equipment, and so one can only vaguely deduce what the ships were like; but such documents are the only clues from that crucial moment of shipbuilding history. And the lists are all the more fascinating because they are exceptionally difficult to read. They are written in a mixture of three languages; they seem as if the men who wrote them were thinking in courtly French, and trying to write in clerkly Latin, but could only find plebeian English words for most of the parts of a ship.

One of the ships in these lists, in 1410, was the *Christopher* (spelt Xprofer), and she is remarkable because she carried three iron guns, stocked, with five chambers. Even this phrase, which is the earliest reference to guns in a British ship, included all three languages: 'iij gunnes de fer stoked cum v cameris.' She also had one hand gun, ten bows and six sheaves of arrows. Among her anchors, ropes and spars, a toppcastell and somercastell were listed as equipment; the former was the crow's nest for fighting men or lookouts at the masthead, and the latter may have been the tent-shaped awning on the after-castle which can be seen in pictures later in the century. She had only one ketill and one ffrying pan – which may not be the best of evidence, but brings to mind a ship of modest size. But also, she had only one mast; and that does indicate that she had not evolved very far from the cogs of fifty years before.

The next ship of particular interest, also in 1410, was called *The Carake*. She was the first British ship which is known to have had two masts – they are listed, one large and one small; and since she was named *The Carake*, it seems likely that she was the first of this Mediterranean type, the carrack, in British possession. She was probably bought by the King from a foreign merchant. And within the next few years, more carracks are listed, the *Andrew*, the *Peter*, the *Trinity* and the *Holigost*. Each had at least two masts, and more rigging and equipment than the *Christopher*. The *Holigost* – the Holy Ghost – of 760 tons was completed in Southampton in 1415, but she may not have been a wholly local product; she may have been an extensive conversion of another foreign ship. She is notable in the accounts for her decoration. £4. 13. 4d. was spent on carving a swan and an antelope for her, and no less than £7. 6. 8d., which must have been most of a year's wages, on painting the ship with swans and antelopes, with diverse arms, and with the King's motto in diverse parts of her.

So far, none of these ships could be said with certainty to have been built in England; and next, the King ordered an even larger ship, of 1400 tons, to be built at Bayonne in France. But she was never finished; and at last, two English yards set to work to outmatch the foreign builders. The *Jesus*, 1000 tons, was built in Winchelsea; and in July, 1418, Huggekyns finished his masterpiece in Southampton, a ship of 1400 tons with two masts or possibly three. She was blessed by the Bishop of Bangor, and named the *Grace Dieu*.

With nothing more than the inventories to go on, and some bills from shipwrights, the sequence of these events can only be guesswork. But it seems that the King demanded bigger ships, five years before Agincourt, and that the English yards were unable to build them. So he bought *The Carake* and other ships from Spain or Genoa, and he placed his first order for building in his domains abroad. That put the English yards to shame, and stung two of them, at least, to show what they could do. Of course, they had the foreign ships as models. These were certainly carvel built, and one would have supposed that the English builders, in spite of their long tradition of clinker building, would have copied this simpler and more effective method. That would have explained their sudden skill in building so much bigger. But there is one more piece of evidence. The bottom of the *Grace Dieu* still exists, and it is clinker built, but built in a manner that has never been found in any other ship.

The life of this great ship was sad. By the time she was launched, the King had secured the mastery of the Channel, and the need for her had vanished. She probably never set sail. She was laid up, with the other big royal warships, in the mouth of the Hamble River at the bottom of Southampton Water. She leaked, and in 1433, without her mainmast, she was warped upstream to a mud berth. In January 1439 she was struck by lightning and burnt, and the remains of her settled in the river mud. And there they still lie, almost buried. But for an hour or so at the bottom of the lowest ebbs in spring and autumn, the outline of her frames and planking can be seen.

Nobody yet has found the money to excavate this unique medieval relic. But by wading in the cold opaque water and delving in the mud, one can uncover a little of Huggekyn's workmanship. She has three layers of oak planking, a double layer of clinker planking outside and a third layer, somewhat like carvel planking, on the inside. The three layers are fastened with an enormous number of square iron nails $\frac{5}{8}$ of an inch in thickness. The frames are massive, roughly 11 inches by 8 inches with gaps of only 5 inches between them; and they have been hewn to fit the inside of the planking and fastened to it with the wooden pins called trenails.

The labour of building a ship in this way would be prodigious, and it has nothing to commend it. Perhaps the use of treble planking helped to prevent the tendency of clinker planks to split; but on the other hand, it provided twice the number of seams. No wonder she leaked.

Why then did they do it? It may have been a mulish prejudice. English ships had been clinker built since Sutton Hoo, eight hundred years before, and shipwrights, like sailors, are slow to change their ways. But there is another oddity about her which suggests a more practical explanation: all her planks, or all those that can be seen, are in very short lengths, not more than 6 or 7 feet. No shipwright would use short planks in a ship of this size if he had enough long ones; and to build a normal carvel ship of such very short planks, and give it sufficient strength, would be impossible.

So perhaps the extraordinary way they built her may have been caused by a shortage of tall straight oaks in the neighbouring forest, or a shortage of time. She was built in under three years; and nobody within that time could have selected the trees in the forest, and felled, transported, sawn and seasoned them. She looks like a rush job, built out of planks already sawn and in stock for much smaller clinker-built ships. With more time, the shipwrights might have done better. But it was several generations before they were given another order for anything so ambitious; while for thirty years, the rest of the lifetime of most of the men who built her, their useless masterpiece lay rotting in the river.

*

So the great venture of English builders suddenly flourished and died; it was fed and then starved, as shipbuilding often has been through the centuries, by political needs. But the spur of Agincourt, and the forceful personality of

Henry V, had some effects on English ships that lasted. The King not only built ships of his own, he gave subsidies to merchants who would build them. Soon, in competition for the Mediterranean trade, they advanced from two masts to three. Sail plans grew more elaborate. The fore and main were square-rigged, but the mizzen carried a lugsail or lateen; topsails appeared on the mainmasts, and square spritsails hung below the bowsprits to balance the windage of the aftercastles.

And English seamen started to stir from their long obscurity. They mastered these complicated rigs and took their ships on ever longer journeys, peacefully fishing off Iceland and trading to the farthest ports of the Mediterranean. Their slow awakening came at a crucial time. In the same generation, the two events occurred which mark the end of the dark ages in seafaring: the ancient Byzantine empire fell to the forces of Islam, and a Prince of Portugal founded a school of navigation. Both these events were far away, but they had a profound effect on the seamen of England.

PART TWO

AWAKENING
1418–1567

*In seeking a route of their own
to the wealth of Cathay,
the British learn the arts of seamanship,
and a single battle
incites them to challenge
their rival, Spain.*

CHAPTER 7

The Search for Cathay

IT seems a paradox that the fall of so distant a city as Constantinople changed the course of the seafaring history of Britain. But it was true; for the fall of the city cut off the source of the silks and scents and spices of the east, and it was the lure of these treasures that drew all the great explorers by sea in the following century, the Portuguese, the Genoese, the Spaniards and the British. Especially, it was for cloves and pepper, not for conquest or power, that seamen started to cross the open oceans and spread their influence to Africa, America and the Arctic, and finally to India and the East.

For two thousand years, the most luxurious of fabrics, scents and spices had come to Europe by two routes of trade: from India by sea to the Persian Gulf and thence by caravan to the Mediterranean; and from Far Cathay, or China, by the Silk Road which led from Pekin, through mountains and deserts, to Bokhara and Samarkand, the shores of the Caspian Sea, and finally Constantinople. The Silk Road had always been a special source of wonder and romance for Europeans: the Three Kings, with their gold and frankincense and myrrh, were a part of its legend, and so were the dreams of the kingdom of Prester John. Trade on this long archaic road had survived the ravages of Alexander, Genghis Khan and Tamurlaine. But between 1420 and 1453 it dwindled and ceased; for the Turks attacked and finally overwhelmed Constantinople and its Christian empire, and the trade was diverted from the Christian to the Moslem world. The road became a route of pilgrimage to Mecca, and so it remained until the rival sects of communism cut it again in the middle of the present century.

It seems paradoxical too that the lure of scents and spices was almost stronger in medieval Europe than the lure of fine clothing and gold. The importance of smell and taste, and the craving to satisfy those senses, is hard to recreate. But it helps if one tries to imagine the pervading stink of even the grandest of medieval castles, and the dullness of medieval food – the unvariable bread and meat, dried fish in Lent and on Fridays, nothing sweet except honey and the local fruit when it was ripe. By the end of the Middle

Ages, the tastes of the rich had grown far beyond the natural products of Europe; they longed for anything that would give more interest to their diet or alleviate the coarseness of their homes, and they were able and willing to pay whatever it cost. Thus great expeditions were planned and made, and thousands of men both risked their lives and lost them, to fetch such things as cinnamon, cloves and pepper from the limit of the world they knew, and search for them beyond it.

That was the quest. The skill to follow it came mainly from Portugal. The seafaring history of any European nation would have to deviate, in the first half of the fifteenth century, to mention Prince Henry the Navigator, because his life's work changed them all. But in a British history it is not a very distant deviation. Henry was a prince of Portugal, but he was half English. His mother was Philippa, the oldest child of John of Gaunt and sister of Henry IV of England; so that he himself was first cousin of his contemporary, Henry V, who built the *Grace Dieu*. And it is said to have been to his mother, a lady of formidable character, that he owed his academic education, and a taste for mathematics and astronomy which was rare in princes.

The title Prince Henry was given in English, the Navigator, is rather misleading. He seldom went to sea, and never on long voyages; nor did he make any new discoveries in navigation. What he did was to encourage other people; especially, he persuaded the masters of ships, hitherto an uncouth and superstitious class of men, to listen to astronomers and philosophers.

For a very long time, such scholars had possessed the knowledge needed for navigation by the sun and stars. But scholars did not go to sea, and seamen were seldom scholars. So on land, men were able to measure latitude with the astrolabe and gnomon, and to construct fairly accurate maps and charts – which included the Mediterranean and the Atlantic coasts of Europe. But at sea, men continued to sail from point to point of the shore, and only ventured out of sight of it on well-known crossings with favourable winds and easy landfalls. The Vikings' methods of ocean navigation had already been forgotten, and scientific methods had scarcely yet been tried.

In his early twenties, Prince Henry had the reputation of a knight; he had fought against the Moors with such success that the Pope and Henry V of England, according to a Portuguese historian, both offered him the command of their armies. But he did not accept those honours of chivalry: he retired instead to the remote peninsula of Sagres, near Cape St Vincent. There he built an observatory and invited philosophers to visit him; and he also persuaded the masters of ships to come and learn to use the instruments for observing latitude, the compass for laying courses, and the use and the making of charts. As a prince, he had the means to fit out expeditions, and the authority to send men to sea on journeys that were more than merely warlike or mercenary. So, under his patronage, masters were able to put to sea equipped for the first time, wherever they went, with the skill to find their way home again. His ships rediscovered the Azores, Madeira and the Canary Islands. But most of their efforts were made to the southward, down the coast of Africa. A known coast which stretches on to unknown distances has always enchanted explorers on the sea; and besides, that seemed the most likely way to the fabulous east.

*

The teaching of the school at Sagres took a long time to reach the masters of English ships. It is hard to imagine that any of them went there. Perhaps some students of Prince Henry came to England; or perhaps the English simply heard what was happening there, and learned independently from scholars of their own. But fifty years after Prince Henry began there were certainly some English masters who knew how to navigate the oceans. Yet it seems they still felt diffident, and inferior perhaps to southern seamen. They needed someone to wake up their latent enterprise and encourage them to the first tremendous act of faith – to set a course not along the coast but right away from it, into the unknown seas that had no landmarks. And probably the man who first encouraged them was Christopher Columbus – but long before he made his own first voyage, while he was still an unknown or derided theorist.

The Portuguese had monopolised the coast of Africa. But by about 1475 the idea of another alternative route to the east was growing in the older seafaring states of the Mediterranean – the idea of sailing west, the other way round the world. A Mediterranean state could not have organised a voyage to the west without the approval of one of the kings of the Atlantic coast – Portugal, Spain, France or England. Columbus brought the idea from Genoa, and spent over ten years in trying to win the support of one of the kings. Very early in his researches, in 1477, he came to Bristol. This was the principal port for the Iceland fisheries, and its seamen knew more than anyone else about the north Atlantic. Columbus certainly had discussions with them, and it is a fair guess that he talked about fabulous riches to be found by sailing west: he always did. And soon after his visit, in June 1480, according to the historian William of Worcester, a mariner named Thomas

Lloyd left Bristol in a ship of 80 tons to search for land in the west. His ship was beaten about by storms, and he came back in September without any sight of land. In the next few years, several more of the Bristol masters set out on the same brave search. But some of them, and probably all of them, were confused by the ancient story of St Brendan's Isle. That mythical island was shown on the latest charts to the west of Ireland; and that was what they looked for, believing no doubt that it was an outlying part of the Khandom of Cathay. So all of them hunted around in the middle of the Atlantic, and none went far enough west to find any land at all.

Meanwhile, Columbus had been rejected in Portugal and met tedious procrastination at the Spanish court; and in 1489 he sent his brother Bartholomew to ask Henry VII of England to grant him crews and ships for a western voyage. On the way, Bartholomew was robbed by pirates and he arrived in England sick and destitute. He did not dare to approach the king until he had made some money and 'gotten somewhat hansome about him'; so he began to work in London, drawing and selling charts. After a long time – it must have been over a year – he ventured to present his petition, and gave the king a map of the world with a dedication in Latin verse. The King accepted Columbus' proposition 'with joyfull countenance' and sent for him at once to come to England. But while Bartholomew was delaying, Columbus at last had achieved an agreement with Queen Isabella, and before he heard of the English offer, he had sailed with a Spanish crew. So through a series of mischances the flag of Castile, and not of England, was the first to be planted in the New World.

By that time another native of Genoa had come to Bristol and settled there, and also begun to talk about Cathay. This was John Cabot. His belief in sailing westward had a direct connection with the old Silk Road: he had become a citizen of Venice, and in some official capacity he had been to Mecca. There he had seen the spices that were brought with the pilgrim caravans, and had asked where they came from. Merchants had bought them, he was told, some other merchants far in the east, who themselves had bought from others farther still. The stories gave the impression, correctly, of enormous distances. Everyone at that time, including Columbus, believed the world was much smaller than it is; and to Cabot, the source of the spices had seemed so far to the east that it could not be far to the west. So he further encouraged the Bristol voyages. In 1493, when the news of Columbus' success reached Bristol, Cabot began to make plans to take part in the search himself. In 1496, he petitioned the King for Letters Patent for the discovery of new lands, and they were granted; and in May 1497 he sailed from Bristol with an English ship and crew, and made landfall on the coast of North America.

This was the first successful voyage of pure discovery made by an English ship, although it was under Genoese command. Remarkably little is known about it, and there are contradictory stories of what happened. The contemporary papers, such as they are, all refer to John Cabot as the leader of the expedition. But his second son, Sebastian, lived to be a highly respected old gentleman; and many years later he told the story to Spanish and Italian historians, and gave them the unanimous belief that he had been the leader. In the Victorian age, English historians argued fiercely about the voyage, some maintaining that Sebastian really led it, and others that he was a rascal who stole the credit due to his father and used it to win a position of authority for himself. Certainly, Sebastian's stories contradicted each other, and some were plainly untrue. And certainly, John was at least the nominal commander, a mature and respectable figure who could gain the King's approval.

John Cabot's petition and the King's reply are still in British archives, but if he wrote an account of the voyage, it has vanished. The only known accounts that were written at the time were by two foreign residents in London: Raimondi di Soncino, who was the ambassador of the Duke of Milan, and a Venetian named Lorenzo Pasqualigo. Both of them sent letters home within a few days of Cabot's return to Bristol, and both had spoken to him and men of his crew.

Putting together these second-hand reports gives a story that is bare but has the ring of truth. John Cabot sailed in a small ship with a crew of eighteen men, and called on the west coast of Ireland. (A much later history of Bristol names the ship as the *Mathew*.) He was forced to sail north-west for a while, and then sailed west, keeping the pole star by night on his starboard hand. He saw no people on the land he found, but he saw some felled trees, and brought back for the King some snares for catching game, and a net-maker's needle. His landfall is usually identified as Cape Breton Island in Nova Scotia; but he and his crew seemed less impressed by the land than by the vast shoals of fish, so plentiful that they hindered the passage of the ship and could be caught by lowering baskets over the side. He was back in Bristol in early August, after only three months at sea.

Both the letter-writers were sarcastic. Soncino wrote to his Duke: 'The said Master John being foreign and poor would not be believed if his companions, who are almost all Englishmen from Bristol, did not testify that what he says is true . . . I have also talked with a Burgundian, a comrade of Master John's, who confirms everything and wishes to return there because the Admiral (for so Master John already entitles himself) has given him an island; and he has given another to a barber of his from Castiglione of Genoa, and both of them regard themselves as Counts, nor does my Lord the Admiral esteem himself anything less than a Prince. I think several poor Italian monks will go with the next expedition, who have all been promised bishoprics. And as I have become a friend of the Admiral's, I would get an Archbishopric if I wished to go there. But I have thought that the benefices your Excellency has in store for me are a surer thing.'

But the King was pleased, and promised to fit out a number of ships for the following summer. He awarded John Cabot ten pounds to amuse himself, and a few months later increased this niggardly gift to a pension of £20 a year.

In 1498, John Cabot made a more extensive voyage. Of course he believed, like Columbus, that he had reached the coast of Asia, and had only to follow it southward to find Cathay. So hopes were high. The King's letters gave him authority to take six ships of under 200 tons, and others from Bristol joined him on their own account. Merchants ventured cargoes of trade goods – 'sleight and grosse marchandizes, as course cloth, caps, laces, points & other trifles' – the first of many pathetic attempts to barter European clothes with unresponsive natives.

This time, Cabot sailed by Iceland, and explored the coast of Greenland as far as the ice allowed him. He must have passed very close to the settlement Erik the Red had founded six hundred years before. Its last few inhabitants were still alive, although they were forgotten by the world and had not seen a ship for four or five generations; but if Cabot sighted their houses, churches and cathedral, he failed to recognise an outpost of Christianity. He crossed the Davis Strait by the Norsemen's route to Labrador, which he named in honour of a Portuguese who had advised him; and he sailed south down the coast of north America for most of 2000 miles, until he ran short of stores in the neighbourhood of Cape Hatteras in Virginia.

Again, he brought back remarkably little information – or little that has survived. The people of those regions, Sebastian said long afterwards, wore animals' skins but were not without the use of reason, and there were bears which caught fish. Cabot, or his captains, brought back a few more souvenirs for the King, including three savages who survived for some years in the

Palace of Westminster. But that was all. They had hoped to find the wealth and civilisation of the east, but had seen no sign of it. Instead, they had traversed most of the eastern seaboard of north America, but that seemed comparatively dull, and the expedition seemed a failure.

John Cabot returned to draw his pension in 1499, but died soon afterwards; and perhaps the most striking legacy of his voyages is the enigma of his son Sebastian: was he a pioneer, or a charlatan, or merely forgetful? For fifteen years after the second voyage, he made no independent mark on history. Then he was appointed captain in the Spanish navy, and in 1518 became Pilot Major of Spain. About 1549, when he must have been over 70, he came back to England and was granted a handsome pension. He lived to be well over 80; and all through this long life, on the basis of his father's voyages, he behaved and was usually treated as a great explorer and the leading authority on the far north-west.

Yet the accounts he gave of the voyages were muddled: he always spoke of a single voyage, combining in it the events of both. And some of his statements, quoted by foreign historians, were certainly false: for example, that his father was already dead at the time of the expedition and that he himself had been granted two ships by the King. It was only when he was abroad that he made these claims. In England there were people who remembered otherwise, besides the royal letters which proved him wrong.

Even in England, he was treated with veneration. But there were discordant incidents. In 1521, Cardinal Wolsey invited him to command some ships that Henry VIII had thought of sending to the Newfoundland. The Livery Companies of London were invited to furnish the ships, but one of them, the Company of Drapers, refused because it was rumoured that Sebastian had never been to the north-west at all – that he had not even accompanied his father, and knew nothing about it except what his father and other men had told him. Five years later, however, he did command a Spanish expedition, the only long voyage he is certainly known to have made. It was a fiasco. He set off to find the western route to the Moluccas and Cathay, which he said he already knew, but he only found the River Plate, which had already been explored. When he came back he was arrested and put in disgrace for a while, and the Spanish historian Oviedo wrote: 'Cabot is skilful in constructing both plain and spherical plans of the world. But leading men is not the same thing as using an astrolabe.'

He was also remarkably skilful in convincing kings and other men of

73

power. From the documents that survive, one would think him an impostor; but if he was, he kept up a successful deception for sixty years.

*

After John Cabot's death, English exploration languished. The Bristol seamen had shown they had the skill for it, and they made a few more journeys to the Newfoundland, but none of them was of any consequence.

The Portuguese went on and found their own route to the east by the Cape of Good Hope, and so did the Spaniards, by Cape Horn and by crossing the Isthmus of Panama – though they lost interest in the seas of Cathay when they found instead the greater riches of the Inca and Aztec civilisations, which could be conquered and robbed. But the British were hemmed in, or felt they were, in the north Atlantic. The ways out to the south were closed by the sovereign claims of Portugal and Spain. To the north there was nothing but ice, and to the west the dull and disappointing coast of America – for nobody was looking then for virgin lands, they were looking for wealthy kingdoms which would barter exotic goods.

Again, after a generation's delay, it was the merchants of England who showed initiative. They resolved to break out of this constriction, and to find their own route to the kingdoms of the east, a route that would be English, just as the others were Portuguese and Spanish. By then the continents of Africa and America were known to be continuous barriers. The southern ends of them had been monopolised, and therefore the only possible English routes were round the northern ends – the hypothetical routes that came to be known as the North-East and North-West Passages. So it came about that the greatest efforts of early British exploration were made not in quiet sunlit seas, but in the most dangerous testing ground of the Arctic.

About 1550 the merchants founded the first company for trade and exploration overseas. It was named the 'Mysterie and Company of Marchant Adventurers for the Discoverie of Regions, Dominions, Islands and Places Unknowen'; and none other than Sebastian Cabot, who was then about 75, was appointed its governor for life.

In 1553, the ships for its first expedition were ready in the Thames: they were well built and armed, provisioned for 18 months and given strangely outlandish names: the *Bona Esperanza*, 120 tons, the *Edward Bonaventure*, 260 tons, and the *Bona Confidentia*, 90 tons. This first attempt was to find a North-East Passage to Cathay. Cabot wrote a set of instructions for the masters and crews, and thereby put historians in his debt; for one of the things he told them to do was to keep a proper journal. This expedition, the first under wholly English command, was also the first to bring home a day by day account of its adventures – the first to evoke, four centuries later, some echo of the excitement of making landfall on an unknown coast, and the hazard of sailing where nobody had ever sailed before.

There were plenty of volunteers as Captain General of the fleet ('and some voyde of experience,' according to one account), but the company chose a knight, Sir Hugh Willoughby, who was considered valiant, well-born, of goodly personage and skill in the services of war – he had served as a soldier on the Scottish border. As Captain General, he was not expected to be a seaman, but the officers and crews were all experienced men. Two of them, Richard Chancelor and Stephen Borough, captain and master of the *Edward Bonaventure*, distinguished themselves as explorers; and Borough's young brother William, who shipped as a boy, grew up to become Comptroller of Queen Elizabeth's navy. There were a minister, three surgeons and sixteen merchants with their wares, 115 men in all, and each was provided with a sky-blue livery – which was to be kept by the merchants and only worn when the captain needed to show his crew in good array.

Each ship carried copies of a letter from King Edward VI, written in English, Latin, Greek and other languages – an interesting letter, because it expressed the hope and ambition of early English exploration, and an idealised philosophy of English trade. It was broadly addressed 'To all Kings, Princes, Rulers, Judges and Governors of the earth, and all others having an excellent dignitie on the same, in all places under the universall Heaven.' God has given mankind, it said, above all other living creatures, the desire for friendship, to love and be loved, and to give and receive mutual benefits. All men ought to show affection to those who come from far countries, and the farther they come, the more do they show their ardent desire for friendship. And of all men, the most deserving is the merchant; for God, in providing for mankind, ordained that all his needs should not be found in any single region, in order that each region should have need of others, and friendship be thus established among all men. For this reason, the King asked all other kings and princes to help his voyagers, and promised his own help to any of theirs who came to his dominions.

The company's orders to the fleet, which were signed by Cabot, expressed the same wide tolerance. The crews were told not to preach their own religion, but to bear with such laws and rites as they found among foreign people. And although they were warned to beware of trickery, ambushes and cannibals, they were also told to treat all nations with gentleness and courtesy, and not to provoke them by laughing, disdain or contempt.

No doubt the King's letter, like the orders, was drafted by the Merchant Adventurers themselves, and it might be said there was a touch of hypocrisy in it; love and friendship were not only the wish of God, but were also good for trade. Yet the English, at that moment of dawning enterprise, did have the merit of addressing all men as equals. They avoided the worse hypocrisy of Spain, which made the spread of Christianity a cloak for conquest, slaughter, robbery and enslavement. The early English explorers were neither conquerors nor preachers, they were simply traders, or the pathfinders of traders. And even when they turned to robbery, a generation later, they made it a practice only to rob the robbers.

*

On 10th May, 1553, with these earnest intentions, the three ships left Ratcliffe, a mile or so below London Bridge. It was a slow start. They were towed downstream on the tide by rowing boats. On the second day they passed Greenwich, where the court was in residence. Courtiers and commoners lined the shore and climbed to the roofs of the palace, privy counsellors watched in dignity from the windows, the crews in their blue liveries cheered and shot off their ordnance, and the echoes came back from the hills around Blackheath. The young King did not see the show but perhaps he heard it, for he lay in the Palace, dying.

In a leisurely fashion, the fleet sailed on, out of the river and up the coast of East Anglia, anchoring every night and often waiting for the wind and tide. In London, the crews had said farewell to their wives and children, and perhaps they were reluctant to commit themselves to the adventure. But the prolonged departure must have made matters worse: six weeks later, they were still on the Suffolk coast, not much more than sixty miles from home. There was nothing wrong, and the rate of progress went without comment in their journals.

On 23rd June, the wind was fair; they hauled off to seaward and set a course to the north. For the next three weeks, they were out of sight of land, and now there was a note of impatience in Sir Hugh Willoughby's own account: 'We sayled with divers other courses, traversing and tracing the seas, by reason of sundry and manifolde contrary windes.' In the middle of

July, land was sighted to the eastward. They closed with it, and Sir Hugh in the *Bona Esperanza* sent his pinnace ashore among innumerable islands. There were little houses, but the people had fled.

This was somewhere on the coast of Norway, and sailing northwards they found inhabited places where friendly, less timorous people were mowing and making hay. They put in to the Lofoten Islands, and learned that they belonged to the King of Denmark; and early in August, in 70° north, they spoke a local skiff and asked for a pilot. Their first objective, and indeed the only one they knew, was a town and stronghold which the English of the time called Wardhouse. This was Vardö, which was then, and still is, the last Scandinavian port before the inhospitable coast of arctic Russia. The pilot was promised, and the men in the skiff escorted them towards a harbour; but trouble began. 'The land being very high on every side, there came such flawes of winde and terrible whirlewinds, that we were not able to beare in, but by violence were constrained to take the sea agayne, our Pinnesse being unshipt; we sailed North and by East, the wind increasing so sore that we were not able to beare any saile, but tooke them in, and lay a drift, to the end to let the storme over passe. And that night by violence of winde, and thickenesse of mists, we were not able to keepe together within sight, and then about midnight we lost our pinnesse, which was a discomfort unto us. As soone as it was day, and the fogge overpast, we looked about, and at the last we descried one of our shippes to Leeward of us: then we spread an hullocke of our foresaile, and bare room with her, which was the *Confidence*, but the *Edward* we could not see.'

The *Bona Esperanza* and *Bona Confidentia* kept company; but their crews, for forty-five days in worsening weather, had a nightmarish experience of being lost at sea. At first, they sailed north-east, expecting to find Wardhouse: 'then wee sounded, and had 160 fadomes, whereby we thought to be farre from land, and perceived that the land lay not as the Globe made mention.' In fact, they had missed North Cape, and sailed out into the open Barents Sea.

It is impossible after that to deduce where they went from the entries in their log. Week after week, as the nights grew longer and the weather colder, they set courses hither and thither, searching with increasing anxiety for a friendly shore. After two or three weeks, land was sighted, but in ice and shallow water they could not reach it even by boat, and there was no sign of habitation. This may have been as far east as Novaya Zemlya. Then, still looking for Wardhouse, they began to set courses from south to north-west, as the wind allowed them. Late in August, they sounded in only seven fathoms, but were still out of sight of land. At last they found another coast, but it was a lee shore, they hauled off it to give themselves sea-room and lost it again; and the same thing happened, the shore was found and lost, four times in the beginning of September. The leisurely start of the voyage had been fatal. Time had run out. The arctic winter was on them, and they did not know where they were.

At the equinox, they found a sheltered bay on a barren coast. 'Remaining in this haven the space of a weeke, seeing the yeare farre spent, & also very evill wether, as frost, snow, and haile, as though it had beene the deepe of winter, we thought it best to winter there. Wherefore we sent out three men Southsouthwest, to search if they could find people, who went three dayes journey, but could find none; after that, we sent other three Westward foure daies journey, which also returned without finding any people. Then sent we three men Southeast three dayes journey, who in like sorte returned without finding of people, or any similitude of habitation.'

That lonely entry was the last in Willoughby's journal. During the winter he and the whole company of the two ships froze to death. The ships and the bodies were found the next summer by Russians. They were 300 miles beyond Wardhouse, on the coast of the Kola Peninsula, which is still a desolate place today.

The ship they had lost, the *Edward Bonaventure*, fared better, perhaps because her captain, Richard Chancelor, was also Pilot General of the fleet. He rounded North Cape, and gave it its present name, and found Wardhouse without any trouble. While he waited there for the others, he had a strange encounter. He met a party of Scotsmen, who did their best to dissuade him from going any farther and told him of every kind of danger. His journal gave no explanation of who they were, or how they had come there, or why they wanted to stop him. But the fact that they were there, at the very edge of the known world, should remind a historian of how little he knows. All the recorded voyages of this period are English, but the Scots had clearly made one very enterprising voyage, and they – and perhaps the Welsh and Irish too – may have made many more, and left no record of them.

Chancelor and his crew were worried at losing the other ships and the Captain General – 'very pensive, heavie, and sorrowfull . . . not a little troubled with cogitations and perturbations of minde' – but they took no notice of the Scotsmen's warnings, and pressed on to the east. They came to the head of the White Sea, where they met some people and treated them, according to their orders, with gentleness and courtesy. So they were welcomed to the town that is now Archangel, where they spent the winter in safety. A message was sent to the Emperor in Moscow, and Chancelor, with some of the merchants, was invited to visit him there. This they did, travelling 1500 miles by horse-drawn sledges. They came home by the same way next summer, in 1554, and so founded a long and prosperous trade between England and Russia.

The Spaniards, in their search for the riches of Cathay, had discovered a source of greater riches in conquering and robbing the Aztec and Inca empires, and they devoted most of their energy to exploiting what they had found. To some extent, the English in the North-East Passage did the same, when they found an unexpected source of profitable trade in Russia. The Company of Merchant Adventurers became the Muscovy Company; its ships made voyages every summer by the route to Archangel that Chancelor had discovered, but few of them tried again to go farther east. Chancelor's route was dangerous enough. 1555, the year after his return, was full of disaster. The Company sent him back, with two extra crews to find and salvage Willoughby's ships. They did so, and took on board the first Russian ambassador to England with his retinue. But on the voyage home, the *Bona Confidentia* struck a rock off the coast of Norway and sank with all hands; the *Bona Esperanza*, Willoughby's own ship, disappeared for the second time and was never seen again; and Chancelor himself, after four months at sea on the homeward voyage, was driven ashore and drowned near Peterhead, north of Aberdeen. The Ambassador himself was one of the few survivors, but all his goods were stolen by the Scots.

Of all the senior officers of the first expedition, only Stephen Borough was left, and it fell to him to make the next attempt at exploration. He sailed from London in April 1557 in a pinnace named the *Serchthrift*, a ship so small that its crew was only eight. His departure gave a last glimpse of Sebastian Cabot, who came aboard at Gravesend. 'The good olde Gentleman,' Borough wrote in his journal, 'gave to the poore most liberall almes, wishing them to pray for the good fortune, and prosperous successe of the *Serchthrift*, our Pinnesse. And then at the signe of the Christopher, hee and his friends banketted, and made me, and them that were in the company great cheere: and for very joy that he had to see the towardness of our intended discovery, he entered into the dance himselfe, amongst the rest of the young and lusty company: which being ended, hee and his friends departed most gently, commending us to the governance of almighty God.'

Stephen Borough was a good navigator, who would never have got lost like Willoughby and his captains. He always knew his latitude, although once in a heavy swell he recorded his noon observation as a 'reasonable gesse'. He must also have been a likeable person, because the most memorable thing about his voyage was his friendship with Russian fishermen, especially with one named Gabriel. He met the Russians in a river mouth just beyond Wardhouse, and they told him they were going to Pechora, which is on the mainland opposite Novaya Zemlya, to fish for salmon. He went with them. The Russians were in open boats which were faster down wind than the pinnace; but whenever Borough fell astern, the Russians struck their sails and waited for him. Once when he lost the wind in a narrow harbour mouth and was drifting ashore, Gabriel came out at the risk of his life and lent him two anchors and a hawser. Sometimes they lost company, and celebrated when they found each other again: 'Gabriel came aboord of us, with 3 or foure more of their small boats, and brought with them of their Aquavitae & Meade, professing unto me very much friendship, and rejoiced to see us againe, declaring that they earnestly thought that we had bene lost. I gave them figs, and made them such cheere as I could.'

With this amiable escort, Borough and his eight men sailed 600 miles along the coast of Siberia, and reached the southern end of Novaya Zemlya; but there, in the middle of July, they were beset by ice. In early August, the Russians made for home. Borough tried for another fortnight to beat through the sound which separates Novaya Zemlya from the mainland. The winds were strong and constantly against him, the ice was thickening, the nights were growing dark. At the end of the month, he turned back towards Archangel through every kind of evil weather, gales, fogs, hail and rain and snow; and he spent the winter there.

In fact he had taken the little *Serchthrift* as far as a sailing ship could go. Belief in a navigable North-East Passage persisted on and off for another hundred years. In 1580, a larger expedition was sent to find it, with the encouragement of the geographer Mercator. In 1607 and 1608, the explorer Henry Hudson tried it, and in 1676 Samuel Pepys sent a solitary ship to try again. But Novaya Zemlya was a barrier that nobody could pass. And in the meantime, a new generation of seamen was seeking Cathay by the opposite way round the pole: the North-West.

CHAPTER 8

The North-West Passage

THE dream of a North-West Passage lasted very much longer: it began in Queen Elizabeth's reign and ended in Queen Victoria's, and then was revived in the late 1960's by an American ice-breaking tanker bringing oil from Alaska to the eastern seaboard of the United States. In fifty years, beginning in 1576, at least fifteen expeditions were sent to find the passage, and English captains scattered their own names, and the names of their friends and sponsors, all over the maps of the far north-east of Canada: Frobisher Bay, Davis Strait, Hudson Bay, Baffin Land, Fox Strait and scores of others. Their wrecks and bones were widely scattered too.

To follow the search will take this narrative right through the Elizabethan age: while the arctic explorers were out on their own, detached from the rest of the world, other seamen were venturing south and meeting the wrath of Spain. It is a side track in the story of Britain and the sea, because these men were looking for something they could not possibly find. But it is important, because it was a far harder test of the awakening strength of British seamanship than most of the southern voyages. So it seems logical to follow it first to the early part of the seventeenth century, when it was abandoned for two hundred years, and then to go back to follow the story of the men who went south.

To judge the hazards of the arctic voyages, one needs to know something of the methods of navigation the captains and pilots used. Willoughby's ships, for example, should not have been lost in the Barents Sea. They observed their latitude before they left the coast of Norway, so somebody in the expedition must have had the proper instrument, the cross-staff. And of course they had compasses. With these, a competent pilot of the time could have found his way back to where he started. There seem to be only two explanations of that grim disaster. Either there was only one cross-staff, and Richard Chancelor had it; or else the masters of Willoughby's ships did not know how to use it. The English explorers never made that mistake again.

An ocean pilot's equipment was simple; it changed very little in 300 years, from the time of Prince Henry the Navigator until the invention of the chronometer in the eighteenth century. He had a compass, a lead and line, a log, a cross-staff or an astrolabe, a table of the sun's declination, and a formula which he could carry in his head for correcting the elevation of the Pole Star. With these, in clear weather, he could always roughly find his latitude, but not his longitude.

The cross-staff and astrolabe were both very ancient instruments, invented for measuring angles – especially the angle of the sun above the horizon at noon and the pole star above it at night. They were more or less complementary. With the cross-staff, the pilot moved a sliding cross-piece along a staff until the lower end of it could be sighted in line with the horizon and the upper end in line with the sun or star; then he read off the angle from a scale engraved on the staff. It was difficult in a moving ship, because he had to glance first at one end of the cross-piece and then at the other; and for a star sight, it could only be used in the few minutes of twilight when the horizon and the star could both be seen. The astrolabe, on the other hand, did not need a horizon. It was a heavy brass disc with a ring on top, and a pointer pivoted in the centre. One man held it with his thumb through the ring, while another turned the pointer to sight the sun or star. But this was primarily a land instrument, and it was difficult to hold it steady in a seaway. At sea, the cross-staff gradually superseded it.

When the sun was approaching south, the pilot watched it with one of these two instruments, and recorded its elevation when it began to dip. Then he looked up the sun's declination for that day in his tables, which were prepared by astronomers; and his latitude was $90°$ plus the declination and minus the elevation. But the tables were rather inaccurate and the instruments much more so, and it needed luck and a calm day to observe the ship's latitude within a degree – that is, within sixty miles.

Pole star observations were probably better. It was known that the pole star is not exactly above the pole, but one degree away from it, and pilots knew from the position of the Little Bear whether to add or subtract a degree or half a degree from their observations. With this correction, of course, the elevation of the star was equal to the latitude.

But the problem of observing longitude remained insoluble until chronometers were invented in the eighteenth century. It was known in theory that longitude could be found by observing the times of eclipses, or the angle between the moon and chosen stars, which were known as lunars.

But eclipses were rare, and lunars needed calculations few practical pilots could manage. And neither the pilots' instruments nor the astronomers' predictions were accurate enough to make these methods any use in practice.

Meanwhile, pilots got some guidance in their east and west positions from the variation of their compass. Since the magnetic pole and the true pole do not coincide, compass north at most places on the globe varies from true north; and the variation could easily be observed by taking a compass bearing of the pole star. In the Atlantic (though not in other oceans) the lines of equal variation run roughly north and south; and so a pilot crossing the Atlantic could very approximately tell from his variation when he was likely to sight the other side. This was no use, of course, to a prime explorer; but anyone who discovered new land recorded the compass variation for the use of men who tried to find it again. However, these observations were so vague that many islands, especially in the Arctic, were shown twice on maps in different longitudes and with different names, according to the estimates of different people who had sighted them.

Apart from this rough empirical observation, a pilot could only tell where he was in an east-and-west direction from his own dead reckoning – by keeping a log-book of his speeds and courses. A seaman who knew his own ship could then, and still can, make a fairly good guess of her speed by looking over the side; and a rather better estimate could be made by a log. The log in use in Elizabethan times was a wooden board weighted on one edge so that it floated upright. It was dropped overboard on a line, and the speed was reckoned from the length of line that ran out in the time recorded by a 28 or 30 second sand-glass. The line had knots at intervals, each representing one nautical mile per hour; hence the word knot as a unit of speed at sea. But the question here was: how long was a nautical mile? By definition, it was one sixtieth of a degree of latitude, or of longitude on the equator; but nobody knew exactly what that represented in land measurements – the league, the statute mile, or the yard. Many geographers made estimates, but none was very close to the truth until 1637, when Richard Norwood, an English sailor who was also a mathematician, took careful observations of the latitudes of the Tower of London and York Minster and then, with commendable patience, measured the distance between them by road, allowing for all the changes of direction and the hills up and down. His figure was 2040 yards to a nautical mile, which is only 12 yards too much; but before that most of the estimates had been much too small, and consequently all the explorers, most notably Columbus, believed the world was smaller than it is. Norwood reckoned the knots in a log line should be 51 feet apart with a 30-second sand-glass. But pilots preferred on the whole to err on the safe side. They put the knots in their log lines closer together, so that their speed was over-estimated and their lookouts were alert for a sight of land too soon – which was better than too late.

All through the centuries when latitude could be observed and longitude could not, ocean pilots set courses by the time-honoured method of the deliberate error. If they knew the latitude of their destination, they set northerly or southerly courses until they reached the latitude, and then sailed east or west along it, as nearly as the wind allowed them, checking it as often as they could with the astrolabe. The compass variation, in the Atlantic at least, gave them some idea when they were nearly there. They looked for birds and seaweed as signs of land, and the colour of the sea. When those gave them warning, the leadsmen were set on watch to take regular soundings, and cautious pilots only sailed by daylight. At last, a look-out gave the cry of land – a moment of excitement that could never be re-created in modern ships whose pilots know exactly where they are.

The captains who searched for the North-West Passage were a diverse set of Englishmen. The first was Martin Frobisher, a rough Yorkshireman who was probably illiterate; the next John Davis, a pious, scholarly and poetic Devon man, and an expert pilot who invented two instruments, the backstaff and the Davis quadrant, which superseded the astrolabe. Henry Hudson was a man of unknown origin who was deserted by most of his crew in the bay he discovered; William Baffin, a Londoner who rose from poverty; and Luke Foxe another north countryman, with a sense of humour and a novel turn of phrase, who called himself North-West Foxe. These men had only two things in common. One, of course, was an inclination to adventure, and the other was humble birth. All of them were self-made men who rose to command through their own ability; for the aristocrats of Tudor England also enjoyed adventure, but looked for it on the whole in pleasant climates.

The search was started by a treatise written by Sir Humphrey Gilbert, a soldier by training, but Elizabethan in the breadth of his interests and the energy of his mind. It was published in 1576: 'A Discourse to prove a Passage by the North-West to Cathaia and the East Indies.' His arguments were convincing, and some were also true. If America and Asia were joined at their northern ends, with no sea passage between, how was it that no Asian people had found their way to America by land, and why did the animals of

America differ entirely from the animals of Asia? And how could the tides and currents of the Atlantic be explained, if they had no outlet to the Pacific in the north? The Spanish and Portuguese, he believed, did not want the passage to be discovered and had forbidden their own pilots to explore it; it was an opportunity for English enterprise. And he ended his discourse with an expression of faith that might stand for all the adventurers of his age: 'He is not worthy to live at all, that for feare, or danger of death, shunneth his countries service, and his owne honour: seeing death is inevitable and fame of vertue imortall.'

Gilbert's eloquence gave Frobisher his chance. Frobisher was a plain sea captain, comparatively inarticulate: he had wanted for twenty years to try the North-West, but had never found a sponsor. But the Queen herself read the Discourse before it was published, and gave Frobisher a licence to explore. The Muscovy Company, absorbed in its own affairs in Russia, declined to take an interest, but other city merchants put up money; and on 7th June, 1576, Frobisher sailed, like Willoughby, from Ratcliffe in London, with two small ships, the *Gabriel* and the *Michael* of 25 and 20 tons, and a 10-ton pinnace. Like Willoughby, he shot off his guns as he passed the palace at Greenwich; and Queen Elizabeth waved to him from a window.

Frobisher sailed northabout round Scotland. He sheltered in the Shetland Islands to fill his water barrels and stop a leak, and then set a course of west and by north, into the unknown ocean. A fortnight later he sighted the south of Greenland, a land rising like pinnacles of steeples over a low lying fog. Somewhere near there, he lost company with the pinnace in a storm, and nothing was ever heard of it again. And the captain and crew of the *Michael* lost heart and turned for home. The *Gabriel*'s mast was sprung and the topmast blown overboard, but Frobisher pressed on alone to the north-west, 'knowing that the sea at length must needs have an ending, and that some land should have a beginning that way.' And on 20th July, six weeks out from home, his faith was rewarded – he saw barren mountains surrounded by floating ice, and named them Queen Elizabeth's Foreland.

All explorers of the North-West Passage let themselves be guided by the tide, reasoning that any sound with a strong tide running in and out must lead to the other ocean. Some were misled because strong tides run in and out of Hudson Bay; but it was the only guide in the maze of sounds and bays which fills the Passage. Frobisher found what he thought was a promising sound and followed it for over a hundred miles, believing that the land to port was America and the land to starboard Asia, and hoping to see the

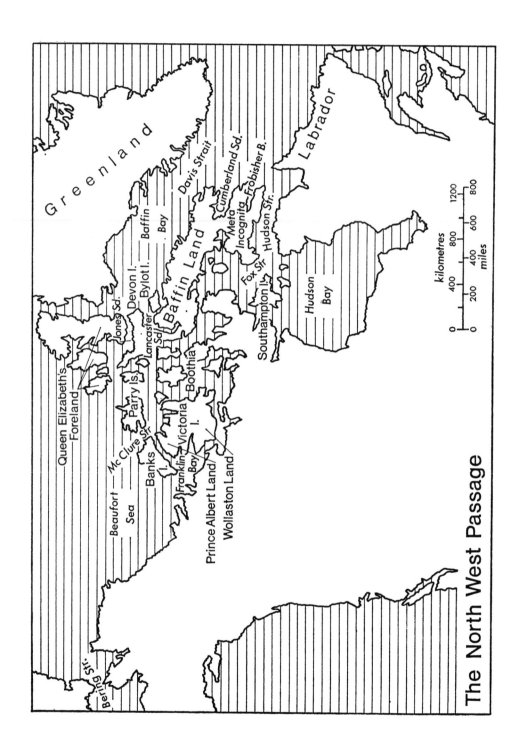

The North West Passage

Pacific Ocean opening ahead. He named his discovery Frobisher Strait, to correspond with the Strait of Magellan at the other end of the continent. Years afterwards, his Strait was found to be only a long inlet, and now it is marked on the maps as Frobisher Bay. But he was spared the disappointment of reaching the end of it, because winter came on and forced him to make for home.

In the early part of the strait it was difficult to land because there was so much ice, and Frobisher told his crew, if ever they reached the shore, to bring him the first thing they found, whatever it was, as a token of the Queen's possession and a proof that he had discovered land. Some accordingly brought him flowers, and some brought grass and one brought a piece of black stone; and all these he took back to England as souvenirs of the voyage.

The black stone was the cause of his second and third voyages, in 1577 and 1578. A piece of it was given to the wife of one of the voyagers. By chance, according to the story, she threw it on the fire, and then for reasons unexplained took it out and quenched it in vinegar. It glistened with gold. So it was taken to experts in London, who said it was a rich gold ore. At once, the Queen put a ship at Frobisher's disposal, merchants offered money, and gentlemen offered their services as adventurers. It was the very same thing that had happened to Willoughby and Columbus: the search for Cathay had discovered a promise of quicker riches, and people had lost interest in the search. Frobisher's new instructions were not to look for the Passage, but to bring back a cargo of the ore.

On both his subsequent voyages he therefore carried miners and assayers; and on the third, in a fleet of fifteen ships, he also took a wooden house in sections, and a hundred men who had volunteered to spend the winter in the land that the Queen had named Meta Incognita. But this was an ill-starred journey. Before it reached land, the whole fleet was caught in the ice. One ship, in sight of the others, was crushed and sank, and everybody laboured day and night with pikes, baulks of timber and oars, to bear off the ice which threatened to sink them all. A fog came down and the skies were overcast. Without sight of the sun, neither Frobisher nor his pilots could find the way into his strait, and they entered another which proved to be farther south. If exploration had been their object, the mistake might have turned to profit, for this was Hudson Strait, which has an outlet to the west. But all they were seeking was the bay within Frobisher Strait where the gold ore could be found.

At length they reached it. The last of the ships turned up when all hope of them had been lost, and the miners went to work. But when it came to building the house for the winter, Frobisher and a council of captains consulted their bills of lading and found that two walls of the house had been stowed in the ship that had sunk, and other parts of it had been used as fenders against the ice. The carpenters and masons were summoned, and asked how long it would take them to build a smaller house with the bits that were left. They answered eight or nine weeks, and it was already August; so the project was abandoned. It was just as well. To winter there was far too ambitious. They did not know what they were undertaking, and most of them would have died like Willoughby.

*

These voyages achieved very little in exploration, and nothing at all in profit; for the hundreds of tons of black stone they mined and carried aboard with prodigious labour turned out in the end to contain no gold at all, and the principal backer of the scheme was sent to a debtor's prison. But in retrospect the voyages do show something the English themselves were only beginning to suspect: that the centuries of inferiority on the sea had ended, and English seamen at their best were second to none in the world. Exploring the Arctic, like Frobisher's or Borough's crews, showed far more bravery and freedom of mind than was needed by Spaniards or Portuguese in their gentler seas. By the standards of any age, their self-reliance was wonderful. To sail out of the Thames in a 20-ton ship without any chart whatever, expecting to find a hypothetical passage three thousand miles away – this strains the imagination of a modern sailor, who would not cross the English Channel so badly equipped. And when they had weathered the Atlantic, and found the distant coast, they were in solitary peril all the time – the ice, the storms and fogs, and the unknown shore itself. They faced these dangers with equanimity – and another which seemed equally real to them. They met Eskimos, and assumed they had the habits of the Caribs the Spaniards had discovered. So they believed they were surrounded by cannibals, who would eat them if they were cast ashore.

It was not the very first time that English seamen had met a primitive race of people: Cabot's crews had some kind of meeting with North American Indians. In the course of time, Englishmen became rulers of primitive people all over the world; but the first they met and studied and wrote about were Eskimos.

English ships at Lisbon from a 15th century English chronicle

Armada Portrait of Queen Elizabeth I
Overleaf: The English Fleet engaging the Spanish Armada

It was Frobisher himself, on the first of the voyages, alone in the *Gabriel*, who saw what he thought were porpoises. They proved to be men in kayaks. With good intentions, and a not unfriendly curiosity, he persuaded them aboard. They gave him raw meat and salmon, and cheerfully bartered seal-skin coats and bearskins for small bells and mirrors which Frobisher, like all explorers, had provided for the purpose. The ship's master learned and wrote down a score of words in their language, they showed their agility by climbing in the rigging, and everyone was merry. But then, five of the crew went ashore in the ship's boat, and they vanished. Without the boat, the remainder could not reach the shore to try to find them, and they supposed the Eskimos had captured them to eat. Frobisher regretted then that he had not captured an Eskimo, who might have been useful as a hostage, or certainly as a trophy to take to England; for nothing was better as proof of a distant journey, or more likely to amuse the courts of Europe, than a genuine living savage. Cabot and Columbus had both abducted Indians, and nobody gave a thought to the suffering of such captives, alone as an exhibit to the curious in an utterly alien world where they could not speak to anyone.

So with patience and cunning he lured one back to the ship: rang one of his bells, and made gestures of offering it as a gift. The man in the kayak was reluctant: Frobisher threw the bell to him, but purposely threw it short, so that it fell into the sea. He held out another, the man was tempted and came close enough to take it – and Frobisher dropped it and seized him, and hauled him kayak and all on board. The man bit off his tongue – they thought in his rage at being captured, but perhaps it happened in the struggle. 'He died not thereof,' the journal of the voyage said with the callous innocence of the age, 'but lived untill he came to England, and there he died of cold which he had taken at sea.'

Next year, the Eskimos seemed delighted to see the ships again; they danced and sang, and waved flags from the hilltops. They could hardly have known they were suspected of having eaten some Englishmen; and from time to time, as the ship coasted along, the Englishmen rowed and wrestled and even played football with the Eskimos. But Frobisher had decided to take a hostage as soon as he came to the place where the five men had disappeared; and while he complained of the Eskimos' trickery, he planned a trick himself. He arranged a peaceful parley, two men on each side, unarmed. He and the master of his ship attended, meaning to overpower the Eskimos' spokesmen. But when they tried, they failed. The two Eskimos slipped from their grasp and reached their bows and arrows first, and one of them with an unerring shot hit Frobisher in the buttocks. The English crew came with their guns, and a sailor from Cornwall, a county well known for its wrestlers, caught one of the Eskimos and brought him down.

That man remained on board for the rest of the voyage. He was quick at sign language, and seemed to do his best to explain to his people ashore what Frobisher wanted. Negotiations came to a point when Frobisher wrote a letter to the missing men, and the Eskimos seemed to understand what it was and said they would deliver it. But suddenly, fear, mistrust and misunderstanding flared up again. There was a skirmish, guns were used, some Eskimos were killed and others fled, and two women were overtaken. One was old and ugly, and was freed because the sailors thought she was a witch. The other was young, and had a small baby on her back; and she and the baby were taken aboard as company for the captive.

The crew installed all three in a cabin together and watched to see what happened, as if they were mating animals. They observed that the two were very kind to each other: the woman attended the man when he was sick, and he always gave her the choicest morsels of their food. But to the sailors' astonishment, the man always sent the woman out of the cabin when he took off any of his clothes, and nothing was ever seen between them that might not have passed between brother and sister. Perhaps, for all anyone ever knew, that was what they were. As time passed, they grew more pleasant and docile with the crew, though they often tried to escape; but as human beings they remained so unimportant that the account of the voyage omitted to mention the fate of the adults or the baby – whether they survived the Atlantic crossing, or where and how long they lived if ever they were brought ashore in England.

*

It was not a good beginning for a nascent imperial power. But Frobisher was a blunt sea-captain who would not have claimed much subtlety in human relations. To explore the sea demanded ruthlessness and courage: to befriend a primitive race of people needed tolerance and patience. Only a man of exceptional breadth of character could succeed in both. Luckily, Elizabethan England bred an astonishing number of men of that kind; and one of them was John Davis, Frobisher's successor in the North-West Passage.

As a Devon man, Davis was an inheritor of the long tradition of piratical independence. But he was a peaceable person, both scientific and devout: so peaceable that he chose to explore the far north-west in 1585, 1586 and 1587, the three years before the attack of the Spanish Armada, when war at sea was plainly imminent and most English seamen were looking forward to a fight. And he was the first explorer to express a mystical devotion for the Arctic. He wrote that it was the place of greatest dignity in the world, and the people who lived there 'have a wonderful excellency, and an exceeding prerogative above all nations of the earth' – a feeling felt and expressed by a few single-minded men in each generation since.

Davis sailed from Dartmouth on 5th June, 1585 with two small barks, the *Sunneshine* and the *Mooneshine*, and forty-two men, including four who signed on as musicians. They made land on the east coast of Greenland, which they named Desolation, and cruised around its southern point, up the west coast and across the strait which still bears the name of Davis. They met Eskimos in Greenland and in the north-west islands, and Davis treated them with a romantic kindness which foreshadowed the eighteenth-century concept of the noble savage. 'They are very tractable people, void of craft or double dealing, and easie to be brought to any civilitie or good order: but we judge them to be idolaters and to worship the Sunne': this was written by John Janes, a merchant who sailed with Davis and wrote the surviving account of the first voyage, but it certainly reflected the view of Davis himself.

The four musicians, whose duty presumably was to entertain the crew and accompany the singing at daily prayers, were also useful with the Eskimos. At the first meeting, they were taken ashore and struck up a tune, the crew danced to it, and the Eskimos were entranced. The savages proved to be able not only to dance in time, but also to pick up an English tune and sing it. This cheerful scene, on a beach in western Greenland, led to jumping, wrestling and football matches, and to bartering satisfactory to all, in which sailors and Eskimos exchanged the clothes they were wearing. Davis was even kindly and understanding about the primitive disregard of the rights of property, which angered European explorers and led to bloodshed all over the world for centuries. 'These people are very simple in all their conversation,' he wrote on his second voyage, 'but marvellous theevish, especially for iron, which they have in great account. They began through our lenitie to shew their vile nature: they began to cut our cables: they cut away the *Mooneshine*'s boat from her sterne, they cut our cloth where it lay to aire though we did carefully look unto it, they stole our oares, a caliver, a boare speare, a sword, with divers other things, whereat the company and Masters being grieved. for our better securitie, desired me to dissolve this new friendship, and to leave the company of these theevish miscreants: whereupon there was a caliver shot among them, and immediately upon the same a faulcon, which strange noice did sore amaze them, so that with speed they departed: notwithstanding their simplicitie is such, that within ten houres after they came againe to us to entreat peace; which being promised, we againe fell into a great league. They brought us Seale skinnes, and sammon peale, but seeing iron, they could in no wise forbeare stealing: which when I perceived, it did but minister unto me an occasion of laughter, to see their simplicitie, and I willed that in no case they should bee any more hardly used, but that our owne company should be the more vigilant to keepe their things, supposing it to be very hard in so short time to make them know their evils.'

But Davis's crews, and especially the Master of the *Mooneshine*, disapproved of his friendliness. While he was absent exploring a river by boat, escorted by scores of kayaks, quarrels broke out on the ships, the Eskimos flung rocks at the *Mooneshine* and succeeded in stealing her anchor. When he came back, he tried to make peace; but in the end the Master captured the man he thought had been the ringleader in the thefts. Davis made signs that he would free the captive when the anchor was returned. But the wind came fair, and the ships set sail, taking the Eskimo with them. 'One of his fellowes still following our ship close aboord, talked with him and made a kind of lamentation. At length this fellow aboord us spake four or five words unto the other and clapped his two hands upon his face, whereupon the other doing the like departed as we suppose with heavie chere. We judged the covering of his face with his hands and bowing of his body downe, signified his death. At length he became a pleasant companion among us.' So Davis wrote, with as much compassion, perhaps, as a captain could allow himself to show. But the man died.

The Eskimos were in fact perfectly harmless people, except when they were frightened. But they still suffered in English eyes from the reputation of the Indians farther south. In the same voyage, Davis coasted southward nearly as far as Newfoundland. Down there, he trustingly sent a party ashore: a volley of arrows, shot by men who never showed themselves, killed two of his seamen and badly wounded others. And he did not know – although he may have suspected – that he had encroached on the country of a wholly different race.

The day of that trial ended with another: a reminder that death and disaster were daily to be expected and only to be averted by seamanship and faith. 'This present evening it pleased God further to increase our sorowes with a mighty tempestuous storme, the winde being Northnortheast, which lasted unto the tenth of this moneth very extreme. We unrigged our ship, and purposed to cut downe our masts, the cable of our shutanker brake, so that we onely expected to be driven on shoare among these Canibals for their pray. Yet in this deepe distresse the mightie mercie of God, when hope was past, gave us succour, and sent us a faire lee, so as we recovered our anker againe, and newe mored our ship: where we saw that God manifestly delivered us: for the straines of one of our cables were broken, and we only roade by an olde junke. Thus being freshly mored a new storme arose, the winde being West north west, very forcible, which lasted unto the tenth day at night.

'The eleventh day with a faire Westnorthwest winde we departed with trust in God's mercie, shaping our course for England, and arrived in the West countrey in the beginning of October.'

Davis was the exemplar of the pure explorer: to find the passage was his life-long hope. But exploration still needed the approval of the Crown and the money of merchants, and he was hampered like his predecessors by the need to show a profit for his sponsors. On his second voyage, he reported a virgin fishing ground which teemed with cod, and consequently on his third, he was provided with three ships but told to use two for fishing and only one, the smallest, for exploration. From that voyage he returned still full of confidence. He had sailed up to 73°, farther north than anyone else, and found the sea still open; the passage, he wrote, was most probable and its execution easy. But by then the Armada was preparing in Spain, everyone was busy, and nobody would finance him for another attempt. He had to turn his attention to southern seas.

*

The North-West Passage was left alone for the following fifteen years. During that time, from 1597 to 1602, the English victory over Spain at sea had made a different world. The Portuguese and Spanish monopolies over the southern routes were broken, the English East India Company was founded, and English ships were trading in the far east by way of the Cape of Good Hope. The search for Cathay was ended: it was found. And the only remaining practical use of exploring the North-West Passage was to find a shorter and quicker way to China and Japan.

But still it fascinated seamen. Everything suggested to them that the passage existed: the common sense of Gilbert's arguments, and in addition the strong tides they discovered, the colour of the sea, the schools of whales they saw swimming purposefully westward, and the little they managed to understand of the Eskimos' stories. Everywhere on the thousands of miles of coast from New York up to Baffin Bay they probed into inlets great and small – and any one of them, so far as they knew, might have opened suddenly into a sunlit ocean. In fact, the explorers discovered no more than the fringes of the passages through the islands. But they still had no method of observing longitude, except by dead reckoning or the variation of the compass, and both were so inaccurate that they were merely misleading. So they had very little idea how far they had travelled round the periphery of the Arctic, or how much farther they had to go – the thousands more miles of impossible icebound sea that still lay between them and the opening of the Pacific. They imagined a single northern headland, sharp like Cape Horn, and success and glory on the other side of it.

Of all exploration by sea, this passage was the most enchanting quest. And the source of its enchantment was that it did in fact exist, but was quite impossible to navigate under sail; so nobody could prove that it was there, but nobody could prove that it was not.

So they persevered. In 1602 the East India Company backed a voyage, but off Greenland there was a bloodless mutiny led by the ship's preacher, and the crew put up the helm and steered for home again. In 1604, another voyage came to grief in Greenland: the ship, a single pinnace, was crushed by ice and lost her rudder, and the captain and master disappeared on a walk ashore; eight survivors patched her up and recrossed the Atlantic in mid-winter. And in 1607 another famous captain began a short and surprising career in arctic waters: Henry Hudson.

Hudson emerged from total obscurity to take his place in English history. Nothing is known of his birth, or of his life except the last four years of it. His story begins on 19th April 1607: on that day, he attended Holy Communion at St Ethelburg's church in Bishopsgate in the City of London, with eleven other men who proposed to go to sea in the next few days to discover a passage by the North Pole to China and Japan. And his story ends four summers later, on 21st June 1611, when he was cast adrift by a mutinous crew and never heard of again. Between those dates, with energy that seems fanatical, he ranged the arctic seas from Novaya Zemlya in the east to the bay in the west that is still named after him. But even within that period, he remains a shadowy character. His own logs were impersonal, and the much more copious journals written by men of his crews are reticent about him – perhaps with intent, because their authors, in the end, connived at his murder.

His first two voyages were made for the Muscovy Company, in a revival of the search for a north-east passage. He explored Spitzbergen and a part of Novaya Zemlya, and the edge of the ice between them, but he made no more progress eastwards than Stephen Borough fifty years before. In 1609, he took service with the Dutch, again to explore the north-east. But this time, soon after he rounded the north of Norway, he abruptly turned back and crossed the Atlantic to Newfoundland, Cape Cod and New York. The journal of this voyage was written by a man called Robert Juet, who was probably second mate – the first mate was a Dutchman. It gives no explanation of the change of plan: on the contrary, it simply omits the events of the fortnight when the change was made, except to mention that there were fogs and snow, and that two of the crew saw a mermaid. But subsequent Dutch accounts say the crew were quarrelsome and complained of the cold. It is likely that Hudson was forced to turn back by a threat of mutiny, the first of many he experienced, and that Juet was among the mutineers.

The American coast was well known by then; it was a place for fishermen, not for explorers, and Hudson passed through fleets of French fishing boats off Cape Cod. But there was one possible source of interest. Indians had often spoken of another ocean, not far to the west – presumably the Great Lakes – and some of the maps of the time showed that part of the continent as an isthmus like Panama. Perhaps Hudson, with a crew who refused to go north, had some hope of finding a passage through the isthmus which nobody else had noticed. At all events, the voyage culminated in his famous but fruitless expedition up the Hudson River.

It was November before he reached England again, and put in to Dartmouth to find himself in trouble with everyone: with his quarrelsome crew, and with the English authorities who forbade him to go back to Holland or to take service with foreigners again. Yet such was his energy that he shook off these worries and sailed again in April with another ship, a wholly English crew, new sponsors and a new objective: the North-West Passage.

Of all the early arctic voyages, this one provides most scope for psychological speculation. The new sponsors were perhaps not entirely content with Hudson's record as master, for they appointed another master as his assistant; but before he was out of the Thames, Hudson sent this man ashore, with a letter, now lost, to the sponsors to explain why he had done so. By the time he reached Iceland, discontent and mutinous talk were rife among his crew, and they grew as he pressed on westward, past Greenland, and started to force his way through the ice in the Davis Strait. His own journal was edited afterwards by the mutineers, and the remaining parts of it make no mention of what happened. A long account of the voyage written by a survivor called Abacuk Prickett only hints at these early dissensions. But a short note was found on board the ship, apparently written by a man named Thomas Wydowse ('a student in the mathematickes') who was cast adrift with Hudson; and that described how Robert Juet was accused by Hudson of incitement to mutiny, and demanded a trial; and how other men on oath bore witness against him, so that he was convicted and degraded from his post as mate. Thus for the rest of the voyage, Juet remained on board, doubly discontented and a source of inevitable strife.

In spite of everything, Hudson found the entrance of a sound where Davis had reported a very strong tide (he had called it a furious overfall). The tide carried Hudson into the sound in a fog. He followed it farther west than anyone had been before, and on 3rd August he emerged into a spacious sea and turned south, 'confidently proud that he had won the passage'. But this, of course, was not the Pacific, it was Hudson Bay. For the next three months, with winter coming on, he sailed here and there all over the bay. The crew could not see any sense in the courses he set, or understand what he was searching for, and they openly began to argue with him: 'Up to the north we stood till we raised land, then down to the south, and up to the north, then downe to the south againe: and on Michaelmasse day came in and went out of certain lands . . .' Long before he gave up searching, he had passed the date of no return when the sound he had come in by was impassable. On 1st November, they hauled the ship ashore on the barren coast, and ten days later they were frozen in.

This was not the action of a reasonable man. To winter there was foolhardy: to do it with a crew already mutinous was asking for disaster. And it was useless too. They had started with only eight months' provisions. Through hunting and fishing they still had six months' left – enough on short rations to get them through the winter, but certainly not enough for another summer's voyage. The whole story reads as if Hudson, in those three months, was suffering from the blind euphoria that has sometimes led other explorers to their death – when the exploration itself becomes more important than life, and more important than the need to reach home with news of fresh discoveries. He seems to have thought he could force his crew to follow him because he was the only man who could find the way home. But he was wrong: at least two of the others thought they could find it. One was Robert Juet, and the other Robert Bylot, the man who had superseded him as mate. And early in the winter, Hudson degraded Bylot too, and appointed as mate a man who could not read or write – in order, the crew believed, that nobody who could understand his charts and logs would have access to them.

The winter was a miserable, sordid story of quarrels and intrigues. They quarrelled over anything: most violently over a grey cloth gown which belonged to a man who died. Hudson's authority was often questioned or defied, and his orders flouted. Something, perhaps the numbing cold and the suffering they shared, kept them from murder while the winter lasted. But when spring set them free, their latent hatred and fear broke out. Hudson shared out the remaining food, a few bits of bread and cheese, and then took the ship's boat in an unsuccessful search for Eskimos, who he thought might barter meat. When he came back empty handed, the crew rose in the night and bound him, and put him in the boat with a boy named John Hudson, who was probably his son. Six men who were lying sick were also dragged up on deck and condemned to the boat: nobody wanted to have to share food with men who were too weak to hunt or fish. And the ship's carpenter joined them of his own free will: he had fallen out with Hudson in the past, but refused to take part in a deed he said was wicked. They cut the boat adrift and sailed away.

It was a plainly murderous act. The men in the boat had never a chance of survival. And those in the ship had a voyage home which presented a series of horrors. Juet and Bylot quarrelled about the course, and the crew chose Bylot as master – luckily, because his idea of the course was right and Juet's wrong. They ran aground on a rock. Escaping from that disaster they had a furious fight with some Eskimos or Indians and five of them were killed or died of wounds – one in particular 'swearing and cursing in a most fearfull manner', according to Abacuk Prickett who wrote the journal. The rest, now only eight of the twenty-three who had started the voyage, set sail across the Atlantic with nothing to eat except some birds they had killed. After eating the birds and making soup of the offal, they ate the skins, and finally the bones fried crisply in candle grease. Robert Juet, who was older than the others, died of starvation. Seven survivors reached Ireland, too weak to stand at the tiller or handle the sails, and they had to employ some fishermen they met to sail them home to Cornwall.

Hanging was the punishment for mutiny, but these seven men were only imprisoned for a little while and then set free; and Robert Bylot, their elected master, together with Abacuk Prickett, sailed again for the same sponsors a few years later. Perhaps they owed their freedom to Prickett: his graphic account of the voyage shrewdly put all the blame for the mutiny on the men who were dead.

As for Hudson, he has come down to history as something of a hero and a victim. He was indeed an intrepid arctic sailor. Yet there must have been something wrong with the man, as a commander or as a judge of men. Quarrels and mutiny dogged his voyages, and the final mutiny, whoever its ringleaders were, can only have been his own making: he had tried his crew too hard. 'He committed many errours,' Samuel Purchas wrote a few years afterwards, 'especially in resolving to winter in that desolate place, in such want of necessarie provision.' And that, so far as one can judge, was the general opinion at the time.

*

Hudson must at least have suspected, before he died, that the sea he was in was not the Pacific Ocean. But people at home, from the mutineers' stories, persuaded themselves it was. His sponsors formed a new company, the Company of the Discoverers of the North-West Passage, under the patronage of the Prince of Wales; and they continued to send out explorers for several years to 'perfect the discovery'. Some discovered nothing new; some pressed a little farther. The most successful of them was William Baffin, but he was also the most pessimistic. In 1615 he crossed Hudson's Bay to its western shore. 'Doubtles there is a passadge,' he wrote when he came back. 'But within this strayte whome is called Hudson's Straytes, I am doubtfull, supposinge the contrarye.' And the next year he sailed much farther north, through Davis Strait and round the shores of the bay named after him. This time, he changed his spelling but not his opinion: 'I entend to shew the whole proceeding of the voyage in a word: as namely, there is no passage nor hope of passage in the north of Davis Straights.'

But hope of a passage was not so easily extinguished. New generations of optimists were always to be found. Baffin was wrong, of course; but exactly the same mistaken conclusion was reached by Sir John Ross, when he searched for the elusive passage just over two centuries later.

CHAPTER 9

John Hawkins and the
Slave Trade

THE searches for the arctic passages had been a direct attempt by the merchants of England to find a way out of the confines of the north Atlantic, into the seas where profits could be made in scents and spices. The only other way out was south, across the routes where Portugal and Spain claimed sovereignty; and with Baffin's discouraging report it is time to turn back again for a hundred years, to the reign of King Henry VIII, and follow the fortunes of seamen who tried that other way.

It is also perhaps a good moment to pause, in order to mention two clergymen who never went to sea at all, except to cross the English Channel, and yet put all historians in their debt. The first and greater of the two was Richard Hakluyt; the second Samuel Purchas.

Hakluyt was Welsh by birth, and some people say he pronounced his curious name in three syllables, Hacklewit. Among other things, he was an Oxford don, and at Christ Church from 1570 to 1588 he studied geography, or cosmographie as he would have called it. This scholarly and sedentary man was a friend of all the men of action of his time – Drake, Raleigh, Sir Humphrey Gilbert, Sir Philip Sidney – and they came to him for help, as a writer and propagandist, in furthering their schemes. And all his life, he collected seafaring stories, mainly English, from the past and present; he delved in archives, translated foreign accounts, and sometimes travelled hundreds of miles to interview an old survivor of an expedition. Towards the end of the century, he started to publish them: the *Principall Navigations, Voyages and Discoveries of the English Nation within these 1500 Years*. His massive volumes are still a rich mine of sea adventures, some trivial and some that marked an epoch, some tragic, some comic and some triumphant – and some, one must confess, repetitive and boring. And modern historians are also indebted to the Hakluyt Society, which began in the nineteenth century to republish what he wrote, and a mass of other early stories of the sea.

Samuel Purchas took over when Hakluyt died in 1616. He was vicar of a parish in Essex and was also an Oxford man, but he seems much less reliable than Hakluyt; sometimes he plainly edited stories to give them a moral of his own. But he inherited all the material Hakluyt had not had time to publish, added a great many other adventures and kept the collection up to date until 1625, when he brought out his volumes called *Hakluytus Posthumus, or Purchas his Pilgrims*. Two years later he died, it is said in a debtors' prison, and there was nobody else who carried on the work; for by then, the winds of Elizabethan enterprise had died away, and English seamanship was in the doldrums of the first of the Stuart kings.

*

Hakluyt provides a brief account of three voyages to the south which were made in the reign of Henry VIII, before even Willoughby tried the Arctic. Like Willoughby's, they were merchant ventures. Some wealthy men of Southampton, between 1530 and 1540, financed them for William Hawkins of Plymouth, the father of John and the first of this distinguished family of Tudor seamen and shipowners. Hakluyt's story, written a generation later, makes it plain that they were unusual: 'Olde M. William Haukins of Plimmouth, a man for his wisdome, valure, experience, and skill in sea causes much esteemed, and beloved of King Henry eight, and being one of the principall Sea Captaines in the West partes of England in his time, not contented with the short voyages commonly then made onely to the knowen coastes of Europe, armed out a tall and goodlie ship of his owne, of the burthen of 250. tunnes, called the *Pole of Plimmouth* wherewith he made three long and famous voyages unto the coast of Brasill, a thing in those days very rare, especially to our Nation.'

Hawkins traded for ivory ('Oliphants teeth') with the Negroes of Guinea on the west coast of Africa, then crossed the Atlantic and traded the ivory to the Indians of Brazil. He became so friendly with the South American Indians that on his second voyage one of their kings took ship with him to England: a Plymouth man named Martin Cockeram was left as hostage for his safe return. The savage king was presented to Henry VIII at Whitehall – 'at the sight of whome, the king and all the Nobilitie did not a little marveile, and not without cause; for in his cheeks were holes made accordinge to their savage manner, and therein small bones were planted, standing an inche out from the said holes, which in his own Country was reputed for a great braverie.' A year later Hawkins sailed again to take the king home and bring back Martin Cockeram. The king died at sea from the change of air and diet, but his people agreed that nobody was to blame, and Cockeram was allowed to go home to Plymouth, where he lived to become an old man.

Whatever story Cockeram had to tell is lost and forgotten now, and so are all the details of the voyages. They were an isolated enterprise. Nobody else of Hawkins's generation is known to have sailed any farther south than Gibraltar. They were a first attempt to start a peaceful trade on coasts that were claimed by Portugal, but of course they were not an attempt to reach Cathay. The most important result they had was to set a family example. When William Hawkins was sailing, his son John was a very small boy; when John grew up, he put to sea to emulate his father; and so began one strand of adventure that runs through the whole of the story of the sea in Queen Elizabeth's time: the association of the Hawkins family and Francis Drake.

John Hawkins began when he was young with several voyages to the Canary Islands, which had been colonised by Spain, after many attempts, in the 1490's. There, it was said, by his good and upright dealing he grew in love and favour with the colonists. He learned all he could from them about the Spanish West Indies, for his plans were more ambitious than his father's: to trade or capture slaves in Guinea, instead of ivory, and to sell his wares to Spaniards instead of Indians in America. It was a reasonable project. He was trading in one of the Spanish colonies, and had no cause to think he could not trade in others. As for the morals of slavery, there had never been a market for slaves in England, but hardly anyone in that era saw any harm in selling them to people who wanted to buy them. The investors in Hawkins's plan were men of the highest repute – among them two Lords Mayor of London and the Treasurer of the Admiralty.

He sailed in 1562 with a hundred men in three small ships of 120, 100 and 40 tons. On the coast of Guinea, he 'got into his possession, partly by the sword, and partly by other meanes, to the nomber of 300. negroes at the least, besides other marchandizes.' With his prey packed into his ships in unimaginable misery, he crossed the Atlantic to Hispaniola,* where the Spaniards eagerly bought the Negroes. With the money he made he bought hides, ginger, sugar, and pearls. The hides were a bulkier cargo than the Negroes, and he chartered two extra ships to carry them, and sent them to Spain itself where he hoped to sell them at a profit. But that was an error. In Cadiz, the cargo was confiscated and the Spanish authorities learned what

* Map on page 124.

he was doing. It touched their most sensitive point, their jealous monopoly of the plunder of the islands and of Mexico and Peru; and orders were sent to the Indies forbidding any more trade with English ships.

If Hawkins was told of this ban, he did not expect the Spanish colonists to take much notice of it: they were far away from their central government, they wanted slaves, and they had often interpreted government orders in ways to suit themselves. And the journey had made a profit in spite of the confiscation. So in October 1564 he sailed again, with identical plans but a much larger ship to accommodate more Negroes, the *Jesus of Lubeck* of 700 tons which was lent by the Queen. Three smaller ships were in his company, and down channel they met by chance with the Queen's ship *Minion*, escorting two others. They also were bound for Guinea and the slave trade.

Together they made an ill-assorted fleet, with ships of widely different speed and ability. In the Bay of Biscay they were scattered by a storm, and when they met again at a rendezvous – at Ferrol in northern Spain – Hawkins issued fleet orders to the masters. The orders seem to have been of his own devising, but they were probably typical; and they evoke the hardship of sailing in company before any system of signals had been invented. The small ships were always to be ahead and aweather of the *Jesus*, and to speak with her twice a day at least. If the ensign were over the poop of the *Jesus* by day, or she showed two lights by night, all the ships were to speak with her. Three lights aboard the *Jesus* showed she was putting about. If the weather were extreme and the small ships could not keep company with the *Jesus*, they were all to keep company with the *Salomon* (his own ship of the previous voyage) and forthwith to repair to the Island of Teneriffe. If any met any misfortune, they were to show two lights and shoot off a piece of ordnance; and if any lost company and came in sight again, to make three yaws and strike the mizzen three times. And the orders ended with eloquent brevity: 'Serve God dayly, love one another, preserve your victuals, beware of fire, and keepe good companie.'

Fire at sea was a terror all through the ages of wooden ships and gun-powder, and the fourth of these instructions was emphasised when the *Minion* came in to Ferrol. A narrative of the voyage was written by one of the gentlemen adventurers on board. 'The *Minion*'s men had no mirthe,' he wrote, 'because of their consort, the *Merlin* . . . By misfortune of fire (through the negligence of one of their gunners) the powder in the gunners' roome was set on fire, which with the first blast stooke out her poope, and therewithal¹ lost three men, besides many sore burned (which escaped by the

Brigandine being at her sterne), and immediately, to the great losse of the owners, and most horrible sight to the beholders, she sanke before their eyes.'

Taking the Negroes was a ruthless business which appears in the narrative without any comment or hint of remorse: 'In this island we staied certain daies, going every day a shoare, to take the Inhabitants with burning, and spoiling their townes.' And of another island: 'We sojourned unto the one and twentieth of December, where having taken certain Negroes, and of their fruites, rise and mill,* as we could well carry away, we departed.' The raiding parties wore armour and went well armed, but it was risky. Hawkins attacked a village where some Portuguese had told him there were only forty men and a hundred women and children, so that he might get a hundred marketable slaves. But the Portuguese had also said there was a great quantity of gold there, and his men scattered to ransack the huts in hope of treasure: the Negroes counter-attacked, seven Englishmen were killed and twenty-seven hurt. And there was a carpenter who went ashore to get some pompions, or pumpkins: 'who being more licorous than circumspect, went up without weapons, and as he went up alone, possibly being marked of the Negroes that were upon the trees, espying him what he did, dogged him, and finding him occupied in binding his pompions together, came beind him, overthrowing him, and straight cut his throat.'

One tenuous excuse for seizing Negroes might have been that the Negroes did the same thing to each other: in tribal wars, they enslaved the men they captured, and some tribes punished their own convicted thieves by judicially selling them to the Portuguese. But it seldom occurred to Englishmen of the time that any excuse was needed. Europeans always interpreted Christian moral teaching in ways to suit their age, and this was an age when cruelty was hardly accounted a sin. Crossing the Atlantic, the fleet was becalmed for three weeks, and they feared they might lose their perishable cargo, or even their own lives, for shortage of water; but then, the same narrator could complacently remark, 'Almightie God, who never suffereth his elect to perish, sent us the ordinary Briese.'

This time, they sailed all over the Caribbean trying to sell their wares, along the north coast of South America, and up to Hispaniola, Cuba and Jamaica. The royal orders had reached the remotest Spanish settlements, and Hawkins was driven to every kind of persuasion and bargaining. Sometimes he argued that the royal houses of England and Spain were in amity; some-

* Rice and millet.

times he pretended the *Jesus* was a royal ship only driven to the Indies by contrary winds, and now in need of money to pay her troops and crew; sometimes he landed with a hundred men in armour and tried to trade by threats. Everywhere, it was the same story: the Spaniards wanted to buy but they had been ordered not to, and they were afraid that if they did, their purchases would be confiscated. And while they argued, the Negroes sickened, and lean ones had to be sold off cheap to poor colonists who could not afford a healthy one. The first had been captured in November, and the last was not sold until May: six months chained in the dark of the holds. Perhaps the crews contrived to enjoy the voyage in spite of the horror they knew was below their decks; but almost the only pleasant incident in the narrative is their first taste of potatoes – 'the most delicate roots that may be eaten, which far exceed parsnips or carrots.'

Hawkins sold all his wares at last, and came home safely; and in spite of all the difficulties he made another journey, the third. He was again in the *Jesus*; but this time the Queen sent her own ship the *Minion* under his command. On 2nd October, 1567 his fleet stood out of Plymouth: among it a small bark named *Judith*, 50 tons, whose captain was one of two figures in English seafaring who stand above all others – Nelson the greatest master of tactics and of men, and Drake the greatest master of the sea.

Drake was about twenty-two, ten years younger than Hawkins, and they are said to have been kinsmen. Whether that was so or not, they were close neighbours at Tavistock in Devon when Drake was a child – the Hawkins family wealthy members of the landed gentry, and Francis Drake a local farmer's son. Through religious persecution in Mary's reign, Drake's father, who was a protestant preacher, had to move to Kent, and Drake learned to handle a boat, like Nelson, among the strong tides and mudflats of the Medway estuary. As a boy and a very young man, he served in coasters, then to the Bay of Biscay, and once to the Indies. But no doubt it was the patronage of the Hawkins family that brought him back to Devon, where pride in the sea still united men of every social level, as it had in the days of medieval piracy.

Hawkins wrote an account of this voyage himself: he called it miserable, troublesome and sorrowful. But the trading went well. One African chief invited Hawkins to help him win a war against another, and promised him all the captives. Between them they set a town on fire and put its citizens to flight. The chief broke his promise and decamped with six hundred prisoners, but the English themselves had taken two hundred and fifty. By other forays, they brought the number up to four or five hundred: not so many as they had hoped, but enough to pay the expenses.

In the Caribbean, the Spaniards had begun to forget the royal order and traded willingly, except in the town of Rio de la Hacha on the coast which is now Colombia. There, the Treasurer who was in charge would not agree to any trade, or allow the fleet to water; so Hawkins attacked the town with two hundred men, and its defenders fired one volley and ran away. By some means this show of force put the Treasurer's mind at rest, and he came back by night with the gentlemen of the town and bought two hundred Negroes.

The origin of the trouble and sorrow was not the trade, but the weather, and the condition of the *Jesus*. She was a very old-fashioned ship. Henry VIII had bought her from the Hanseatic league fifty years before and she had the huge forecastle and aftercastle of her period. In structure she was long past her prime: some years before the Queen lent her to Hawkins as a slaver, she had been condemned in the navy as beyond repair. At the beginning of the voyage she was in difficulties. A severe storm in the Bay of Biscay dispersed the fleet. The small ships weathered it, but the *Jesus* was in such distress that they thought she was unfit for the voyage and turned for home. A change in the weather made them change their minds and set course again for the Canary Islands, where they caught up with the others.

The Atlantic crossing, Hawkins said, was harder than usual, and it took them seven weeks from land to land. And then, on the way home in July, between the coasts of Cuba and Florida, they were caught in a hurricane: 'which so beat the *Jesus*, that we cut downe all her higher buildings, her rudder also was sore shaken, and with all was in so extreme a leake that we were rather upon the point to leave her than to keepe her any longer.' Another account said that some of her leaks – or presumably the gush of water coming through them – were the thickness of a man's arm, and that live fishes were swimming among her ballast. They searched for a harbour on the Florida coast, but the sea was too shallow. Driven west by another storm, on the edge of despair, they sighted the little Spanish port of San Juan de Ulloa and entered it.

Coming into this haven, battered and tired, they were surprised by the chief officers of the country, who approached with ceremony and came aboard. These gentlemen thought the ships were forerunners of the fleet of Spain, which was expected daily with a huge consignment of treasure. When they found their mistake they were greatly dismayed; but they were comforted when Hawkins asked for nothing but victuals, for which he could pay, and time to rest from the sea and repair his ships. One night passed in peace: but in the dawn, thirteen great ships were sighted outside the harbour, the treasure fleet, laden according to rumour with nearly two million pounds' worth of gold and silver.

Hawkins described his own dilemma. He could, he believed, have defied the fleet and kept it out of the port. But the roadstead was dangerous and the weather uncertain, and he feared the Queen's indignation if the Spanish fleet were shipwrecked through his action. On the other hand, if he let it in, he feared the treachery which Englishmen expected of the Spaniards. After thinking it over, he sent a messenger out to the fleet to offer conditions for its entry.

On board, it turned out, was no less a person than the Viceroy of Mexico, Don Martin Henriquez, a man who later introduced the Inquisition to the country he ruled. He replied that he had heard of Hawkins's fair dealing on the coast; and after three days of negotiation, he and Hawkins signed an agreement that the two fleets should both lie in the harbour at peace. They met to ratify it, and exchanged ten hostages to guarantee it; and the Spanish fleet sailed in, saluting the English with guns according to custom.

The ships filled the harbour, moored alongside each other with their bow anchors ashore on an island. The peace between them lasted only two days. On the third, the English saw troops being moved on shore and from ship to ship. Hawkins sent word to the Viceroy to ask what was meant by it. The Viceroy renewed his promise that no harm was intended. The English were still suspicious: a great number of men seemed to be hidden in a ship of 900 tons moored next to the *Minion*. Hawkins then sent the master of the *Jesus*, who spoke Spanish – and the Viceroy had him seized, a trumpet was sounded and the Spanish attacked from all sides. Hundreds jumped ashore from the bows of their ships and slaughtered the English who were on the island. Others boarded the *Minion*. But in the half-hour of suspicion, she had prepared: her crew fought off the boarders, cast off her headropes and hauled her off by her stern anchors. The attack then fell on the *Jesus*, but with heavy losses she also was defended and warped astern for two ships' lengths.

At that range, an artillery battle began. Hawkins's men were hopelessly outgunned, but they fought back with everything they had, and thought they set the Spanish flagship on fire and sank another. But their own smallest ships were also sunk, and the rigging and masts of the *Jesus* were soon so cut up that she could not have carried sail. Hawkins hauled her round until she sheltered the smaller *Minion*: he had a hope of holding out like that until the night, and then stocking the *Minion* with provisions from the *Jesus*. But next, the Spaniards set two of their own ships on fire and let them drift down on the *Jesus* and the *Minion*. Fireships were a fearful weapon within a harbour: some men on the *Jesus* wanted to take to the *Minion* and sail her clear, others to wait and see if the wind would carry the fireships past. But the *Minion's* men made their own decision. Without waiting for orders, they cast off and set some sail. Hawkins jumped aboard her as she went. Other men left it too late. Some of them, still unwounded, piled into a boat and rowed after her; the rest had to wait for the mercy of the Spaniards, which was small. And as the *Minion* cleared harbour, Drake brought his own small bark, the *Judith*, out of the fire. The *Minion* anchored two bowshots from the Spanish ships, but the *Judith* stood out to sea: 'which barke,' Hawkins wrote, 'the same night forsooke us in our great miserie.'

Then began one of the nightmare voyages the sea sometimes imposes. The *Minion* was impossibly overcrowded by two hundred men, and she had almost nothing to eat on board. For the first fortnight, she wandered in the Gulf of Mexico, a sea unknown to anyone aboard her. Men caught seabirds, and ate the mice, rats, cats and dogs that were in the ship, and the prized parrots and monkeys the seamen had bought as pets. Some men wanted to surrender to the Spaniards somewhere else, for the colonists, unlike the Viceroy and the fleet, had been friendly enough; some wanted to join the Indians, and some to abide the mercy of God at sea. At length they made land, somewhere in the bottom of the gulf, but they found neither people, food nor harbour. About half their company asked Hawkins to put them ashore, and he did so. On the 16th of October, the rest set sail again. Two and a half months later, a remnant so few and weak that they could scarcely work the ship made land again in Spain. Many had died of cold and starvation in the winter sea; now, with fresh meat from the shore, more died by gorging themselves. Twelve fit men were recruited from English ships in Vigo, and these brought the *Minion* back to Cornwall with the outworn survivors. Hawkins was among them.

Drake was already there. He had brought the *Judith* home, equally overcrowded, after a voyage almost equally fraught with suffering.

*

The fight at San Juan de Ulloa was no great affair in itself, but it had the most momentous results. By English standards of honour and the custom of the sea, the Spaniards had shown the foulest treachery. Elizabethan England never forgot it or forgave them for it, and anger was renewed from time to time years afterwards, when solitary broken survivors of the hundred who went ashore made their way home with ghastly stories of imprisonment and torture. This was the incident that put an end to the diffidence of the seamen of England: no Englishman ever again felt he was inferior to the Spaniards on the sea.

Especially, it changed the temper of the two commanders, Hawkins and Drake. Hawkins was desolated by the loss of so many men under his command. He seldom went to sea again; instead, he took his revenge by accepting the post of Treasurer of the Queen's Majesty's Marine Cause. In that capacity he was in charge of the royal ships. And his single-minded rule brought the most profound change that was ever made in the design of fighting ships under sail – the change that alone enabled British seamen to beat the Spanish Armada twenty years later.

As for Drake, this affront at the age of twenty-two was the start of his career, and his revenge for it was to cause his name to be whispered in fear and sometimes shouted in panic, yet often remembered with gratitude, in Spanish seaports everywhere in the world.

CHAPTER 10

Tudor Ships

Of all the results of San Juan de Ulloa, one can look first at the revenge that Hawkins took: the years he spent in changing the Queen's ships to make them fit, and more than fit, to challenge the fleets of the King of Spain. But to appreciate what a radical change he made, one has to go back again to the start of the Tudor age, to look at the ships his predecessors built.

On the whole, the Tudors had much more feeling for ships and the sea than the earlier kings of England. Seaborne trade had proved its own value, and they understood the need for royal ships to protect it, either by fighting or by a display of magnificence at sea. In a century of Tudor inspiration, the design of the royal ships achieved a double climax: first a peak of totally unpractical splendour, and then, under Hawkins's regime about fifty years later, a peak of fighting efficiency which far outstripped the ships of rival nations.

Yet the Tudors still had no fighting navy as a separate service; that did not begin until Stuart times. The word navy was still often used to mean the whole seafaring resources of the realm. Merchant ships were armed, and they still took a major part in battles; and their masters and crews made a habit of changing their roles, sometimes trading as peacefully as they could, sometimes fighting and plundering on their own account, and sometimes taking service under the crown. The last of the Stuart kings, a century later, had professional naval officers; the last of the Tudors still had amateurs when it came to war – but amateurs of incomparable brilliance.

Henry VII began the new evolution of ships with the *Regent* and the *Royal Sovereign*, launched in 1488 and 1489 – before Columbus's voyage. Not much is known about them: ships were still built by eye, or by rule of thumb. The *Regent*, the larger of the two, was certainly the largest built in England since the *Grace Dieu* in 1415, although she had only half that monster's recorded tonnage. She had four masts, with topmasts on the main and fore, and also a main top-gallant mast; and she is said to have carried more guns than any other ship in history – 225 of them, all mounted on the upper deck and castles. But they were only serpentines; they had a bore of only an inch and a half, and they fired a half-pound shot. Nobody yet had put heavy guns in ships. Ships were still conveyances for soldiers; and indeed the *Regent* was lost in a hand-to-hand fight, when she grappled a French ship off Brest and both of them caught fire.

These two were almost certainly carvel built. Some time in the past century, clinker building of large ships had quietly been abandoned by the English shipwrights, and carvel building had become the normal practice. A large clinker-built galley is recorded in 1515, but she seems to have been unusual. It was said of her that she was the 'dangeroust ship under water that ever men sailed in', and in 1523 orders were given to 'break her up and make her carvel'.

Unexpectedly, the Scots were the next to enter the field of large prestigious ships. In 1506, they built the *Great Michael*, which is said to have been 240 feet in length, with sides that were ten feet thick. With those dimensions, she would have been one of the largest and heaviest wooden ships ever built. All the shipwrights in Scotland, and some of other countries, took part in building her, and all the oak woods of Fife were felled to supply such astonishing frames and planking, besides other timber that was brought from Norway. She was built in a year and a day, and they claimed that no cannon shot could go through her; but she lived only six years, and was lost on her way to France in the same year as the *Regent*.

Henry VIII inherited a well-found navy and built a good many more ships in his reign; and like earlier kings, he built one, presumably for the sake of prestige, which was much bigger than any of the others. This was the famous *Henri Grace a Dieu*, or *Great Harry*, a ship of 1000 tons. At least three paintings or drawings of her by contemporary artists still exist. In the eyes of shipwrights and sailors, artists are often distressingly inexact; but three separate artists' impressions of a single ship must give a fair idea of what she looked like.

The most widely known of them is the painting by Volpe of the King's embarkation at Dover in May 1520, on his way to the Field of the Cloth of Gold. It most clearly shows her decoration. She is caparisoned with all the pomp of ancient heraldry – and not merely because the King was aboard her, for the other pictures confirm that this was her normal adornment. 'The royal standard of England flies on each of the four angles of the forecastle, and the staff of each standard is surrounded by a fleur-de-lys Or. Pennants fly from the mastheads, and at each angle of the poop is a banner of St

George. Her quarters and sides, as well as her tops, are hung with targets, charged differently with the Cross of St George, Azure a fleur-de-lys Or, party per pale Argent and Vert a union rose, and party per pale Argent and Vert a portcullis Or, alternately and repeatedly . . . Beneath the break of the forecastle are shown, party per pale Argent and Vert, within the garter, the arms of England and France, quarterly crowned; the supporters, a lion and a dragon, being those then used by the king.' The King himself stands in the waist, dressed in cloth of gold and crimson. Yeomen of the Guard are on watch, and trumpeters are sounding on the poop and forecastle. The pennants stream bravely in the wind; and one of these, as it appears in the accounts for her building, was 51 yards long and cost £3, compared with a flag for 10d, a boathook for 4d and a compass for 2/-. The sails are golden.

In short, this picture, confirmed by the others, shows that the ancient trappings and ornaments of chivalry had been transferred or extended, from castles and horses to ships. It suggests a social approval of ships and the sea, as if the world of chivalry, which for so long had scorned the world of ships, had decided at last to take it over. But it was a phase that seems not to have lasted very long. Queen Elizabeth's ships were more mundane and workmanlike in their decoration, and though those of the Stuarts a century later were highly ornate, their ornament was more baroque than heraldic. Yet it might also be said that ships have never quite lost the last vestige of chivalric art, for sailors still make more ceremonial use of flags and pennants than anyone in other walks of life.

The *Henri Grace a Dieu* has another particular interest: she is a ship in transition. She still has the huge medieval forecastle and aftercastle. To any sailor they make her look like a prehistoric monster which has evolved to a size that dooms it to extinction. And yet she also has cannon on the lower decks, which fire through gunports. So she lies between two epochs of fighting at sea. The castles take her back to the days when soldiers fought hand-to-hand to board an enemy ship, and threw down missiles on their opponents from a superior height. The gunports belong to the coming age of naval artillery.

Of course, heavy guns had been used for a long time ashore, but they could not be used on the upper decks of ships, because their weight would have upset the ship's stability and their recoil strained its structure. It is said the King himself suggested the answer to this problem: to mount them lower down, and fire them through ports which could be closed securely in heavy weather. It was not an entirely new idea: the same thing had been done fifty years before in the Mediterranean. But it was a novelty in northern waters. When the *Henri Grace a Dieu* was launched, she was equipped with 21 brass guns of calibres from the cannon, 8 inches, down to the falcon, 2½ inches, in addition to the smaller weapons called slings, fowlers, bassils, top-pieces, hail-shot pieces and hand-guns. She was rebuilt in 1540, and by then the technique had advanced; she was re-fitted with 19 guns of brass and 103 of iron – the latter cast in the Sussex foundries. But still, she did not rely entirely on gunnery. In her stores there were also 500 bows of yew, ten gross of bow-strings, 400 pikes and bills, and great quantities of darts and arrows.

With this dinosaur of a ship, the time was clearly coming for a seamen's rebellion, for someone to insist that ships were meant to sail and should be designed to sail as well as science and art permitted. It is impossible to believe the *Henri Grace a Dieu* was fit for distant voyages. An admiral wrote to tell the King she was one of the best and most weatherly ships in his fleet; but if that was true, and was not only said to flatter the King, it can only have meant that the others were even worse. Yet her guns gave a promise of something better. To fight with guns at a distance, instead of grappling and fighting hand to hand, would set seamen free of two encumbrances: soldiers and their castles.

Another generation passed before the growing experience of English seamen began to make itself felt. During the reigns of Edward and Mary Tudor and the early years of Elizabeth, the royal ships went into another of their periods of decline. But when the Queen appointed Hawkins as Treasurer, she put an experienced seaman in charge of her ships, and one moreover who was obsessed with revenge for San Juan de Ulloa. With him was William Borough, who had sailed as a boy to the far north-east with his brother Stephen and made many more voyages since. Behind them was the knowledge of other deep-water seamen, and the skill of a new generation of master shipwrights, most notably Matthew Baker and Peter Pett. And these practical men evolved for the Queen an entirely new kind of fighting ship.

It was sometimes called a race-built ship; and whatever that phrase may have meant, it conveys the essence of the new design. It was a ship that relied entirely on gunnery. It was not very large or imposing in appearance, and beside the older ships it looked smaller than it was; for the freeboard was less, the old forecastle was swept away and the aftercastle lowered. If this kind of ship had ever been boarded and forced to fight hand to hand, it would have been at a hopeless disadvantage against the older kinds; but it was meant to avoid that situation. Without the windage of the top-hamper soldiers had demanded, it was faster, more weatherly and quicker on the helm. So it could outsail the older ships on any point of wind; it could choose and keep its range and beat them with its guns. In short, it was a seaman's weapon, no longer a mere floating fort for landsmen.

If one were to look for the sources of Britain's supremacy at sea, the first would perhaps be the skill of her seamen, but the second would certainly be the new conception of a royal ship that began in the years that Hawkins held his office. To stake everything on the evolution and practice of naval gunnery was the boldest of decisions. But it put England far ahead of any rival in fighting power. When the Spanish Armada came, with its ships of the old design, its officers were appalled to find that the English could sail rings round them. And English seamen, armed with this new weapon, won a self-confidence in battle which they never lost.

*

The design and building of Tudor ships was a family affair; shipwrights kept their methods secret and handed them on to their sons. The Pett family, for instance, produced at least ten master shipwrights in four generations, between 1560 and 1660 – most of whom, to the confusion of historians, were named either Peter or Phineas. If Tudor shipwrights drew plans of the hulls they designed, they kept them to themselves, and so there is no direct evidence of how they went to work.

But in the next century, from 1620 onwards, several treatises on hull design were written. They laid down accepted rules which seem to have been the well-established practice and had probably been in use for at least a hundred years. These rules were remarkably simple – so simple that a man who used them could design and build a ship of any size without drawing any plans at all. And that is almost certainly what the shipwrights did.

Since their major ships were carvel built, the frames were made and set up first, and the shape of the frames dictated the shape of the ship. And the frames, or cross-sections, it was now revealed, had none of the parabolic curves of a modern design; they were constructed in circular arcs, which were known as sweeps. On each side of the keel, the floor of the ship AB was flat. The first sweep BC was drawn from a centre O1 vertically above the end of the floor. The second sweep was of greater radius. To avoid a discontinuous curve where the two sweeps joined, the second centre O2 had to be in line with O1 and the end of the first sweep C. With the same geometrical con-

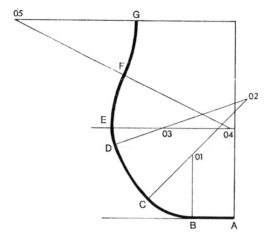

Midship section constructed by Anthony Deane's rules

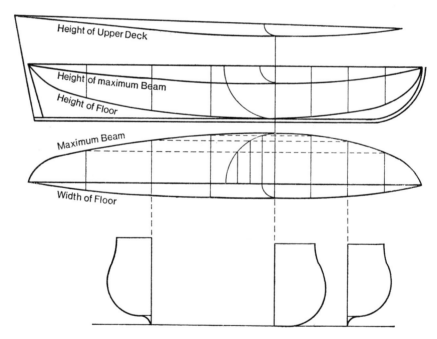

The fore-and-aft ellipses and three sections obtained from them

struction, the third sweep brought the side of the ship to the vertical a little above the waterline, and the fourth gave it a tumble-home. The fifth was reversed, and brought the side almost vertical again at the height of the upper deck.

The art of design lay in the choice of the radii, and a manuscript by Anthony Deane, a famous shipwright of the 1650's, gave the formula:

Radius of the first sweep: $\frac{1}{4}$ of the beam
Radius of the second: 20/36 of the beam
Radius of the third: 7/9 of the first
Radius of the fourth and fifth: 17/36 of the beam.

For a ship of a given beam and draught, this formula fixed the shape of the frame at the point where the beam was greatest. This point of greatest beam was not amidships; from the example of ducks and fish, it was placed farther forward, about 2/5 of the ship's length from the bow.

The shapes of all the other frames, except at the extreme bow and stern, were derived from the fore-and-aft curves of the ship, and these were almost as simple: they were either circles of large radii or ellipses – an ellipse being the easiest curve to construct from a circle, and the easiest to translate into practical terms in the building dock. To find the beam at any point, for example, a quarter circle was drawn with a radius of half the greatest beam. The bottom radius was divided into a number of equal parts, and per-pendiculars measured up to the circumference of the circle. The forward two-fifths, and the after three-fifths of the keel, laid in the dock, were then divided into the same number of parts, and the length of the perpendiculars gave the half-beam at each of them. Other smaller quarter circles gave the other dimensions that were needed: the breadth of the floor, which decreased towards the ends of the ship, and the heights above the keel of the floor, the point of greatest beam and the upper deck, which all increased.

By using these rules and some elementary arithmetic, it was possible for the master shipwright to tell his sawyers the radius of every part of the main framework of the ship, leaving only the frames at the bow and stern to be shaped and fitted by eye. And to make all the frames in circles was a practical plan which would greatly have simplified the sawing of the timber; for all that was needed was a large pair of compasses, or simply a piece of string and a piece of chalk, to choose curved logs and mark them out and saw them, either in the shipyard or else in the forest itself.

Given the rules, the only difficult parts of a ship's design were to choose her beam in relation to her length, and to estimate the waterline at which she would float – which was then called the swimming line. Shipwrights often seem to have made mistakes in these. Anthony Deane was credited with an extraordinary power to estimate the swimming line: others, less gifted, corrected their swimming lines with ballast. As for the beam, it was believed then and for long afterwards that a narrower ship was faster, which is not wholly true. Consequently, ships were often built too narrow in the beam; they were crank, they heeled too much under sail. This was such a common fault that there was a recognised term for the method of putting it right: they had to be furred, which meant that an extra layer of planking was added above and below the waterline to increase the beam and make them more stable.

Ships designed by these primitive rules must always have had a somewhat primitive shape, and been far from perfect in their sailing ability. And it is a question how exactly the rules could be followed. English oak is intractable stuff which warps unpredictably. It was always thought wise to let the frames stand as long as the contract permitted before they were finally faired off and planked – Nelson's *Victory*, in 1759 and 1760, stood a year in frame. Probably, after the sawyers had finished and the frames were erected, the men with adzes had to do plenty of fairing; and certainly, lean frames sometimes had to be furred to bring them into line. In 1620, there were complaints that shipwrights never succeeded in building two ships alike, and Samuel Pepys, later still, said most of them were gouty, illiterate, intemperate and ill-conditioned men who understood their own craft so imperfectly that they could not explain it to anybody else. Wooden ships are fascinating; but a dispassionate study of English ships, at least as far as the end of the eighteenth century, leaves a strong impression that the secrecy of shipwrights often hid their ignorance, that botched-up jobs were not at all uncommon, and that even the best and most famous of ships were perforce designed on simple lines which very simple workers could understand, and so could not have attained the sea performance which more subtle curves might have given them.

But still, whatever faults the English ships possessed, the ships of other nations had them too. All countries, including England, had mathematicians in the sixteenth century who could have improved the rules of hull design; but it was not until very much later that science and scholarship made any mark on the empirical family traditions of the shipwrights. The race-built ships of the Elizabethan navy won their superiority not by novel lines, but by their confident dependence on gunnery, and by stripping away the unseamanlike upper works that armies had imposed on fighting ships. With those advances, they set a pattern among the warships of the world which lasted without any fundamental change for all the remaining centuries of fighting under sail.

PART THREE

MASTERY

1567–1603

*The British discover
they can master the sea.
With new confidence, they harass
the Spaniards as a sport,
and then beat them in battle.*

CHAPTER II

The Sport of Baiting Spaniards

THE treachery of San Juan was the biggest mistake the Spaniards could have made. In Hawkins it induced the methodical hatred which designed the race-built ships for their overthrowing. In Drake it caused a more direct reaction. To judge by all his later life, it would be wrong to say it made him hate the Spaniards. He was not a man for hatred. But it made him utterly despise them. He never killed a Spaniard except in the necessity of battle. But he delighted to make them look foolish – to scare them out of their wits, provoke them to impotent rage, deflate their reputation as seamen and mock the pompous manners of their officials – and also of course to rob them of the treasures they themselves had stolen from simpler people. And under his example the English found an entirely new motive for going to sea. It was neither trade nor conquest: it was not organised by the merchants, nor by the Crown. It was sport, the greatest sport of Elizabethan England: baiting Spaniards.

It was in this sport that the English found their mastery of seamanship and shook off for ever their feeling of inferiority: the supremacy which built a world-wide empire started as a game. Looking back, it seems that such a great historical movement should have begun with some more serious intent, but it did not; the seamen who started it thought of it as sport, and it fits no other sphere of human activity. It was not war, although it led to war after fifteen years; nor was it piracy, although it came rather near it. It was organised by the men who took part in it, simply because they enjoyed it and it was fun. They were only a few score captains and a few thousand men, and almost all of them were very young. But the whole of the rest of the nation followed it precisely as they follow football now: they celebrated its wins and suffered in its losses, and made heroes of its most successful captains.

As a sport, it excelled the outright piracy of the centuries before. It was very exciting and very dangerous, it needed skill and stamina and a kind of

121

team spirit, and it took its players on long adventurous journeys to exotic shores. It gave a chance of unimaginable wealth and yet seemed perfectly moral, for all the treasures plundered from the Spaniards had already been plundered by them. It had the spur of religion, of Protestant against Catholic, and also something of the ancient spur of chivalry – because it was played at the pleasure of a Queen who was feared and loved, a woman who took the place, on distant voyages, of the romantic lady-loves of the earlier knights. And it was played according to strict unwritten rules. Every sea captain knew he could go so far but no farther. If his behaviour to the Spaniards was too outrageous, the Queen would disown him to preserve her tenuous peace withSpain; if he failed, her scorn would put an end to his career; but if he came home with trophies and a good story to tell, she would gladly take her share of the booty and reward him with her favour.

*

Within two years of Drake's return from San Juan, he was granted a privateer's commission by the Queen. Strictly speaking, privateers were privately owned ships commissioned to act as warships against a hostile power, and their status in international law was not abolished until 1856. But Queen Elizabeth used her commissions freely. In legal terms, Spain was not a hostile power, and the Queen had no intention that her privateers should act as warships. Her commissions meant that men could claim her protection if they were captured – provided they had not exceeded the rules of the game. With a letter of marque from her on board his ship, a captain could tell a Spanish court he was not a pirate, and with luck could save himself and his crew from the gallows.

Drake laid his plans with extraordinary patience. To harass the Spaniards in the Indies, he wanted bases where he could rest and refit, and the first two voyages under his independent command were reconnaissances. When he met Spanish ships at sea he captured them, in order to help himself to their food, but he always let them go again, or put their crews ashore in places where they could find their way home. In these voyages, he made himself a reputation all over the Spanish Main for quick irresistible attacks and quite unexpected generosity. But he avoided Spanish ports, and explored the coasts unseen. The settlements were far apart; between them, he found plenty of natural harbours where small ships could lie in secret. The one he liked best was on the coast of Darien, the eastern part of the isthmus of Panama: it was entirely hidden by jungle, and he named it Port

Pheasant because of the number of birds his seamen caught and cooked.

In May 1572 he was ready, and he sailed from Plymouth straight to Port Pheasant, only stopping to water on the way, with two small ships, the *Pasco* (which was a Plymouth name) and the *Swan*, and seventy-five adventurers who mostly were neighbours in Devon. He was twenty-six or twenty-seven, and all the others were younger than him except one man of fifty. And of all voyages ever made, this must have been the most exciting for a youthful crew: a year and three months of pure adventure on an empty coast, through tropical jungle, in and out of Spanish harbours, under a captain who could always sail a boat a little better than anyone else alive and always go farther in sheer audacity than either his friends or his enemies expected. It had failures and disappointments, enough to enhance its triumphs. It had extreme hardships also: half the men died on the way. But adventure does not exist without danger; any Englishman sailing to the Spanish Main would have been content with a fifty-fifty chance of coming back alive. And over it all was the air of gaiety, good humour and overflowing self-confidence which was the mark of the best of the Elizabethans.

Drake's voyages are so well-known that people are apt to think they were unique. But already, other English captains were playing the same game, and two of them turned up at Port Pheasant. Entering the harbour which he supposed was secret, Drake saw a column of smoke among the trees. There was nobody there, only a dying fire. Prowling around, his men found a sheet of lead nailed to a very large tree, with a message scratched on it: 'Captain Drake, if you fortune to come to this Port, mak hast away, for the Spaniards which you had with you here the last yeere have bewrayed this place, and taken away all that you left here. I departed from hence, this present 7. of July, 1572. Your verie loving friend John Garret.'

Five days before. Everyone knew John Garret, he was a Plymouth man, and Port Pheasant, of course, was an open secret in Plymouth: but nobody knew, or knows now, what he was doing there, or where he had gone. Drake was not much disturbed. He landed the parts of three pinnaces he had brought in his holds from home, and his carpenters started to hammer them together.

Next day, another ship came in: an English bark from the Isle of Wight, Captain Rance, escorting two captured Spaniards. This was a nuisance, the place was getting crowded: Drake had to confide in Rance and tell him his plans.

They were typical. The Spaniards by then had exhausted the gold of the

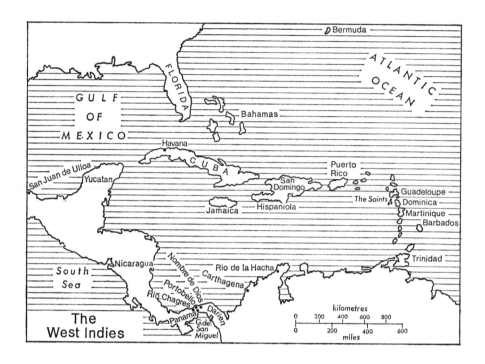

The West Indies

Caribbean Indians, and almost exterminated the Indians in doing so. Now, they were exploiting their discoveries in the Pacific: the gold and jewels of the Incas, the silver of the mines of Bolivia and the pearls of the South Sea. All this inestimable wealth was brought from Panama, on the Pacific side of the isthmus, to the town of Nombre de Dios on the Caribbean, by a single mule-track through the jungle. Nombre de Dios and the track itself were the centre and hub of all the Spanish operations; and consequently, those were the objectives Drake had chosen. Rance said he would like to join him, and Drake was obliged to agree.

In a week, the pinnaces were ready. Fifty-three of Drake's men embarked in them, with twenty of Rance's in a boat of their own, to row and sail along the coast to Nombre de Dios, 150 miles away. Their arms, packed in casks to keep them dry, were 'sixe Targets, sixe Firepikes, twelve Pikes, twentie four Muskets and Callivers, sixteene Bowes, and sixe Partisans, two Drums and two Trumpets.' It was an outfit he had carefully considered. Bows were more reliable than muskets in a wet climate. The arrows had been 'made of purpose in England, not great sheafe arrows, but fine roving shafts, very carefully reserved for the service.' The drums and trumpets were

124

to signal to friends and intimidate enemies; and the firepikes were ordinary pikes with a twist of tarry tow on the end, used both as torches and weapons. From his captives in the past two years, he had a clear idea of Nombre de Dios. It was a considerable town, bigger than Plymouth, with streets and a market place, main buildings of stone and houses of wood, a wall all round except on the seaward side, and a single gate where the trail from Panama came in: not a small undertaking for seventy-three men in open boats, but not a small prize if they won it.

After five days, at dusk, they sighted the watchtower on the point of the bay, waited until it was dark, and quietly rowed to the harbour mouth, below the loom of the hills that surrounded it. Drake meant to attack at dawn, but the men began to whisper about the size of the town and its garrison. Most of them had never been in a fight before; the odds against them were heavy, and with nothing to do but wait they looked heavier still. So he cut the waiting short. The moon was rising. He said it was the dawn, and gave the word to go.

The crew of a ship saw them coming, and put off a boat for the shore. Drake cut in ahead of it and ran the pinnaces aground below the houses. Twelve men, in his plan, were to keep the pinnaces, sixteen under his brother to double round to the far end of the town, and himself with the others to march up the main street with firepikes lighted and the sound of drum and trumpet. And in the eye-witness account of what happened, there is the elation of the torchlit, moonlit skirmish:

'The Souldiers, and such as were joyned with them, presented us with a jolly hot volley of shot . . . we stood not to answer them in like tearmes: but having discharged our first volley of shot, and feathered them with our arrowes, we came to the push of pike, so that our fire-pikes being well armed and made of purpose, did us very great service. For our men with their pikes and short weapons in short time tooke such order among those Gallants, some using the but-end of their Peeces in stead of other weapons, that . . . they, casting downe their weapons, fled all out of the Towne by the gate aforesaid.'

The town was emptied, the church bell still ringing the alarm. Drake sent some men to stop it, but the church was locked and he told them not to force it. He made for the Governor's house, where the treasure that came from Panama was counted. The door was open, a horse stood saddled, and a candle was lighted inside. There was nobody there. By the light of the candle, they saw a huge heap of silver, twelve feet high and seventy feet in length, piled against the wall of a lower room. Drake told them to leave it, it was too heavy, and the gold and jewels, he believed, were in the King's Treasure House, nearer the water's edge.

After a lull, the uproar in the town began again, but then it was stilled by a thunderstorm and a heavy shower of rain. Everyone took shelter to keep their powder dry, Drake's men beneath the eaves of the Treasure House itself. As soon as the rain began to ease, he told his brother's troop to break open the treasury, and the rest of them to follow him to hold off the enemy. Stepping forward, he fainted and fell; and then they saw he was wounded in the leg, and standing there all that time had filled the footprints they had made with blood. They tied his scarf round his leg, and begged him to give up the treasure to save his life. He refused, but grew weaker, and when he could not resist, they carried him back to the pinnaces, launched them and rowed away.

They only retreated three miles, to an island which was the market garden for the town. Next morning, the Governor sent out a courtly official – 'a proper Gentleman of mean stature, good complexion and fare spoken' – to ask after their health. He was the kind of Spaniard the English thought most ludicrous: Drake assumed he was a spy, but asked him to dine. Was it true, the emissary asked, that he had the honour to meet Captain Drake? The townsmen had been delighted that their attackers were English, not French: the English might steal their treasure, but the French were cruel. But were the English arrows poisoned? And what victuals or other necessities did Captain Drake desire? Drake gave him the obvious answers; as for his needs, he said, he wanted nothing but the special commodity the country yielded, gold, and if God lent him life and leave, he proposed to reap some of that harvest. After dinner, the gentleman departed, protesting that he had never been so honoured in his life.

Before the fight Drake's crew had been hesitant; but they had won, and could have taken the treasure if they wished, and now they were almost over-confident. Captain Rance, on the other hand, lost heart and went away, to nobody's regret. Drake had no idea what to do next. But he had found an ally, a runaway Negro slave who said his name was Pedro: he begged to be taken on board, and offered his life and service to the English. In the jungle, he said, there were thousands of men like himself who would gladly help the English to rob the Spaniards.

In fact, the Negroes who had escaped from their Spanish owners had created a civilisation of their own in Panama. They had secret towns: the largest was called Ronconcholon, and it kept 1700 men under arms. They were so many, and made themselves such a menace, that the Spanish had a name for them: cimarrones, wildmen, a word that was shortened later in English to maroons. Drake found some of them, with Pedro's help, on an empty stretch of coast. They said it would be easy to seize a train of the mules that carried treasure across the trail from Panama to Nombre de Dios, but they also told him a fact he did not know; that in the rainy season the trail became impassable, and no more treasure would come across it for the next four months.

So he waited, but not in idleness. He hid his ships and put to sea in the pinnaces. At that time the Spaniards had about two hundred ships in the local coasting trade, and his crew claimed afterwards that they captured them all in those four months, and some of them several times, and always let them go again after taking food and ammunition, and anything else of value they had on board. Perhaps in their enthusiasm the story grew a little, but Drake did not deny it; and certainly they had astonishing success – the sighting almost every day, the chase, the short symbolic fight against a token opposition, and then the pleasure of rummaging in the ships for anything useful: maize, wine, sugar, bacon, cheese, live hogs and hens, once a whole cargo of honey and once, less welcome, of soap. Sometimes they met the fiasco of an empty ship; sometimes they were wet and cold and hungry, sometimes they feasted; always they had the hope of a chest full of gold. Whenever ships were scarce at sea, they sailed right into the harbour of Carthagena, the strongest of the cities on the Main, captured ships inside it and sailed them out, and always kept to windward of their enemies. And between times, when the pursuit of Spanish men-of-war grew hot, they vanished into hidden bays to rest, and Drake set half of the men each day to mending gear and the other half to gentler sports than robbery: bowls, quoits, archery and skittles.

They succeeded simply because they were incomparably better seamen than the Spaniards, and knew they were. But their run of luck had a sudden disastrous end – not from the Spaniards, but from something nobody understood, the tropical diseases of the coast. All of them sickened and twenty-eight of them died, probably from yellow fever and malaria.

Nevertheless, when the rainy season ended twenty of them set off, escorted by maroons, the Negroes who had escaped from slavery, on a march of three weeks through the jungle towards the Spanish trail. On the way there was a famous incident: the maroons took Drake to a very high tree in which they had built a look-out post. From the top, he saw both seas, the first Englishman to do so, and he prayed God to give him leave to sail an English ship in the South Sea. He called up his men to see the inspiring sight, and one of them in particular, a man called John Oxenham, declared that unless he beat him from his company he would be with him on the voyage he had prayed for.

The attack was another failure. They laid an ambush on the trail, but it was ruined by a man named Robert Pike, who had fortified himself with brandy and made his only mark on history by jumping out too soon. All of them marched two hundred miles and came back to the ships again hungry and footsore and no richer than they had started, but not very much dismayed.

By then the Spanish colony was like a hive of angry bees, and Drake had only thirty-one men left to assault it. He must have faced the likelihood of going home a failure, empty-handed, of earning the Queen's displeasure and coming to the end of his career. But again he found an ally: a French privateer called Captain Tetu, who hailed him out at sea and asked for food. Tetu lent him twenty men in return for a promise of half the proceeds, and with a mixture of Englishmen, French and maroons he took to the jungle again.

He had learned there was no need to march so far, and he laid his second ambush close to Nombre de Dios: so close that his men, lying silent in the undergrowth, could hear the hammers of shipwrights in the town, who were working by night to avoid the heat of the day. And then they heard bells, the bells of a mule train coming down the hills from Panama. The maroons rejoiced, and promised more treasure than they could carry away. They waited breathless. The first of the mules came past, tied head to tail. Drake blew a whistle, everyone jumped out of the bushes, seized the leading mules and brought them all to a halt. A few shots and arrows were fired, for a minute or two the trail was full of a milling mass of mules and shouting men, and then the muleteers and their escort of soldiers fled. One maroon was killed, Captain Tetu was wounded in the stomach, and Drake was in possession of two hundred animals laden with gold and silver. His men spent two hectic hours in burying silver bars, and then heard the garrison of Nombre de Dios coming up the track. Laden with all the gold they could carry, they made their march back to the coast. Poor Captain Tetu lagged behind and was overtaken and killed. And when they came to the rendezvous appointed with the pinnaces, nobody was there and a storm was blowing, and seven Spanish ships were patrolling to cut them off.

Even Drake thought the worst – that the Spaniards had taken the pinnaces and must now be putting the crews to torture to learn where the ships were hidden. This, he said, was no time to fear, but rather to hurry to prevent what was feared. Overnight, he had them build a raft of trees with a sail of biscuit sacks. Drake could sail anything, and he put to sea with three volunteers in this crazy equipment and covered nine miles before the storm, sitting up to his waist in the water, and up to his shoulders at every surge of the waves. At last they saw the pinnaces, which disappeared behind a point of land. He still had the surplus energy to think of a practical joke: he landed on the near side of the point and ran round it full speed on the shore, pretending he was being chased by the enemy. Successfully alarmed, the crews of the pinnaces hurried to take him on board; he answered their questions so coldly that they were sure he had met with another and final disaster. And then he undid his shirt, and pulled out a bar of gold.

That night, he rowed back to the rendezvous against the gale and rescued the men and the treasure. And soon after, with his fortune made and everything to lose, and every Spaniard ashore and afloat on the hunt for him, he decided to go back again to the scene of the ambush, to look for Captain Tetu and dig up some silver. The Captain, of course, was dead, and most of the silver was gone, but they found another Frenchman, lost and despairing, who fell on his knees in the jungle and thanked God for the day that Captain Drake was born.

English reports were evasive about the worth of the booty; the Spaniards said it was £50,000. Drake divided it equally with Captain Tetu's crew, and parted with the maroons on friendly terms. The adventure needed a final gesture to round it off, and the Spanish fleet was riding in all its strength and glory at the entrance of Cartagena harbour. 'Thus we departed, passing hard by Carthagena, in the sight of all the Fleete, with a flag of Saint George in the maine top of our Fregat, with silk streamers and ancients downe to the water, sayling forward with a large wind.' On Sunday 8th August, 1573, they sailed into Plymouth at sermon time. The news spread through the town and through the church, and few of the congregation stayed to hear the preacher.

*

That early voyage was a prototype of the sport. Perhaps nobody, not even

Drake himself, was ever quite so successful again in mixing gaiety and profit, or in winning his fights and taking his plunder with such courtesy and magnanimity. Many other captains joined the fun and hoped to make a fortune. Many came back with nothing to show for their exploits, and their names are forgotten; some disappeared entirely and their fate was never known; and some fell into Spanish hands and their stories were found long afterwards in Spanish archives. One of the latter, by way of example, was John Oxenham, the man who climbed the tree with Drake and saw the South Sea with him.

All the treasure that came across the trail to Nombre de Dios had first been brought to Panama by sea, either up the Pacific coast from Bolivia and Peru or down it from Mexico and Nicaragua. Both Drake and Oxenham either knew or guessed that Spanish ships were only lightly guarded in the safety of the Pacific. Drake began to lay plans to attack them by rounding Cape Horn; Oxenham independently made up his mind to hide his ship on the coast of Darien, march across the isthmus again with the help of the maroons and build himself a ship when he came to the other side. And he succeeded. Nothing is recorded of his crossing, but it was a considerable feat: there was limitless timber, of course, to be felled on the Pacific coast, but all the rest of the makings of his ship, and the tools to build it with, must have been carried for fifty or sixty miles across the mountains and through the steaming jungle: the bolts and nails, oakum and tar, rigging and sails, anchors, ropes and cables, and the hammers, axes, adzes, saws and augers. He launched the ship in a river and sailed it out to sea in 1578, so that he, not Drake, became the first Englishman to navigate in the Pacific.

Scarcely anything is known of John Oxenham. He was another Plymouth man, and a Spanish description says he was thick of speech and grave in his demeanour, much feared and respected by his men. On what evidence there is, he was lacking in Drake's unerring flair, and his genius for getting out of trouble. Within a week or two, he captured a treasure ship on its way to Panama and landed on some islands demanding gold and pearls from the Spanish settlers. Probably none of his crew had seen a Catholic home before, and in the first house they entered the shock to their narrow Protestant minds overcame their interest in gold. They spent the night giving stern but crude lectures to the owners and their family on the evils of popery. Oxenham found a crucifix in a box and threw it at the master of the house, but it missed him and broke in pieces. A man called John Butler, who was second-in-command and interpreter, read out the ten commandments from a lesson-book which belonged to the children, and laughed raucously when he came to 'Thou shalt not steal.' The ship's cook put on a vestment and cut off the skirt of it so that he could use it as a shirt, and when a Franciscan friar had the misfortune to turn up in the middle of the fracas, they put a chamber pot on his shaven head and made him eat his wafers.

All this was reported as a solemn scandal by the Spanish authorities, and it was indeed a coarse example of intolerance. But Oxenham's men at least did no physical harm to the Spanish families, and when they had as much gold and pearls as they could carry they began to walk back across the isthmus by the way they had come.

But then everything went wrong. In the Spanish reports, Oxenham is said to have promised the maroons they could have all his captives to kill or keep as slaves, a thing, if it was true, that Drake would never have done. But when it came to the point, he set his captives free: one account says he fell in love with a beautiful Spanish woman he found on a ship, and she made him change his mind. For breaking this promise, the maroons turned against him when he needed them most, to guide him back through the jungle.

As soon as his depredations were known in Panama, a force was sent to pursue him, and another went along the Caribbean coast to cut off his retreat. The pursuers, faced with a choice of rivers he might have used, picked the right one because they saw chicken feathers and bacon rind floating down it. They caught up with the Englishmen, skirmishes were fought, and Oxenham's command broke up, some men being killed, some captured, some scattered in small parties and lost for ever in the jungle. The maroons, caught between the European opponents, suffered most of all; the Spaniards found their hidden town of Ronconcholon and laid it waste. Of all the English, there were no survivors except some boys the Spaniards thought too young to execute. Oxenham was captured and taken to Lima in Peru. He had to admit he had no commission from the Queen, and so he was legally a pirate; and he came to a pirate's end.

CHAPTER 12

The World Encompassed

WHILE Oxenham was facing trial in Lima, Drake was on the other coast of South America, sailing south for the Straits of Magellan, intending to harass the Spaniards in the Pacific, and contriving the trial of his own friend Thomas Doughty.

The right and wrong of his enigmatic quarrel with Doughty will never be known, but it marked an epoch in the history of the sea. It showed Drake in a new light, apparently unsure of himself and harsh in his judgment through his own unsureness, yet enforcing a principle that was also new: that a captain at sea, whatever his status ashore, was absolute master of his ship and its company.

Now, at the outset of his voyage round the world, Drake was no longer a happy pirate, enjoying life with a crew of Devon youths; he was Captain-General, with the Queen's authority, of a fleet that included gentlemen-adventurers, and he dined off silver plate and was attended by his own musicians. But in spite of this ostentation, he was not a gentleman and never could have been; and men like Doughty, who were, believed they had authority too and should have their say in decisions about the voyage. By all the old conventions, they were right. The Judgments of Oléron, 350 years before, had said that masters should consult their companies, and that was still more or less the custom in English ships. Moreover, when medieval knights embarked, ships' masters did their bidding, and that was another custom of which the vestiges still survived: Sir Hugh Willoughby, for example, was a gentleman and a knight but not a seaman, and the practical seamen were his subordinates.

Between Drake and his gentlemen, all down the coast of Africa and across the Atlantic, there had been a clash of wills. There were hints and suspicions, after the voyage was over, that secrets of state were involved, though nobody said what they were. The Queen had certainly known that Drake was heading for the Pacific and meant to rob the Spaniards there;

and she had strictly said that nobody was to tell her Treasurer, Lord Burghley, who was the advocate of peace with Spain. Doughty confessed to Drake that he had told Burghley, and it may be that Burghley had encouraged him to disrupt the voyage and restrict it to a harmless exploring expedition in the south Atlantic. At all events, the company had taken with it, all the way down to Patagonia, a microcosm of the intrigues of the court, and Drake was out of his depth in it.

Down there, on a beach in the harbour Magellan had named San Julian, Drake brought the quarrel to a head: he accused Doughty, the leading gentleman, of mutinous talk, empanelled a jury and condemned him to death on evidence that seems trivial in itself – and then took Holy Communion with him and dined with him before his execution; and finally dismissed all the officers and appointed them again. His famous speech to the company was only reported by a supporter of Doughty; yet the furious eloquence of its phrases set the style of the English sea-service ever after: 'My masters, I am a very bad orator, for my bringing up hath not been in learning . . . Here is such controversy between the sailors and the gentlemen and such stomaching between the gentlemen and the sailors, that it doth even make me mad to hear it. But, my masters, I must have it left. For I must have the gentleman to haul and draw with the mariner, and the mariner with the gentleman. What! Let us show ourselves all to be of a company, and let us not give occasion to the enemy to rejoice at our decay and overthrow . . . And now, my masters, let us consider what we have done, we have now set together by the ears three mighty princes, as first Her Majesty, the Kings of Spain and Portugal; and if this voyage should not have good success, we should not only be a scorning or a reproachful scoffing-stock unto our enemies, but also a great blot to our whole country for ever . . . To say you come to serve me I will not give you thanks, for it is only Her Majesty that you serve.' There would be no more executions, he promised: if any men wanted to go home he would give them a ship, but if they got in his way he would sink them. Nobody went. Particular offenders whom he named knelt down in submission before him; the whole company accepted his absolute command.

There in that distant harbour, farther from home than any Englishman had ever been before, Drake defied sea conventions that were centuries old: he insisted once and for all that things were not decided at sea by consultation or by social rank, but by an unchallengeable power which did not exist on land, except in the will of a determined king or queen. Ever since his lifetime, captains and masters of ships alone at sea have had extraordinary power. Perhaps it has been to the good, because it would be hard to run a ship without it, but in the days when voyages lasted for years it was often misused by weak or cruel men.

There were some signs that Drake's conscience was uneasy after the execution, but the voyage was transformed. Crossing the Atlantic, it had been a miserable affair for everyone; in the Pacific it was like his earlier adventures. He scrapped two of his ships, and took the other three through the Straits of Magellan with the skill that made men glad to have him as their master: his own ship the *Pellican*, which he renamed the *Golden Hinde*, was 100 tons, about 95 feet in length, the *Elizabeth* was 80 tons and the *Marigold* only 30. His prime intention was to plunder Spanish ships on their way to Panama, and he had no recorded plans for getting home again. The Straits were likely to be closed by the Spaniards as soon as they knew he was there, and the North-West Passage was still a doubtful chance. But if he had thought of sailing round the world he told nobody else, and as guide to that venture he had nothing but a wildly inaccurate map of the world and the journal of Magellan's voyage fifty years before, with its daunting record of sudden death and starvation.

It was August, and his crew seem to have been surprised to find it was winter in the southern hemisphere. Astronomers had known it in theory for hundreds of years, but if Drake knew it himself it is hard to see why he chose that time of year. Coming out of the Straits, they expected the Pacific Ocean to deserve the name the Spaniards had already given it; instead, they met the force of the Roaring Forties in winter, a storm which lasted fifty-two days and seas that no mariner had seen or imagined before. Behind them was a lee shore, so steep that they could find no place to anchor: they were forced to fight it out at sea. 'The violent storm without intermission; the impossiblity to come to anchor; the want of opportunitie to spread any sayle; the most mad seas; the lee shores; the dangerous rocks; the contrary and most intollerable winds; the impossible passage out; the desperate tarrying there; and inevitable perils on every side, did lay before us so small likelihood to escape present destruction, that if the special providence of God himselfe had not supported us, we could never have endured that wofull state.' The *Marigold* foundered with all hands. The *Elizabeth*, running before the wind, found the entrance of the Straits again, passed through it, gave up the struggle and made for home. The *Golden Hinde* survived by the grace of God, and 'by the great and effectual care and travell of our Generall, the Lord's instrument therein.'

That danger passed, and the plundering along the Pacific coast was up to his highest hopes. Spanish ships in the Atlantic were armed to the teeth; in the Pacific, as he had expected, they were scarcely armed at all, and the harbours were unguarded. What was more, the Spaniards had no suspicion that a hostile ship had invaded their ocean; time and again, they greeted the *Golden Hinde* as one of their own, and in their astonishment at finding she was not, they surrended without a fight. Ashore, Drake's men behaved as rudely as Oxenham's; but none of them were cruel, and he always treated his captives with courtesy. 'In the moonlight,' one Spanish captain reported to the Viceroy, 'I saw a ship close alongside. Our helmsman shouted to her to stand clear. They pretended to be asleep and did not answer. He shouted again, and asked them where they hailed from. From Peru, they said. Suddenly she crossed our poop, ordered us to strike sail and fired some arquebuses at us. We thought it was a joke, but it turned out to be very serious. They boarded us with as little risk to themselves as if they had been friends . . . I found Drake walking his deck, and kissed his hands. He received me kindly, showed me into his cabin and asked me to sit down. "I am a friend of people who tell me the truth," he said, "but with those who do not I get out of humour. So tell me how much silver and gold you are carrying." "None," I said, "except some small plates I use, and some cups." He is a man of about 35, not tall, with a fair beard, and he is one of the greatest mariners at sea. He treats his men with affection and they treat him with respect . . . I managed to ask if he was well liked, and they all said they adored him.' This man, like all the others, was entertained with food and drink and music on the *Golden Hinde* while his ship was searched, and then sent peacefully on his way. He had nothing much worth taking, as it happened: unlike the captain of the *Cacafuego*, a ship the Spaniards called the *Glory of the South Sea*. That ship, to quote the English account, was searched 'to do him the kindness of freeing him of the care of those things with which his ship was laden . . . some fruit, conserves, sugar, meal and other victuals, and (that which was the especiallest cause of her heavy and low sailing) a certain quantity of jewels, thirteen chests of reals of plate, eighty pounds weight in gold, twenty-six tons of uncoined silver, two very fair silver drinking bowls and the like trifles, valued in all at about 360,000 pesos.' The rummaging took three days, and when it was finished Drake and the captain parted with expressions of friendship that seem to have been sincere.

By the time the *Golden Hinde* had reached the latitude of Panama, she was ballasted with silver and had all the booty she could stow. Drake sailed her north, by one account as far as 48°, which is near Vancouver. At that stage, he evidently hoped to find the other end of the North-West Passage. But from one of the prizes he had taken a book of Spanish charts of the South Sea, and in face of a cold and contrary wind he changed his mind, turned back and put the ship ashore for careening in a creek near San Francisco.

While they were there, Drake and his crew had the same embarrassing experience as Captain Cook two centuries later in Hawaii: they were mistaken for gods. Drake carried it off very creditably; he was always gentle with primitive people after his early experience in the slave trade, and he allowed the Californian Indians to dress him up in feathers, and listened to their long and tedious speeches. The ship's chaplain, Francis Fletcher, disliked their sacrifices and the women's way of tearing their own hair and faces with their finger nails, and he did his best to convert them by praying and singing psalms. But as Drake understood it, they were offering him their kingdom; so he accepted it for the Queen and named it Nova Albion. Before he left – to the evident despair of the people – he put up a brass plate on a post, 'whereon is engraven her graces name, and the day and yeare of our arrivall there, and of the free giving of the province and kingdome, both by the king and people, into her majesties hands; together with her highnesse picture and armes, in a piece of sixpence currant English monie, shewing itselfe by a hole made of purpose through the plate.' In 1933, just such a plate was found, a mile and a half inland from the creek now known as Drake's Bay, by a chauffeur who had nothing to do while his employer was hunting. He kept it for a while, then threw it away. In 1936, it was found again by a man on a picnic, who kept it to mend a hole in his automobile. When he started to use it, he saw writing on it and showed it to other people, and at length it reached the University of California. Of course it was suspected of being a fake, and the most elaborate tests were devised to discover its age. All of these strongly suggested it was genuine, the original plate inscribed on the *Golden Hinde*.

It may be a trite observation, but it is also a fact to bear in mind, that the chroniclers of pioneering voyages wrote for their own times; so they made much of things that were novel to their readers, and left out the things that everybody knew. Since then, the novelties have become familiar and much of what they knew has been forgotten. For example, they wrote more about penguins than about their daily life at sea, or the means they used to cross unknown oceans. It was in his creek near San Francisco that Drake told the

Lord Howard of Effingham,
by Mytens

Sir Francis Drake

The Galie Subtile.

Tunnage._____ 200.

Menn {Marrynars. 242 } 250.
{Gonnars _____ 8 }

Overleaf. An English galley of the mid 16th century, Anthony Anthony's Roll

Shipbuilders at the end of the 16th century, from Fragments of Ancient English Shipwrightry

crew he was going to cross the Pacific. They gladly agreed. They sailed on 26th July, and through the whole of August, September and October they were out of sight of land. Nobody complained, but it must have needed some strength of mind to go on believing, like Frobisher in the north-west, that 'the sea must needs have an ending'. Yet the journal, which had devoted half a page to the curious conies of Nova Albion, dismissed the feat of navigation in a single sentence: 'And so having nothing in our view but aire and sea, without sight of any land for the space of 68 dayes together, wee continued our course through the maine Ocean.'

But what course? Drake was aiming for the Moluccas, where the Portuguese were already trading for spices by the other route, round Africa and across the Indian Ocean. One account, by John Drake who was his nephew or cousin, says they set a direct course but changed it when they were near the equator because they met an east-going current. But it was impossible, with the knowledge of those days, to set a constant compass course, or a direct or rhumb line course, over such an enormous distance – over a quarter of the whole way round the world. Drake would have known the latitude of the Moluccas from the Spanish charts he had captured, or from his map of the world, but he could only have had the vaguest idea of their longitude, or of his own, or of how far away they were. A direct course would have been too rough an estimate to be practical. It is much more likely that he was using the time-honoured method of the deliberate error: that he set a course to take him safely down to the latitude of the Moluccas before he reached their longitude, then to sail along the latitude, checking it every day with the astrolabe, until he reached them. The alteration of course that John Drake recorded was made in $1°30'N$, which is exactly the latitude for entering Ternate, the port of the Moluccas. After making it, Drake must have been driven north again, for the first land they saw was in $8°N$ – it is thought to have been the Pelew Islands. From there, he crossed to Mindanao in the Philippines and then stood south from island to island until the Moluccas were in sight.

On sighting any land, they identified it in the simplest possible way: they asked the natives where they were. The Portuguese before them had done the same, and some of the native names, in various spellings, appeared on the Spanish charts. But another thing they omitted to mention, like all the early explorers, is the means they used to communicate with people who spoke a totally unknown language.

From the Moluccas home, the Portuguese had a well established route through the Macassar Straits; but Drake was driven south of it by contrary winds, and had to find his own way by trial and error through the Java Sea and archipelago, which is still reckoned a difficult passage. After three weeks of beating round the shoals, they saw the Indian Ocean clear ahead of them; and running free at last with all sail set and a monsoon wind astern, they brought up with a hideous crash on a sunken rock which was twenty miles from land.

The ship, the treasure and their lives were suddenly in jeopardy: their boat could carry less than half the crew, and the land was dead to windward. Drake called all hands to prayers. Then, lest they should seem to tempt God by failing to try any means of salvation He offered, they got to work with a kedge anchor; but the rock was so steep they were out of soundings just astern of the ship. They spent the night in prayer that she would hold together till morning. She did, but still stuck fast. They resigned themselves to God, and the parson administered the Sacrament and preached a sermon. Again combining prayer with seamanship, they jettisoned some food, eight guns and some of the cargo. Then they sounded again; she drew thirteen feet, over the larboard side there were only six feet of water, and a short way to starboard they found no bottom at all. The wind was holding her upright. In the afternoon it abruptly dropped, she heeled over and it seemed the end had come: but as if by a miracle she slid off the rock and righted herself in deep water.

That scene of despair dissolved into a macabre kind of comedy. Drake had the parson seized and chained by the leg to a staple in the forehatch, and sitting cross-legged on a chest with a pair of slippers in his hand he solemnly excommunicated him, and condemned him under a threat of hanging to wear an armband inscribed with the words 'Francis Fletcher, the falsest knave that liveth.' Nobody knows what the wretched man had done. Perhaps when they all expected to die, his sermon had dwelt with rather too much relish on the sins of the captain and crew, which in the parson's eyes had earned the wrath of God. Certainly, he had always been a pompous fellow, and Drake had always had a sailor's sense of humour.

That was the last recorded incident of the voyage. From Java they reached home in six months, and only seem to have landed once for wood and water on the way, in Sierra Leone. From San Francisco to Plymouth they sighted only a single ship, a Portuguese which outsailed them, to their chagrin, off Mindanao; and at anchor in Plymouth Sound after nearly three years at sea they noted, as a kind of proof they had really been round the world, that it was Sunday by their reckoning, but Monday for their friends who had stayed at home.

*

That was the greatest of Elizabethan voyages, in seamanship and in profit: it put England on the map as a first-class maritime nation, it paid its supporters £75 for each pound they had invested, and it made Drake the equivalent of a millionaire. But for some time, its profit hung in the balance. Mendoza the Spanish ambassador demanded that Drake should be punished and the plunder returned to Spain, and he was supported by Burghley and his followers, and by the powerful city merchants who were still trading with Spain. Privately, the Queen was delighted by Drake's audacious story and by the jewels he brought her, and he was constantly in her company; but it was six months before she made up her mind to defy the ambassador and the King of Spain by the famous ceremony when she knighted Drake on board the *Golden Hinde* at Deptford.

From the long historical point of view, the voyage had another kind of importance. As an afterthought, it achieved the objective the merchants of England had peacefully sought so long: an English ship had broken out of the north Atlantic and reached the seas of Cathay, sailed among the Spice Islands and safely come home again. In the Moluccas, Drake had actually taken on board three tons of cloves, but he jettisoned them when the ship ran on the rock. And the grip of the Portuguese on the islands had seemed to be weaker than anyone had expected. The rajah had said he was at war with them and had made a treaty with Drake; and during the voyage the King of Portugal had died, and the King of Spain had successfully claimed his throne.

So the merchants hastily organised a second expedition, to establish a trading post in the islands before the Spaniards had time to send out a fleet. Frobisher offered to command it. But the Muscovy Company put up most of the money, and they insisted on having as second in command a man named Edward Fenton, a soldier who had already sailed with Frobisher and quarrelled with him. Frobisher resigned, and Fenton became the commander. Merchants, carpenters and bricklayers sailed to set up the trading post. Fenton was given the power of life or death, subject to the kind of trial Drake had used against Doughty, but he was not given the power to dismiss the captains. His orders were to avoid any hostile action, to go by the Cape of Good Hope – the old Portuguese route – and not to provoke the

Spaniards by attempting the Straits of Magellan unless he was forced to do so.

These were normal arrangements for a merchant voyage; but the command by a soldier, and the orders not to fight, were exactly the things that Drake most strongly disapproved. He had not been invited to command, which was wise; but the organisers made a mistake that turned out to be fatal. They let him send one of his ships and a good many of the men who had sailed with him: among the captains were John Drake and John Hawkins's nephew William. So the voyage became a trial of strength between two fundamentally different outlooks, the sporting plunderers' and the sober merchants'. Drake's men had no intention of taking orders from a soldier, or of missing a chance of booty if they saw one. They despised Fenton, and suspected him of being in league with the Spanish ambassador. When the time came, Fenton sailed without them, apparently in the hope of leaving them at home, but John Drake collected them all in his ship and caught up with the fleet. They seem to have tricked Fenton, by sailing impossible courses, into believing the wind was contrary for the Cape of Good Hope, and they took the whole fleet to the coast of South America.

All the way, there were bitter and furious quarrels between the factions. Fenton tried setting the course himself, and according to Hawkins he was 'laughed at by every man almost because all knewe that he understoode not what he did.' In South America he captured a small ship with seven friars on board, and some women and children, bound for a settlement far up the River Plate: and they told him a Spanish fleet was then on its way to found a colony in the Straits of Magellan and fortify it. He called a council. 'Their opinions were as diverse as their names; & as much differed, as before this time they were wont usually to do.' After hours of argument, Fenton decided to sail north for the Portuguese port of St Vincent, where he hoped to trade. The next night, John Drake deserted and sailed south, intending to try the Straits of Magellan alone.

This was a forlorn endeavour, presumably born of anger: he commanded a pinnace of forty tons, with a crew of eighteen men. And in the mouth of the River Plate, she ran on a reef and was wrecked. The men all got ashore, walked a few miles inland and had a fight with some Indians. Five of them were killed, and the rest captured and enslaved. Fifteen months later, Drake and two others escaped. 'They took a very little canoa, which had but two oares, & so passed to the other side of the river, which is about 19 leagues broade, and were three days before they could get over without meat: and coming to land, they hit upon a highway that went towards the Christians: and seeing the footing of horses, they followed it, and at last came to an house where there was corne sowed, and there they met with Indians servants unto the Spaniards, which gave them meate, and clothes to cover them, for they were all naked, and one of the Indians went to the towne, and tolde them of the Englishmen; so the Captaine sent foure horsemen, who brought them to the towne behind them.

'This Captaine clothed them, and provided lodging for them, and John Drake dieted at the Captaines table, and they were all very well entreated, the Captaine purposing to sent them for Spaine. But the Viceroy of Peru having newes thereof, sent for them, and so John Drake was sent to him, but the other two were kept there, because they were married in the countrey.' Drake never reached home again, but there were stories that he lived to old age in captivity.

The Spanish fleet on its way to the Straits of Magellan was also in desperate trouble. It had left Spain with twenty-three ships, 3500 men and an unspecified number of women. In a series of storms, six ships with 1100 men had been lost at sea. Two more were abandoned on the coast of Brazil. The commander pressed on with the ten ships that were still seaworthy, 'and into the other three ships which were old, and shaken with the storme, hee put all the women and sicke men in all the fleete, and sent them to the river Jenero'. This pathetic remnant, exhausted by months at sea, put in to St Vincent; and there were Fenton and his three remaining ships. A desultory battle was fought and one of the Spaniards sank, but Fenton broke it off as soon as he could escape and sailed for home. According to his orders, he was right. His captains had told him he could not go by the Cape of Good Hope, and he knew he could not go by the Straits of Magellan without a fight. It may have been true that Doughty tried to disrupt the first of these voyages: it was certainly true that Drake's men disrupted the second.

CHAPTER 13

Defeat of the Armada

FENTON's voyage was doomed by the same divided policy that Drake, on his own expedition, had stamped out when he executed Doughty: the policy represented on one side by Burghley and the merchants, who favoured expansion overseas through peaceful trading, and on the other by Walsingham, who supported Drake's piratical escapades. Drake's was the expression at sea of Elizabethan genius, and beside him the ambitions of the merchants seem prosaic. But trade, after all, was the only lasting object of going to sea, and it could have been pursued much farther without provoking Spain. There was plenty of room in the world; at that very moment, Gilbert was making the first attempt to settle a colony in Newfoundland, and Raleigh in Carolina, and the trade of India and of China or Cathay itself had scarcely been touched by anyone. The English, it must be admitted, were behaving rather like jackals; the merchants coveted the Moluccas simply because the Portuguese already had them, and Drake and his followers preferred to rob the lion of its kill. If the whole genius of Elizabethan seamen had been allied to the wealth of Elizabethan merchants, both trade and exploration might have advanced in peace. But the sport of baiting Spaniards had diverted the brightest of the genius; it had been fun, but it had succeeded too well and gone too far. War came – in the eyes of Hawkins and Drake, the final revenge for San Juan de Ulloa; and the hopes of the merchants were set back for twenty years.

There were less than five years between Fenton's failure and the execution of Mary, Queen of Scots. Within that time, Drake led his next two expeditions, the attack on San Domingo and Cartagena in the Indies, and the attack on Cadiz. There was nothing novel about them in seamanship, but they were famous feats of arms; and they made Drake into a national hero of a different kind – not only the captain of marauders, the 'thief of the unknown world', but a naval commander. So he was able to impress his ideas, or some of them, on the navy that England was bringing into being. They were ideas that were stamped on the Royal Navy ever after. And they were the opposite of the old-established system the Spaniards were using in the great Armada they were making ready.

The first was what he had insisted on with Doughty: that the practical seaman was supreme at sea. In the Spanish navy, ships were commanded by soldiers, and sailors were more or less despised as descendants of galley slaves. In the nascent English navy, ships were to be commanded, as a general rule, by captains who had served their time at sea, with soldiers – or later, Royal Marines – and gunners as part of their crew. It still remained true that a great fleet would need a great nobleman to command it in the name of the Queen, because nobody else could command a set of jealous, proud and unruly sea-captains; and that was a fact that Drake admitted gracefully enough when he had to serve under Lord Howard of Effingham in the fleet that opposed the Armada. And of course a rich man, who could buy or build a ship and find a crew, could still put to sea as its captain if he pleased.

The difference in outlook showed in every way, in strategy, tactics and the design of ships. The Spanish military captains still demanded ships with high bulwarks and imposing fore and after castles. Some of these were still in service in Elizabeth's navy, but English captains already preferred the race-built ships Hawkins had caused to be created.

In tactics, most Spaniards still held to the medieval soldier's idea of grappling and boarding, for which the older, higher ships had been designed. Guns, in that view, were used to disable an enemy ship by cutting its masts and rigging. The English had come to regard the great gun as the primary naval weapon, to be used not only to disable an enemy ship but to put it out of action by shooting low. The race-built ships, they had begun to find, could fire one broadside, then quickly tack or wear and fire the other. A fleet of them could make this manœuvre one after the other: and so the idea was just beginning of the line of battle, the formation used by every fleet at sea from the seventeenth to the nineteenth century.

These two ideas, the design of ships and the tactical use of them, were agreed by almost all the captains who came together from their different trades to form a navy for the Queen. Drake's was merely the leading opinion among them. It was in strategy that his personal influence was strongest: so strong that it gave the navy a fighting philosophy to which it returned in times of crisis for centuries to come. Naval strategy had hardly existed before him; to exist, it needed a certain mastery of the sea itself.

Drake came into the navy with a wider experience of the sea than any Englishman had ever had, and with an unrivalled confidence that he could keep the sea whatever weather came. So his strategic ideas had a freedom nobody had dared to express before. He passionately argued that the proper place to fight an enemy in defence of England was not off the English coast but off the enemy ports – the same strategy, based on the same confidence, that guided the navy of Nelson's age in the great blockade before Trafalgar. Ever since they began, the English had been diffident at sea, and had seldom fought far out of sight of the shores of home; but Drake put an end to that, and made them arrogant.

The attack on Cadiz had shown what he meant, but when imminent invasion threatened he had a harder job to convince the Queen and her Council. In Spain, the greatest fleet that had ever been assembled by the greatest naval power – in the Spanish Netherlands, the strongest army in Europe under the Prince of Parma – these were menaces to make the English draw back by instinct to the fortress of the island. In the winter of 1587, Drake was in command of half the fleet at Plymouth, and Lord Howard of the other half at Queenborough in the mouth of the Medway. This was the Council's disposition to prevent the Armada coming up the Channel and joining Parma's army. There was no logic in it, and Drake spent the winter fretting impatiently for leave to sail to Spain, and struggling to keep his fleet in fighting order against a chronic shortage of food and ammunition.

At the end of March he wrote a long dispatch. He never learned to express himself clearly with a pen in his hand, and the thoughts he wrote down are tangled. But phrases stand out among them. 'To seek God's enemies and her Majesty's where they may be found . . . With fifty sail of shipping we shall do more good upon their own coast than a great many more will do here at home . . . If there may be such a stay or stop made by any means of this fleet in Spain, so that they may not come through the seas as conquerors, which I assure myself they think to do, then shall the Prince of Parma have such a check thereby as were meet.'

Perhaps the dispatch was even less clear to the Queen and Council than it is to a modern reader who knows what he meant. It made them think he proposed to attack the Armada in the river Tagus, where it was making ready under the forts of Lisbon, and that was impossible. He was summoned to court to explain, and found Howard opposing him. But he was far more convincing as a talker than a writer. He persuaded the Queen, and Howard came round to the idea when he understood it: not to attack Lisbon, but to lie off the port and attack the Armada there if it dared to come out. In May, Howard was sent down Channel with open orders and most of his fleet, leaving fifty ships in the east to watch for any move from Parma's army.

So almost all the famous captains of the age were met in Plymouth, and ships with names that have come down through generations of warships ever since: Lord Howard flying his flag in the *Ark Royal*, which the Queen had bought from Sir Walter Raleigh; Drake as vice-admiral in the *Revenge*, of 450 tons, 92 feet in length and 32 in beam; John Hawkins, rear-admiral in the *Victory*, at sea again after 20 years ashore; Frobisher in the *Triumph*, an old-fashioned ship of 1100 tons, the biggest in the fleet and no smaller than the Spanish men-of-war; Sir George Beeston in the *Dreadnought*; Drake's captains Thomas Fenner and Robert Crosse in the *Nonpareil* and the *Hope* – ten thousand men and over a hundred sail, 69 of them galleons and great ships, 16 of them the Queen's, and the rest from merchant owners, 'the gallantest company,' Howard wrote, 'of captains, soldiers and mariners that I think ever was seen in England.'

Lord Howard's council of war was formed by Drake, Hawkins, Frobisher and Fenner. At its first meeting the whole question of sailing to Spain was opened again and one of the members opposed Drake's strategy; probably it was Frobisher, who never had much love for Drake. After a long discussion, they all left the council convinced. But there were other troubles. That summer was stormy, the wind was south-westerly, Howard's royal ships had only three weeks' food and his supply ships were stuck up the Channel. 'God send us a wind to put us out,' he wrote to Burghley; 'for go we will, though we starve.' At the end of May, the wind showed signs of changing and the whole of the fleet put to sea, to find the Armada and fight it where it lay. Before they reached Ushant, they met with a southerly gale. They fought it for seven days: then it veered to the west with equal fury. While it was blowing, they spoke a merchant ship which had sighted a huge fleet standing out from Lisbon. It seemed that the weather that held the English might bring the Spaniards into the Channel at any moment. The English were in danger of being driven to leeward of Plymouth and leaving it unprotected; so they put back to the Sound.

There in Plymouth were new dispatches from London: the Queen had changed her mind. They were not to go to Spain, but to 'ply up and down in some indifferent place between the coast of Spain and this realm.' The whole of Drake's reasoning was still not understood at court: Howard replied with an angry sarcastic letter which no lesser man would have dared to write, explaining it all again in simpler terms. He waited for an answer, and for a shift of wind. Every day, the Armada was expected. But a fortnight passed, and nothing was sighted by the pinnaces that were scouting in the Channel. In the wind that was blowing, it would certainly have arrived – unless it had been scattered by the gale and driven back in disorder to Spanish ports. Now was the moment to strike: so Drake insisted, and there was nobody now in the fleet who disagreed. Another attempt was made, but in the face of another gale, and perhaps in deference to the Queen's decision, it was carried no farther than the coast of Brittany.

Back in Plymouth, new orders were received: the Queen had relented, and confirmed that Howard should use his own judgment, subject only to the advice of his council of war. The weather began to lift. Howard's supply ships came in, and men worked without sleep or rest to get the stores on board. Pinnaces and horsemen were constantly coming in to report that the Armada was on the coast: yet nobody claimed to have seen the whole of it. Surely, it seemed, the gale had broken up the Spaniards into separate groups. On 24th June the wind came fair from the north east. They did not wait to complete the victualling, but gave orders for the store ships to follow them, and stood away for Spain.

Off Ushant, the wind headed them yet again – a fair wind for the Spaniards, foul for them. They beat against it for ten days, between Ushant and the Scillies, with pinnaces out to port and starboard to watch the widest front, and provisions running shorter all the time. Then again it changed, and stood fair for Spain. But Howard hesitated. Evidently, Drake was desperate: aboard the *Revenge*, he wrote a protest – an act he would have condemned in anyone else – and sent it across to Howard in the *Ark Royal*. The message itself is lost, but it must have been emphatic. Howard called a council of war at sea, and on 7th July there was a long discussion. The question they had to answer was clear: but the answer needed a kind of inspired conviction. Was the Armada still in port, or had it used the shift of wind ten days before to put to sea? If it had, and the English fleet stood south, there was every chance of missing it on the way and leaving England bare of sea defences. Moreover, most of the English ships had scarcely enough provisions to reach the coast of Spain, and certainly not enough to lie there. Drake was insistent: from his own intuition, from all the meagre intelligence they gleaned, from his own knowledge of the sea and of the Spaniards, he had convinced himself the Armada was still in Vigo or

Corunna, recovering from the gale, open to an attack that would cripple it. As for provisions, he had always fed his crews by plundering prizes. His argument prevailed; that evening, Howard signalled the fleet to make sail and the whole of it set course down wind across the Bay of Biscay.

It was perhaps the greatest gamble ever taken with the fate of a nation as the stake, and it failed. Sixty miles off the coast of Spain the wind fell away and left the fleet becalmed; and then it got up again from the south. Without food, there was no chance of hanging on in the teeth of the weather and waiting for it to change. There was nothing for it but to put about and run for the coast of England.

Back in Plymouth on 12th July the fleet began to revictual. This was becoming more difficult all the time: food was scarce, and so was money. And before it was finished, on 19th July, the news was brought in by a pinnace that the whole of the Armada had been sighted off the Lizard. Drake had been right. At the moment when the English fleet approached the Spanish coast, the Armada had been lying vulnerable in Corunna. It had been badly damaged and scattered by the gale; some of its transports had pressed on to the Scillies, and sightings of them had caused the confused reports before they were recalled. If the wind of the 7th had lasted a few more hours, the Armada would certainly never have sailed for England, but in the end would have been destroyed on the coasts of its own country. The course of history has often been changed by a change of wind.

The rest of the story is better known. Yet it is still surprising how little is known of the seven day battle along the coast of England and across to Calais – less than of any important battle in English history. There are two reasons. First, nothing remotely like it had ever happened before, or indeed has ever happened since; and secondly nobody, not even the admirals, was able to see the whole of it at once. About two hundred and fifty ships were engaged in it and scores of others were hovering round its outskirts, bringing out supplies from the English ports, carrying messages back, or simply trying to get out of the way. No single man on any single ship, or even among the spectators on the headlands, could possibly watch so many sail at once and analyse their movements.

Nor can anyone prove, of course, that Drake made his legendary comment when the game of bowls on Plymouth Hoe was interrupted by the news: 'Time to finish the game, and beat the Spaniards after.' The story only appeared in print in the eighteenth century, but it is just the sort of thing he would have said in a moment of desperate urgency when people around him were excessively excited – a moment also when he knew that all his efforts of the past six months had failed. It is much easier to believe he said it than that somebody else invented it in after years.

It certainly was a moment for urgent action, and also for keeping cool: the enemy almost in sight, the wind south west, and the course out of Plymouth Sound directly south. To all appearances the fleet was trapped: a council of war on the Spanish flagship was even then deciding to attack it with fireships in the harbour. But during that afternoon, sixty-five of the English galleons beat down the Sound and reached the open sea. Some, under Frobisher, started to tack along the coast, close inshore and directly into the wind. Most, under Howard, Hawkins and Drake, stood on south across the bows of the Armada, and worked up to windward in the night. To get to windward of the enemy, to gain the weather gage, was the essence of tactics then on the sea, and by dawn both parts of the fleet had achieved it. It was a feat of seamanship the Spaniards had discounted as impossible, a feat that would still have been surprising two hundred and fifty years later in the final days of the navy under sail. Seeing the fleet to seaward and to windward in the dawn, the Spanish command abandoned the Plymouth plan and altered course to clear Start Point and stand across Torbay.

But when the English fleet had won the dominant position of the weather gage, there was really not much more they could do. They had a problem without any precedent or any possible answer. The English had put their faith in gunnery, which was a wise and forward-looking policy; but still, even a single ship, if it had a determined crew, could be pounded all day by naval guns and still be afloat at the end of it. To do any lethal damage to a hundred and twenty ships would have needed more ammunition than had ever existed in the whole of England, and at best would have taken weeks. And the Armada was in a very close formation, well disposed for defence. Such a solid mass of ships was invulnerable, so long as it remained under way and its wind was fair.

They did what they could: they menaced and harried it, ran in to attack any ships that lost their station, herded it very slowly along the coast, past each of the vulnerable places where landings had been feared – Plymouth, Torbay, Weymouth, the Isle of Wight. Every day, there were battles, great or small, around the margins of the fleet. The English used their guns far better than the Spaniards, and were careful to keep out of range of grappling-irons. Spanish ships were damaged, some hundreds of their men were killed or wounded. But only two ships were captured, and both of them through accidents; one had been crippled by an explosion and the other by a collision in the night. From Plymouth to the Isle of Wight, the Armada progressed at an average speed of two knots. South of the island, both fleets were becalmed. Howard and Hawkins had their ships towed into musket-range by their longboats. And during the calm, when all the hundreds of ships were lying motionless, Howard invited the admirals and senior captains aboard the *Ark Royal* and used his prerogative to knight half a dozen of them, including Hawkins and Frobisher.

Two prizes were not much to show for six days' fighting, but they had had more success than they knew. The Spaniards had meant to wait at the Isle of Wight and use it as a sheltered base until they made contact with the Prince of Parma in the Netherlands and heard that his army was ready to embark. But under the threats and attacks of the English, they could not detach a ship or a pinnace and send it ahead with the slightest hope of taking a message to Parma; nor could they safely come to anchor. They were driven on to leeward of the island and into the narrow seas, where they were doomed.

Moreover, they gave up hope. Nearly twenty thousand soldiers had been embarked: they cannot have had much idea of what was going on, except that they were under fire and were never given a chance of the boarding they had been told to expect. But the sailors knew very well: they had met an enemy who could outgun, outsail and outmanœuvre them all the time. 'The worst of them,' a Spanish master wrote, 'without their maincourse or topsails, can beat the best sailers we have.'

After the calm, the wind came up more strongly from the west-south-west; the Armada set course away from the coast of Sussex and through the Straits of Dover, with the English under easy sail still on its heels. On 27th July, eight days after the sighting off Plymouth, it came to anchor off Calais, and the English also anchored a mile to windward. And the whole problem was changed, for a fleet at anchor could be attacked by the only other long-range weapon of the time: fireships.

Now the Spaniards sent their messengers to Parma, requesting him to embark without delay and asking for help, food, fast boats and ammunition. While they waited for answers, the better informed of them knew they were in peril. The weather was breaking up, they had no port to go to, and to leeward was a dangerous shallow shore. 'We rode there at anchor all night,' one of their gentlemen wrote, 'with the enemy also anchored half a league from us. We had made up our minds to wait, since there was nothing else to be done, but with a great presentiment of evil from that devilish people and their arts. On Sunday also we waited all day, watching them the whole time.' They saw nothing to give them courage. During the day another squadron of 36 sail was seen to be joining the English. It was the squadron that had been left to guard the Thames under Lord Henry Seymour. The entire maritime force of England was gathered. The Spaniards counted 136 sail: they were outnumbered. And Parma replied that his army would not be ready for a week. The news was kept secret for fear of its effect on the fleet's morale.

It was Lord Henry, or so he believed, who first suggested fireships when he reported to Howard aboard the *Ark Royal*. But other people had thought of the possibility. Walsingham, watching the progress of the fight from London, had ordered fishing boats, faggots and pitch to be collected at Dover. At a council of war that day, in the *Ark Royal*, it was agreed there was no time to bring the boats across the Channel: the attack should be made that night. Eight ships were hastily chosen and filled with whatever would burn. After midnight, when the tide turned towards the Spanish fleet, the crews made sail, set them on fire and scrambled down into boats that were towed alongside.

The Spanish lookouts saw the fires flare up where the enemy lay. Soon every man on watch could see the fireships bearing down with wind and tide, 'spurting fire and their ordnance shooting, a horror to see in the night.' To stay there was destruction, but every ship was lying to two anchors: there was no time to weigh. Panic orders were given to cut the cables, and as the ships fell astern, made sail and wore, they fouled each other and drifted to leeward with spars and rigging tangled. Disordered, in a slowly loosening mass, the Armada struggled to make its way to sea. The fireships passed over a deserted anchorage and burned themselves out; but they had done their job. At dawn, the Armada was seen to be scattered miles along the coast. Some ships had anchored again, some were aground, and most were still working to bring up spare anchors and cables. Its defensive formation was gone.

The English accounts of the battle that followed are very confused. Howard, Drake and Seymour all wrote or told their own versions of it; so did Sir William Wynter in the *Vanguard*. All of them were more or less jealous of the others; and Frobisher, who was a tough old fighter and seaman but no tactician, misunderstood what Drake had done and called him a cowardly knave. Moreover, they were all disgruntled because they took no prizes. The Spanish accounts were more consistent, but written to excuse defeat; and putting them all together, no historian has ever done more than make a rough impression of the day. The fact was that nobody who was there had any clear idea of what had happened.

It began with a charge – and the word was their own, still with a ring of the horsemen of chivalry. Each of the squadrons charged the enemy, except Howard's, which turned aside to plunder a galleasse aground on the Calais bar. Drake led them all in the *Revenge*, fired his bow guns and then a broadside at the Spanish flagship *San Martin*, then left her to the others and pressed on to intercept the body of the fleet which was trying to make up wind to her assistance. As more and more of the ships came into action, a gigantic melée began, under the gunsmoke drifting with the wind. The Spaniards were trying to regain their close formation, or at least to herd together for protection: the English were trying to stop them, and to pound to pieces any ship they could isolate.

Yet even to say that much suggests a kind of concerted tactics and plan which could not have really existed. There was no system of signals. Captains had to do whatever seemed best at the moment, unless they happened to come within hailing distance of their admiral. Among hundreds of ships all milling around in the smoke, they just had to take whatever chance they saw of firing a broadside; and by the time they reloaded, that chance had disappeared and they had to go on to the next. The only plan was that all the captains were more or less trying to do the same thing. Sometimes they pressed their attacks to the length of a pike: the Spaniards tried to board, but never succeeded in grappling the nimbler English ships. By afternoon, sixteen of the Spanish ships were out of action but none of the English. But what was more, the whole battle had drifted to the leeward of Dunkirk, the last port where the Armada could have made contact with Parma and his army.

Over it all was the threat of the shoals down wind to the east, along the coast of Flanders. The *San Martin*, which was under fire all day and riddled with shot holes, recorded her soundings: by midday, they were down to eight fathoms and falling. And in the late afternoon, a squall was seen coming up from the west. Torrents of rain came with it, and the English broke off the fight and hauled to the wind, probably needing most of their hands aloft to shorten sail. But the Spaniards drove before it; many were too badly shot in the rigging to do anything else. And so the fleets were separated, and beyond a few scattered shots the battle ended.

The English could afford to take a rest. By better gunnery, more weatherly ships and more skill in handling them, they had done far more damage than they had received. And they had forced the Spanish fleet to take a course that seemed certain, at dusk that day, to lead it to complete destruction by the rising wind and sea on the Flemish banks.

Three Spanish ships ran aground that night, and another sank. The crews of all the others spent a night of horror, the first of many. In the pitch dark and rain, with nothing in sight but the menacing lights of the English fleet to windward, unable to anchor again or else afraid to be caught where they were next morning, they stood on as close to the wind as they could and expected every minute of the night to feel their own ship strike. Leadsmen in the chains were calling soundings of five fathoms: at that depth, the keels were stirring the sand and mud, and ahead was the curving coast of Holland.

At dawn, the English were still to windward. They made feints at the nearest Spanish ships but did not attack them. The Spaniards thought they also were afraid of going aground, and perhaps they were; but also, they had scarcely any ammunition. They simply waited for the Spaniards to be wrecked. 'It was a day of fear,' a Spaniard wrote, 'everyone was in utter despair and stood waiting for death.' Aboard the *San Martin*, the commander-in-chief and his officers made their confession and prepared to die.

And during the morning the wind suddenly backed to the south of west. To the Spaniards it seemed a divine intervention. They bore up to the north towards the open sea. Their immediate peril was ended; but still, they were far to leeward of England and of their army, and they were unfit to fight again. There was nothing they could do except to go farther and farther to the north. The English followed them, sending urgent messages back to the Thames for supply ships with food and water, and above all ammunition. But none came. The English navy had outrun its own resources. In the latitude of the Scottish border they gave up the chase and left two pinnaces to shadow the enemy up to the Orkney Islands. For two or three weeks there were rumours and alarms that the Spaniards were coming back; but then the stories began to come in of shipwrecks all along the Atlantic coasts of Scotland and Ireland.

'Flavit Jehovah et Dissipati Sunt' was engraved on the medal the Queen decreed should be struck to commemorate the victory: God blew with his winds and they are scattered. It was the custom to ascribe all victories to God, and regard a fleet or an army as an instrument of His will. But even according to custom it was a strange inscription. All through the Bay of Biscay, the

Channel and the North Sea, the winds of heaven had favoured the Spanish Armada. The change of wind off Flanders had saved it when its crews had resigned themselves to death. Even the Atlantic gale it met off the north of Scotland would not have driven its ships ashore if they had not been damaged by gunfire and forced to cut away their anchors. The English fleet at least had been an effective instrument.

CHAPTER 14

Last Voyages of the Elizabethans

IN the 900 years since the Norman conquest, the threat of invasion has always united the British more strongly than anything else. Each time it has been tried, by Spain, France and Germany, the sea defences of the island have reached a peak of skill. And each time, when the threat has been beaten, the navy has shrunk again to a state of neglect and querulous argument. Before the remains of the Armada were back in Spain, most of the English ships had been paid off. In the arts, the Elizabethan age continued to flourish, but at sea it degenerated. England remained a leading power, but almost entirely on the fame of that single victory; for the ghastly fate of the Armada had badly shaken the pride of the Spanish navy, and there was no other rival. English exploration languished, and world-wide trade had scarcely yet begun; and the war against Spain, in the remaining years of the life of the Queen, showed more failures than successes on the sea. This rise and fall was exactly in parallel with the career of Drake. He rose in confidence and skill until the great climax of the Armada, and fell in disgrace and failure afterwards. He lost the touch of genius, and so did Elizabethan seamen as a whole.

In the summer after the Armada was beaten, Drake put to sea again with an Armada of his own – a fleet which rivalled the Spaniards' in size, and in the total disaster of its voyage. He had 130 sail of ships, which nominally carried no less than 4000 seamen, 1500 officers and gentlemen and 17,000 soldiers. Its organisation broke all the principles he had insisted on before, except his forceful strategy. The soldiers were under the command of Sir John Norreys, 'Black John', a famous swashbuckling veteran of French and Irish battles; and Norreys and Drake were made equal in authority. Indeed, the whole huge project was their own idea. It was a major effort of war, committing a large proportion of the nation's strength; yet it was organised, like the trading and privateering voyages, as a joint stock company in which Norreys, Drake and the Queen were principal shareholders. To be a success, it therefore not only had to do some serious damage to the enemy, but also make a profit for its backers.

Its intention, in the eyes of Norreys and Drake, was to capture Lisbon and the Azores in the name of Don Antonio, the pretender to the throne of Portugal, who was said to have an ardent following in his country, and to oust the King of Spain from those possessions. But the Queen insisted they must first destroy the surviving ships of the Armada which had reached the northern ports of Spain.

Perhaps Drake organised the voyage as a private venture to free himself from the vacillations of the Queen and her Council and the noble command of Howard. At all events, when the two adventurers were clear of the land, they began a capricious course of action that took no account of the orders the Queen had given. First, they attacked Corunna. In harbour, there was only one of the Armada galleons, and the Spaniards burned it. But Norreys laid siege to the town and captured part of it after long and costly fighting. It was a useless acquisition. All they got out of it was wine and brandy, so much of both that thousands of soldiers were incapable and speechless, and many were afterwards said to have died of drink.

Next, they entirely neglected the Queen's instruction to attack the Armada ships, of which about fifty were lying in ports to the east; instead, they sailed for Lisbon and landed the army some distance up the coast to march on the city. By then the troops were in very poor shape through drink, disease and malnutrition; and the Portuguese turned out to have no love at all for Don Antonio, and joined the Spaniards to defend their capital. Norreys and the army retreated to the ships without achieving anything. The Earl of Essex, who had run away from court to join the fleet, offered a single-handed challenge to the best man the enemy could produce, but nobody bothered to answer; and Drake and Norreys blamed each other for the failure.

Then the Azores: Drake tried for two or three weeks to take the fleet to the west, but contrary gales scattered them and pinned them to the coast of Portugal. At last, most of them were forced to enter the harbour of Vigo. At sea, disease had made havoc, and only 2000 men were fit to fight; but they took the town without any opposition, burned it to the ground and laid waste the surrounding country. At sea again, the gale began afresh; two ships were wrecked, some were forced back to Vigo, others driven as far to the south as Madeira. The *Revenge* sprang a leak, and Drake came back to Plymouth alone with his ship on the verge of sinking. Others returned at intervals over the next two months. It was said that 16,000 men had died, some of wounds but more of disease and drink.

Ever since that dreadful failure it has been easy to criticise the folly of it. But it is only fair to remember that this was a time when sea power was being extended very quickly away from the coasts of home, and mistakes were bound to be made in testing the limits of what could be done. In this voyage, Drake's ambitious strategy had overreached itself, just as the Spaniards' had overreached itself the year before. Both nations were taught the same lesson: huge fleets of ships, especially those encumbered by soldiers, could only be managed when the wind was light and fair, and to send them far from home relied too much on the luck of the weather. Neither nation made quite the same mistake again.

Drake and Norreys both had to answer for what they had done. They seem to have been acquitted, but Drake was in disgrace with the Queen and kept ashore for the next seven years. At sea in that time, the English confined themselves to smaller expeditions, some of the Queen's ships and some of privateers, and mainly to attacks on Spanish merchantmen at sea. Drake had the mortification of seeing his own flagship the *Revenge* commanded by jealous rivals who were certainly not displeased at his eclipse: first Frobisher, and then Sir Richard Grenville, who lost her in his famous single-handed fight against a Spanish fleet in the Azores – the only royal ship the Spaniards had taken since the old *Jesus of Lubeck* in the fight at San Juan de Ulloa. Of all the privateers the most persistent was the Duke of Cumberland, who fitted out nine expeditions, and himself commanded many of them in a celebrated ship which he named the *Scourge of Malice*. And of all the prizes taken in those years, the greatest was the carrack *Madre de Dios* in 1593.

She was captured by a privateering cruise which reveals every oddity of Elizabethan enterprise. It was organised by Sir Walter Raleigh, who to some degree had succeeded Drake as a popular hero. Two of the Queen's ships took part in it, with thirteen privateers, and the merchants and landed gentry subscribed to its cost. It was delayed for two or three months in Plymouth by contrary winds, as so many others had been. But it sailed on 1st May, with Raleigh in command. On the very next day, it was overtaken by Frobisher in a pinnace, with letters from the Queen revoking Raleigh's command and appointing Frobisher instead, and ordering Raleigh to come back to court; and after a few days while his anger and disappointment cooled, he obeyed her summons.

But several of the captains, including those of the Queen's two ships, were unwilling to serve under Frobisher. And certainly no two commanders could have been less alike: Raleigh the courtier, poet and visionary, and Frobisher the rough sea-captain, known for his stern discipline, who probably could write no more than his name. So about half the ships left the squadron to cruise on their own account.

Frobisher went to the Spanish coast, with no success; and it was one of the defectors, Captain Robert Crosse of the Queen's ship *Foresight*, who boarded the *Madre de Dios* off the Azores, after a long fight between a Spanish fleet and half a dozen English ships, mostly the Duke of Cumberland's, which he happened to have met there. It was no mean achievement: the *Foresight* was 300 tons, 120 men, and the *Madre de Dios* a seven-decked ship of 1600 tons and 600 men. And it was no mean prize: they took her to England, her cargo was partially looted, and what remained was valued at £150,000 of Tudor money, equivalent to several millions now.

But it was a question who had a right to a share of this glorious fortune: Raleigh or Frobisher, who had not been there; the merchants who had financed the original expedition; Crosse and his crew; Cumberland, whose ships had been in the fight; or the Queen, who owned the *Foresight*. The Queen had the simplest answer; she took it nearly all.

*

Drake was active ashore, as Mayor of Plymouth and a member of Parliament, but he never stopped trying to restore himself in the favour of the Queen so that he could go to sea again. Among other persuasions, he gave her a written account of his first successful attack on Nombre de Dios, and put up a plan to go there again with an army instead of a few dozen men, and to march across the isthmus of Darien and take the city of Panama on the other side. In 1592, she half-heartedly approved, but only with the condition that Sir John Hawkins should share the command with him. For three years, she kept postponing her final permission to sail. But in August 1595, news came that the principal ship of the Spanish treasure fleet was lying dismasted in Puerto Rico with a cargo said to be worth two and a half million pounds. And abruptly, the Queen told Hawkins and Drake they could go, and capture Puerto Rico on the way.

Perhaps she expected to temper Drake's impetuous behaviour with the sober caution that was Hawkins's nature. But the two men, who had known each other well since they were boys, were too unlike. They could not share command. Their combined fleet was 27 sail, with 2500 troops commanded by Sir Thomas Baskerville; and a captain in his force named Thomas Maynard wrote a wise and perceptive account of the voyage. Drake was about 54, and Hawkins over 60: 'a man oulde and warie,' Maynard wrote, 'entering into matters with so laden a foote, that the other's meat woulde be eaten before his spit could come to the fire: men of so different natures and dispositions, that what the one desireth the other would commonly oppose against . . . Whom the one loved, the other smaly esteemed.' After a few days at sea, the two commanders were openly quarrelling in front of other officers and sailors, and Baskerville was having to try to calm them.

The names of Draque and Aquines were still the two most dreaded in the ports of Spain, and warnings that they were planning to sail together had been sent by spies to Spain and thence to the Indies long before they did so. And after they sailed they took no trouble to keep their destination secret. Hawkins let every sailor in the fleet know where they were going. Drake and Baskerville insisted on trying to land in the Canary Islands but were beaten off; and off Guadaloupe a small bark of Drake's squadron lagged behind the fleet and was taken by the Spaniards. So the governor of Puerto Rico knew they were coming, and had time to call up his militia, reinforce his defences and take the treasure ashore and bury it. And the day the island was sighted, Hawkins died, dictating on his death-bed a letter to the Queen which foretold disaster for the expedition.

The rest of the voyage was a most pathetic story of a genius that failed: Drake, the man above all for instant decisive action, had grown muddled, unsure and hesitant, and so ineffective in command that it seems he must have had a chronic sickness that could not be recognised – something which had begun to affect his brain. He began the attack on Puerto Rico, but broke it off although some officers thought it could succeed. Then he sailed for Nombre de Dios, but stopped on the way to burn the small town of Rio de la Hacha, where he and Hawkins had sold their slaves when they were young. So warnings of his approach went ahead of him all along the coast. Nombre de Dios was taken without any trouble: its people had abandoned it and taken everything of value into the jungle or across to Panama. And there Baskerville landed with 750 men to march by the Spanish trail across the isthmus.

Drake himself was probably the only man who had seen that trail before. It was fifty miles in length and nine feet wide, just wide enough for laden trains of mules to pass each other, brushing the virgin jungle on either side. And the jungle for most of its length was so thick – it still is – that it could only be entered by hacking down the undergrowth. It was the most complete defence against an invading army that could have been devised. If Drake had been himself he must have known his troops could not possibly cross it in face of Spanish ambushes, and come out fit to fight at the other end. And indeed, less than half way there, they gave up the task and came straggling back again, exhausted and discouraged, and bringing with them malaria and yellow fever.

At that reverse, Drake seemed to lose hope. For the first time in his life, his optimism failed him. 'Since our return,' Maynard wrote, 'he never caried mirth nor joy in his face.' Futile plans were discussed for further raids in Nicaragua and anywhere else they could think of, but the officers had grown cynical about both Drake and Hawkins: 'Our blinded eyes began now to open, and wee founde that the glorious speeches, of an hundred places that they knew in the Indies to make us rich, was but a baite to draw Her Majestie to give them honourable employments and us to adventure our lives for theyr glory.' The wind was boisterous and contrary, and men were sickening and dying. They struggled on a little way, past the bay of Portobello, where the Spaniards were building a new town to supersede Nombre de Dios, and they anchored in the lee of a waterless island where they found nothing to eat but tortoises. Here Drake admitted defeat: 'He resolved to departe, and to take the winde as God sent it.' It brought them back to Portobello, and in that beautiful fever-ridden bay, on 28th January 1596, he died. The next day he was buried at sea: a burial made romantic in songs and verses, but in truth a grave of lost youth, lost hope, lost reputation.

If England mourned for Drake and Hawkins, and the era which they represented, there was soon a chance to forget the loss in celebrating a surprising victory. This was the sacking of Cadiz; and its success is surprising because it was not led by seamen, but by the flower of the gentry and nobility, men who jealously vied with each other in personal feats of daring. The seafaring exploits of the reign of the Queen had evolved: they had started as a popular sport for humble seamen, and they ended now as a pastime for the rich.

The fleet was under the joint command of Lord Howard and the Earl of Essex. Their council of war included Lord Thomas Howard, Sir Walter Raleigh, Sir Francis Vere, Sir Conyers Clifford and Sir George Carew. Ten of the fourteen ships the Queen provided were commanded by knights, and so were several of the privateers; young nobles and courtiers served among the gentlemen, and nearly sixty men were knighted for their prowess in the fight.

It is hard to believe such a distinguished set of amateurs could have won a sea-battle, but that was not the plan; their battle was fought, like the battles of medieval fleets, inside a harbour, and no knowledge of naval tactics was involved. Perhaps Howard and Essex had taken note of the failure of Hawkins and Drake, for they skilfully took precautions to keep their plans a secret, and to avoid being sighted as they passed down the coast of Portugal. So they arrived off Cadiz in the morning of 20th June, 1596, with the advantage Drake had wasted: complete surprise. At a council of war that day, Essex claimed the honour of leading the fleet into harbour, and had to be persuaded out of that idea by Howard, who had promised the Queen not to let him take unnecessary risks. At length, positions of honour were allotted, by a balance of social rank and martial skill; and at dawn the next day, the English fleet sailed into the Spanish harbour in face of the galleys and forts that guarded it and the powerful warships within. By night, they had taken the town and sunk, burned or captured some forty Spanish ships, and Essex in person was gallantly escorting the ladies of Cadiz to safety, with their richest clothes and jewels. It was a remarkable feat of arms, if not of seamanship.

*

Among all the minor voyages in the last years of the Queen, one especially deserves to be remembered, because it seemed to recapture for a moment the spirit of Drake's early enterprises. It was led by yet another Plymouth man, William Parker, and he wrote an account of it himself. He set off in November 1601 to spend the winter looking for profit and amusement in warmer climates: his own ship, the *Prudence*, 100 tons, manned by 130 'tall men', the *Pearl* of 60 tons with 60 'lustie fellows', and a pinnace with 18 men of a size and strength he did not specify. And he took with him 'divers Gentlemen of much towardliness and valour'.

Off the coast of Spain in a terrible gust of wind the pinnace sank and only three of her crew were rescued. But the others went on to the Cape Verde Islands and took the town of St Vincent which they burned and looted. Across the Atlantic, they captured a small Spanish island and ransomed it for £500 in pearls. And the captain of a Portuguese ship with a cargo of Negroes paid another £500 for his freedom.

So far, it was pure piracy. But on the coast of Darien, Parker seems to have taken Drake's first attack on Nombre de Dios as a model. Nombre de Dios itself had been almost abandoned; the building of Portobello had been finished, and this was now the end of the Spanish trail across the isthmus, a town with three strong forts and a new Royal Treasure House, all elegantly built of stone.

Parker hid his ships, somewhere not far from Drake's Port Pheasant, and embarked 150 men in two small pinnaces, which he must have captured, and two shallops which he had brought in sections from Plymouth. Like Drake, they rowed and sailed along the coast, and picked up some Negro guides; and at two o'clock in the morning, one moonlit night, they boldly entered the harbour of Portobello. A sentinel in the first of the fortresses hailed and asked where they came from. Parker had men with him who spoke good Spanish: from Cartagena, they shouted back. They were ordered to anchor. An hour later, Parker himself took thirty men in the shallops and made for the town. Soldiers ran along the shore, shouting to him to stop. But he took no notice, landed the men and marched right into the town and up to the Treasure House, where a squadron of troops confronted him with two brass cannon.

There were running fights through the streets and houses of Portobello all that night. By dawn, the mayor had fled to the jungle, wearing his gold chain of office, the military governor was a prisoner, wounded in no less than eleven places, and the garrison had retreated outside the walls. The rest of Parker's men had come ashore. Triumphantly they forced the Treasure House itself. At some times of year, according to rumour, it held five or six million ducats, but they found in it a mere ten thousand, which Parker took for himself. The rest of the pillage of the town he gave to his crews.

They held the place all day – a stately and new-built town, Parker said, with two goodly churches and five or six fair streets. 'I might speedily have consumed it all with fire, but I willingly abstained from the same: knowing that though I could have done the King of Spaine great hurt, and have undone a number of the Inhabitants, yet the good that I should have done myself and mine thereby should have been very small in comparison of their damage.' As for the Governor: 'in regard that he had valiantly carried himself in making resistance untill he had ten or eleven wounds upon him, I did not only at length dismisse without any peny for his ransome, but also caused my Chirurgion very carefully to dresse and trimme his wounds.'

It was in a good tradition to show respect to an enemy who had fought well. And perhaps it showed an unusual sensibility to forgo the pleasure of burning a Spanish town. Parker would probably not have been so forbearing, if he had had time to bargain over its ransom. But the forts were still in action, and his little boats were in an impossibly dangerous position. 'The day being spent, I embarked my men, enriched with the chief spoils of the Towne, and set sail to depart with my owne two Pinnasses and two shallops and two Spanish frigats which I had wonne: but in going out I was shot in at the elbow, and out at the wrist with a Musket shot which came from the Wester shoare, whereof there were many shot over us: besides eight and twentie great shot from the chiefe and Easter Fort.' They passed over the spot where Drake's coffin had been thrown overboard six years before, and they sailed past Cartagena; whose governor, Parker said, 'when he heard that I had taken Porto Bello, one of the chiefest places of the West Indies, with so small a force, he pulled his beard, and sware that he would give his Mules lade of silver, but to have a fight of mee and my companie.'

That summed up the Elizabethan ambition: to be able to boast of winning a fight, with a few well-chosen men against enormous odds, and of annoying the Spanish authorities. A few thousand ducats, of course, added sweetness to the victory.

*

Half a century of distant expeditions had left a good many Englishmen shipwrecked and stranded, alone or in dwindling groups, on the Atlantic coasts of Africa and America. Their chance of reaching home was very small. Most of the native people they met had learned to attack a European stranger before he could do any harm, and if they met Spaniards or Portuguese they were likely to spend their lives in prison. But of all the thousands who sailed and met disaster, a few did come back after years in the wilderness, and some were able to tell coherent stories which reached the ears of one of the tireless collectors of seafaring history, Richard Hakluyt or his successor Samuel Purchas. The journals and accounts of successful voyages were written by captains, masters or gentlemen, but these stories of escape were told by the humblest seamen, who show themselves to have been a resourceful breed and, on the whole, remarkably acute observers.

One of them, for example, was Peter Carder, who came from St Veryan in Cornwall and sailed with Drake in the *Golden Hinde* on the voyage round the world. In the storm when the ships had passed through the Straits of Magellan, Drake for some reason ordered the ship's boat away with eight men in it. In the night, the men in the boat lost sight of their ship and never found her again. Five west country sailors, two Londoners and a Dutch trumpeter were lost, alone in the South Pacific in winter in an open boat with no sail, no food or chart or compass. But they had eight oars, and they rowed; and after two days in heavy seas they sighted land. And then they rowed back through the Straits and up the coast of South America, beyond the mouth of the River Plate, a distance of about 2000 miles, living on oysters, mussels, crabs, penguins and seals.

But then, in the same district as John Drake and probably a year before him, they landed and went foraging in the forest and were attacked by Indians. All of them were wounded and four were taken prisoner and very likely eaten or enslaved: the other four took the boat to a small island ten miles offshore. Two died there of their wounds, leaving only Peter Carder and a Londoner named William Pitcher. And the boat was driven on to some rocks and wrecked.

On the island, these two survivors found crabs, and creatures like eels which buried themselves in sand, and a kind of fruit like an orange. But there was no water and no rain. They kept themselves alive for two months until their wounds had healed by drinking their own urine. And then they found a plank which they supposed had drifted out of the mouth of the river, and they lashed some other bits of wood to it with withies and took two poles for oars; and after three days in the sea they reached the mainland. 'We found a little River of very sweet and pleasant water,' Carder wrote, 'where William Pitcher my onely comfort and companion (although I diswaded him to the contrary) over dranke himselfe, being pinched before with extreme thirst, and to my unspeakable griefe and discomfort, within halfe an houre after dyed in my presence, whom I buried as well as I could in the sand.'

The next day, all alone, Peter Carder started to walk up the shore towards Brazil, which he knew was somewhere to the north of him. Very soon, he was surrounded at a distance by dancing Indians, armed with bows and arrows. But this was a different tribe. They hung a white cloth on a post, and retreated to see what he would do. He went to it and took it in his hands and then put it back on the post. That pleased them, and they beckoned and called to him to join them, and took him to their town, where he reckoned four thousand people lived in four enormous houses.

Parker seems to have charmed these people. He lived with them long enough to learn their language and understand their ways, and he helped them in their wars. Before he came, they had only used bows and arrows, but he taught them to make themselves shields and clubs. And he also introduced the idea of military uniform: he advised them each to paint one leg with red balsam before a battle, so that they would know friends from enemies. Consequently, they were often victorious and well provided with prisoners, whom they killed and ate. And indeed, when some Portuguese came trespassing in their country, they killed and ate them too.

At length he told the chief he wanted to march on towards the equator. Four men were sent with him to guide him and find food for him; according to his story they marched for nine or ten weeks and came to the coast again at Bahia de Todos os Santos. As the crow flies, that is 1800 miles, and perhaps he had lost account of time. But at all events, he did undoubtedly emerge there from the Brazilian jungle, having rowed and walked for almost the entire length of South America; and he was promptly put in prison by the Portuguese.

However, they must have liked his story, for they sent a dispatch to Lisbon to ask for instructions, and in the meantime he was allowed to live and work with a man who had befriended him. He became an overseer of sugar plantations, and then the skipper of a local coasting boat. It was three years before an order came from Lisbon, and the only Englishman he met in those years was a surgeon called David Leake, who had also been ship-wrecked and had set up in practice there. His friend warned him about the order: he was to be taken to Portugal as a prisoner – and that often meant a life as a galley slave. So he borrowed a boat and went even farther north, to Pernambuco. There at last, he heard of a ship that was bound for England. Off the Azores, it was captured by two English men-of-war; and so he arrived in Chichester in 1586, nine years after leaving Plymouth. Lord Howard heard of him, and took him to tell his story to the Queen.

*

In the Queen's old age, the seamen of England were on the verge of their centuries of power. The exuberant genius of her middle years had faded, and settled down to more sober confidence. They had proved no sea in the world was too dangerous for them to try. The Spaniards' voyages, with only a few exceptions, had been made in temperate climates across the Atlantic and Pacific. The Portuguese, in rounding the Cape of Good Hope and crossing the Indian Ocean, had often run the risk of stormier seas. But the English, starting later, had been forced to practise their seamanship in the parts of the world that were left. So they had ranged from Novaya Zemlya to Cape Horn, and encountered every kind of wind and sea and every possible hazard of exploration.

In warfare, they had designed a kind of ship and invented a kind of tactics which had beaten the greatest navy in the world and won the respect of the others. And they had discovered at least one thing they could not do: they could not manage large fleets too far from home. They excelled in small ships and small fleets, which allowed every captain and sailor to show his own skill.

So they knew they could master the sea, and were proud of it. But they had scarcely begun to make any use of their power. The old trade routes were still being used, to Iceland, the Baltic and the Mediterranean. Crossing the north Atlantic had become so commonplace that all the maritime nations had fishing fleets off the American coast. But the colonies there had failed, and so far the only steady substantial trade that had come out of Tudor exploration was with Muscovy, the result of the north-east expeditions.

The rewards of skill at sea awaited another century and another ruling house. In the year 1600, the aged Queen was persuaded to grant the first charter to the Governour and Company of Merchants of London trading into the East-Indies. So, very slowly at first, the East India Company began, the vast commercial enterprise which sailed farther in distant seas, in the next two centuries and a half, than the Royal Navy itself, designed its own ships and fought its own wars, and came in the end to rule two hundred million people.

PART FOUR

RIVALRY

1603–1759

*Merchants show
more enterprise than kings,
but the royal ships in a century of war
win dominance
that all their rivals recognise.*

CHAPTER 15

East Indiamen

DOMINANCE in any walk of life is a quality that has to be acknowledged, not only claimed. Ever after the Armada, the British could have claimed to be a dominant power at sea; but it was still almost two hundred years before their dominance was acknowledged by all their rivals, and in that time they often had to defend it, in war and trade, against the French and Dutch, the Spanish and Portuguese.

At the death of Queen Elizabeth the country began a dismal period when royal ships were allowed to decline again, and naval power sank to its lowest ebb, and only the merchants, still doggedly searching for their profits, kept Britain's claim to a place on the sea alive. Their ambition to trade in the east had never quite been abandoned in the war with Spain. It had risen after Drake's voyage round the world and been thwarted by Fenton's failure. And then it had been revived by the voyage of Thomas Cavendish, who followed Drake's route in 1586.

Cavendish was not a trader himself: like Drake, he was a plunderer. But unlike Drake, he was a ruthless, violent man, and Englishmen cannot look back on his voyage with any pleasure. In the Straits of Magellan, he found fifteen starving men and women, the only survivors of the colony the Spaniards had tried to plant in that desolate place at the time of Fenton's voyage four years before. He promised to rescue them; but the wind came fair, and he sailed away and left them there to die. And after that, he left a trail of burning towns and slaughtered populations up the Pacific coast of South America. 'All the Villages and Townes that ever I landed at, I burnt and spoyled,' he reported with satisfaction. But he passed through the East Indies and came back to England full of enthusiasm for the profits that might be made there; and he arrived just after the Armada victory, when English self-confidence was boundless.

He sailed again in 1591, but failed to get through the Straits and died on the way home after a series of mutinies. In a pathetic letter he wrote when he was dying, he blamed everyone for the mutinies but himself; but he seems to have caused them by trying to deceive his crews. Especially, he blamed John Davis the arctic explorer, who was captain of one of the ships. Davis did pass through the Straits, searching for Cavendish, who had disappeared. But he was beaten back by storms on the other side, and had to make an epic journey home. The account of it reads like the voyage of the Ancient Mariner. His ground tackle had been lost, except one anchor with a broken fluke and one cable which had already parted and been spliced. His rigging was rotten, most of his sails had blown away, and most of his provisions had been eaten; and he seems to have been so badly equipped that he had to build a forge for making nails, and set his men to fishing with bent pins. In the Straits, he made salt by evaporating sea water in pools on the rocks, and his crew dried and salted fourteen thousand penguins.

But coming back through the tropics the penguins rotted and infested the ship with a plague of innumerable worms which bit the men in their sleep and also (they said) ate the timbers. Some men disappeared in Patagonia and were assumed to have been caught by cannibals. Others were ambushed and killed by Portuguese off Rio de Janeiro. More died of scurvy until sixteen were left of whom, in the end, only five were able to move; Davis himself, the master, two other men and a boy. For a while, only Davis and the master had the strength to climb the rigging and work aloft – perhaps their diet had been better – but then they also had to give it up and allow the topsails to be blown to rags. And these two men took the helm, watch and watch, brought the ship back across the Atlantic to Ireland and ran her ashore in Bantry Bay, where they had to employ the local fishermen to furl the last remaining sails.

That voyage put an end to English attempts to go through the Straits of Magellan; probably, after the survivors' stories had been told, it would have been hard to man another fleet to go that way. But in the same year, 1591, three ships had sailed to try the other route to the east, round the Cape of Good Hope. And this was the first of a series of enormously long and dangerous adventures which are hard to imagine now; for their only specific objective was still to trade for spices, especially pepper and cloves.

Above all, it was the passion for pepper that still sent men in thousands to risk their lives. The Portuguese had almost a monopoly in pepper, and sold it in Lisbon at a net profit of 500 per cent. That in itself was enough to tempt any merchant. But in the aftermath of the Armada battle, the King of Spain, now also the ruler of Portugal, put a ban on the sale of spices to

Protestant countries – and thereby, in the end, lost the whole of his pre-
dominance in the east to two Protestant powers who refused to do without
pepper on their meat; the Dutch and the British.

The three ships which set forth to break the monopoly and follow the
Portuguese route were the *Penelope*, the *Merchant Royal* and the *Edward
Bonaventure*. No doubt this last ship was named in succession to Richard
Chancelor's, which had been wrecked in Scotland on her way home from
the North-East Passage. Her captain was James Lancaster, a citizen of
Basingstoke, who had also commanded her under Drake in the fight against
the Armada.

The expedition had an unusually tentative air. Its crews may well have
been aware they were trying something that England had scarcely done
before: to come to terms with people of ancient civilisations which were
wholly separate from Europe, and to sail on coasts well known to strange
seafaring races, the Arabs, Indians, Malays, Chinese and Japanese. Especially,
they must have been aware of being novices in seas where the Portuguese
had a hundred years' experience and knew the courses, currents and prevailing winds, and the landmarks and safe havens. The Portuguese, like every
other nation, kept that kind of knowledge to themselves, and only scraps of
it at second-hand had spread to England. There was a letter, for example,
from an Englishman named Thomas Stevens, who had taken passage in a
Portuguese ship in 1579 from Lisbon to the colony of Goa in India. Going
down to the Tropics, he said, the Portuguese sailed from island to island –
Madeira, the Canaries, and Cape Verde. But south of that, they did not try
to follow the coast of Africa, or sail direct for the Cape, because there were
zones of contrary winds; instead, they set a course as near south as they could
until they were in the latitude of the Cape, $35\frac{1}{2}°$S. Then they turned east,
estimating their longitude by the variation of the compass, and their distance
from the Cape by the kinds of seabirds they saw. From the Cape, if they
could, they sailed inside the island of Madagascar, so that they could get
water and fresh provisions at places they knew on the coast of Mozambique.
But late in the season they had to sail outside the island to catch the monsoon
wind. Stevens's ship was forced to take that course, 'a way full of privy rocks
and quick sandes, so that sometimes we durst not saile by night.' These
would have been the islands and shallow seas between Mauritius and Sey-
chelle, with the Maldive Islands as a threat to starboard. After re-crossing
the equator, Stevens and his companions expected to sight India, and they
rejoiced when they saw two hawks. But so vague was their measurement of

longitude that the first land they found was Socotra, in the mouth of the Gulf of Aden, almost 20° too far to the westward. The voyage took seven months, although it was sometimes made in five; but only 27 people died of scurvy, which was less than usual.

Against scurvy, the English ships fared worse. Knowing less of the route, they crossed to Brazil before they set their easterly course for the Cape; and by the time they reached it so many men were too weak to work that the *Merchant Royal* was sent back to England with the sick. The *Penelope* and the *Edward Bonaventure* rounded the Cape, the first English ships to do so from west to east, and embarked on the hazards of the Indian Ocean. Soon after, they lost company in a storm; and the *Penelope* was never heard of again. The *Edward Bonaventure* was struck by lightning, which split her mainmast and killed four men, 'their necks being wrung in sonder without speaking any word, and of 94 men there was not one untouched, whereof some were striken blind, others were bruised in their legs and arms ... others were drawen out at length as though they had been racked. But (God be thanked) they all recovered saving onely the four which were slaine out right.'

They sighted the coast of Madagascar on a moonlit night; and putting about to avoid it, they came to land on the island of Comoro. The natives there seemed friendly, and the king came aboard and was entertained, and several parties went ashore for water. But then, for no reason they could understand, the final shore party was set upon in sight of the ship and slaughtered – the master and thirty-two men. Depressed by that ghastly sight and puzzled at what had caused it, the rest of them sailed on up the coast of Africa and stopped again in Zanzibar. And there for the first time they learned the kind of thing they were up against; for the Portuguese had heard they were coming, and warned the local people that Englishmen were dangerous cannibals.

Like Stevens's ship, the *Edward Bonaventure* was set almost into the Gulf of Aden by unexpected currents and a north-easterly wind; but in May 1592, just over a year from England, she passed the southern point of India. From there, with a very large wind and heavy rain, she ran down to the Nicobar islands, 1000 miles in six days. Her master, who must have been promoted when the first was killed, made a mistake in observing the latitude and she missed the islands, but found instead the western end of Sumatra, the principal source of pepper.

But having found the place after so much tribulation, Lancaster made no attempts to trade, or none that were recorded; nor did he go ashore to meet the local rulers. All he did was capture some ships with Portuguese goods on board and rifle them for anything worth having, including some pepper – which he might have done, and indeed had done, without going much farther than the coast of Portugal. Almost the only things they bought ashore were ambergris and the horns of the Abath, 'a beast which hath one horne onely in her forehead, and is thought to be the female Unicorne.' Its horn, they were told, was a sovereign remedy against poison; but perhaps they had misunderstood, and had bought rhinoceros horn, a well-established aphrodisiac.

One can imagine why Lancaster showed so little enterprise, and felt unable to face the problems of foreign kingdoms or match his own wits against those of the Portuguese. He must have been very lonely. He had only one ship, and few if any men he could confide in: he had lost his Captain General in the *Penelope*, and his master in the massacre at Comoro. He himself fell sick, and the remainder of his crew lost heart. While he was lying in his cabin and seemed likely to die, the men decided they were going home and refused to hoist a sail for any other purpose. Single handed, there was nothing he could do to stop them.

So with little to show for the journey, they crossed the Indian Ocean again, rounded the Cape and called at St Helena, where they found some fruit and goats, and a solitary Englishman who had been put ashore there eighteen months before by the *Merchant Royal* in the hope that he might recover from a sickness. And indeed he had; but the excitement of being rescued seemed to drive him mad: he refused to lie down and after a week without going to sleep he died.

In the Doldrums, the ship lay still for six weeks without a useful breath of wind. Only a quarter of the crew was still alive, and those were still insisting they were going home and nowhere else. But starvation forced them to try for Trinidad. They failed to find it, and sailed aimlessly through the Caribbean; landed here and there to catch crabs and tortoises or turtles; spoke a French ship which had no food to spare but sold them some hides, which they ate; tried to run up the coast to Newfoundland; lost sails and foremast and sprang a dangerous leak in a storm off Barbados; and at length drifted back down wind to the Spanish islands. On one small island, Lancaster and fifteen men went ashore to forage, leaving only five men and a boy on board the ship. They stayed there several days, searching vainly for something to eat; and the carpenter who was on board must either have thought they had gone for ever, or else that he would be better off without them. He cut the cable of the ship, and she drifted away and left them.

The remnant of the expedition disintegrated into little groups of desperate starving men. Two went to look for birds' eggs and fell down a cliff; a few were killed by Spaniards; Lancaster lived for a month on the island eating the stalks of purslane. He and about a dozen others were picked up in the end by French ships. But for one man even then the adventure was not over; the ship that rescued him was wrecked in Jamaica, and he and the Frenchmen had to build a boat to escape from the island.

*

That voyage had been an almost complete disaster: of all the men who rounded the Cape of Good Hope, not as many as one in ten saw home again. But the next was worse. In 1596, an expedition entirely vanished, and no one came home at all. Years afterwards, stories were heard in Spain and Portugal of another final shipwreck in the Caribbean. It is surprising that the English did not give up the idea of sailing east. But the Dutch, in the same few years, had entered the trade with far more success; and London merchants, to their chagrin, were having to bid high prices for pepper in Amsterdam. This was the more annoying because the Dutch relied on English pilots. John Davis piloted a Dutch fleet to the east in 1598. In the same year, an Englishman named Malis took one round the world; and in 1599 William Adams, another English navigator, took one through the Straits of Magellan and was made a kind of prisoner in Japan. This unlucky man, the first Englishman to reach that fabled country, made himself so useful to the Emperor as a shipbuilder that he was not allowed to leave. In 1611, he smuggled out two letters, one to his wife in London and one addressed to all his countrymen, begging for a ship to come to fetch him; but he died there after twenty years in exile.

So the merchants of London were still determined to win a share of the profits. At the end of the century, they combined to subscribe about £70,000. The Queen procrastinated, as was her custom, when they asked for a charter which would give them a monopoly of the trade. But they went ahead and bought four ships, and fitted them out in the Thames. The largest, 600 tons, was the Duke of Cumberland's *Scourge of Malice*, the old privateer, which was given a less provocative name, the *Dragon*. The others were the *Hector*, the *Ascension* and the *Susan*, and there was also a supply ship named the *Guest*. James Lancaster was appointed General of the fleet and John Davis its chief pilot; and the Queen gave Lancaster powers of court martial and

flattering letters to kings in Sumatra and Java. Victualled and stocked with
trade goods, the fleet left the Thames in February 1600; but it was delayed
in the Channel by unseasonable calms and did not get away, from Dartmouth
in Devon, before the beginning of April. Nine months later, the Company's
charter was signed.*

In May, the ships were in the Canary Islands, at the end of June they
crossed the equator and lost the Pole Star; and beset by calms, it was
9th September before they reached the bay which is now the site of Cape
Town. By then, all of the crews except one were so stricken with scurvy
that they could not hoist out their boats and could scarcely let go their
anchors. The exception was Lancaster's. Since his first voyage, he had somehow learned the cure. He took bottles of lemon juice with him and dosed
every man with three spoonfuls every morning on an empty stomach. So
they reached the Cape comparatively healthy. And yet, although the
treatment was so simple and known so long ago, sailors continued to suffer
and die from scurvy for at least two centuries more.

A little over a year out of England, still intact, Lancaster's fleet let go its
anchors off Sumatra. Lancaster sent a delegation ashore, and the King sent a
procession of elephants to bring him, with Queen Elizabeth's letter, to a
banquet. 'The biggest of these Elephants was about thirteene, or fourteene
foote high, which had a small Castle, like a Coach upon its back, covered
with Crimson Velvet. In the middle thereof, was a great Bason of Gold, and
a peece of Silke exceeding richly wrought to cover it: under which her
Majesties letter was put. The Generall was mounted upon another of the
Elephants.' All went well. Lancaster found, as he already had at other ports
of call, that the Portuguese had warned the native people of the evil intentions of the English and also of the Dutch. But something in the Englishmen's
behaviour pleased the King, and he agreed to trade with the English and oust
the Portuguese. The same thing happened in Java, where the King turned
out to be a boy of ten.

The ships stayed almost another year in these exotic places, very slowly
filling their holds with pepper. A large proportion of their crews had died

---

* There is some confusion about these dates, although they might be said more justly than
many others to mark the birth of the British Empire. Some authorities give 31st December
1599, the last day of the century, as the date when the Queen signed the Charter; but the
document itself is dated 'the three and fortieth yeare of Our Reigne', which was 1600. Others
have assumed the ships sailed in 1601, but the narrative of the voyage is clearly dated in February 1600. So it seems certain that the Company sent out its ships before it received its Charter.

of accidents or tropical diseases; but this was accepted as a normal thing, and only caused comment when the manner of their deaths was strange or their rank was high. Such was the fate of Captain Brand of the *Ascension*. He took his boat to go ashore for the funeral of the Master's Mate of the *Dragon*: 'and as it is the order of the sea, to shoote off certaine peeces of Ordnance at the buriall of any Officer, the Gunner of Ordnance shotte off three peeces, and the bullets being in them, one stroke the *Ascension* boate, and slue the Captaine, and the Boatswaines Mate starke dead.'

In February 1602, Lancaster began to make ready for the voyage home. He acquired or built a pinnace of 40 tons and sent her with trade goods to the Moluccas, to wait there hopefully for the next expedition the Company might send; and he left three factors and eight other men in Java to accumulate cargoes there. The *Susan* and the *Ascension* were sent in advance to England with letters; and last, he sailed in the *Dragon* with the *Hector* in company, deep laden with pepper and carrying letters and gifts from the Kings to Queen Elizabeth.

Two months later, south east of the coast of Africa, the *Dragon* was in desperate distress; and the anonymous chronicler of the voyage wrote one of the best Elizabethan accounts of a crisis at sea. It deserves to be read at length:*

'The fourteenth day of April we were in 34 degrees, judging the land of Madagascar to be north of us. The eight and twentieth day we had a very great and a furious storm, so that we were forced to take in all our sails. This storm continued a day and a night, with an exceeding great and raging sea, so that in the reason of man no ship was able to live in it. But God in his mercy ceased the violence thereof, and gave us time to breathe, and to repair all the distresses and harms we had received; but our ships were so shaken that they were leaky all the voyage after.

'The third of May we had another very sore storm which continued all the night, and the seas so beat upon the ship's quarter that it shook all the ironwork of her rudder; and the next day in the morning, our rudder broke clean from the stern of our ship, and presently sank in the sea. This struck fear in the hearts of all men, so that the best and most experienced of us knew not what to do: and especially in such a tempestuous sea and so stormy a place, that I think there be few worse in all the world. Now our ship drove up and down in the sea like a wreck, whichever way the wind carried her:

---

* The spelling and punctuation here are slightly changed to make the story clearer.

so that sometimes we were within three or four leagues of the Cape, then cometh a contrary wind and driveth us almost to 40 degrees to the southward, into the hail and snow and sleety cold weather. Yet all this while the *Hector* kept by us carefully, the company whereof was some comfort unto us.

'At the last it was concluded to take our mizzen mast and put it forth at the stern port, to try if we could steer our ship to some place where we might make another rudder and hang it. But this was to small purpose, for when we had fitted it and put it forth, it did so shake the stern and put all in such danger that it was needful to make all haste to get the mast into the ship again; which we were very glad when we had brought it to pass. Now we were without all remedy, unless we made a new rudder and could contrive to hang it in the sea: let every man judge how easy a thing it was, our ship being of seven or eight hundred tons, and in so dangerous a sea as this was. Then the General commanded the carpenter to make a rudder of the mizzen mast; but at such time as we lost our rudder, we lost also most of our rudder irons wherewith to fasten it. But yet we went forward and made all the haste we could; and one of our men dived to search what rudder irons remained, and found but two, and one that was broken. Yet, by God's help, finding a fair day, we made fast the said rudder and sailed on our course homewards. But within three or four hours, the sea took it off again and we had much ado to save it; and with the saving of it, we lost another of our irons, so that now we had but two to hang it by. And our men began to be desirous to leave the ship, and go into the *Hector* to save themselves. Nay, said the General, we will yet abide God's pleasure, to see what mercy he will show us: for I despair not to save ourselves, the ship and the goods by one means or another, as God shall appoint us. And with that, he went into his cabin and wrote a letter for England, purposing to send it by the *Hector*. And he commanded her to depart and leave him there; but not one of the company knew of this command. The letter was very brief, and the tenor more or less as followeth:

' "Right worshipful, what hath passed in this voyage, and what trades I have settled for this Company, and what other events have befallen us, you shall understand by the bearers hereof. I will strive with all diligence to save my ship and her goods, as you may perceive by the course I take in venturing my own life and those that are with me. I cannot tell where you should look for me if you send out any pinnace to seek me, because I live at the devotion of wind and seas. And thus fare you well, desiring God to send us a merry meeting in this world, if it be his good will and pleasure."

'This letter being delivered, the General thought the *Hector* would have been gone in the night. But the ship kept some two or three leagues from us: for the master was an honest and good man, and loved the General well, and was loth to leave him in so great distress. Then the carpenter mended the rudder we had saved, and within two or three days the weather began to be somewhat fair, and the seas smooth. So we put out a sign to the *Hector* to come near us, out of which the master came, and brought the best swimmers and divers that he had in his ship, who helped us not a little in the business we had to do. Thus, by God's good blessing, we hung our rudder again upon the two hooks that were left. Now we had been beaten to and fro in these mighty seas, and had more storms of weather than are here expressed, sometimes for one whole month together, so that our men began to fall sick and diseased: and the wind fell so short that we could fetch no part of the coast of Africa, which was nearest to us. Committing ourselves therefore to God, we set sail straight for the island of St Helena. As we were in our course, the main-yard fell down, and struck one of our men into the sea and he was drowned. This was the end (God be thanked) of all our hard fortunes.'

In September, 1603, the two ships anchored in the Downs after nearly three years at sea. The Queen was dead. Plague was raging in London, commerce was at a halt and there was a glut of pepper, most of which belonged to the new King, James I, who insisted his should be put on the market before the Company's. For some time, the Company could not raise the money to pay its crews. But at length the pepper was sold and the voyage proved to have made a handsome profit. Nobody counted what it had cost in lives.

*

The Reverend Samuel Purchas, who continued the life's work of Richard Hakluyt in collecting narratives of English expeditions, was apt to make moral and patriotic comments on the stories he published; and his fourth volume was entitled

ENGLISH VOYAGES

BEYOND THE EAST-INDIES, TO THE ILANDS OF JAPAN,
CHINA, CAUCHIN-CHINA, THE PHILIPINAE WITH
OTHERS, AND THE INDIAN NAVIGATIONS
FURTHER PROSECUTED.
Their just Commerce, nobly vindicated against

East Indiamen

*Turkish Treachery, victoriously defended
against Portugall Hostility, gloriously
advanced against Moorish and
Ethnike Perfidie:
hopefully recovering from Dutch Malignitie;
justly maintayned against ignorant and
malicious Calumnie.*

English sea captains, indeed, who on the whole were simple straight-forward men, had entered a world of intrigue, bribery, swindling, slander and literally cut-throat competition; and the only fault of Purchas's title was its suggestion that the English did not do their best to outwit their rivals in trickery. Yet their best, in the early days, was seldom quite good enough; they seem by their own accounts slightly less ruthless than the Dutch, slightly less devious than the Portuguese, often aggrieved and bewildered by the stratagems of international trade. For the Portuguese and the Dutch persistently whispered malignant lies about each other, and about the English, in the ears of the Eastern rulers. The rulers judged Europeans by the gifts they brought, and often demanded things that were hard to supply: a Sumatran King told Lancaster to bring him a Portuguese maiden for his harem, and an Indian rajah asked for an English racehorse. Hierarchies of officials expected well-graduated bribes. Chinese traders, who had been there for centuries, pushed up the price of pepper as soon as a European ship was sighted, and native merchants hid dust and stones in their bags of peppercorns. And Portuguese and Spanish Jesuits, who were active in making proselytes from India to Japan, appear in all Protestant accounts to have been more crafty and treacherous than anyone. The ordinary Javanese were astonished by the amount of pepper the Europeans wanted, and it was a standing joke that these strangers came from cold countries and mixed the hot spice with mortar to plaster the walls of their houses and keep them warm.

In the beginning, the first decade of the seventeenth century, the Protestant Dutch and English often ganged up on the Portuguese. The Portuguese were less determined fighters; their ships and cargoes were often captured, and they were slowly ousted from the islands where they had worked so long. But then the Dutch turned on the English. The English company sent out eight expeditions between 1600 and 1611, some of four ships and some of only one; but the Dutch, with more money behind them and the support of their government, sent a strong fleet every year. So they were always more numerous in ships and men, and were able to make both life and trade very hard for the English. The English expedition of 1611 succeeded in sailing to the Moluccas and Japan. Its commander, John Saris, made a long and adventurous journey through the country to see the Emperor and he was well received; but through Dutch and Jesuit opposition, he failed to set up permanent bases for trade.

That was the apex of the English effort: from time to time there were meetings in London and Amsterdam, and resolutions were passed to end the fearsome rivalry. But news of decisions at home took at least a year to reach the islands, and longer still to reach the farthest outposts. In the oppressive climate tempers were short and life was cheap, and profit was the overriding aim. Desperate skirmishes, mysterious fires in warehouses, brawls between seamen, shots and knives in dark alleys in the night – all these continued; and they reached a climax in 1623 on the island of Amboyna. That was one of the clove islands, where the Dutch had installed a governor and the English, by agreement, had a number of resident traders. The Dutch governor rounded up ten Englishmen and accused them of plotting to seize his fortress. He put them to torture and extracted confessions which were certainly false, and after long ill-treatment he executed them all. News of this atrocity came to England a year after it was over, and caused such an outrage that there were demands for war. The Dutch government apologised and the offenders were withdrawn. But English traders living alone and far from help had already begun to retreat for their own safety; and in 1626, after 25 years of struggle, the English company abandoned the Spice Islands to the Dutch and only retained one trading post, at Bantam in Java where the king had been consistently kind and friendly. The Dutch founded colonies in the islands and remained until modern times. But English voyagers turned all their attention to India.

*

These enterprises, which led to three hundred years of British dominance in India, took place in the reign of the peaceable and hesitant King James I: the initiation of distant voyages, and the effective use of the sea, had passed again from the Crown to the city merchants, as it often had in the past. The navy of royal ships, in the same twenty-five years, was a melancholy remnant which seldom sailed beyond its own home waters. And its administration fell into a state of corruption.

It is a strange fact that naval affairs through the ages have been subject to periods of swindling, much more blatant than in other spheres of public life. Napoleon once accused his admirals of hiding their own inefficiency behind their technical terms; and although the accusation was unjust and only revealed his own ignorance of the sea, it is true that ships and the sea are an esoteric world in which it has always been easy to hide dishonest dealings from the eyes of landlubberly accountants. So it was in the reign of James. The King was charged for the maintenance of ships that had long before been scrapped; positions of trust were sold and bought, at prices in accordance with the scope they gave for cheating; imaginary men were added to ships' companies and their pay divided among the officers; there was a busy trade in stolen boatswains' stores, ropework, paint and canvas; even the guns of ships were taken away and sold to foreign bidders; and pursers made such profits on the sale of clothes to seamen, and took such bribes from the contractors who supplied them, that seamen could only afford to dress in rags.

In the reign of James, these subtle practices were a product of the morals of the age, and perhaps were also aided by another recurrent affliction of the navy: control by men who were far too old for the job. Lord Howard was no youngster at the time of the Armada, but as Earl of Nottingham he was still the Lord High Admiral in 1619, when he was 82; and he seemed content, or more than content, with what was happening under his command. Twice, when scandals grew too outrageous, commissions of enquiry were appointed. But they were composed of landsmen, and seldom understood or unravelled the skeins of deceit; more often, the commissioners themselves came under suspicion.

At sea, the navy spent most of what energy it had in chasing pirates. A good many of these were ex-naval men themselves; for when James abruptly concluded his peace with Spain, they felt defrauded of the quarry that had been legitimate so long, and they turned to the ancient sport instead. They attacked whatever shipping came their way, whoever it belonged to; one of them openly adopted Lundy Island in the Bristol Channel as his base and proclaimed himself king of it. The Scots, now subjects of the same king, also showed a taste for piracy; so did the Irish. And most active of all were the Barbary pirates from the north of Africa. They invaded the Channel, sometimes in fleets, and even landed in England from time to time and took off the people of coastal villages to slavery. In seven years in the middle of James's reign, no less than 466 British ships were known to have been captured, with their crews. One Barbary ship was found and defeated in the Thames itself, but the great majority escaped whatever ships the King could send against them. The reason was simply that the pirates' ships were faster. Of course, they never built their ships; they captured them, and then cut down all the top hamper, sometimes removing most of the upper deck. So the hulls had less windage and could beat up to windward better than any normal ship. Pirates were also said to take out most of the knees (which join the frames to the deck beams), so that the hulls were flexible; for it had been a belief since Viking times that a ship which flexed to the waves was faster than one which was rigid – 'like a man that is tight trussed and hath his doublet buttoned, that by loos'ning it he is able to run the faster': the graphic simile was made by Sir William Monson, who was Admiral at the time in the English Channel. And it did not worry the pirates that the ships soon fell to pieces; they simply captured more.

In 1620, a naval expedition of eighteen ships ventured as far as the Mediterranean to attack the pirates' ports, but it was a gloomy failure. It waited there for six months, mostly in friendly harbours, and sallied forth to make three visits to Algiers, where most of the pirates lay. The first time, it tried to negotiate with the local ruler for the release of his British slaves: he was polite, offered refreshments, admitted he had forty captives and gave them up – a derisory gesture, for he had hundreds or thousands more. The second time, the fleet attacked with fireships: whatever fires were started were put out by a shower of rain. The third time, a boom was found across the harbour mouth, and boats were rowing guard. The fleet had failed without those obstacles; in face of them, it did not even try. It sailed away; and the next night, a fleet of pirates and their prizes sailed jubilantly in.

That year, 1620, marked the lowest ebb of enterprise at sea that Britain ever sank to. In the Far East, the English company was retreating from the Dutch. In the north-west, William Baffin had just concluded that there was no passage, and the long search had lost its ardour. In the Pacific, no English ship had been seen for thirty years. In the Mediterranean, the King's fleet was making itself a laughing stock; in home waters, pirates had more control than the royal ships, which were crippled by fraud ashore; and barely two years before, the last of the great Elizabethan navigators, Sir Walter Raleigh, had been beheaded on the orders of the feeble King, a crime that put out the final glow of gallantry on the sea. It was a failing of spirit, not of skill, and the causes of such changes of national temperament always defy any true analysis. But certainly this was epitomised by the strength of the Queen and the weakness of her heir. In later years, sea-enterprise survived and even flourished under kings as futile as James. But in his reign, it was like a newly planted tree, and through his neglect it wilted before its roots grew deeper.

And that was also the year, 1620, when a humble and undistinguished ship crept out of Plymouth on a voyage more momentous in its consequence than any that had left an English port. It was appropriate that the *Mayflower* should have been a perfectly ordinary ship of her time. But her voyage, it must be admitted, was not an important achievement in itself; it was only its result that was important. By 1620, to cross the Atlantic was a commonplace event. For over a century, fishermen had casually done it every year, in much smaller and simpler ships, with no greater reward than the cod they brought back in their holds. And many of the East India Company's ships, successfully making the long haul to the islands of the east and back again, were more or less the same size as the *Mayflower* and much the same, so far as one can judge, in their design. The *Hector*, for instance, which stood by the *Dragon* so bravely through the storms in the Indian Ocean, was only a little bigger; the *Darling*, which traded and fought from the Red Sea to Sumatra, had only half the tonnage of the *Mayflower*. To the Pilgrim Fathers, the North Atlantic may well have seemed a menacing waste of waters, which indeed it is; but seamen of the time made light of it, and perhaps the greatest risk the *Mayflower* really ran was of meeting a pirate before she was clear of the land.

In the history of the British and the sea, the Pilgrim Fathers' voyage has many reflections. Religious feeling drove them to sea like the ancient Irish monks, or like the crusaders of Richard Cœur de Lion; social discontent like the Anglo-Saxons'; land hunger like their predecessors in Elizabethan days who failed, and their millions of successors. But no voyage in all this history can be recognised quite so precisely as the start of an era: an era which first extended British influence on the sea, then challenged it, and finally shared its burden, in its most desperate trials, between two national navies and two distinct traditions.

CHAPTER 16

Pepys and
the Stuart Navy

ALTHOUGH the royal fleet of King James I had sunk to such dismal depths, at least two great ships were built in his reign, one for him and one for the East India Company.

The Company's ship was the *Trade's Increase*, of about 1100 tons: one of the largest ships in the world, and the first of a noble series the Company built in the 250 years it existed. But her history was short and sad. She was built at Deptford on the Thames, and her hull was ready in December 1610, together with a smaller ship called the *Peppercorn*. The King and a retinue of lords came down the river for the launching, and feasted with a banquet of sweetmeats on board the ship in the dock where she was built. But the tide was lower than it was expected to be. The great ship refused to move, and the *Peppercorn*, built on a slipway alongside, stuck on her launching ways. The King had chosen the names, but the ceremony had to be abandoned; it was recorded that his Majesty was somewhat discontented, and the failure may have seemed a bad omen. On her first voyage in 1611 she struck a rock off Sumatra and was so badly holed that she had to be beached for repair in the harbour of Bantam in Java. And there she seems to have fallen on her side, to have filled with water and lost her masts. She was abandoned, and her captain died soon after: it was said of grief.

The King's ship was the *Prince Royal;* and hers was a history less tragic but more controversial. Her builder was Phineas Pett, a member of the remarkable dynasty of master shipwrights who had already been leaders in their craft for half a century. The Phineas Pett of King James's reign was more of a courtier than a ship designer, and he was probably deeply involved in the swindles of the period. The King's commission accused him of building a ship for himself, using timber and rigging from the royal dockyards, and of sailing it to Spain in company with a royal fleet, where he sold to the Spaniards some cannon and six hundred pounds of biscuit, the property of the King. But the King was a forgiving man, and let him off with a lecture;

Englishmen in a skirmish with Eskimos, 1576-8

Portrait of Charles II, 1684-5 by M. Laroon
Overleaf: Sovereign of the Seas, 1637. Coloured engraving
by John Payne

and he established himself in the royal favour by building for Prince Edward, the King's eldest son, a little replica of the *Ark Royal*, 25 feet in length of keel, which the boy could sail in the Thames above London Bridge.

In 1607, Pett built what he called 'a curious model for the Prince my master, most part whereof I wrought with my own hands; which being most fairly garnished with carving and painting, and placed in a frame arched, covered and curtained with crimson taffeta, was, the 10th day of November, by me presented to the Lord High Admiral.' That was the first known case of building a model of a ship of new design; for it represented the great ship Pett wanted to build for the King. Lord Howard arranged for the King to see it, the King was exceedingly delighted, and Pett was commissioned to build it. A year later, the keel was laid at Woolwich.

But Pett, so far as is known, had only built two ships before, the illicit ship for himself, which was small, and the replica for the Prince, which was almost a toy. Other shipwrights were incensed, and when the ship was in frame they wrote such a damning report that the King himself had to come to Woolwich and hold a formal enquiry. The design was said to be full of mistakes, and the construction showed 'gross errors and absurdities'; the frames, for example, were sawn out of straight timber so that they were cross-grained, the limbers were so large that the frames were weakened, the scarphs too short, the planks were unseasoned and some of the timber was rotting and weak with age. Pett claimed that these attacks were merely spiteful; and yet, to a modern builder of wooden ships, the report has a ring of truth.

However, the King supported Pett and the ship was completed. The cost of her was enormous. Shortly before, a ship of nearly the same size, the *Merhonour*, had been built by contract for £3600; but Pett's bill for the *Prince Royal* was nearly £20,000, including £1309 for painting and carving. Her design was never put to a serious test; like the rest of King James's ships, she never went far abroad, and the longest voyage she made was to Spain. When she was ten years old, the Navy Commissioners said she needed expensive repairs which 'will but make her ride afloat and be able to go to sea upon our own coast rather for show than for service'. And ten years later, she had to be wholly rebuilt, at a further cost of £16,000.

*

It was twenty years before Phineas Pett built another great ship, and by then his son Peter, at the age of twenty-five, was in charge of the yard at Woolwich. Phineas kept his connection with the court, and in 1635 Charles I, like so many kings before him, felt the royal need to build a grander and larger ship than anybody else. Phineas got the job, and he and Peter between them produced the family's masterpiece. She was named the *Sovereign of the Seas*.

The *Sovereign of the Seas*, like the *Prince Royal*, the *Henri Grace a Dieu* and the other great ships of kings, had a double purpose. She was a fighting ship; but she was also designed to express the majesty of the realm. In both respects, she surpassed any ship that had gone before. As a fighting ship, she was the biggest that had ever been built in England: her official tonnage was 1637 – which was also the year she was launched, a coincidence that enthralled the superstitious. She was also the first three-decker, in the sense that she carried three complete tiers of guns, at least a hundred in all; for the *Prince Royal*, which has sometimes been claimed as the first, only carried a third tier on her after deck.

And in the trappings of majesty, she far exceeded even the *Henri Grace a Dieu;* her ornament was more lavish than any before or since. She was covered all over with gilded carving, from the equestrian statue on her beakhead of the peaceful King Edgar trampling seven prostrate kings under foot (the same perhaps that had rowed him on the River Dee) to the carved reliefs on the stern of Victory, Jason the Argonaut, Hercules with his club and Neptune riding on a sea-horse – and the stern lantern in which, it was said, ten men could stand upright without shouldering or pressing each other.* Between these extremes an exuberant riot of figures flowed over her sides and her bulkheads; Greek and Teutonic gods, females twice life size who represented nautical virtues, satyrs and caryatids, signs of the zodiac, lions, unicorns, greyhounds and dragons cavorting among the roses of England, the thistles of Scotland, the fleur-de-lys of France and the royal monogram entwined with swags and garlands; and a frieze the length of the middle gun deck of trophies of war, guns, shields, swords, battleaxes, linstocks, rammers, suits of armour, trumpets, drums, muskets, flags and banners. The stem-head was crowned with a lion, ridden and tamed by a cupid.

Like the *Prince Royal*, the *Sovereign of the Seas* had critics. They were the Elder Brethren of Trinity House. The Corporation of Trinity House had been founded by Henry VIII for the training of sea-officers and pilots, and Elizabeth had made it responsible, as it still is, for the lighthouses, beacons

---

* In 1661, Mr Pepys shut five ladies in it, and then went in himself and kissed them all.

and seamarks on the coasts of England; so its executive court of thirteen Elder Brethren was a respected body. When the King's intention was reported, it wrote a curious letter to his principal secretary. 'The art or wit of man,' it stated firmly, 'can not build a ship well conditioned and fit for service with three tier of ordnance'. And furthermore, no port in the kingdom except the Isle of Wight could harbour so large a ship. 'Then it followeth, if she be not in port then is she in continual danger, exposed to all tempests, to all storms, that time shall bring. In a desperate estate she rides in every storm; in peril she must ride, when all the rest of her companions (his Majesty's ships) enjoys peace, rides quiet and safe in port . . . Yet anchors and cables must hold proportion, and being made, they will not be manageable, the strength of man can not wield nor work them, but could they do it, yet the ship little bettered in point of safety, for we are doubtful whether cables and anchors can hold a ship of this bulk in a great storm.'

It was a strange outburst, an early example perhaps of the excessive and passionate conservatism that naval experts showed in later ages. And it was very soon proved wrong, for the King took no notice of it, the great ship was launched – after several attempts – and she had an exceptionally long and useful life.

It was true the Brethren were justified in one respect: she was cut down, after many years, from three decks to two because the weight of the top tier of guns made her crank. But she remained the greatest ship in the navy for many years. In Cromwell's time, her name was shortened to the *Sovereign*. After the restoration she became the *Royal Sovereign*, and she fought through the Dutch wars of the second half of the century. She was still a flagship at the Battle of Barfleur against the French in 1692, when she was 56 years old. Indeed, if ships could have lived so long, her size and armament would have fitted her for a ship-of-the-line at Trafalgar. But she was burnt in the Medway at the age of 60 because a cook left a candle in his cabin.

*

The name of the *Sovereign of the Seas* was not only meant to describe the ship herself. It was a restatement of the royal claim to be sovereign of the seas which kings of England had made on and off since the reign of King John; and the seas still meant the Narrow Seas around the Straits of Dover. King John had expected foreign ships in the straits to salute his own by lowering their sails. King Charles expected them to dip their national ensigns, which is still a salute at sea. And there was a particular point in the claim in the seventeenth century. The Dutch were outdoing the English not only in the Far East but also in the coastal trade of Europe; yet they had to bring almost all their commerce through the Narrow Seas, in sight of Dover Castle. So command of those seas by either of the rivals was a possible stranglehold on the other, and the name of the great ship was a pointed gesture in defiance of the Dutch. The rivalry in trade, inflamed by memories of affronts like the massacre of Amboyna, was certain in the end to lead to war; but the immediate pretext of the first of the wars with the Dutch, in 1652, was that the Dutch admiral Tromp, who was passing Dover, refused to lower his flag in salute to the castle, or to the English admiral Blake.

This, of course, was under the Commonwealth, and Cromwell's more disciplined rule had gone some way towards curing the inefficiency and swindles of naval affairs under James and Charles I. The navy was ruled no longer by elderly noblemen, but by commissioners who were appointed by Parliament; and an infusion of army officers into the highest ranks had brought back a certain amount of pride to the naval service. An exception among the generals-at-sea, as they were called, was William Penn, the father of the founder of Pennsylvania; he had commanded a ship when he was 23, was rear-admiral at 27 and a general-at-sea at 32. But Robert Blake, the greatest and most successful of them all, never went to sea until he was nearly 50. It is sad for a naval person to think that the navy ever sank so low that it had to be brought back to life by the army, but so it was.

It was under these army generals, oddly enough, that the English first fought what might be called professional naval wars. They were wars unlike any other, in that they were fought in a very small area of sea. There were a few distant forays, one of which captured New Amsterdam and renamed it New York; but otherwise, everything happened in the hundred miles of water between the coasts of England and Holland. Within that narrow compass, the battles of these wars were some of the fiercest ever fought at sea; they ranged from one shore to the other, with sometimes the English and sometimes the Dutch in retreat, and often a hundred ships a side, all hammering each other.

In 1666, for example, there was the Four Days' Battle. Part of the English fleet, under the Duke of Albemarle – one of the soldier-admirals – encountered the Dutch off Dunkirk, under their admiral de Ruyter. The Dutch were stronger in numbers, and they forced the English out to sea in a series of short-range artillery fights – for both sides, by now, were relying on gunnery. During the night, as usual, the fighting stopped, and the Duke called his captains to a council of war and made a speech that included the memorable sentence, 'To be overcome is the fortune of war; but to fly is the fashion of cowards.' Next day, he gave battle again, now with only 44 ships against 80. By evening, both fleets had suffered badly, but fresh ships were sighted coming up from the coast of Holland, and the English began a fighting retreat which went on through the third day. The Duke sent the most shattered ships ahead, and defended them with what he had left; but one of his newest and finest, the *Royal Prince*, ran aground on the Galloper Shoal twenty miles off the coast of East Anglia, and the Dutch surrounded her, set her on fire and took the whole of her company prisoner. That evening, another fleet was sighted, approaching from the Channel; it could have been friend or enemy, and there was an anxious hour before it was seen to be the rest of the English fleet, fresh to battle. So reinforced, on the fourth of these hectic days, the English turned on the Dutch again and attacked with 'trumpets sounding, and drums beating in every ship, the seamen waving in defiance their hats, and the officers their plumed beavers.' That was another day of furious fights, until a thick summer fog came down and put an end to them; which perhaps was just as well, because the English and Dutch were too well matched in stubborn bravery, and would have fought on until nobody on either side was fit to fight.

And indeed they started again as soon as the fleets were repaired. The Four Days' Battle, on the whole, had gone against the English, but two months later the same admirals, and largely the same ships, met again off the North Foreland, the eastern point of Kent; and this time it was the Dutch who retreated and the English who chased them back to the harbours of Holland – and anchored there for a week, burning and pillaging villages and a huge number of merchant ships. The Dutch took their revenge in the following year, when lack of money, and the disasters of the Plague and the Fire of London, made Charles II keep his ships at moorings in the Medway. De Ruyter sailed into the river, broke the chain that was stretched across it in defence, silenced the forts, burned many of the ships and chose the *Royal Charles* to take and tow back to Holland – the most daring and successful sea-raid that was ever made on the homeland of England after the Norman conquest.

With an enemy equally matched in skill and stubbornness, the fighting navy was put on its mettle, and forced to develop and evolve. It was in these wars that it first became a separate service from the merchant navy, and was equipped entirely with ships that were built to fight. Both the Dutch and the

English put more and more gun-power into their fighting ships, until they were so weighted with cannon and shot that they could no longer be converted, in time of peace, to earn their keep in trade. In merchant ships at the same time, the trend was the opposite, especially on distant voyages. They still had to be armed, but the less they carried in guns the more they could carry in cargo, and therefore their merchant owners sent them to sea as lightly armed as they dared. The distinction had been coming for quite a long time: in the fleet that fought the Armada, the merchant ships had not been much use except for show. And to look further back, it was only a return to what the Vikings had known – that a good fighting ship had to be fundamentally different from a good cargo ship. In the stress of the Dutch Wars, that fact was rediscovered, and the two kinds of ship were never interchangeable again.

And tactics also evolved in the hard-fought battles of those wars. Ships began to manoeuvre in squadrons. The manoeuvres were still elementary, because no comprehensive system of signals had been invented – that invention was only made in Nelson's time. But large fleets were commonly divided into three squadrons each under its admiral, the admirals of the red, the white and the blue. Each admiral flew a flag or a pennant or both in his own colour; and by hoisting the pennant in different positions in the rigging, sometimes in combination with another flag, he could give a few simple orders either to a single ship or the squadron as a whole – to make or shorten sail, to chase to windward or leeward, to take up a specified formation. The signal for line ahead, to take an example, was the union flag and the admiral's pennant hoisted at the mizzen peak. To fight as a squadron needed a specialised skill outside the duties of a merchant captain. And so, like the two kinds of ships, the two kinds of officers grew apart. By the end of the reign of Charles II, most naval officers entered the service as boys, intending to make it their life's career. With these professional officers, and ships designed solely for war, the fighting service had an entity, and in his reign, about 1670, it was first called the Royal Navy.

*

It was very lucky, at the birth or rebirth of the navy, that one of the generals-at-sea was Edward Montague, later the Earl of Sandwich, and that one of Montague's servants was his impoverished young cousin Samuel Pepys. Through Montague's influence, Pepys at the Restoration became Clerk of the Acts of the King's Ships; and that ancient title – though Pepys hardly knew it when he was appointed – gave him most of the responsibility for building the ships, maintaining the dockyards, and feeding and clothing the crews. It was a hard task for an unknown and humble young man of twenty-seven: even after Cromwell's cleansing, the departments Pepys had to control were the most outrageous of all in their firmly established corruption.

Pepys knew nothing at all about ships when he started, and had only just come back from the first sea trip he had made in his life – to accompany his master to Holland and bring back the King from his exile. For quite a long time, he could hardly believe his luck, and felt amazed at his new importance; and he made up his mind that he could only keep his post by hard work. 'Chance without merit brought me in,' he wrote in his diary, 'and diligence only keeps me so, and will, living as I do among so many lazy people.' He set himself to learn, with his astonishing industry, getting up at four in the morning to study mathematics and memorise the multiplication tables, finding out about different kinds of timber, tar and rope, taking lessons in ship design from Anthony Deane, working half the night in his office, and yet enjoying the life of London to the full. At first he was flattered by the exalted company of the other members of the Navy Board, but as he learned the job he also began to learn their weaknesses. Sir William Batten, the Surveyor, he described in the private diary as a knave and a sot: Sir William Penn the distinguished admiral as a doating knight and a counterfeit rogue; others as rotten-hearted false vapourers and incompetent idlers.

The fact was that they were all busy making themselves rich men. So was Pepys. But he made a distinction between the perquisites of office and the downright swindling he began to find all round him. He was a good servant, first to Montague and later to the King, and he always remained a good servant even when his service had made him a powerful man – rather like a good butler who would expect to finish an open bottle of his master's wine but would not dream of taking a case of it. When somebody he had found a job for gave him a letter – it often happened – he knew it would contain the 'proceed' of his help and only opened it in private, 'not looking into it till all the money was out, that I might say I saw no money in the paper if ever I should be questioned about it.' And when somebody else, for a similar favour, gave him a pair of gloves for his wife, wrapped up – 'When I came home, Lord! in what pain I was to get my wife out of the room without bidding her go, that I might see what those gloves were; and by and by, she being gone, it proves a payre of white gloves for her and forty pieces in good gold, which did so cheer my heart that I could eat no victuals almost for dinner for joy to think how God do bless us every day.'

Such blessings were the recognised fruit of office; Montague himself had explained, when he introduced Pepys to the royal service, that it was not the salary of a place that made a man rich, but the opportunity it gave him for making money. What Pepys could not bear was laziness, incompetence and sheer dishonesty. And he set himself to weed them out of the navy. He made a habit of turning up unexpectedly in dockyards, sometimes so early that the men who should have been in charge were still in bed. With his new-won learning, he inspected their books and stocks, and he was ruthless with men who had gone too far in trickery. Even his seniors were pursued and subtly menaced with hints of exposure. As for serving officers, it annoyed him extremely that any young man of good birth could buy a commission and go to sea without any knowledge at all, and as soon as he had the power to do it he introduced an examination for the rank of lieutenant which he knew very few of them would pass.

That was one of the permanent marks he made on naval affairs. Another was in cartography. Hitherto, the English had been backward in making charts. When the Dutch wars began, the English fleet was using Dutch charts, even of the coasts of England. That rightly offended Pepys' feelings: it was neither patriotic nor practical. So he appointed a captain named Greenvile Collins to survey the British coast and harbours. The result was an atlas far better than the Dutch possessed, which is still a source of pleasure to connoisseurs of maps. And this was the beginning – a very late beginning – of the evolution of marine cartography in Britain: in the age of Cook, a century later, it surpassed all other nations', and by the nineteenth century everyone in the world relied on British Admiralty charts.

Pepys has been called the saviour of the navy. Perhaps that is going a little too far. The navy was suffering rather acutely from the malaise of the times, and no doubt it would have survived and recovered when the standard of honesty in the rest of English society took a turn for the better. But he very much speeded the recovery. With this strange and wonderful little man at the head of affairs, incredibly energetic, humorous, the best of company, yet implacably strict and a source of terror when he was much displeased, the navy had a core of uncomfortable conscience, and was freed of most of the dead weight of thieves and rogues ashore which had crippled it so long. 'At my office till 3 o'clock in the morning,' he wrote on a winter's night in 1664, 'having resolved to sit up, and did till now it is ready to strike four o'clock, all alone, cold, and my candle not enough left to light me to my owne house; and so, with my business however brought to some good understanding, and set it down pretty clear, I went home to bed with my mind at good quiet.'

That was the greatest of all his services: in a selfish and cynical age when most men did as little as they could, he worked like a beaver for the navy and his master. Yet it was always like the task of Hercules. When he was put out of office for five years in the later 1670's, everyone contentedly relapsed and everything was soon as bad as ever. In 1684, when he made his only long sea voyage, to Tangier, he observed that naval captains were defying their orders, using their ships to carry bullion for their own profit, and spending months in gay festivities at the King's expense in foreign ports; while ashore the navy was deep in debt again, the stores were empty through theft, and new ships were rotting away from neglect in the royal dockyards. Under King James II, he started all over again.

*

Pepys seems to have stayed aloof, on the trip to Tangier, from the life of the ship he was in. He was a very distinguished passenger and besides, was busy trying not to be sea-sick. It was a pity; one would have liked to have had his comments on life at sea. But that was the great age of diarists, and several of them, especially chaplains, recorded the life in the very earliest days of the Royal Navy. One of these was the Rev. Henry Teonge, a country parson who went to sea in 1675 to escape his debts. After riding to London, Mr Teonge pawned his horse, his saddle, bridle, boots and spurs, for 26 shillings, and bought instead a small bed, and a pillow, blanket and rug. So equipped and penniless, he joined the royal ship *Assistance*, 56 guns, in Long Reach in the River Thames. The captain and lieutenant welcomed him with bottles of claret, and that night he helped them to drink three bowls of punch. The crew had their wives and sweethearts on board and were equally well provided as the ship dropped down the river to pick up moorings at the Nore: 'So that our ship was that night well furnished but ill man'd; few of them being able to keep watch, had there beene occasion.' She was commissioned for yet another attack on the Barbary pirates.

'To prayers at 10, and to dinner at 12,' he wrote after three weeks at sea (when they had only reached Beachy Head); 'no life at the shoare being comparable to this at sea, where wee have good meate and good drinke provided for us, and good company, and good divertisments; without the least care, sorrow or trouble; which will be continued if wee forget not our duety; viz. loyalty and thankfullness.' And pure enjoyment of his new life, free from the duns who had pestered him at home, runs through the whole of his journal. 'Punch and brandy since I cam on board have run as freely as ditchwater.' On Sundays he preached a sermon, but not if the weather was too bad, or the ship was busy, or the captain was indisposed; on weekdays there were often delightful parties, and every Saturday night without fail the officers drank the healths of the King and their own and each other's sweethearts, wives and friends. Evidently this excellent chaplain was himself the best of company. He was often invited to dine in other ships; he played the viol, and entertained his friends with humorous verses about the events of the voyage, or the merits of Mediterranean wines, which cost threepence a quart. 'Wee were full merry,' he often wrote in his journal. 'And this night also' was sometimes the only entry on the following day.

This may have been a different view of the debauchery Pepys condemned; more likely, it only reflected the pleasure of escaping from the rigours of the parsonage. At all events, the parties do not seem to have interfered with the business of the ship. She cruised all over the Mediterranean in the search for pirates of Tripoli, and blockaded that town in company with the rest of the fleet; and the expedition was successful, in that the ruler of Tripoli at last was obliged to sign a treaty of friendship and peace with King Charles. The *Assistance* fired few guns in battle, but an enormous number in salutes and celebrations. She saluted every ship she met and every port she entered with five, or seven or eleven guns; the other ship, or the shore defences, always replied with an equal number, or two less, and the reply was acknowledged with another three. The King's birthday was greeted with 21; the wives of the crew when they were put ashore with 7; the British consul in a Turkish harbour with 15; and when the admiral came into harbour in Malta, the whole of the fleet let fly and the noise and smoke continued for at least two hours. The number of guns was always odd except at funerals, for odd numbers, except thirteen, have always been lucky at sea. Besides eating and drinking, to let off the guns appears to have been the major pleasure of the naval officers of the time, and prodigious quantities of powder must have been used for protocol and for fun.

*

Even Mr Teonge and his fellow chaplains wrote very little in their diaries about the common seamen, except when they did something comically foolish, or when they were buried at sea. They were a neglected class of men, and so they remained until the latter part of the nineteenth century. The navy which gave its officers a steady career in 1670 did not do the same for its seamen until about 1860. Meanwhile, they were recruited or impressed for each ship's commission and simply put ashore to fend for themselves at the end of it: such an astonishing waste of manpower and training that it is a wonder the navy survived, and much more a wonder that it was ever efficient or successful. Men were always reluctant to join it, because its pay was less than the merchant navy's and its discipline was stricter. In time of peace, when it was small, enough men could usually be found and persuaded to volunteer, but in times of war, when it suddenly had to grow, press gangs were always needed, and vagrants and minor criminals had to be sent to the ships instead of prison to make up the numbers. So for 200 years, in every time of crisis, the navy was largely manned by the outcasts of society, and by men who were put aboard its ships against their will. And yet, by the end of the same 200 years, it had become the most successful navy the world had ever known.

All through that time, the navy continued to have good periods and bad, good leadership and bad: the only thing that never seemed to change was the infectious and almost indestructible pride of its seamen. Once a man had been dragged aboard a ship, he was totally cut off from the world ashore; whether he liked it or not, the ship became the only home he had. To make his own life bearable, he had to become a member of the ship's community, and the first thing it taught him was that a seaman was a cut above any landlubber. He might have been a rogue, but he had to become a seaman. With the smallest encouragement, men grew to be proud of their calling and their ship. Of course the life was hard, sometimes incredibly hard by modern standards; but life ashore was hard for a poor man in those centuries. The naval food was disgusting, but there was usually plenty of it and there was seldom plenty ashore. The officers might be martinets, but so were civil officials. And whatever happened, a ship was a man's world, and her crew had a stronger companionship than men in other walks of life. They shared discomfort, boredom and danger: they kept themselves alive by their common skill. And they accepted the need for stringent rules and ruthless punishments: nobody, after all, wanted to be shipmates with a thief, a man who was often too drunk to pull his weight, or one who endangered them all by sleeping on watch. They often grumbled, and they deserted if they could, but they never rebelled except at unfairness – at captains who punished

CHAPTER 17

The Royal Society

ON the last day of the seventeenth century, a small naval ship called the *Paramour* was at sea, alone in the south Atlantic. She was a portent of the century to come: for she was commanded not by a naval officer, but by Dr Edmund Haley, a well-known astronomer. And in the history of the century which was just beginning, the dichotomy can first be seen which was the merit of British power on the sea. The ships of the Royal Navy were put to two uses which seem opposed in philosophical intent: one, to smash and wreck the almost identical ships of other nations, and two, to search for knowledge.

It was a lucky chance that the British at sea, who proved to be the most effective in battle, were also the most inquisitive in research and the most ingenious in invention. Their wars at sea were fought through dynastic quarrels or rivalries in trade – one might say, for power or riches. But their research was unselfish. It was either purely scientific – in geography, astronomy, biology and the knowledge of the ocean – or else it was intended to make seafaring safer, not only for themselves but for seamen of any nation, including their enemies. The causes the wars were fought for ceased to exist when they were won, but the search for knowledge brought benefits to seamen ever after.

The Royal Society was the British institution that gave the impetus for research. It was founded under the patronage of Charles II in 1675: The Royal Society of London for Improving Natural Knowledge. By the eighteenth century it was a club of immense prestige, its Fellowships the highest of scientific honours and its weekly meetings the scene of formidable erudition. Ever since, it has been consulted by governments in need of scientific advice, and it organised most of the great endeavours at sea, apart from war, in the following centuries. In explorations, the Society was the brains and the Navy the instrument; and just as the city merchants sponsored distant voyages in the cause of trade, so now the Society sponsored them, in the cause of science.

Freedom for research was a privilege conferred by victories in war. The long wars of the early part of the eighteenth century against the old enemies, France and Spain, were followed by the golden age of exploration, the age of Cook. And the war against Napoleon, which made the supremacy of Britain even more secure in the nineteenth century, was followed by the explorations of Ross and Franklin, and the vast researches and discoveries at sea of the industrial revolution. It was natural that the Navy's greatest efforts in research were made in times of peace. But in one field of knowledge the search continued all the time, through peace and war; and that was in navigation.

From ancient times until the fifteenth century, the science or art of navigation had been an international affair, which spread from the Mediterranean first to Portugal and Spain and then to Holland, France and Britain. In the sixteenth and seventeenth centuries astronomers everywhere slowly improved their theories, observations and predictions, and cartographers vastly improved their maps. But the practice of navigation showed very little change. There were only three specific advances in those two centuries, and all of them happened – perhaps by coincidence – in Britain. There was the quadrant invented by John Davis the Elizabethan explorer, which did the same job as the old astrolabe and cross-staff but did it more exactly; the measurement of the yards in a degree by Richard Norwood; and logarithms, the astonishing invention, so early as 1614, of the Scottish laird John Napier of Merchiston, thinking alone and immobilised, it was said, by the gout, on his estate near Edinburgh. But of these, only the quadrant was in use at sea. Practical seamen still doubted Norwood's measurement; and it was many years before logarithms became an essential part of an ocean pilot's training.

Those centuries of stagnation had made a gulf even wider than usual between the practical seamen and the scholars who took an interest in the art. Old captains who had spent their lives at sea laughed at young ones who used new-fangled inventions, including the quadrant, 'and when that they dyd take the latitude would call them starre shooters and sunne shooters and would ask if they had striken it.' Some were ashamed to use log lines in case people thought they lacked experience in estimating speed. 'A number of them doeth but grope as a blind man doth, and if that they doe hit well, that is but by chance and not by any cunning that is in him.' That was written in 1573. The same sort of thing was still being said about seamen a century later. 'They content themselves that those that know no more have yet brought their ships home safe. Whence they conclude that any further Art, as they call it, is superfluous.' And indeed, seamen have always been the same, at least in the eyes of scholars. Captain Lecky in *Wrinkles in Practical Navigation*, the best-known handbook of the nineteenth century, wrote about the observation of stars, 'It is within the reach of all who choose to try: there are, however, men who won't try, and who for downright double-barrelled, copper-bottomed, bevel-edged bigotry are matchless in all other professions . . . hopeless cases, whose pig-headed obstinacy is only equalled by their ignorance.'

So scholars who hoped to make practical advances in the art had hard work ahead of them. Seamen could always argue that Drake and Cavendish had gone round the world with nothing more than the three L's – latitude, lead and look-out. Yet in the early eighteenth century, navigation suddenly flourished. And it is fair to say that all the most important new ideas were British, with occasional contributions from France.

*

When the King's ship *Paramour* left England in 1698, it was probably the first time a scholar had put to sea in command of a scientific expedition. Dr Halley was a colleague of Sir Isaac Newton. He had already made a journey to St Helena in a ship of the East India Company, to observe the stars of the southern hemisphere, and in 1682 had recorded the comet named after him and predicted, correctly, that it would be seen again in 1759. He had always had an interest in the variation of the compass, which was still the seaman's only indication of longitude at sea: it was said that while he was still a schoolboy he had observed for himself that the variation in London was changing. The object of this voyage was to chart the variation all over the Atlantic.

The first attempt was not a success. He was shot at by another British ship in the Cape Verde Islands which mistook him for a pirate; and, which was worse, his junior officers resented being commanded by an amateur, however learned. So he put back to Plymouth, and wrote to the Secretary of the Admiralty to complain of 'the unreasonable carriage of my mate and Lieutenant who, because perhaps I have not the whole Sea Dictionary so perfect as he, has for a long time made it his business to represent me to the whole ship's company as a person wholly unqualified for the command their Lordships have given me and declaring that he was sent on board because their Lordships knew my insufficiency.'

It was a special case of the age-long disagreement. The mate was court-martialled, and Halley sailed again. This time he was away two years. He quartered the whole Atlantic and made his observations all the way from the antarctic ice to Newfoundland; and when he came home he was able to publish a chart which showed the lines of equal variation all over the ocean.

This was a great improvement on the haphazard observations that seamen had been recording since Columbus. With Halley's chart and Davis's quadrant, a pilot anywhere in the Atlantic could estimate his position. But variation could never give anything more than a rough idea of longitude, and in 1714 a Board of Longitude was established by Act of Parliament. It offered huge rewards to anyone who discovered a better method of observing longitude: £10,000 for a method accurate within a degree, £15,000 within two thirds of a degree and £20,000 within half a degree.

Rewards for solving this ancient problem were nothing new; Spain and Holland had offered them a hundred years before. But the Dutch and Spanish offers did not lead to anything. The British offer did.

The crux of the problem was to find the difference between local time and time on the prime meridian: since the earth revolves 360° in 24 hours, the difference in time was a measure of difference in longitude. Local time on a ship could be observed from the sun. In theory, as astronomers had known for a long time, it was also possible on a ship to observe an astronomical event for which the prime meridian time could be predicted – the method known as lunars. The first applicants for the award were astronomers who had improved these predictions, and the first payment was made to the widow of a German professor who sent the Board a set of new lunar tables before he died. But the observations and calculations were far beyond the scope of the average pilot.

An alternative, much easier for the pilot, was to carry a clock which was set to the prime meridian time. Some clockmakers spent their lifetimes trying to make a clock that would keep time well enough – within two minutes to win the highest prize, on a voyage perhaps of six months – and would do it in spite of the movements of a ship and changes in temperature and humidity. The one who succeeded was John Harrison. He was a Yorkshireman of little education who started life as a carpenter; the first clock he made had wooden wheels. But he became a craftsman of extraordinary patience, ingenuity and skill. He invented the gridiron pendulum, which stays the same effective length at any temperature. Other people had made forlorn attempts to mount pendulum clocks in ships but none had succeeded;

and so Harrison applied his ideas of temperature compensation to a balance wheel. He designed a new kind of escapement and a way of keeping the clock going while it was being wound up, and after years of meticulous labour he finished a clock he thought would satisfy the Board. He took it to London in 1735 and showed it to Dr Halley, who by then was Astronomer Royal, and Halley sent him on a voyage to Lisbon to test it. On the way back, the clock disagreed by $1\frac{1}{2}°$ with the ship's dead reckoning, and when land was sighted the clock was proved to be right. The Board gave him £500 to make more experiments. He worked for another twenty years, and made three more clocks, each slightly better than the last. In 1758, he applied to the Board for a sea trial to the West Indies, which the Act of 1714 had prescribed as a test for the winning design. By then he was 68, and he had to wait three more years before the test was arranged. Then his son took the clock to Jamaica in HMS *Deptford*, surrounded by precautions against fraud – the case of the clock was locked by four different keys which were kept by four different people. Five months later, he was back in Portsmouth, and the error of the clock was 1 minute 53 seconds.

Faced with such a humble claimant for £20,000, the Board acted with caution that seems excessive and even mean. Perhaps they were influenced by the distinguished astronomers working on lunars, who always believed their method was on the verge of success. The Royal Society came out strongly in Harrison's support, but the Board insisted on another similar trial in case the first had been a lucky chance. After thinking it over for no less than seven years they agreed to pay half the money, and the other half if other clocks could be made to prove the principles were right. Harrison then was almost 80, and his eyesight was failing. At last the King, George III, intervened with the words 'By God, I'll see you righted', and in 1773, nearly forty years after the first of his clocks was tested, Harrison had his reward. But he only lived three years longer to enjoy it.

*

Just before the first of Harrison's clocks, another new instrument marked an epoch in navigation. On 13th May, 1731, a man called John Hadley published a description of a reflecting octant he had invented, and soon after he gave a demonstration of it. This, except for the length of its scale, was the sextant which has been used ever since for observing angles, and it was a vast improvement on Davis's quadrant.

In its invention, there were mysteries that have never been wholly solved.

One week after Hadley's announcement, at a meeting of the Royal Society, Dr Halley said he remembered that Sir Isaac Newton had invented something very much the same and given the Society an account of it in 1699, at the time when Halley was at sea in the *Paramour*. But when people looked up the minutes, no details of Newton's proposition could be found. Halley could not remember much about it, the question was dropped, and Hadley was given credit for a new invention.

But in May the next year, the Governor of Philadelphia, who happened to be a mathematician, wrote to tell Dr Halley that a poor Philadelphia glazier named Thomas Godfrey had fitted two pieces of looking glass to an ordinary quadrant and greatly improved it. This turned out to be precisely the same invention. In America, tempers were roused on Thomas Godfrey's behalf. Next year, two affidavits were presented to the Royal Society, sworn before the mayor of Philadelphia, proving that Godfrey had made his invention in 1730, a year before Hadley, and that his quadrant had been used, that year and the next, on voyages to the Indies and Newfoundland. This must have been true; but Godfrey's protagonists went on to try to suggest that Hadley had stolen the idea. They said Godfrey's brother, a captain in the West Indian Trade, had sold the prototype quadrant to a captain or lieutenant in the British navy whose name was Hadley, and that this man had brought it to London for his brother who was an instrument maker in the Strand. But this allegation was never quite made to stick. Hadley, so far as is known, had no brother in the Navy, or in the instrument trade.

But the story was not yet over. In 1742, Dr Halley died, and among his papers was found the document he had half-remembered – a description, in Newton's handwriting, of an instrument that was almost exactly the same. So did John Hadley invent it, entirely out of his own head? Or had he heard of Newton's invention? Or had he seen Godfrey's instrument and nefariously pretended it was his own? His opponents could see no reason why he should have invented such a thing. He was what was known as a country gentleman of independent means, and although he was an amateur mathematician and astronomer, he had no known connection with the sea. It is quite likely, of course, that three separate men could have thought of the same idea. But if that happened, Hadley was only the third: first, as an inconsiderable trifle, the greatest scientist of the age; next the poor colonial glazier with bits of looking glass; and last, the dilettante.

Perhaps the oddest part of the story is that neither Dr Halley, with a life-long interest in navigation, nor Newton himself, should have recognised

Newton's proposal of 1699 for what it was: an instrument that would give new safety to seamen and new freedom to exploration. This it certainly did. It was so much more accurate at sea than the older quadrants that it brought observations of latitude to within a mile or two, and also made lunars, in the hands of a really expert navigator, a feasible method of finding longitude: Captain Cook used lunars, rather than Harrison's clock, on his first expedition.

So the old problem was solved. With the sextant and lunar tables, a well-trained navigator by the latter part of the century could calculate his longitude whenever the sky was clear: with the sextant and Harrison's clock (later given the more pretentious name of chronometer) almost anyone could do it. Distant voyages took on a wholly new character. Hitherto, for example, men had crossed the Pacific only on east and west courses in the latitude of their objective, and had seen only land that happened to lie near their track. Henceforth, once an island was sighted, it could be put in its proper place on the charts of the world, and pilots could approach and find their destinations from any point of the compass.

The astronomical tables that pilots used were prepared by the Royal Observatory, which was another foundation of Charles II. It was in 1675 that he was persuaded, by early Fellows of the Royal Society, that British navigation needed its own observatory, and it was he who chose the site of it on the hill overlooking the Thames behind the palace at Greenwich. In 1710, the Society took over the running of it, and it soon became the foremost producer in Europe of pilots' information. In 1767 it published the first Nautical Almanac, which told the pilot all he needed to know for the coming year. France, Spain and Germany followed its lead within the next twenty years, but they used many of the British tables, especially the lunars; and the British almanac always remained the most widely used at sea.

But it was not for a very long time that Greenwich was accepted by other nations, or even by British seamen, as the prime meridian. Hitherto, longitude had officially been measured by the makers of charts from all kinds of different places: from the Pope's division of the world between Portugal and Spain, a hundred leagues west of the Azores; or from the Azores themselves, because the compass variation there was supposed to be zero; or from the Cape Verde Islands or the peak of Teneriffe – a choice that dated back to Ptolemy in the second century A.D. While longitude could not be observed at sea, it did not matter very much where it was measured from, and pilots often recorded it from their last landfall – so many degrees west of the Scilly Islands, or east of the Cape of Good Hope – or else from their own capital city, which was the custom in making land maps.

The tables in Nautical Almanacs were reckoned from the longitude of the observatory that made them, and French pilots before the Napoleonic Wars were burdened with two kinds of tables, some based on Greenwich and others on Paris. Very slowly, Greenwich superseded London in the thoughts and calculations of British seamen, but it offended the pride of other nations, especially France, to chart the world from a base in England. It was not until 1884 that Greenwich was fully accepted as the prime meridian; and oddly enough, its acceptance had nothing to do with the sea. It was the chaotic time-tables of American railroads, using arbitrary local times across the continent, that pointed the need for agreement on zone times all over the world; and it was a conference in Washington that finally chose the building behind the palace at Greenwich as the source from which all longitude is measured. The reasons for the choice were practical, not historical; but this was, after all, the palace where Willoughby, with his crew in their sky-blue livery, fired his ordnance on his way down river, and where Queen Elizabeth waved from a window to Frobisher, and generations more of explorers outward bound saluted kings and queens.

All the scientific advances of the eighteenth century came to their practical culmination in the voyages of Captain Cook, the greatest of navigators, cartographers and explorers. But before one comes to the story of his adventures and achievements, one must follow the story of the wars that gave Britain the freedom to explore.

CHAPTER 18

Wars in the 18th Century

IN spite of the new inventions, plenty of captains and masters continued to 'grope as a blind man doth': it was perfectly possible then, as it always had been and still is, to roam round the seas with nothing more than luck, a compass, a lead and some common sense. But captains and masters of naval ships could no longer afford to do so, because naval warfare spread out, in the eighteenth century, far from the coasts of home.

This was a steady historical evolution. The Dutch Wars, in the century before, had been fought in the narrow seas between the coasts of Holland and England; they could have been fought, and probably were, without even an observation of latitude. In the War of the Spanish Succession, from 1702 to 1713, the sea-fighting spread to the Mediterranean. In the Wars of Jenkins' Ear and the Austrian Succession, from 1739 to 1748, most of it was in the Caribbean, and for the first time the navy sent an expedition round the world. In the Seven Years' War, 1756 to 1763, it ranged from Canada to India.

And while the scope of its actions spread, the Royal Navy can be seen to have evolved – not in its methods but in its skill and spirit. In the first of these eighteenth century wars, it had at least as many failures as successes. In the second, an admiral still could not depend on determined fighting from his captains. In the third, Britain expected and got a very much higher standard. An admiral was shot for mere lack of decision, and the navy ended by scorning the Spaniards and chasing the French with total self-confidence. Before the end of that war, in 1763, the navy had won the world-wide dominance which it kept until the twentieth century.

These wars were fought by officers who, in modern eyes, look less like seamen than any before or since. It was in 1748 that naval officers first wore a uniform dress. It was designed by several captains, but King George II chose the colour of it. It is said that he had seen and admired the Duchess of Bedford riding in the park in a habit of blue edged with white, and the sight

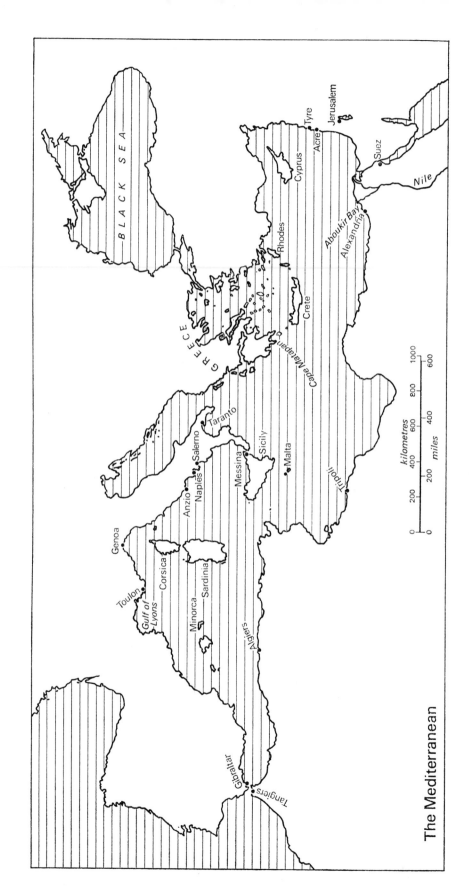

The Mediterranean

of her decided the sober colours that have been worn by sailors all over the world ever since. But the first uniforms, although they were navy blue, had all the elaboration of the highest fashion of the age: waistcoats resplendently embroidered with gold or silver lace, coats equally superb with enormous white cuffs cut short to show the frills and lace beneath them, three-cornered hats with silk cockades, set upon curled and powdered wigs of shoulder length or more. It is hard to believe such clothes were not only worn but laundered through Atlantic gales and tropical calms, but it seems to have been so, and one has to imagine bloody battles and perilous voyages commanded by men in peacock finery. And it is hard to believe the overfed, plethoric and gouty faces of most of their portraits belonged to hardy and capable seamen; but most of them did.

The uniforms must have given emphasis to the division of the organisation of naval ships. They were only prescribed for admirals, captains, commanders, lieutenants and midshipmen – the men on the superior ladder of promotion which alone could lead to the highest ranks. For another hundred years, there was no uniform for men on the humbler ladder, by which a seaman might rise to be boatswain, gunner, coxswain or master.

In the same period, another convention helped to perpetuate this division; and that was the number of servants a senior officer was allowed to take to sea. An admiral could have 30, and a captain 4 per hundred men of his crew – which in a large ship could mean as many as his admiral. Some captains took with them a retinue of tailors, barbers, footmen and musicians, but all of them also took boys from 11 or 12 years old, the sons of their friends, whom they trained to become the officers of the future. By the end of the century, almost every officer had entered the navy in this way. So officers in the course of time became a close-knit clique, all drawn from a narrow social class – by and large, the minor landed gentry; and it was very unusual (though Captain Cook was a well-known example) for any man, however clever, to cross from the lower ladder of promotion to the higher. It was a system that did not pretend to be fair, but it only reflected the rigid class distinction of the age, and the navy throve on it.

But through all this evolution of naval activity, warships remained the same. For sheer size, only the first-rates of 100 guns were as big as the *Sovereign of the Seas* of Charles I, and before the Napoleonic Wars the navy never possessed more than six or seven of those. The great majority were those called fifth-rates up to third-rates, of 30 up to 80 guns, ships from 600 up to 1350 tons and 125 to 160 feet in the length of their gundecks. In appearance, armament, structure and rig they were still very much the same as the race-built ships of the Elizabethans. The only innovation in the eighteenth century was the frigate. This was a word that covered a fairly wide variety of ships, but all of them were smaller, handier and faster than the major warships. They depended for their safety rather on keeping out of gunshot than on fighting, and they came to be used in every navy as scouts and messengers. There have always been naval officers who prefer small ships, which pose their own problems of seamanship and offer a freer, more independent and more audacious life. Expert frigate captains became a class of their own, and some of them, by the end of the century, were seamen of genius under sail.

Since the ships had not changed for so long, the tactics of battle could not change. Almost all the guns of a ship could still only be brought to bear through a fairly narrow arc on either beam; the ship was vulnerable from the bow, and even more so from the stern, where the windows of the officers' cabins allowed an enemy's well-aimed shot to enter and make havoc on the gundecks. So the line ahead, which was just beginning at the time of the Armada and became a formality in the Dutch Wars, still remained the standard order of battle throughout the eighteenth century. To protect each other's bows and sterns, ships of the line sailed into battle as close together as the weather, the sea and the skill of their crews permitted. All navies did the same, and so fleets continued to approach a battle, whenever they could, in lines which slowly converged until they were in range, broadside to broadside. The French stuck more strictly to their line of battle than anyone, and none of their captains was allowed to leave it. The British were slightly more flexible in their fighting instructions, and British captains used more discretion when battle was joined. But it needed the genius of Nelson to break free of this ancient plan – first as commodore at the Battle of Cape St Vincent, and then as commander-in-chief at Trafalgar.

*

In the War of the Spanish Succession, the first of the series of eighteenth century wars, there were not many full-scale battles at sea, and all that were fought were indecisive. This was the first time the British navy was used – under Marlborough's influence – as a strategic weapon to support the army's campaigns in Europe. To that end, it needed a base in the Mediterranean, and most of its actions were concerned with winning one. So most of them were attacks on shore positions, rather than enemy fleets.

The first, in the autumn of 1702, was a huge amphibious expedition against Cadiz, which was not unlike the worst of the similar Elizabethan efforts. Again, there was a fleet too big to manage – 80 warships and 50 transports, including a good many Dutch, who were now the allies of Britain – and again the long councils of war and the irreconcilable views of navy and army commanders. The Admiral, Sir George Rooke, was sick and spent much of his time in bed, and with such a fleet on his hands he was anxious, all through the voyage, to get home before the winter. Troops were landed and they invested the town, but the navy did very little to help them; and after three weeks, distinguished by drunken roistering, they gave it up and embarked again, and the fleet set sail for home.

But luckily, some ships on the way put into Lisbon for water, and some officers went ashore. Among them was a chaplain, who happened to meet the French consul and astutely engaged him in a conversation; and the consul boasted that an invincible French fleet was escorting a Spanish treasure-fleet into Vigo Bay. The chaplain hurried on board and told his captain, the ship put to sea and found the main body of the British fleet, and an attack on Vigo was agreed.

Spanish treasure was the lure no British sailor had resisted for 150 years; this was a project much more to everybody's liking, and it was tackled with spirit. There was a boom across the harbour with a guardship and a fort at either end of it. The army landed and took one of the forts, and HMS *Torbay*, the leading ship of the British line, charged into the boom and broke it. At that moment, the wind fell calm, and the following ships drifted into the wreckage of the boom and left the *Torbay* to anchor between the guardships and engage them both at once. When it freshened again, the next two ships, which were Dutch, got through the boom and boarded one of the guard ships; but the French sent out a fireship, which drifted aboard the *Torbay* and set her rigging on fire. Inevitably, after a while, the fireship blew up; and she must have been hastily prepared, for she still had her cargo in her hold. It was snuff. There is not much record of the effect it had on the combatants, but the snuff fell so thickly on the *Torbay* that it put out most of her fires.

The fight did not last for much more than half an hour. Then the French admiral, seeing the enemy fleet pouring into the bay through the broken boom, ordered his captains to burn their ships. Most of them did so, but some did not do it in time. There cannot ever have been a quicker or more thorough naval victory. In the harbour were 21 French warships and 17

Spanish galleons, and every one of them was either burned or captured. Some of the Spanish treasure had already been taken ashore, but cargo to the value of 13 million pieces of eight was taken or destroyed, and four or five French ships were safely brought to England.

That was a stroke of luck for the British navy; without much loss of life on either side, it weakened the French navy and deprived the Spaniards of a fair amount of gold. An event of more lasting importance was the capture of Gibraltar two years later. As Gibraltar has been a British naval stronghold ever since and has been claimed by Spain in recent years, its capture has a special interest.

It was held at the time by Spaniards in the name of Philip V, one of the two claimants of the throne of Spain; and it was the other claimant, Charles III, who proposed that the British should take it. A fleet of 22 ships of the line was in the Straits at the time, and it attacked Gibraltar mainly because it was delayed by contrary winds and had nothing much else to do. A force of 1500 Royal Marines was landed under cover of a bombardment, but the place turned out to be almost deserted of defenders – there were over a hundred guns in its fortresses, but less than a hundred soldiers. They fought very well and did a surprising amount of damage, but of course they had to surrender; and a garrison of marines was left to look after the place. If the war had ended in favour of Charles, the British nominee, the British could hardly have denied his right to keep Gibraltar; but it ended in favour of Philip, who was supported by the French. And part of the price he had to pay for British recognition was the cession of the rock. So Britain not only took it by arms, but also won it by treaty.

But Gibraltar, when the British took it, had no safely sheltered harbour and no reliable water supply, so it was not very useful as a naval base. Each winter, the British commander-in-chief came back to England, taking the biggest ships, and left only his second-in-command with a small more manageable fleet in the Mediterranean. And it was when the commander-in-chief Admiral Sir Cloudesley Shovell was on his way home for the winter, on the night of 22nd October, 1707, that the famous shipwreck occurred in the Scilly Islands. The flagship *Association* struck on the rocks and broke up, and everyone on board was drowned – the Admiral, the captain of the fleet, the captain of the ship and eight or nine hundred officers and men. Three other ships of the line went ashore astern of her and two of them foundered, also with all hands. The disaster gave point to the need for a winter base, and also to the research in navigation. And next summer, the fleet took the island of Minorca, where it could winter safely.

All in all, it was not a brilliant naval war: it certainly produced no genius in command on the sea, as it did on the land. Yet it brought great gains in sea power. The French, the Dutch and the Spanish were far more weakened by it than the British, and at the Peace of Utrecht in 1713 Britain was not only left with Gibraltar and Minorca but also, on the other side of the ocean, received the lands that France had begun to settle in Newfoundland, Nova Scotia and Hudson's Bay.

*

The War of the Austrian Succession was a vastly complicated struggle of dynasties on land, but at sea it was simply another round in the ancient rivalry with Spain, and in its later years with France. It was that part of it that became known in English history as the War of Jenkins' Ear. Richard Jenkins was master of a brig of Glasgow named *Rebecca*, one of a great many British ships, from home and from the colonies, which were trading by then with the Spanish possessions in central America. There had been a spate of complaints of the way the Spaniards treated lawful traders, and Jenkins found his own road to immortal fame by displaying his ear in a jar of pickle to a committee of Parliament, and saying it had been cut off by a Spanish coastguard. There was some doubt if his story was true, and of course it was only one complaint among many; but it did rouse a popular outcry for reprisals, and it pleased historians to think that ambassadors could be recalled and fleets mobilised at such a farcical affront to British pride.

At any rate, the King in 1739 proclaimed that Spain had committed depredations, and had promised recompense but failed to make it; and in the autumn of that year, war was declared again.

This time, Britain did find admirals of distinction, although they were men of widely different characters: Vernon, Anson and Hawke. The war began with a very ambitious plan to attack the Spanish colonies in South and Central America from both sides, Vernon from the Caribbean and Anson from the Pacific.

Edward Vernon was one of those irascible and outspoken men who are popular with their subordinates, difficult with their equals and impossible with their superiors. It is said that on the lower deck he was known as Old Grog because he wore an eccentric cloak of the material called grogram. It was in the West Indies that he began the ration of rum and water which was named after him: the grog that became the seaman's only solace and also the commonest source of drastic punishment when men who drank it were found to be groggy on duty. Among other things, he was a Member of Parliament, and when war was imminent he insisted that the Spanish West Indies could easily be captured, and offered to go and do it. The Government was glad to get rid of him, and perhaps expected to take the credit if he succeeded and to disgrace him if he failed; so it accepted his offer. He sailed in the summer of 1759 with a squadron of seven ships, and by chance he arrived in Jamaica on the day that war was declared.

Vernon's first deed in the Caribbean was yet again to capture Portobello. He used six ships of the line, and made a meticulous plan which he explained to his captains with model clarity and wisdom. 'From the men's inexperience in service,' he wrote in his orders, 'it will be necessary to be as cautious as possible to prevent hurry and confusion, and a fruitless waste of powder and shot. The captains are to give the strictest orders to their respective officers to take the greatest care that no gun is fired but what they, or those they particularly appoint, first see levelled, and direct the firing of; and that they shall strictly prohibit all their men from hallooing and making irregular noise that will only serve to throw them into confusion, till such time as the service is performed and when they have nothing to do but glory in the victory.' It was a portent of a new and more formal discipline in the navy, and it was successful: he bombarded one castle from a range of two hundred yards, and landed a party who climbed on each others' shoulders and entered its embrasures; and during the night the town's governor hoisted a white flag and surrendered on Vernon's terms. The people and the Spanish troops were treated well. Ten thousand dollars were found in the treasure house, and Vernon distributed them among his crews; and he spent three weeks demolishing the castles.

They were still the same three castles that had defended the place when William Parker took it with 150 men in 1601; so Vernon's action was not a tremendous achievement. But news of it was hailed with joy in England; Vernon was voted the thanks of both Houses of Parliament, and the freedom of the city of London in a gold box – and the victory gave its name to the street market of Portobello Road. The government decided to follow it up by sending reinforcements and a large body of troops.

But once again, as soon as things started to grow big, they started to go wrong. It took a year to recruit the men, provision the naval ships and transports and get them across the Atlantic in the face of frequent storms. Meanwhile, Vernon repeated his success by taking the castle at the mouth of the River Chagres, which defended the Spaniards' only alternative route across the isthmus of Panama. That was the sort of thing the navy, like the Elizabethans, could do extremely well. But when the new fleet arrived, Vernon had to begin to try to operate with over a hundred ships, including transports; and that had always proved to be impossible. Such a fleet, without any adequate system of signals, was far too clumsy a weapon – it took a week merely to get it out of harbour in Jamaica. But Britain had still not learned the lesson: people still persuaded themselves that what could be done by ten ships could be done ten times as well by a hundred. It simply was not so.

Vernon's temperament was certainly not a help. With a small force he was in his element, giving precise instructions to his captains, amusing his men by his eccentricities and keeping them happy with grog. But now he had to cooperate with an army commander. He had been prepared to respect the commander-in-chief, Lord Cathcart, but Cathcart had died of dysentery on the Atlantic crossing, and the senior army officer was a Brigadier General named Thomas Wentworth. Vernon despised him, and the two of them quarrelled incessantly.

The result was further great amphibious operations which ended in ignominious muddles. The first was against Cartagena, the strongest city on the Spanish Main, which nobody yet had captured.

When Vernon anchored his fleet off the city in March 1741, it was by far the largest that had ever been assembled in American waters: 126 ships, which carried eight regiments of Royal Marines and soldiers from England and several thousand men from the colonies. It lay there six weeks, the troops were landed, men died in hundreds by fighting and in thousands by disease, especially the ghastly yellow fever which was graphically called Black Vomit. In the end the survivors had to be re-embarked and the fleet had to sail away in failure. It was an ample force to take the city, and it would be easy to say the whole operation was incompetently led; but in truth, even without the fever, it was simply beyond the capabilities of the age. To issue a general order to a fleet of such a size took far too long. Sufficient copies of an order had to be written, and then distributed by officers in boats; and even to find an individual ship among so many might have been a day's work, for they covered miles of sea and – excepting the flagships – carried no better marks of identification than the names which were carved among the decorations on their sterns. The fleet lay at Cartagena for five days before it could even be told what to do, and in that time, of course, the Spaniards mobilised all their defences.

In practice, decisions were hammered out at councils of war, and each member of the council saw to it, if he could, that the decisions as he understood them reached everyone in his squadron or regiment. But the councils on this occasion were stormy from the beginning; Vernon flung angry insults at Wentworth and at the army in general, Wentworth grew more and more morose, and the enmity between army and navy spread steadily down through the ranks. It was a special case of a longstanding difficulty. Navies are usually confident that they can look after themselves, and they resent having to look after armies; and armies at sea grow confused at having to depend on navies. But gentlemen of the baroque age were the last to have the patience to solve such delicate problems, for their manners, whether good or bad, were often as flamboyant as their arts. At last, Wentworth had to ask Vernon to send sailors ashore as reinforcements. Vernon refused, stamped out of a council meeting in his cabin and sat in a rage on his stern-walk, where he could hear the discussion and shout furious interjections from time to time.

That was the end at Cartagena. Exactly the same thing happened later in the same year, in an attack on Cuba, which the British had confidently expected to take from Spain as a colony. And it happened again next spring. The same two commanders planned, like Drake, to put the army ashore in Darien and march it across to attack the city of Panama; but Wentworth, to Vernon's disgust, gave it up before his troops were even landed, on the advice of an old pirate who said he knew all about it. By that summer, 1742, the flaming rows of the admiral and the general had become so scandalous that both were recalled to England; and the campaign in the Caribbean died away.

*

The British in the twentieth century have been accustomed to think of the navy as a symbol of reliability, and so it is hard to avoid seeming over critical of the eighteenth century navy. Yet it would be absurd to suppose that the navy sprang into being, perhaps in the Elizabethan era, with the tradition of efficiency it won at the time of Nelson. It did not. It had every kind of internal trouble and made most of the mistakes it could (except in its seamanship), before it achieved its final quality. But the important point, of course, is that no other navy was better. Whatever failures the British navy had, whatever mistakes can be seen in the unfair light of history, it came out of every war it fought a little stronger and a little wiser, and always on top of its rivals.

A battle in the Mediterranean in 1745 was a case in point. It was fought off Toulon against a combined fleet of France and Spain, and both sides had 28 ships of the line. Both sides, as usual, formed a line ahead and the British had the weather gage; but the rear division of the British fleet was some miles astern of the rest. The admiral, whose name was Thomas Mathews, signalled at dawn on the day of battle for the rear-admiral to make more sail; but he believed the enemy was trying to escape, so he did not shorten sail himself to allow the rear to come up. Half way through the morning, slowly over-hauling the enemy, he hoisted the signal to engage, and he bore down on the Spanish flagship and began a violent bombardment at the range described as pistol-shot, perhaps fifty yards. The ships next ahead and astern of him did the same; so did one other, whose captain was Edward Hawke, the future admiral. But the rest stood on, still in their line ahead, firing at such a long range that their shot did not do any damage. As the fighting slowed the fleets, the British rear division came up, but it did not engage at all. Several ships on both sides were put out of action, one Spaniard was taken and another blew up in the night; but the following day, Mathews broke off the fight. As soon as he reached port, he suspended his rear-admiral and sent him back to England. Soon after, he also was ordered to resign.

This affair led to a series of courts-martial, more of them than any other battle in naval history. The rear-admiral and some of the captains made a technical excuse: the admiral had hoisted the signal to engage the enemy without hauling down the signal for line ahead, so they could not engage without disobeying the formation signal. On this, the rear-admiral was acquitted, but Mathews himself and seven or eight of the captains were cashiered, and most were dismissed the service.

But France and Spain were equally disgusted with their own navies' part in the battle. The French and Spanish admirals laid complaints against each other, and the Frenchman, who was commander-in-chief and was nearly eighty, was removed from his post. And the fact was that although the British had attacked half-heartedly and badly, they had at least attacked; while the French and Spanish, who were in equal strength, had done nothing but try to escape. The British fleet had again been far from perfect; but once again, it had been better than its enemies.

*

At the time when this dismal battle was being fought, a solitary naval ship, the *Centurion*, 60 guns, was homeward bound round the Cape of Good Hope, bringing an epic story which not only showed the navy's faults but also gave some sign of its coming greatness. She was the only survivor of Commodore Anson's squadron, sent out four years before to attack the Spanish colonies from the Pacific while Vernon attacked them from the Caribbean.

The faults that this voyage revealed were the navy's backwardness in health precautions, and its haphazard ways of manning its ships: its virtue was the astonishing perseverance which preserved the *Centurion* as a disciplined naval ship through year after year of hardships and disasters.

This was one of the periods when naval administration was almost as muddled and corrupt as it had been under the Stuarts. Anson was given his orders for a Pacific voyage in November 1739, and it was September in the following year before his ships were fitted out and manned. The plans were often changed, and there were always delays in delivering stores and equipment. Worst of all was the perennial problem of finding crews and a body of troops for expeditions ashore. The crews were still short-handed when they sailed; and as for the troops, somebody had a uniquely stupid idea. Five hundred Chelsea pensioners were drafted to the ships, 'soldiers who from their age, wounds, or other infirmities, are incapable of serving in marching regiments.* But instead of five hundred, there came on board no more than two hundred and fifty-nine; for all those who had limbs and strength to walk out of Portsmouth deserted, leaving behind them only such as were literally invalids, most of them being sixty years of age, and some of them upwards of seventy. Indeed, it is difficult to conceive a more moving scene than the embarkation of these unhappy veterans: they were themselves extremely averse to the service they were engaged in, and fully apprised of all the disasters they were afterwards exposed to.' To replace the pensioners who had managed to walk away, 210 marines were then supplied; they had only just been recruited, and had not yet been taught to fire their muskets.

With these grumbling ancients and rustic youths as his land force, and still short of 200 seamen, Anson put to sea, knowing that the delays would oblige him to face Cape Horn at the stormiest time of year. In company with the *Centurion*, 60 guns, were two 50-gun ships, the *Gloucester* and the *Severn*, the *Pearl*, 40 guns, the *Wager* 28 guns, the *Tryall* sloop and two victuallers – 1500 officers and seamen, and 470 invalids and untrained marines.

Five and a half months out from England, the squadron approached Cape Horn. In the tropics, an unusual number of men had died of fluxes,

* The account of the voyage was written from Anson's papers and published under the name of Richard Walter, who was chaplain of the *Centurion*.

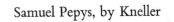

Samuel Pepys, by Kneller

Phineas Pett, 1st Master of
the Shipwrights Company

INTRA CAMERAM STELLATAM.

The Royal Observatory, 1675
Overleaf. Burning of the *Royal Prince*, June 1666,
by W. van Diest

fevers and delirium on the stinking lower decks, but otherwise the voyage had not been remarkable. Anson did not try the Straits of Magellan, but passed through the shorter Strait of Le Maire at the south-east end of Tierra del Fuego. It was a beautiful day when they went through the Strait with a following wind and tide; and they believed – or some of them at least – that the most dangerous part of the voyage was over and the calm of the Pacific lay ahead. 'Animated by these flattering delusions', Richard Walter wrote, 'we passed those memorable Streights, ignorant of the dreadful calamities which were then impending, and just ready to break upon us; ignorant that the time drew near, when the squadron would be separated, never to unite again; and that this day of our passage was the last chearful day that the greatest part of us would ever live to enjoy.'

It was early March, the beginning of the southern winter, and a southerly storm hit the squadron before the last two ships were clear of the Strait. It continued, with short deceptive calms, for three months. For all that time, the ships were in tempestuous seas. In the calms, they rolled gunwales under, men were thrown overboard from the rigging, or lost their hold below and broke their bones. In the storm, they were often forced to lie to under a reefed mizzen or bare poles. Snow froze on the rigging and sails, and men working aloft lost fingers and toes from frostbite. Sails were blown to bits and the ships themselves began to break up; masts, yards and standing rigging were always under repair. The *Centurion* started to work and spew her oakum, and nothing was dry below decks. The *Gloucester* broke her main yard, and in a moment of calm carpenters were put aboard her. A pump was sent to the *Tryall* which was making more water than her own pumps could clear. Early in April, the *Wager* rolled so heavily that her starboard chain-plates carried away and the mizzen mast went by the board.

All this time, there was an easy way out of the ordeal – to run before the storm back to the lee of the land – but nobody seems to have thought of giving up. After a month of peril and distress, Anson's dead reckoning put the squadron well clear of the land, and he began to set northerly courses to reach the calmer water of the Pacific. But on 14th April, in a dark and hazy night, the moon came suddenly clear of the clouds: and two miles ahead was a rocky promontory. Leeway and easterly current had set them 400 miles back on their course, and they were still not clear of Tierra del Fuego. In desperate disappointment they had to stand away to the south to start the struggle again. The *Centurion* lost sight of the *Severn* and the *Pearl*. And on 24th April, 'the wind began to blow fresh and soon increased to a prodigious storm: and the weather being extremely thick, about midnight we lost sight of the other four ships of the squadron, which, notwithstanding the violence of the preceding storms, had hitherto kept in company with us. Nor was this our sole misfortune; for the next morning, endeavouring to hand the top-sails the clew-lines and bunt-lines broke, and the sheets being half flown, every seam in the top-sails was soon split from top to bottom . . . However, at length some of the most daring of our men ventured upon the yard, and cut the sail away close to the reefs, though with the utmost hazard of their lives; whilst at the same time, the foretop-sail beat about the yard with so much fury, that it was soon blown to pieces: nor was our attention to our top-sails our sole employment; for the mainsail blew loose, which obliged us to lower down the yard to secure the sail.'

All through these terrible weeks, the scurvy had been increasing, and men lay sick and dying in their swaying hammocks in the darkness and stench of the lower deck, where nobody could attend them or keep them clean. On board the *Centurion*, forty-three men died in April, and double that number in May. Most of the Chelsea pensioners met this miserable end: only four of them survived the Horn.

But the ship crept out of the latitude of storms towards the end of May, meeting a final hurricane off the coast of Chile, when such a sea broke over the quarter that several shrouds were carried away by the shock and the stores and ballast shifted, and the master and chaplain were left to man the helm while everyone else who could stand on his feet was working to save the masts. On 9th June, at daybreak, the island of Juan Fernandez was sighted. When the ship left England, her complement had been six hundred men: rather over two hundred were still alive, but that night in the middle watch only two quartermasters and six fore-mast-men were capable of duty. The officers' servants and boys, who were not watchkeepers, were called out to help to wear ship; and it took two hours to trim the sails. As they neared the land, they saw green valleys and a cascade of clean clear water which fell a hundred feet into the sea. 'Even those amongst the diseased, who were not in the very last stages of the distemper, crawled up to the deck, to feast themselves with this reviving prospect.'

It was almost a century and a half since Captain Lancaster, on his second voyage to the Spice Islands, had kept the scurvy in check with lemon juice. Yet naval ships still went to sea without that simple remedy, and indeed it was another century before the navy finally adopted it as a preventative. Scurvy remained a very confusing disease. Most people agreed it was something to do with diet; and they must have noticed – although it was seldom mentioned – that officers suffered much less from it than seamen. But they had not understood there was simply something lacking in the seamen's salt provisions: they thought there was something positively poisonous in them. No doubt there often was, but that caused other ailments.

And there was added confusion because fresh food was not an infallible cure. Sometimes, of course, crews were given food that was fresh but did not contain the vitamin they needed; and sometimes, to judge by the symptoms they described, other diseases were combined with scurvy and mistaken for it. Everyone who wrote about it described the ghastly swellings, the discoloration of the skin, the lassitude and depression which could advance to coma and could make a man fall dead if he had to make a sudden effort or had to be moved. But the flux or dysentery, constipation, fevers, hysteria and rheumatic pains were also put down to scurvy; and probably, when scurvy was rife in a ship, men were all the more likely to sicken and die of the many other diseases seamen were prone to. All this caused further doubt about its origin. Some people put it down to the fetid stink of the decks where men were lying sick, and some to a kind of steam in the ocean air which was absent from air on land. Good captains insisted decks should be ventilated when it was possible; but in bad weather it was not.

For both these latter reasons, it was held to be part of the cure to get a man on to dry land, and the first thing Anson did in Juan Fernandez was to set all the able men to the work of putting up tents on shore. It took a long time, because there were so few men. But when it was done, 180 sick men were carried ashore in their hammocks, a labour shared by Anson himself and the officers. A dozen men died in the boats, and in the next ten days they buried many more. But on a diet of seal meat, fish, birds, watercress, and turnips that were growing wild, men began to recover. And one by one, the *Tryall* sloop, the *Gloucester* and one of the victuallers were sighted. All were in a desperate condition. The *Gloucester* in particular had so few men alive – one quarter of the crew – and so few who could go aloft that they could not work the ship, and had the added horror of being in sight of the island for a month before they could make the anchorage.

Anson had the reputation of being quiet, calm, fair-minded and even taciturn – a contrast to Vernon – and he must have been a leader of very remarkable talent; for nobody in this terrible situation, or at any other time in the voyage, seems to have had any doubt he would know what was best to do. A sketch made on shore at Juan Fernandez shows him still the immaculate naval officer, still wearing the wig, the three-cornered hat and the elegant coat and waistcoat, still the symbol of discipline and order. As for his thoughts, it was obvious the remnants of the squadron could not do all it had come for. It could not risk losing men in attacks on land: there were only just enough to sail the ships. But he decided it could go on with its mission, and could take prizes at sea. And as soon as men were fit to crawl out of their tents, he set them to work. The strongest cut timber, others on crutches hauled it down to the shore. Some were sent fishing, and two Newfoundland fishermen were appointed to salt the catch. They hunted seals and sea-lions, and rendered down the blubber as lamp-oil and tallow for paying seams. A large tent was set up for the sailmakers, and a forge was landed to mend the broken ironwork. The victualler was beyond repair; she was broken up, and her rigging, masts and sails were used for the other three. And of course a watch was kept for any Spanish sail. None was sighted until mid-September, and by then everyone was in a mood to put to sea and chase it. They lost it, but the *Centurion* found another. It turned out to be a merchantman which struck its topsails after four shots in the rigging. Its passengers and crew were terrified and had to be reassured that they would not be put to death, but when they calmed down, they gave some encouraging information. A fleet that had been sent from Spain to deal with Anson's had failed to round the Cape and met with complete disaster in the south Atlantic; and the Spaniards believed the same thing had happened to Anson.

So the prize was taken back to the island, and fitted out with guns from the victualler. 'And now the spirits of our people being greatly raised, and their despondency dissipated by this earnest of success, they forgot all their past distresses, and resumed their wonted alacrity, and laboured indefatigably in completing our water, receiving our lumber, and in preparing to take our farewell of the Island.'

Anson ordered the ships to cruise separately, with a rendezvous near the equator. By the time they met again, they had three more prizes. Their cargoes, apart from food, were not much use to the British – 'steel, iron, wax, pepper, cedar, plank, snuff, rosarios, European bale-goods, powder-blue, cinnamon, Romish indulgencies and other species of merchandize' – and the number of ships and prisoners was an embarrassment. The *Tryall* had sprung both her masts, so she was scuttled and a much more power-ful prize was commissioned into the navy as a frigate. And to get rid of the prisoners, Anson decided to attack the small town of Paita, where a large sum of money was said to be lodged in the custom house.

That was an easy victory and profitable. A party landed in boats by night, and marched like Drake at Nombre de Dios up the main street with the sound of drums; and the garrison and inhabitants fled from the town as quickly as they could. The prisoners were put ashore, profuse in their thanks for the treatment they had received. £30,000 in plate and cash were found in the custom house, and the sailors who ransacked the town all dressed themselves there and then in laced and embroidered coats and hats and wigs: the late-comers, when all the men's clothes were gone, paraded the town in women's gowns and petticoats. The governor refused to ransom the town, although Anson's price was only some cattle on the hoof, so it was set on fire. In the harbour were two 36-oared galleys, meant to defend the place, and three or four other ships. All were sunk except the largest, which was given to the lieutenant of the *Tryall* with a crew of ten. The fleet then numbered seven sail; and everyone's thoughts, as their confidence increased, began to turn towards the Manila Galleon.

The Manila Galleon was a ship of legendary size and riches. It sailed every year from the port of Acapulco in Mexico across the Pacific to Manila in the Philippines, taking millions of dollars in Peruvian silver and bringing back the goods of the east to the Spanish American colonies. And to make use of the seasonal winds, it always left Acapulco at the same time of year, in March. It sailed due east down the trade wind in the latitude of Guam; and after loading at Manila it sailed again in July to go up with the westerly monsoon, past Formosa and Japan, across the north Pacific towards the Californian coast, and so back to Acapulco.

On 1st March, Anson's flotilla took station to cover a wide arc of sea about 40 miles off Acapulco, and the cutters of the *Centurion* and *Gloucester* were posted closer in to watch for the galleon. There they lay until 23rd March, and nothing happened. But their water ran short. Anson left one cutter on watch, and took the flotilla to look for a watering place they could enter unobserved. After a tedious search they found a place a buccaneer had recommended fifty years before. While they were lying there, a cook, who was a Frenchman, went to the woods to look for limes for the Commodore's table, and was seized by Indians and taken to Acapulco. Of course he was imprisoned; and then he was sent to Mexico City and Vera Cruz and shipped from there to Spain. The ship he was in had to put into Lisbon; he escaped and found the British consul, who sent him to London, where he brought the first news of what had happened to the squadron and then, after all his adventures, was almost immediately killed in a drunken brawl.

Anson had come to believe the governor of Acapulco knew he was in the offing, and had cancelled the sailing of that year's galleon. If the galleon was kept in port, every other ship with a worthwhile cargo would stay there too, and there was no more chance of finding prizes on the coast. So he scuttled the four he had, put all his remaining men in the *Gloucester* and *Centurion*, and sent his prisoners ashore. And he sailed down to latitude 13°N and set a course of west to cross the Pacific.

Then came more weeks of frustration and suffering – enough to have made any lesser captain and crew think of nothing but getting home. This was the latitude that almost everyone had always used to cross the Pacific from east to west – Drake, Cavendish and the Spaniards and Portuguese. Normally, there was a steady north-easterly trade wind; but that year, for seven weeks, the winds were variable or westerly. Seven weeks was the normal time for the whole of the crossing; but at the end of it, they were only a quarter of the way. Both ships were described in the chronicle of the voyage as extremely crazy. Both had a sprung mast; in mid Pacific, the *Gloucester's* main mast was on the point of falling, and had to be cut away. And both were leaking. Worst of all, the scurvy began again. It surprised everybody, because they had fresh food. There were still live pigs and fowls which they had taken at Paita, and the sick were fed on them; and they caught so many bonitos, dolphins and albacores that the whole crew often had fish to eat. It rained so much that there was plenty of drinking water. The sea was calm enough for the gunports to be opened to ventilate the decks. And yet the men weakened, took to their hammocks, and died.

They found the trade wind at the end of June, and made good progress in July. But at the end of the month, they met a westerly wind again and a heavy head sea. In a calm, the *Gloucester* rolled her fore-top mast overboard, and in falling it broke her fore-yard. And then a westerly storm: the *Centurion* sprang a serious leak in the bows which could not be stopped from inboard, and all her fit men and the officers manned the pumps. The *Gloucester* lost her jury mainmast, and when the storm abated and the two could come within hailing distance, her captain told Anson he had seven feet of water in the hold.

It was a serious matter to abandon a ship-of-the-line, but there were not enough men to save the *Gloucester*. Her captain and all the officers signed a declaration of her defects, and Anson sent his own carpenter on board to verify them. She was falling to pieces. She had 77 men alive, including her officers, but only 16 men and 11 boys were able to work and several of those were very weak. All of them were taken on board the *Centurion*, and some of the stores which were still above water. Then she was set on fire and the captain left her, and the *Centurion* stood away as fast as the wind allowed her. Early next morning, 16th August, the *Gloucester* blew up. And ten days later, three months after leaving Mexico, land was sighted again, and the *Centurion* came to anchor off a verdant island.

It turned out to be the island of Tinian, north of Guam. There was nobody there except one Spaniard and a party of Indians who had been sent by the governor of Guam to slaughter cattle, and it provided everything the destitute travellers needed: water, meat, coconuts, limes, oranges and breadfruit, watermelons, dandelions, scurvy grass and sorrel. It pleased them almost as much by its beauty: 'a great number of the most elegant and entertaining prospects, according to the different blendings or these woods and lawns, and their various intersections with each other, as they spread themselves differently through the vallies, and over the slopes and declivities in which the place abounded.' So in this second paradise, the healing treatment of Juan Fernandez was repeated. Even Anson had scurvy, and after some days of securing the ship, he followed the rest of the sick men ashore.

After some peaceful weeks, the cure was brought to an end by a stormy night. At dawn, the ship had vanished. Anson and about half the crew were left on shore, the other half on board. Ashore, the men contemplated ending their lives on the island, or worse still being caught defenceless by the Spaniards: 'they were at least six hundred leagues from Macao, which was their nearest port . . . and the chance of their being taken off the Island by the casual arrival of any other ship, was altogether desperate; as perhaps no European ship had ever anchored here before, and it were madness to expect that like incidents should send another here in an hundred ages to come.' The only boat on the island was a small Spanish bark, which would not hold more than a quarter of their number.

'In the midst of these gloomy reflections,' the chronicler wrote, 'Mr Anson, though he always kept up his usual composure and steadiness, had doubtless his share of disquietude.' He made a speech, and proposed they should haul the Spanish boat ashore and saw it in half and lengthen it by twelve feet, which would make it big enough to carry them all to China. Two carpenters with their chests of tools were on land, and so was a smith, with his forge but without his bellows. So the laborious task began – first by catching cattle, tanning their hides and making bellows, 'which answered the intention tolerably well, and had no other inconvenience than that of being somewhat strong scented, from the imperfection of the tanner's work.' The bark was cut in half, Anson himself led parties which cut down trees and sawed them into planks, sailmakers cut up the tents and made sails, and anyone who had nothing better to do collected coconuts for the voyage. Somebody found a toy compass in a chest. 'And a few days after, by a similar piece of good fortune, they met with a quadrant on the sea-shore, which had been thrown overboard amongst other lumber belonging to the dead. The quadrant was eagerly seized, but on examination it unluckily wanted vanes, and therefore in its present state was altogether useless; however, fortune still continuing in a favourable mood, it was not long before a person through curiosity pulling out the drawer of an old table, which had been driven on shore, found therein some vanes, which fitted the quadrant very well.'

It seems doubtful if Anson could really have hoped to make a successful voyage of 1800 miles in such a small and overloaded vessel. At best, there would only have been room for half the crew below deck, and if they had all been on deck at once she would probably have overturned. But at least it kept everyone busy on ingenious improvisations. And after 19 days of their isolation, a man came running down from a hill and 'saw some of his comrades, to whom he hollowed out with great extasy, The ship, the ship. The Commodore, on hearing this pleasing and unexpected news, threw down his axe, with which he was then at work, and by his joy broke through for the first time, the equable and unvaried character which he had hitherto preserved.'

The ship had parted one of her cables and dragged the other anchor into deep water, and then drifted through the pitch-dark night with the anchor hanging Judas, her gun ports open and her yards sent down. But she survived that night, and the men on board had spent the rest of the 19 days in raising the anchor (that took them a day and a half), getting sail on her and beating back towards the island. She was still leaking, but at least she was intact.

So to Macao in China. As the port for Canton, Macao often saw trading ships of all the seafaring nations, but it had never before seen a British man-of-war. The *Centurion* lay there six months, and Anson was able to give her a fairly thorough refit, only hampered by the red tape of the neighbouring mandarins and the bargaining skill of Chinese merchants and custom officers. And here, after two years at sea, the crew met other Englishmen and heard news of home that was only six months old. When at last she was ready for sea, it was April again and the westerly monsoon had set in. No ship had ever tried at that time of year to beat to the westward for Batavia and Europe, but Anson persuaded his crew, and the people of Macao, that a British warship was perfectly capable of doing it, even with only a third of her normal complement.

But really, that was not what he meant to do. This tenacious man had decided, in spite of all the past disasters, to go back to the Pacific and try again to intercept the Manila Galleon. He had been right in believing she had not sailed the year before, because of his presence off Acapulco. This year, he reasoned, she would have a cargo even richer than usual; and if she left Acapulco in March, she would be due off the northern end of the Philippine Islands in June. And there he went, and lay to intercept her, and exercised the men while he waited in gunnery and small-arms.

They had lain off the islands three weeks when at sunrise on 20th June a sail was sighted from the masthead. It bore down on them. By mid-morning, they were certain this was the galleon; by noon, she was too close to escape. But she did not mean to try: she brought to under top-sails, and hoisted Spanish colours, accepting the encounter.

Yet the Spaniards seemed not to believe they were going to be attacked in a part of the ocean so utterly remote. As the *Centurion* closed, she hoisted the commodore's pennant and her colours, and it was only then that the Spaniards began to clear for action. Anson saw them throwing lumber and cattle overboard, and he opened fire with his chase-guns to hinder them. The galleon returned the fire with her stern chasers. But the *Centurion* over-hauled her, and came abreast within pistol-shot.

Necessity made Anson use novel tactics. He had thirty marksmen with muskets in the tops. On the gundecks he had only two men to each gun. They did nothing but load it, while gangs of a dozen men went from gun to gun to run them out and fire them. The result was a more or less continuous fire, instead of a more or less simultaneous broadside; and it disorganised the Spaniards, who had always been accustomed to lie down when they saw that a broadside was coming, and get up again safely when it had been fired.

As the *Centurion* passed her to lie on her bow, the hammocks and mats in the galleon's netting caught fire. That horrified the *Centurion*'s crew: the last thing they wanted was to burn the galleon, and there was danger she would drive down on the *Centurion* and destroy them both. But the Spaniards at last cut the netting away, and pushed the whole blazing mass of it into the sea. That left their decks unprotected from musketry and grape shot. All the officers on their quarter deck were hit: their confusion could plainly be seen from on board the *Centurion*. The galleon's colours had burnt off the ensign staff. But after a gunnery duel that lasted an hour, she struck the standard at her top-gallant masthead.

It was a fight that was won entirely by the discipline and training Anson had managed to keep intact: the galleon was a much larger ship than his own, with roughly the same armament and three times the number of men: yet she had 67 men killed and the *Centurion* only two. 'Of so little consequence,' the chaplain wrote, 'are the most destructive arms in untutored and unpractised hands.'

Anson took her back to Macao with a prize crew on board and the unfortunate prisoners crammed in the hold of the *Centurion* – a grim necessity, because they so far outnumbered their captors. 'Their sufferings, though impossible to be alleviated, were much to be commiserated; for the weather was extremely hot, the stench of the hold loathsome beyond all conception, and their allowance of water but just sufficient to keep them alive.' They had to stay there a month. None of them died, but when they were taken out they looked like ghosts and spectres.

And the treasure was also transhipped and meticulously counted: 1,313,843 pieces of eight and 35,682 ounces of virgin silver. In Macao, Anson landed the prisoners and sold the galleon, and sailed for home by the Cape of Good Hope. Six months later, after nearly four years at sea, the *Centurion* came to anchor at Spithead, and the chaplain made the only sententious comment in his journal: 'That though prudence, intrepidity, and perseverance, united, are not exempted from the blows of adverse fortune; yet in a long series of transactions, they usually rise superior to its power, and, in the end, rarely fail of proving successful.'

*

Anson's voyage illustrates a very important aspect of naval life. His astonishing perseverance, and his crew's, may partly have been due to patriotic feeling; but to judge by the chaplain's account, the hope of prize money was a very much stronger motive. The capture of the galleon made Anson rich for life, and gave each survivor of the voyage a worth-while bonus. But it was not really an ignoble motive – or if it were, the same could be said of any naval action in most of the seventeenth, eighteenth and nineteenth centuries. It was in Cromwell's time that naval officers and crews were first given a formal right to the value of the ships and cargoes they captured. The shares were varied from time to time by Acts of Parliament, and the seaman's share was always a minute proportion of the captain's or the admiral's. Many captains made fortunes in a single happy fight, while their seamen only got enough to get drunk on; but once in a while a prize was so rich that even the seaman's share was worth more than years of his pay.*

It was a practical arrangement. A seaman's reward, whatever his rank, was a wage which was very small, but on top of it he had, as it were, a ticket in a tremendous lottery. It was always hard to man the naval fleet: without the lure of this gamble it would have been impossible. Without it, the boredom and discomfort of life in wartime would have been much harder for seamen to bear. And without it, the navy would certainly not have fought so eagerly as it did against such heavy odds. Even their tactics and gunnery training were designed for the winning of prize money. The navy did not fight or shoot to sink the enemy's ships, it fought to capture them and bring them home intact. No doubt British seamen were as patriotic as anyone else, but what they talked about when they sighted an enemy fleet was not the victory they might win for Britain, it was the prize-money they could hope to win for themselves; they counted it and spent it in anticipation. Soldiers fought from a sense of military glory that was drilled into them, but in naval annals the thought of a glorious victory is far less often found than the thought of a profitable prize. And on the whole it was perhaps a healthier frame of mind; certainly naval wars were fought with less hatred and bitterness, and with more courtesy and compassion, than wars on land.

*

So Anson's capture was a tonic to the navy: people forgot the hundreds of men who had died, but remembered the profit of those who lived to come home. And it had another good result: Anson never forgot the inefficiency at home that had forced him to round the Horn in winter. Some years later, he became First Sea Lord, and he used his patience and tenacity to reform the navy's administration, as Pepys had reformed it a hundred years before; he dragged it up to a state of honesty and capability which it maintained on the whole until its supremacy over its rivals had been won.

And Anson had more success at sea. Towards the end of the War of Jenkins' Ear, there were two victories over the French which were almost

---

* In 1799, for example, three frigates brought two Spanish ships into Plymouth, laden with 2,811,526 dollars and a cargo of cocoa. Each frigate captain got £40,730, lieutenants £5,091, warrant officers £2,468, midshipmen £791 and seamen and marines £182 4s. 9½d. A seaman's pay at the time was about £14 a year.

identical. The first was commanded by Anson and the second by Admiral Hawke, who had distinguished himself as a captain in Mathews' half-hearted fight in the Mediterranean.

The French had been active in North America and in India, trying with some success to capture territory from the British, and in 1747 they sent out a large convoy. Half of it was bound for Canada and the other was meant to attack the East India Company's posts on the Coromandel coast of India. British intelligence was improving, and the plans of the French were known; and Anson was sent with 14 ships of the line to intercept the convoy. On a morning in May he sighted it, 70 miles north-west of Cape Finisterre. The French escort shortened sail and formed a line of battle, while the convoy set all possible sail to escape to the westward.

Anson's first signal was also for line of battle, but when he saw what was happening he hauled it down and hoisted a signal that was profoundly different: general chase. Its meaning was that every ship should carry all the sail she could. A line of battle could only move at the pace of the slowest ship. But in a general chase, the fastest British ships were certain to overhaul the slowest French, so that the French either had to abandon their laggards or wait and accept a battle. And this signal implied a growing confidence: the confidence that any single British ship both could and would engage whatever enemy forces it could catch. It was a signal the French, at this time, would not have dreamed of using against the British.

The result, at last, was an overwhelming victory in a fair fight in the open sea. The firing began at four in the afternoon. Only eight of the British ships were engaged, against nine in the enemy line; but by seven o'clock every one of the nine had struck her colours and been taken. Anson sent three of his own to pursue the convoy. They came up with it just before dusk and took three more of its remaining escort. And all of these dozen prizes were brought back to England.

In the autumn of the same year, Hawke did the same thing: he intercepted an even bigger convoy, 252 merchant ships, again off Cape Finisterre. Again he hoisted general chase, changed it to line ahead when he saw the huge number of ships ahead of him, then changed it back again when the French escort formed a line. This time, the French escort was outnumbered. It fought a brave battle and lost many hundreds of men in defence of the convoy, but six of its ships were taken. Most of those were dismasted, and the British fleet was badly damaged. Hawke sent a sloop to the West Indies with a warning that the convoy was approaching. He lay a long time out in the

Atlantic, getting up jury masts on the prizes; and in the end, he brought them all in to Portsmouth.

*

So that war ended; British skill and confidence riding high, the French navy weakened and somewhat demoralised, the Spaniards a spent force. Among merchant ships, extraordinary numbers, over 3000, had been captured by both sides. But most of the causes the war had been fought for were still left undecided, and eight years later, in 1756, it all began again. This was the Seven Years' War; and it was in this war that the British navy won world-wide supremacy on the sea.

It began badly with the loss of Minorca and the execution of Admiral John Byng. The French invaded Minorca with a large fleet and an army of 16,000 men; and they did it before war had been declared. The British Government had known for at least six months that the attack was being prepared in Toulon, but they were preoccupied with fears that England might be invaded; and Admiral Byng was sent to the Mediterranean with a force that was much too small and much too late. He reached Minorca to find only the town of Port Mahon holding out, and that under heavy fire. And before he could make any contact with the shore, the French fleet came into sight.

The two fleets fought in the usual formal manner, in two converging lines ahead. But one ship in the British line had its foretopmast shot away, came up into the wind and was taken aback. The ships astern, including the flagship, had to back their topsails to avoid running each other down. But Byng was still flying the signal for line ahead; and remembering that Mathews had been blamed eleven years before for breaking line, he hesitated to bear down on the enemy. So the van of his fleet bore the brunt of the fighting and was badly damaged, and the battle ended without a decisive result.

Before doing anything else, Byng called a council of war, and it endorsed a decision he had already made: it was too late to save Minorca, and he ought to go back to Gibraltar, which had been left without any naval defence.

Unluckily, the French admiral's dispatch reached London first, so that authority there was prepared to be critical of Byng's when it arrived. And when it did, it was not a convincing statement. He was called back to England under escort and court-martialled. The court of twelve naval officers inevitably found he had not done his utmost to relieve Minorca or engage the enemy. Under one of the Articles of War, this was a capital offence, and the court had no discretion to change the sentence. It made a strong recommendation for mercy; and its members were horrified when their advice was disregarded. Byng was shot on the quarterdeck of a ship in Portsmouth harbour, and history books still tell how he tied his own blindfold and gave his own signal to the firing squad. The navy has resented this execution ever since, and rightly. But it demonstrated, at the beginning of a long-drawn war, that England now expected not only courage and loyalty from its naval officer but also instant tactical judgment and strategic wisdom.*

In this war, the navy lived up to that high expectation. It played its part, at last, in perfectly successful combined operations at Louisburg and Quebec; demolished French fleets at Lagos and Quiberon Bay; blockaded and attacked the ports of France; drove out the French in India and the Spaniards in Cuba and the Philippines. And in innumerable minor encounters it showed the spirit that sustained it for two centuries to come: in the West Indies, to take a single example, on 21st October, 1757, when three British ships were cruising to intercept a convoy and found themselves confronted by seven enemy warships. The senior British captain called the other two on board, and a short significant conversation was recorded. 'Well, gentlemen, you see they are come out to engage us.' 'It would be a pity to disappoint them.' 'I agree.' 'Very well, go on board your ships again.' The signal was hoisted, 'Bear down and engage the enemy,' and the three ships did so, and fought until the French flagship and several others had to be towed away by frigates. One of these three captains was Maurice Suckling, who was the uncle of Nelson and his first patron; and when Nelson was approaching battle at Trafalgar on the same day 48 years later, he mystified his friends on the quarterdeck of the *Victory* by saying, without any explanation, that it had always been the happiest day of the year in his family.

The taking of Louisburg on Cape Breton Island in 1758 was the beginning of the navy's part in the great strategic plan, devised by Pitt, to seize control of Canada from the French and prevent the junction of their forces in the north and on the Mississippi, which would have hemmed in the British colonists and stopped their expansion to the west. It was a model of helpful cooperation between the army and the navy, distinguished by a particular feat of naval arms. In harbour, there had been five French ships of the line but one had blown up, for reasons unexplained, and set two more on fire.

---

* 'Dans ce pays-ci,' Voltaire wrote in *Candide*, 'il est bon de tuer de temps en temps un amiral pour encourager les autres.'

The guns of the other two were annoying the army, and so the admiral sent 600 sailors into the harbour in boats by night. They were fiercely attacked by the guns of forts and by the ships themselves, but they boarded them both and cut their cables. One drifted ashore, so they burnt her, and the other was towed by the boats to a distant corner of the harbour, where she remained a prize.

The capture of Louisburg gave the navy access to the St Lawrence River, the route to Quebec. The capture of Quebec in the following year has always remained a celebrated battle, because of the unprecedented daring of both the army's and the navy's tactics. Nothing bigger than a frigate had ever navigated the river. The defenders had removed the buoys and leading marks, and were free to man or fortify the banks. The only charts were French and unreliable. Yet Charles Saunders, the admiral commanding the British fleet, seems never to have doubted his captains and crews could reach the city; or at least, he did not hesitate to try.

It was a methodical business which began as soon as the ice broke up that spring. Ships' masters were sent up the river in boats to survey it – among them Mr James Cook, who had joined the navy as a seaman and only recently been promoted. Marine surveying at the best of times needed patience and care: to correct whatever maps had existed of the river banks, and traverse it again and again under oars, taking soundings with the lead at proper intervals, always observing the boat's position, allowing for stream and tide, and methodically writing down the depths. And this survey, in water that had just unfrozen, was made entirely under the enemy's observation: a large proportion of it had to be done at night. But between them the masters drew charts which were perfectly adequate, and Cook in particular founded his reputation as a cartographer.

With that preparation, the whole of the battle fleet entered the river in June and anchored a hundred miles from the open sea and sixty miles below Quebec: 22 ships of the line, 27 frigates and smaller warships, and the transports carrying over 9,000 soldiers. This was already much farther than General Wolfe had expected the ships to escort him, and also much farther than the French had thought a fleet could come. Above that point, the river narrowed to its most dangerous passage. Saunders shifted his flag from a 90-gun to a 60-gun ship, left the largest there and proceeded with four ships of the line, the frigates and transports. Below the narrows, the fleet picked up some French pilots who had been captured by an advance squadron. They were distributed among the ships, but of course nobody was willing to give them any credit for what happened. It was said no master took any notice of them, and indeed any patriotic Frenchman might have been expected to run his ship aground.

But none ran aground. Mark boats were sent ahead and moored on the edges of the channel. Some masters conned their ships from the forecastle, watching the look of the water. The fleet passed through the narrows without mishap and came to anchor again while the army began to reconnoitre the defences of the city. At midnight, seven fireships and two burning rafts came down the river, a sight that might have appalled the crew of any wooden ship, but men went out with confidence, threw grappling irons on board the flaming ships and towed them clear. Next day, a little over a week after entering the river, the first of the ships were anchored in sight of Quebec.

It was undoubtedly a great feat of seamanship, or to be more precise of ship-handling: it must have needed not only an admiral who would try it, but also captains, masters and men right through the ranks who knew without exception exactly what they were doing. And in this feat, and the two-month siege that followed it, was the first example of an attitude of mind that came to distinguish the navy: a will not merely to do what the army or anyone else expected, but to go one better, and astonish landlubbers by doing something they thought was impossible – and then, of course, to make light of it. It was an attitude the navy often showed in years to come, and still was showing in the last war it fought. And if it began at Quebec it is pleasant to recall that an army commander deserves some credit for it; for General Wolfe was absurdly young – he was only 32 – brave, enthusiastic, appreciative, and free from the cantakerous prejudice of some older men, the kind of general a navy likes to serve.

*

While the fighting was going on in Canada, the French at home were preparing an invasion of Britain, as they often had in the past; and the two greatest battles at sea in this war were both fought to prevent it. This invasion got further than most; and at sea, the moves and countermoves were so like Napoleon's and Nelson's that they have the air of a dress rehearsal. The main French fleets were in Toulon in the Mediterranean and Brest on the Biscay coast. They were meant to combine and escort an army to land in the Clyde, then sail round Scotland, pick up another army which was ready in Ostend and land it in the Blackwater estuary in Essex.

But Toulon and Brest were both blockaded by British fleets, as they were in Nelson's time. The fleet off Toulon, like Nelson's, had no base that was nearer than Gibraltar, and the fleet off Brest, standing off and on in the open Atlantic and among the rocks and tides of Ushant, was driven off its station from time to time by westerly gales.

The Mediterranean fleet was commanded by Admiral Boscawen, a Cornishman who had commanded at Louisburg and had had an adventurous naval career all over the world – he had the distinction, in this series of wars, of defeating and capturing the same French captain, whose name was Hocquart, three times in eleven years. Off Toulon, he did his best to lure the French out of port but they would not come, and in July 1759 he had to go back to Gibraltar for food and repairs. The French took the chance, hoping to pass Gibraltar while the British were out of action. But a frigate sighted them. The British were re-rigging and Boscawen's flagship had not a single sail bent, but they got out of harbour in two hours and he signalled General Chase.

The chase was distinguished by a strangely patchy wind. In the first morning, the British had a following breeze while the French were becalmed. By afternoon, the British overhauled but then fell into the calm themselves, and an artillery battle began between ships that were almost motionless. The sternmost French ship was crippled and forced to strike, and Boscawen's flagship lost her mizzen mast and both her topsail yards. At the height of the battle, Boscawen ordered his barge to take him to an undamaged ship. On the way, the barge was holed by a shot, and the Admiral snatched off his wig and stuffed it into the hole and stopped the leak. Night fell, the breeze sprang up and two French ships escaped unseen to Cadiz. At dawn the remaining four were three miles ahead on a course for the coast of Portugal. They ran for the bay of Lagos; and there, as she entered the bay, the French flagship ran aground with the breeze behind her and all her sails set, so that all three masts in a dreadful tangle of rigging fell over her bows. She and another damaged ship were boarded and burnt. The other two were taken as prizes, and one had a name that won fame in the British navy: *Temeraire.* Boscawen's comment on the battle was essentially naval: 'It is well, but it might have been a great deal better.'

Three months later the other fleet, which was blockading Brest, won a victory which indeed was better. This was under Admiral Hawke. It was winter, and a gale had driven him to shelter across the Channel in Torbay. The same gale imprisoned the French in the harbour of Brest. But on the day it began to moderate, they put to sea; and on the same day, Hawke got under way from Torbay. Off Ushant he learned from a frigate that the French had sailed – the same frigate, as it happened, which had sighted the fleet off Gibraltar. News from merchantmen made him head for Quiberon Bay, 120 miles down the Brittany coast, and at midday on 20th November, twelve miles off the coast, the fleets were in contact. The weather was vile and growing worse, the wind blowing straight on shore in heavy squalls. The French admiral bore away for the bay, which is full of islands, shoals and rocks.

Perhaps he expected Hawke in that kind of weather would keep clear of a lee shore for which he had no pilot. But blockade was a stern training in seamanship. The British ships set far more sail than the French thought it safe to carry, and as the French entered the bay, rounding the notorious rocks called the Cardinals, the British were overhauling them and engaging them as they passed. The flagship of the French rear-admiral was shot to pieces and struck her colours after an awful loss of life. A 74-gun ship overturned and foundered because she had her lower gunports open in the heavy sea. Another sank after broadsides had holed her between wind and water. As dusk was falling, Hawke entered the bay and met the French flagship *Soleil Royal*, desperately trying to beat her way out again, and in spite of his master's protest he ordered his ship laid alongside the enemy and drove her down to leeward among the shoals. At dark, he made the signal to anchor. But that signal, in the primitive book of those days, was simply the firing of two guns. Among the other gunfire in the bay and the thunder of breakers on the rocks all round, a good many ships did not hear it, and one, the *Resolution*, still under way in the pitch dark later at night, ran ashore on a shoal and was wrecked.

It was a wild night of storm: the reports and flashes of guns of distress could be heard and seen from every part of the bay. At dawn, the *Soleil Royal* was found to have anchored in the midst of the British fleet: she cut her cable and ran ashore, and her crew set her on fire. So did another ship that had struck the night before. The *Essex*, sent to engage them, ran on the same reef as the *Resolution*. Seven French ships were embayed in the mouth of the River Vilaine and could not beat out again. To escape from British attack, they jettisoned guns and provisions and managed to cross the bar, but four of them broke their backs in the shallow water.

*

At home, the succession of three victories set the navy on a pedestal. Each of the three officers sent back with dispatches was received by the King and given £500 'with which to buy a sword,' and each of the admirals was voted the thanks of Parliament and a pension or a sinecure appointment as a general of Marines. And the simplest sailors, with such stories to tell, were sure of an admiring audience in any inn, and all the free drinks they could stomach. 'Rule Britannia' was written in 1740, the year when Anson started round the world, and was more an expression of hope than of fact. But 'Hearts of Oak' was written this year by David Garrick, and in spite of its deplorable verse it held some truth:

> *'We ne'er see our foes but we wish 'em to stay,*
> *They never see us but they wish us away.*
> *If they run, why, we follow, and run 'em ashore,*
> *For if they won't fight us, we cannot do more.'*

The immediate effect at sea was that French possessions fell like ninepins: Guadaloupe, Dominica and Martinique in the West Indies, Calcutta and Pondicherry in India. And when France dragged Spain into the war, the British took Havana and Manila, the keys to Spanish wealth in the west and east. To the merchants of England, it must for a moment have seemed a golden opportunity. But Britain could not absorb and administer this sudden empire, and perhaps did not want to try. When peace was signed in 1763, she gave back most of the places she had conquered to the nations who owned them before. But she kept Canada.

The long-term effect was vastly more important. If one had to put a date on Britain's ultimate supremacy at sea, it would be that autumn and early winter of 1759. It was those three victories within four months that won the unspoken recognition of the only possible rivals. Ever since Queen Elizabeth's reign, the British had always managed to put a fleet to sea which held its own, or did a little more than hold its own; but Holland, Spain and France, each in its turn, had also fought at sea with hope of winning. With the three battles of 1759, the balance was irrevocably changed. The Dutch had been out of the running for many years; the morale of the Spaniards was already low; now the morale of the French was shattered, and it never really recovered. Henceforth, even through the great age of Napoleon, it was always without exception the British who sought a fight, because they were sure they would win, and the French and Spanish who tried to escape it, because they were sure in their hearts they would lose. The Royal Navy was in command of the seas, and everyone knew it was.

PART FIVE

SUPREMACY

1759–1945

*Napoleon in his fall
leaves only Britain as a power on the seas,
and the British conceive that the seas should be free for
the ships of every nation.*

CHAPTER 19

The Age of Exploration

'WHEREAS nothing can redound more to the honour of this Nation as a Maritime Power, to the dignity of the Crown of Great Britain, and to the advancement of the Trade and Navigation thereof, than to make Discoveries of Countries hitherto unknown: His Majesty taking the Premisses into His Royal Consideration, and conceiving no Conjuncture so proper for an Enterprise of this Nature as a Time of Profound Peace which His Kingdoms at present happyly enjoy, has thought fit to make those Attempts which are specified in the following Instructions . . .' These words were written in June 1764, within a few months of the end of the Seven Years' War. The instructions which followed were signed by the Lords of the Admiralty and given to Captain John Byron of the frigate *Dolphin*, with orders that they must not be opened until he was at sea. But he knew very well what was in them before he read them: he was to search for new lands in the south Atlantic, then make his way round the Horn, explore the coast of New Albion or California, and try to find the entrance from the Pacific to the North-West Passage.

These orders began a new era of seafaring which was totally different from any before it, the era in which a navy designed for war was used for exploration. Within the next generation, the navy penetrated every sea that still remained unknown, and left no major mysteries unsolved, except the old mystery of the North-West Passage.

It is not surprising their Lordships began their instructions by offering reasons for such a naval activity; for conquest, the normal business of a navy, was not among the reasons. They must have expected to have to convince the King and parliament that exploration was a proper use for naval ships; and perhaps they also had to convince themselves. Nobody had ever been in such a position before, in command of a navy which had beaten all its rivals and – so far as anyone could foresee – had finished the work that navies existed for. Yet one feels the reasons they gave – the honour of a maritime power, the dignity of the Crown, the advancement of trade and navigation – were really only arguing points. The more probable reason was pure inquisitiveness, the longing to know what lay beyond horizons: and specifically the wish to investigate, before the French could do so, the huge antarctic continent which for centuries had been marked on maps as Terra Australis Incognita. The Lords of the Admiralty had the ships, the crews and the navigators, the oceans were theirs by virtue of victory: and what was more, they had the sextant and the chronometer, which never yet had been used in exploration. But if they were bitten by the bug of exploring, they need not have troubled to excuse themselves. With the first successes, the whole nation became infected.

Like many another British enterprise, this age of exploration ended very well but started badly. Byron scarcely even tried to carry out his orders. He did go to the Falkland Islands, which had been sighted first by Davis in 1592 and claimed for Britain by Richard Hawkins two years later. And he landed and formally took possession of them in the name of the King – his crew were given half an issue of brandy to drink His Majesty's health; but he did not discover that the French explorer Bougainville had already made a settlement in another bay. And his act of taking possession was exceptional. The Falkland Islands were uninhabited, and the Admiralty wanted a British base, rather than Portuguese ports, as a starting point for voyages round Cape Horn. Elsewhere, possession was no part of these British explorations.

Byron searched for an island farther north which had been reported by a buccaneer and named after Samuel Pepys; but he could not find it and concluded, correctly, that it did not exist. (It was a pity Pepys had no other memorial in the atlas of the world than a non-existent island.) But after that, Byron made no exploration of the Atlantic, and he did not go near California or the North-West Passage. He crossed the Pacific to Tinian, which Anson had already discovered, and went home as fast as he could by the Cape of Good Hope. He made a record time for the voyage round the world, twenty-two months, but he did not discover anything except two atolls which he aptly named the Islands of Disappointment. In mid-Pacific he saw flocks of birds which flew off each evening to the southward, but he did not turn aside to follow them. If he had, he could not have failed to sight the mountains of Tahiti, which were just below the horizon.

Byron (he was the poet's grandfather) must have been lacking in the qualities that other explorers possessed. He had plenty of experience, and had served on Anson's expedition in the *Wager*, which lost company with

Anson off the Horn. She had been wrecked on the coast of Chile, and he had suffered fearsome privations before he came back to civilisation; and perhaps that experience had shaken his nerve. But to command an exploration in the eighteenth century must have needed extraordinary stability of mind. A captain then was lonelier in command than anyone, even in outer space, could be today; no help or word of advice or encouragement could conceivably reach him within a year. It is not so surprising that Byron failed as that anyone succeeded.

Perhaps the Admiralty understood this. Byron was not blamed, but within a few months the *Dolphin* was sent out again with another commander, Samuel Wallis; and a very small sloop, the *Swallow*, Lieutenant Philip Carteret, went with her as a tender. Wallis was not more daring than Byron, but he was luckier: he crossed the Pacific on a rather more southerly track, and found Tahiti. He only stayed six weeks, not long enough to begin to understand the Tahitian people, but long enough first to fight them and then to come to friendly terms with them: long enough also for the crew to discover, to their amazement, that the girls were beautiful and had never learned to look upon sex as anything but a pleasure to be shared. And in the report of the voyage was the first fatal application of European judgments to Polynesian customs: the women were described as wanton prostitutes who would 'sell their favours' for a nail. From Tahiti, Wallis went on, like Byron, to Tinian, and so home.

Philip Carteret in the *Swallow* was the only one of these three captains who really showed enterprise. He had sailed with Byron, and in the Straits of Magellan Wallis sent him ahead of the *Dolphin* because he had been there before. But the *Swallow* was thirty years old and a very sluggish sailer, much slower than the *Dolphin*; and as soon as the end of the straits was in sight, Wallis set his topsails and simply left the *Swallow* behind. All day, the crew of the *Swallow* watched her drawing ahead. Next morning, only her topmasts could be seen, and then those disappeared. For this extraordinary behaviour, there was no explanation in Wallis's journal except that he had to carry sail to clear the straits. He made no attempt to wait for his consort or go back to find her, and he had not appointed a rendezvous.

It was the more extraordinary because Wallis knew the *Swallow* was not equipped to look after herself. Before they sailed from England, whenever Carteret asked for anything – a forge, for example, or trinkets to trade with natives – he was told the *Dolphin* had plenty; and as he had not been given any orders, he came to believe his ship was not intended to take any part in exploration. Abandoned in the straits, he might have taken the short way home, but he did not; he went on, to cross the Pacific all alone in his crazy old sloop. First, through weeks of storm, he went to Juan Fernandez for food and water; but he found that since Anson's voyage the Spaniards had fortified the island, and he stood away again, as he 'could not suppose the Spaniards well disposed to receive English visitants.' Desperate for water, he made for the neighbouring islet of Masafuego. It had no sheltered anchorage, and a heavy surf was breaking.

This recalled to Carteret an adventure in Madeira on the voyage out, when some of the seamen swam ashore to get, as they put it, a skinful of liquor. When they came back, he had only remarked that he was glad to know he had some good swimmers aboard; and three of them now, in gratitude, volunteered to swim ashore with some water casks. But while they were there, a storm blew up and they could not swim off again: they had to spend the night naked in the gale. 'In order to preserve a living portion of animal heat, they lay one upon another, each man alternately placing himself between the other two.' At dawn, they walked and swam round the island and at last were brought aboard, where the captain gave orders they should have 'all proper refreshments, and remain in their hammocks the whole night'; and the chronicler of the voyage, recalling the Madeira episode, defined the character of English sailors as 'consisting in a contempt of danger, a love of strong liquor and a girl, and an aversion to be possessed of any coin when embarked on a long voyage'.

Pressing on to the north and west, in the wet and stormy weather of midwinter, Carteret discovered Pitcairn Island, and named it after the midshipman who sighted it at dawn. He passed south of Tahiti, but named and put on the map at least a score of smaller islands. Somehow he missed the large groups of Fiji and Samoa, and after eight months alone in what was described as 'a dull, shattered vessel', he was among the Santa Cruz and Solomon Islands. Most of the crew were sick, and so was he, and he sent the master ashore with a boatload of men to seek provisions.

He had missed the Polynesians, and now was among the more warlike Melanesians. Nevertheless the men were well entertained by them until the master began to hack down a coco-nut palm, an action which would still be intensely resented in a south sea island. The natives plainly protested, but he refused to stop; and so the boat's party was attacked with arrows and fought back with their guns, many were wounded and the master and several others died.

This stupid episode seems to have broken Carteret's will to explore much farther. He was hardly able to get out of bed, and his lieutenant, the only other man on board who could navigate the ship, was so ill he was not expected to recover. Even so, he went on meticulously charting and naming the masses of islands to the north of Papua, not knowing which of them had already been seen and named by the Spaniards or Portuguese. At length he reached Macassar, where the Dutch refused to help him and he drew a little satisfaction from entertaining the governor's envoys with rotten biscuit and bad salt meat. From there, he was in well-known seas, and in two and a half years he brought the old *Swallow* safely round the world.

None of these three captains, Byron, Wallis or Carteret, had a chronometer, perhaps because chronometers were still very rare and expensive; but all of them were able to fix their longitude by lunars. Yet in setting their courses they made little use of this new ability. They sailed almost straight across the Pacific from east to west, as everyone always had before them. On first thoughts, it seems unenterprising, but there was some reason for it. Even when things were going well, they were always aware they might urgently have to find land to cure an outbreak of scurvy. But the few islands that were already known were marked on the charts with a fairly accurate latitude but quite unreliable longitude, so that even a captain who knew his own longitude could only be certain of finding them on an east-to-west course. Indeed Carteret, seriously short of food and water, tried to sail north to find Easter Island, which had already been sighted, but he failed because its longitude had been wrongly reported.

But when they did see land, they fixed its position. So through these three voyages – or at least the last two of them – a few places were entered on the Pacific charts which an explorer could always find again from any direction in case of need: especially, near the middle of the ocean, the hospitable island of Tahiti. And this was the salient fact that set future explorers free to roam the Pacific at will, including the greatest of them all.

*

The three expeditions of James Cook, which followed on Wallis's return, are probably the best-known voyages ever made, and it would be redundant to try to compress all his adventures into the bounds of a history of British seafaring. But in this context, two of his achievements mark the start of an epoch. First, he avoided the scurvy. Second, his own navigation was so confident and precise that latitude sailing, even in unknown oceans, became a thing of the past. These achievements gave him a freedom nobody had ever had before. And of course one must add the perseverance which enabled him to keep his crews contented and enthusiastic. And in a more general sense, the most absorbing aspect of his first journeys has always been – as it was at the time – the manner of life of the people he found in the Pacific, which made the British and the French question the morality of exploring and the standards of their own society.

Before Wallis came home, the Royal Society proposed three expeditions, to the North Cape, a point in Hudson Bay, and an island in the south Pacific. The object was to calculate the distance of the sun, which they hoped to do by observing from these distant places the transit of Venus across the sun which was due on 3rd June, 1769. There was some hesitation in choosing the Pacific site, because there was no island whose position was exactly known. But when Wallis arrived with his reports of Tahiti, the problem was immediately solved.

The choice of Cook to command the Pacific expedition was extraordinary. In an age of class consciousness, he was a man of the humblest birth, and he came from a distant corner of Lincolnshire far beyond the orbit of London society. He still held only the warrant rank of master, and had to be commissioned a lieutenant before he could command a naval expedition. And no doubt there were plenty of naval captains who would have jumped at the chance. But in the St Lawrence and on the coast of Canada he had proved his uncommon skill in navigation and surveying, and the Admiralty had the wisdom to recognise his skill in command before it had even been tried.

So in July 1768 he sailed from Plymouth in the converted Whitby collier which was renamed *Endeavour*, 368 tons and 106 feet long, with a company of seventy; and nine months later he anchored off Tahiti, after a voyage as uneventful as any could be in the days of sail, and with his crew as healthy as when they started. And to appreciate that achievement, one has only to compare the voyage with Anson's.

Oddly enough, it is still impossible to say exactly how Cook succeeded in keeping his people free from scurvy, when almost everyone hitherto had failed. Of course, he knew no more than anyone else what caused it: that problem was still being argued well into the twentieth century. So his precautions had to be empirical, and he took so many that one cannot tell which of them succeeded. His distinction was that he had a profound and continuous interest in the health of his crews and persuaded them, through the respect they had for him, to try new remedies, and take an intelligent care of themselves.

The first precautions, of course, were in food. In the journal of his second voyage, Cook described the normal naval diet of the time. Each man had a pound of biscuit a day, and as much small beer as he could drink, or a pint of wine, or half a pint of brandy, rum or arrack. And each mess of four men shared the following:

Monday, Wednesday and Friday (called Banyan days in the navy), $\frac{1}{2}$ lb of butter, 10 ounces of Cheshire cheese and as much boiled oatmeal, wheat or pease as they could eat.

Tuesday and Saturday, two 4 lb pieces of salt beef, or one piece of beef, 3 lbs of flour and 1 lb of raisins or $\frac{1}{2}$ lb of suet.

Thursday and Sunday, two 2 lb pieces of salt pork with pease. Sometimes sugar and olive oil were issued instead of butter and cheese; and if provisions ran short, the men were paid for what they did not get.

But for Cook's voyages, the Admiralty provided extra stores of things that were thought to be specifics against scurvy. They were pickled cabbage (sauerkraut); salted cabbage; portable broth, which was a kind of beef essence; saloupe, which was a powdered root used as a hot drink like coffee; mustard; marmalade of carrots, which was concentrated carrot juice 'recommended by Baron Storsch of Berlin'; malt; and the 'rob' of oranges and lemons. These were mainly intended for the sick, but Cook issued sauerkraut and portable soup to everyone on Banyan days. Also, he bought and issued 20 lbs of onions for each man, and wherever he touched land he sent parties ashore to look for vegetables; he even collected wild celery and scurvy grass, which was a sort of mustard, among the barren rocks of Tierra del Fuego.

The Admiralty stores, of course, were not Cook's invention, they were the choice of naval doctors and other theorists who took an interest in the problem. Cook's achievement in the sphere of diet was to make his men eat all these unfamiliar things. Seamen, conservative in everything, were devoted to their salt meat and biscuit, their various sorts of porridge, and their solid plum duff; there had been at least one case in another ship of men being flogged for refusing to eat fresh meat when there happened to be some. But Cook managed to create a general opinion in his ships that everyone ought to eat their cabbage, whether they liked it or not.

He took other health precautions too, and these seem to have been entirely his own idea. The whole crew had to take cold baths and wear clean shirts, which was probably unheard of, and they had to change their clothes when they were wet. He kept the men in three watches whenever the work of the ship allowed it, so that they had enough unbroken sleep and had time to get dry and warm before they were called on watch again. He insisted that the decks where they lived, and the cooking utensils they used, should be clean, and he had the decks aired and dried by charcoal stoves below the gratings, even in the hottest weather.

The result of it all was a standard of health which was totally different from anything before, a standard that every captain on long voyages afterwards tried to emulate. On the first voyage, the good health lasted until he put in to Batavia on the way home, where the crew met an epidemic of tropical disease that no precautions at the time could check. On the second voyage, the record was even more astonishing. 'On Saturday the 28th,' he wrote, as the last sentence in his journal, 'we made the land near Plymouth and the next morning anchored at Spit-head. Having been absent from England Three Years and Eighteen Days, in which time I lost but four men and only one of them by sickness.' He might have added that the single death from sickness was a man with tuberculosis which he had certainly contracted before he put to sea. Cook seems in his writings to have been prouder of this record than of any of his discoveries, and with reason; for the discoveries would not have been possible if he had not been able to lay the spectre of scurvy.

The choice of East Coast colliers for these voyages, instead of naval ships, has been put down to the fact that Cook had served his apprenticeship in them. No doubt that had something to do with it, but there were solid reasons for the choice; and they came to light, after the first of the voyages, in letters between the Admiralty and Joseph Banks. The rich young amateur botanist who sailed with Cook on the first of the voyages wanted to go on the second. But the first had made him famous, and also seems to have made him impossibly pompous and conceited. When the second was contemplated, Cook was sent to the Pool of London to choose two ships, and again decided on colliers like the *Endeavour* – the two that were bought and named *Resolution* and *Adventure*. Banks insisted on so much extra accommodation for himself and his suite that the *Resolution* became top-heavy and could not safely be sailed out of the Thames. Her new upperworks all had to be taken off again. Then Banks said the choice was wrong: the *Resolution* was 'if not absolutely incapable, at least exceedingly unfit for the intended Voyage.' He wanted a naval frigate or a three-decked East Indiaman. The Admiralty was anxious to please him; but they were utterly outraged when they found he really expected to command the expedition with Cook as his subordinate. A letter from Lord Sandwich, First Lord of the Admiralty, is a model of how to be crushingly rude in the very politest language: and a memorandum from Sir Hugh Palliser, Comptroller of the Navy, reveals the risks that explorers foresaw and the means they thought best to overcome them.

Banks or his supporters had pointed out that a frigate was more weatherly than a collier, and therefore more able to claw off a lee shore. Palliser answered that no prudent captain in any kind of ship would try to explore an unknown lee shore or let himself be caught on it. The greatest danger to be expected was of running ashore on desert or savage coasts; and therefore the best kind of ship was one designed, as a collier was, to take the ground, with a shallow draught and flat bottom so that she would sit upright. She must also be small enough to be set ashore for repairs without the help of a dockyard. And she needed a very large capacity in proportion to her crew, to stow enough provisions to keep her at sea for several years. 'In such a Vessel,' he wrote, 'an able Sea Officer will be more venturesome and better enabled to fulfill his Instructions than he possibly can (or indeed would be prudent for him to attempt) in one of any other sort or size.' And he added in a final dig at Banks: 'It may further be observed that to embark a great Number of Passengers, claiming great Distinctions and spacious Accommodations with vast quantities of Baggage, is incompatible with the Idea of a Scheme of Discovery at the Antipodes: If such Passengers do go, they must be content with the Kind of Ship that is fittest.' But Banks would not be content; he withdrew in a huff, and on the second voyage Cook sailed without him.

As to the problems of navigation, Cook had no chronometer on the first of his voyages. It was only nine years since Harrison's clock had passed the tests of the Board of Longitude; there were still not many chronometers in existence, and there was still a strong inclination to trust the heavenly bodies in preference to a man-made apparatus. But Cook had an astronomer, who shared the labour of observing and calculating lunars, and he surveyed the coasts of New Zealand and eastern Australia with amazing accuracy. On the second voyage, he had four chronometers. One was a replica of Harrison's, made by a craftsman named Mr Kendall, and the other three were a newer design by Mr Arnold. They were treated with reverence: each of them, like Harrison's original, was kept in a box with three different locks, and the captain, first lieutenant and astronomer, who each kept one of the keys, were required by an Admiralty order to be present every day after noon when the clocks were wound. For one reason and another, all three of

Arnold's failed during the voyage, but Kendall's was perfectly reliable. Cook sometimes referred to them in his journal as watch machines, which gives a clue to the naval origin of the word for a pocket clock; and he used affectionate phrases about Mr Kendall's watch – 'our trusty friend,' 'our never-failing guide.' In charting and surveying, he and his astronomer used the watch in conjunction with lunar observations. But as the voyage went on, he began to put faith in the watch alone for his navigation. When he left Cape Town homeward bound, after nearly three years at sea, he set course for the island of St Helena: 'Depending on the goodness of Mr Kendals Watch, I resolved to try to make the island by a direct course, it did not deceive us and we made it accordingly on the 15th day of May at Day-break.' And one of his midshipmen wrote that the day before the island was sighted they spoke to an East Indiaman who 'said they were afraid that we should miss the Island, but Captn Cook laugh'd at them, and told them that he would run their jibboom on the Island if they chose.' The problem of longitude had certainly been solved, but there were still two reservations: Mr Kendall's watch cost £450, which was far too expensive for an ordinary ship; and a watch, like any machine, could still go wrong, and oblige its owner to fall back on whatever he knew about lunars.

A chart of the world with the tracks that Cook left on it is his most impressive memorial – the line right round the Antarctic to prove that no habitable land existed, and the web all over the Pacific from the ice in the south to the ice in the north. He added far more to geographical knowledge than any man before him or after him. But in reading his own journal, or the many journals written by people who sailed with him, one is struck even more by the character that brought him through these immense enterprises. He was modest and always calm – reasonably calm even in the extraordinary scene when the *Resolution* struck on the reef off Tahiti, and the prim Swedish naturalist Sparrman distributed speaking trumpets to 'those officers who appeared to me most efficient in handling the vessel . . . I should have preferred, however, to hear fewer "Goddams" from the officers and particularly the Captain.' He seldom seems to have been annoyed, even by the ebullient Banks or the impossibly boring and pedantic Dr Forster. In command of his crews he seems fatherly. He knew his own mind, and could be formidably stern when sternness was needed. But he was also humane and kind. Of course there were misdeeds, and men were flogged for them; but then they were forgotten, and one never in all those years sees any sign of a lasting grudge. When two of the crew deserted in Tahiti they were given a

English Ships at Fort William, Calcutta, in the 18th century,
by Lambert & Scott

John Harrison's No. 1 Marine Timekeeper, 1737 and later chronometers
Overleaf: Cook's Second Expedition:
the *Resolution* and *Adventure at Tahiti* by W. Hodges

dozen lashes, which was probably less than they expected; and one of them sailed with Cook again on both his later voyages. On the second visit to the island another man tried it, a footloose character called Marra. Cook merely put him in irons until the ship was clear of the land, and wrote in the journal: 'I know not if he might not have obtained my consent if he had applied for it in proper time . . . Where could such a man spend his days better than at one of these isles?' He was a captain, in short, who understood how the minds of his seamen worked, perhaps because he had been a seaman himself; and they always knew he did. When he died, one of them wrote 'He was our leading-star, which at its setting left us involved in darkness and despair,' and that man seems to have spoken for them all.

His compassion and understanding showed even more clearly when it came to dealing with primitive people. He appreciated something that may be obvious now but was far from obvious then: that simple people may have beliefs and taboos which deserve as much respect as anyone else's. Of course he loved the Tahitians, like everyone else who met them in those early days – 'the most obligeing and benevolent people I ever met with.' But even with people who were not immediately attractive – the Maoris, Aborigines, Melanesians and Alaskans – he took endless trouble to avoid unwittingly giving offence. His men were ordered to show native people 'every kind of civility and regard', and he was hard on any whose clumsiness and ignorance made them fail. He almost went so far as to see the sense of property as a European taboo that other people could not be expected to understand. 'One ought not to be too severe upon these people when they do commit a thieft sence we can hardly charge them with any other Vice.' (This was in the journal of his second visit to Tahiti, and he added the remarkable judgment: 'Incont(in)ency in the unmarried people can hardly be call'd a Vice sence neither the State nor Individuals are the least injured by it.') Of course, the people's habit of taking whatever they fancied was a nuisance to him, as it was to all explorers. Most of the time, like Davis among the Eskimos two hundred years before, he put up with it and simply told his own people they ought to be more careful with their property. But when things were stolen that the ship could not do without, he took chiefs aboard and kept them as hostages until the things were returned. It was a bluff, because he certainly would not have imprisoned anyone very long, but it always worked, until the last occasion in Hawaii. Then, it was a boat that was stolen, and the mutual misunderstanding suddenly flared up in a fight, and Cook was stabbed to death.

Paradoxically, it might have been better for the people of the Pacific if the first European they met had not been so just and friendly. If the first had been oppressive, they might have been more on their guard when others came. As it was, the Polynesians gave the same impulsive welcome to the people who followed the explorers: the whalers who descended with drink and rape, escaped convicts who could rule like kings if they had a few muskets, the missionaries who demolished the Polynesian customs and imposed, as it happened, a particularly dour and joyless kind of Christianity; and finally, long afterwards, the colonists, French, British or American. Cook foresaw a disaster. 'We introduce among them wants and perhaps diseases which they never before knew, and which serve only to disturb that happy tranquillity they and their forefathers had enjoyed.' And again: 'I own I cannot avoid expressing it as my real opinion that it would have been far better for these poor people never to have known our superiority in the accommodations and arts that make life comfortable, than after once knowing it, to be again left and abandoned.' But nothing in the eighteenth century could have halted the process of exploration or guarded against its results whatever they might be.

*

One remarkable thing about this age of British exploration is that it never stopped, until there was nothing important left to explore. When Cook sailed on his last voyage, the War of American Independence had already begun. There was a short gap in naval exploration when France took a part in that war; but then it began again, and right through the age of Nelson and Napoleon the navy felt itself strong enough to spare a few ships and crews to go exploring. Cook founded a sort of dynasty of explorers. After him, every officer who commanded an exploration had sailed on one before in a junior rank. In the 1780s, two of his officers made names for themselves in the Pacific, William Bligh and George Vancouver. One of Vancouver's lieutenants was William Broughton, who mapped the north-east coasts of the Pacific in the next decade. A midshipman under Bligh was Matthew Flinders, who explored the coasts of Australia from 1795 to 1803; and in turn, one of Flinders' midshipmen was John Franklin, who disappeared in the North-West Passage in Queen Victoria's reign. These four generations of explorers covered eighty years, and all of them inherited Cook's regard for meticulous accuracy.

The extraordinary case of Lieutenant Bligh and the mutiny on the

Bounty was not strictly speaking a matter of exploration, although he charted a good many unknown islands. The object of his voyage was itself the most extraordinary use that had yet been made of a naval ship and crew: to collect breadfruit seedlings in pots and take them to the West Indies, where it was thought they might be established to feed the negro slaves. The idea had come from West Indian plantation owners who had read about breadfruit in the explorers' journals, and it had the support of Banks, who by then was President of the Royal Society. The Admiralty supplied the ship and crew.

In modern times, Bligh has been given the Hollywood reputation of a cruel tyrant; but the evidence against him was given by men on trial for their lives, and he may well have been no worse than an average ship's captain of his time. Certainly, he and Cook were very different men, although he had served successfully under Cook as his sailing master; for while Cook looked for and brought out the best in every man, Bligh looked for and brought out the worst. Reading between the lines of the contradictory statements, one sees him as a self-centred man, rude, insensitive and tactless, and given to bursts of bad temper which never lasted long. But Fletcher Christian, the mate who led the mutiny, seems neurotic and childish in the secret grudges that he bore; while John Fryer the master was certainly a weak, mean-spirited man who hated Bligh simply because he was strong. And all the ship's company, when they reached Tahiti, had been packed together in a close confinement that would have tried the patience of anyone.

The *Bounty* was a very small ship, 90 feet in length overall, and 24 in beam. Her main cabin had been fitted to carry the pots of plants and extended to take up a third of her length, and everyone lived in the remaining effective length of her, about forty feet: Bligh himself, 11 warrant officers, 32 other hands and two gardeners appointed by Banks. Bligh had intended to sail by way of Cape Horn, and he tried; but it was too late in the season, and the *Bounty* could make no headway against the westerly gales. So he turned and went round the world the other way. And in all that tremendous outward voyage, 27,086 miles by the log, and a little over ten months, he only touched land three times, in Teneriffe, the Cape of Good Hope and an uninhabited bay in Tasmania.

And then Tahiti. He stayed there nearly six months, apparently waiting for the seedlings to grow. It was too long – long enough for his crew to learn to talk with the Tahitians, to fall in love, to compare the life of the island with life on a naval ship, or life in poverty in an English seaport. Bligh himself was affected. 'I left these happy islanders in much distress,' he wrote in his first dispatch to the Admiralty, 'for the utmost affection, regard and good fellowship was among us during my stay. The King and all the Royal Family were always with me, and their good sense and observations joined with the most engaging dispositions in the world, will ever make them beloved by all who become acquainted with them as friends.'

Bligh's account of their stay is typical of the man: it is well written, detailed, observant, but it is entirely concerned with his own experience and scarcely mentions the experience of his crew. When the time came to sail, three men ran away with their girls and had to be caught; but that had happened to Cook, and it never occurred to Bligh that his crew was under a temptation some of them might not be able to resist.

Nothing might have happened if he had not had one of his tactless rages soon after they sailed. There was a heap of coconuts on deck: he thought it had grown smaller, accused the officers of helping themselves without permission, and made them all bring up on deck all the coconuts in their berths and cabins. It was stupid of him to treat his officers like naughty schoolboys, and perhaps he knew it was; for as soon as his anger cooled, he asked Christian and some of the others to dine with him. Christian was sulkily resentful and he refused; and that trivial episode seems to have made him feel he could not face the months of the voyage home. He meant to desert in one of the boats alone; but during his watch, between four and eight o'clock the next morning, he discovered three or four other men who wanted to go with him, and the idea was born of taking the ship and putting Bligh in the boat. By midday, the most famous of all mutinies was over. Some men were forced into the boat with Bligh: the rest, in that short time, had to make the choice. On one side was the safety of the ship and the prospect of going back to Tahiti; on the other, what looked like certain death in an overloaded 23 foot boat. Yet the crew was equally divided. Twenty-five men stayed on board, including four who said they did not want to; seventeen crowded into the boat.

It was really a small affair. But it has always seemed more than a revolt against an unpopular captain; it has seemed a revolt against all the miseries and indignities of an underdog in eighteenth century England, a revolt in favour of the freedom of the 'happy islanders'. The mutineers went back to Tahiti. Christian and four others went with some Tahitian men and women to hide from retribution in the remote uninhabited island that Carteret had charted and named Pitcairn; and their descendants are still there. But Bligh, on the other hand, proved the value of the discipline they disliked. In his voyage in the boat, 3700 miles to the Dutch settlement in Timor, by nothing but the strength of his will and the prestige of a captain, he kept the men on the ration he reckoned would last the journey: three times a day, one twenty-fifth of a pound of biscuit, which he carefully weighed against a pistol-ball, and a quarter of a pint of water. One man was killed by natives at the start of the journey, but all the others ended it alive, and Bligh survived to serve as one of Nelson's captains at the Battle of Copenhagen twelve years later.

The retribution, when it came, was ghastly. HMS *Pandora*, Captain Edward Edwards, was dispatched from England to capture the mutineers. Edwards found fourteen of them in Tahiti, but he did not find Christian or the ringleaders, because nobody knew where they had gone. After two years on the island, the fourteen men were taken aboard the *Pandora*, handcuffed and shackled on both legs, and locked by Edwards into a box on deck which was eleven feet long. In the Torres Strait on the way back to England the ship struck a rock and foundered. While she was sinking, Edwards refused to let the prisoners out. But at the last moment, his master-at-arms dropped the keys of the shackles into the box and another man unlocked the trap-door which was its only exit. Ten men, still handcuffed, crawled out in time: the other four were drowned. A year later, still in captivity, the ten were landed in England. Bligh was away by then on a second attempt to collect the bread-fruit, in which he succeeded; but on his written evidence, six men were found guilty. Of those, three were pardoned, and the other three were hanged.

*

The traders were never far behind the explorers, and one of the strangest and most distant merchant ventures was functioning within a few years of Cook's last voyage. It was a trade in furs between Canada and China, and it operated from a post on a sound called Nootka on the west coast of Vancouver Island. Nothing much was recorded about it, but the name of Nootka found a place in diplomatic archives; for the Spaniards, annoyed by so much British activity in the Pacific, sent an expedition north and seized the trading post. When the news reached England, a very powerful fleet was assembled, and it made some threatening movements towards the coast of Spain. Spain then agreed to give the place back to the traders, and the Admiralty sent an expedition to see that they did so. It was appropriately commanded by George Vancouver, whose name, when he was a midshipman, had already been given by Cook to that stretch of coast.

Vancouver's report of his voyage included a list of the food and medicine the Admiralty provided in the light of Cook's experience. He was given sauerkraut, portable soup, wheat instead of oatmeal for breakfast, essence of malt and spruce, hops and dried yeast for making beer, flour and seed mustard. The medicines were Dr James's Powders, vitriolic elixir, the 'rob' of lemons and oranges in quantities specified by the ship's surgeon, and a hundredweight of Peruvian bark. With these, Vancouver did his best to follow Cook's precepts, and he succeeded for a long time; but he had a serious outbreak of scurvy on the way home. He also took with him a botanist, and a greenhouse built on the quarterdeck to bring back plants for Kew Gardens; and the Admiralty equipped him with four three-pounder field pieces to defend his camps against hostile natives and 'an excellent assortment of well-prepared fireworks for the amusement and entertainment of such as were peaceably and friendly disposed.' He called at Tahiti, like almost every explorer who could possibly think of a reason, and he let off the fireworks. They filled the Tahitians with a kind of delicious alarm; and luckily, he had no use for the guns.

A secondary aim of the voyage was exploration, for there had been a new outcrop of rumours and theories of a North-West Passage. The traders in Nootka had said there were many deep inlets on the Pacific coast. The Spaniard Juan de Fuca had been into the strait which is still named after him and now forms the border between the United States and Canada, and people persuaded themselves it might lead to the Atlantic. And more mysteriously, a man from Boston named Nicholas Shapely had claimed to have sailed by inland waters from the Atlantic to within a few leagues of the Pacific, and there to have met a Spanish admiral who had come from the other side.

There were always people in England eager to pounce on such claims as proof that the Passage existed, very much as the same kind of people nowadays collect reports about visitors from outer space. Vancouver, as a disciple of Cook, was scornful of all the speculations, which he put down to 'the enthusiasm of modern closet philosophy'. But his orders were to explore all the inlets of the Pacific coast, and the rivers as far as they were navigable by an ocean-going ship; and he spent three summers painstakingly doing so, retreating each winter to the Sandwich Islands. The result was the first complete chart of the American coast from Alaska down to San Francisco.

*

It remains amazing to a modern sailor that people could explore such unknown coasts in such unhandy ships with any hope of not being wrecked in doing it. Shipwreck was still a common enough event, even in charted seas. During eight years of the war against France, from 1793 to 1801, 123 British naval ships were wrecked or foundered, and 10 were accidentally burnt, while only 50 were taken by the enemy (though the British took over 300 warships from the French). Explorers ran the greatest risk at night in a following wind, when breakers might be sighted too late to alter course. That happened to Vancouver's lieutenant William Broughton, who in 1797 was filling in the uncharted coasts of the east Pacific. His ship was the large sloop of war named *Providence* that Bligh had used for his second breadfruit expedition. She ran on a reef at night with all sails set off the coast of Formosa, and she went to pieces. But she had a small schooner as consort, and the whole of her crew sailed back to Macao. Broughton sent most of them home from there in East India Company ships, and he went on with his exploration in the schooner, and surveyed the coasts of Japan, Korea and eastern Russia.

An earlier and stranger shipwreck happened in 1789, just after the penal colony at Botany Bay was founded. A naval ship, the *Guardian*, was on passage from the Cape of Good Hope to Australia with a great many convicts on board, and being short of water, somewhere far to the south, she approached a big iceberg for blocks of ice. She struck a ledge of it under water. They got her off, but her rudder was damaged and she was making water so fast that her captain (it was Edward Riou, who had a distinguished career and was killed at Copenhagen) gave the crew permission to take to the boats. He stayed on board, because there was no room in the boats for all the convicts. By an extraordinary chance, one of the boats was picked up by a French ship a fortnight later: the others were lost. But as for the *Guardian*, she had her hold full of barrels, and most of them were empty; and most of her ballast fell out through the holes in her bottom. So the barrels kept her afloat, though she must have been very unstable. She drifted for two months with sixty-two men on board: and then they sighted the Cape of Good Hope again, and beached her safely.

It was the settlement at Botany Bay that led to the exploration of the Australian coast. But it began in a pleasantly unofficial and amateurish way. Matthew Flinders, who had sailed with Bligh on the second breadfruit trip, was 20 and still a midshipman when he arrived in a naval ship in Botany Bay in 1795. He was youthfully enchanted with the thought of the hundreds of miles of unexplored coast on either side. Cook, of course, had sailed up the east coast and left a general chart of it; but to the west the coast had only been sighted here and there – most notably by the Dutchman Tasman in the 1640s. Nobody encouraged Flinders; but he and a friend called George Bass fitted out a very small boat which they named *Tom Thumb* (she is said to have been eight feet long), and the two of them went exploring unofficially with a boy as crew. They did so well that they were given a whaler with a crew of five convicts, and in that they discovered that Tasmania was an island. In 1798 they went one better; in a sloop with a crew of eight naval volunteers they surveyed the whole of Tasmania and the strait, which they named Bass Strait, that separates it from the mainland. And perhaps nobody else has ever enjoyed exploring more than these two young men, who had a virgin coast entirely to themselves.

But there was nothing amateurish about the charts they made. In 1800, Flinders had to go home, and when his charts were published they came to the notice of Banks, who was still the President of the Royal Society (he held that exalted position for 42 years) and was still the patron of explorers. Banks told the Admiralty the work should continue; and in spite of the war against France the Admiralty commissioned a ship and put Flinders in command of it. During the short uneasy truce of the Peace of Amiens, the French government gave him a passport to explore without being molested.

The ship was an old North Sea collier like Cook's *Endeavour*, and she was called *Investigator*; and the task that Flinders set himself was to sail right round Australia within sight of the breakers, surveying as he went, so that no possible harbours would be left uncharted. He was escorted for part of the voyage by a brig called the *Lady Nelson*, Lieutenant John Murray. (This was in 1801, after the Battle of Cape St Vincent when Nelson was knighted; but it was a meagre compliment, for the brig was very small and a very poor sailer.) Soon after the voyage started, the brig lost company for several days, and in Flinders' journal there were two revealing phrases: 'Our course at night was directed by the fires on the shore (lit by aborigines); and the wind being moderate from the south-westward, it was continued until ten o'clock; after which we stood off and on until daylight . . . Mr Murray not being much accustomed to make free with the land, had kept it barely within sight, and had been much retarded.' Poor Murray: it must have been hard to keep in touch with a senior officer who sailed a square-rigged ship like a dinghy.

Flinders pursued his course round more than half the coast, surveying and sounding every harbour in rowing boats, distributing names, climbing innumerable hills to take bearings, talking as best he could with the naked natives, and landing his scientists – for even he had what he called botanical gentlemen on board: 'A boat was dispatched with the botanical gentlemen to the north side, where the hills rise abruptly and have a romantic appearance.' But on the north coast, hundreds of miles from anywhere, the *Investigator* began to leak, and when the carpenters inspected her they reported she was so rotten she would certainly go to pieces if she grounded or met heavy weather. Very reluctantly, Flinders abandoned his close survey and sailed on, keeping safer distances off shore until he came to Botany Bay again, or rather to Port Jackson. The *Investigator* was condemned as beyond repair, and there was no other suitable ship in Australia; so he took passage to England to ask the Admiralty to give him one. And while he was a passenger, he suffered the disaster he had avoided so long: the ship, like Broughton's, ran on a reef at night with a fresh wind astern. So did another which had sailed in convoy, and a third, a merchantman, disreputably sailed away and left the two crews marooned on a sandbank.

Flinders was a resourceful man. He sailed and rowed six hundred miles back to Port Jackson in one of the ship's boats, and took a relief expedition which rescued the men on the sandbank, and then he borrowed a 26-ton schooner and set off again for England. But his luck ran out. In the Torrse Strait the little schooner also sprang a leak. He crossed most of the Indian Ocean, but had to put in to Mauritius, which was French and was governed by an officious army general. Flinders showed his French passport, but *Investigator* was entered on it as the name of his ship, and the general would not believe he had come from Australia in the small and unseaworthy schooner. So he was imprisoned in the island for six years. When he was released he reached England, but he never sailed again, and only lived long enough to write up the journal of his voyages.

While he was shut up, Trafalgar had been fought and the navy had reached the zenith of its power under sail. And in the same period, the age of grand exploration was merging into the age of meticulous surveying which followed it: an age more mundane, perhaps, but certainly no less useful. In 1795, the Admiralty appointed its first Hydrographer, and began to build up the department which, in the nineteenth century, charted all the coasts and oceans of the world.

CHAPTER 20

The Age of Nelson

In the great wars at the turn of the century, the French army won most of its major battles, but the French navy never won any. This extraordinary contrast was not entirely the navy's fault, it was more the fault of the policies and character of successive governments of France. All through these years, from 1778 to 1815, there were opposite ideas in France and Britain of the proper use of a navy. The French sent fleets to sea with particular objectives, to escort a convoy perhaps, to land an army or support a war on shore; but always with orders to avoid a battle at sea against an equal or stronger force. The British used fleets with the same objectives, but always with orders to seek out enemy fleets and fight them at any odds. So unless a battle was inevitable, the French were always being chased or lurking in harbour, and the British always chasing or blockading the ports of France. This undermined the self-confidence of the French and made the British almost over-confident, so that they had some minor but healthy shocks in the War of 1812, when their opponents were not French but American. The French policy lasted until Napoleon suddenly changed it in a fit of anger just before Trafalgar, with the immediate result that the British succeeded once and for all in what they had expressly tried to do – to annihilate the enemy. The choice of the word was Nelson's.

Two other aspects of government weakened the French at sea. They started, in the American War of Independence, with good admirals, good crews, and ships that all the connoisseurs of the time considered the best in the world. But the navy had been a vocation, not only for the gentry, as it was in England, but also for the aristocracy. So in the revolution, many naval officers were executed or driven into exile, and the ranks were filled by merchant service captains and by sudden promotions: some lieutenants became rear-admirals and warrant officers became captains. The navy which survived was divided in social and political groups that mistrusted each other. That was a serious misfortune: Napoleon was a worse one. The most eager

Bonapartist cannot really deny that Napoleon was absurdly ignorant of the sea and would never admit he was, so that he often gave orders and made plans that were quite impossible to execute. Every French admiral under his rule knew this was so, but none of them dared to say it to his face until a few days before Trafalgar, when the Minister of the Navy, Admiral Decrés, found the courage to speak his mind; and then it was too late.

While the French deteriorated, the British improved. They began with a political division, Whig against Tory, and with quite a number of officers who would not fight against the American colonists; but this dissension vanished in the stress of war. In ships also, they started poorly. After Anson's time, there had been another of the navy's periodic fits of corruption and inefficiency ashore; ships had rotted through neglect, and also, it was said, because there was a shortage of English oak and inferior foreign timber had been used as a substitute. But during the war, things changed for the better, so that the country ended the Napoleonic war with by far the greatest fighting fleet that had ever existed, over 700 ships and 140,000 men.

This may be called the age of Nelson because he grew up in it, although his tremendous influence on the navy was only exercised in the last eight years of his life. When the series of wars began, in 1778, he was 20 and had just received his first command, the brig *Badger*. His first claim to fame was at the Battle of Cape St Vincent in 1797, and he died at the moment in 1805 when all the centuries of war at sea between France and Britain came to their final end. But he was only one, though certainly the brightest, of a galaxy of celebrated admirals – Rodney, Howe and Keppel in the older generation, Samuel and Alexander Hood, Jervis, Duncan, Cornwallis and Collingwood, and in the administration Middleton. It cannot only have been chance that gave the navy so many excellent admirals all at once, but one can only guess the reason. It may have been that success breeds success, and these were the first senior officers who had joined, as small, impressionable boys, when the navy was already aware of its own supremacy, shortly before or after the end of the Seven Years' War. Most of them were rewarded with peerages, which always add confusion to British history. Rodney, Howe, Samuel Hood, Nelson and Collingwood kept their own names, but Alexander Hood is better known as Lord Bridport, Jervis as Lord St Vincent, and Middleton as Lord Barham.

*

In the snail's-pace evolution of fighting at sea, there had been a few innovations, and they need a moment's consideration to set the scene of these wars. Through their different policies, the two fleets by now had evolved quite different ideas of gunnery. The French aimed high to cut the masts and rigging, so that they could escape from their enemies, and they used several kinds of chain and bar shot designed for the purpose. But the British almost always stuck to round shot and aimed at the hull. Given time, this destroyed the enemy's gun batteries and forced him to strike his colours. But it was unlikely to immobilise a ship or damage it beyond repair. Gunfire very seldom sank a wooden warship; the shot holes could be patched and plugged, and the captured ship sailed home for the prize money.

Two inventions in gunnery helped to give the British the upper hand: the flintlock and the carronade. The flintlock, of course, was not new in itself, but its application to naval gunnery was. It replaced the slow match, which had been used to fire guns since their very beginning, and it made naval gunfire much more accurate. The elevation of a gun in a ship depended on choosing the right moment to fire as the ship rolled. A slow match lit the powder with a time-lag which could not be predicted, so that elevation was partly a matter of chance. But a flintlock was almost instantaneous, if it worked at all; and so the gunner could choose his moment exactly. Even at Trafalgar, the French were still using slow matches, while the British merely kept them handy on the gundecks in case a flintlock failed. For this reason, and through much more constant training, the British gunnery by then was far and away more effective than the French – to judge by the casualties it caused, it was at least ten times as efficient – and for this reason, apart from any other, the French and Spanish fleet at Trafalgar had never a chance of victory.

The carronade was a short-barrelled gun of large calibre in proportion to its weight, originally cast in Scotland. The largest, which its inventor called a smasher, weighed less than a normal 12-pounder, but it fired a 68-pound ball; and it could be double-shotted with this tremendous ball and a keg of 500 musket balls on top. It was also used with a lighter hollow shot which broke up when it went through the side of a ship and made havoc with splinters of wood and iron; and one good reason for the hollow shot was that a 68-pound cannon-ball was not the simplest of things to handle in a ship with a lively motion. As an experiment in 1782, an old frigate called the *Rainbow* was entirely equipped with carronades – 68-, 42- and 32-pounders – and was sent to sea to find a French ship to try them on. She searched for four months in the Bay of Biscay before she came up with a large French frigate. It was dead ahead of her, so she fired some ranging shots from the carronades on her forecastle, which were the smallest of them all. Some shot fell on the Frenchman's deck, and the size of them – a 32-pound shot from a forecastle gun – so astonished him that he fired his broadside once to preserve his honour and hastily struck his flag. Of course the carronade had a very short range, so it did not replace the normal long gun; some captains who disliked it said it hardly threw its shot over the side of the ship. But after the early 1780s all ships were equipped with a few of them – a weapon that suited the British, who liked to fight within pistol-shot, but was useless to the French, who preferred to keep their distance.

And there was one other innovation that must be mentioned. This was in signalling. The lack of a system of signals had been a hindrance ever since ships began to fight in fleets – almost from the Armada, and certainly from the first Dutch wars. The uses of flags had slowly been extended; a comprehensive code was brought into use by Howe and Kempenfelt in 1782, and a revised system invented by an Admiral named Sir Home Popham was adopted in 1800. Nowadays, it seems so simple that one can hardly believe the united brains of the navy had taken two hundred years to perfect it. Briefly, there were coloured flags or pennants which indicated numbers from 0 to 9, and also a few important words, such as points of the compass. The same numbered flags were used for letters of the alphabet, from 1 to 26. Each ship had a code book, in which common words and phrases were given numbers, from 26 upwards. If possible, ships used the standard phrases, of which there were several hundreds. If none of those suited, any other message could be composed by using words that were in the code book and spelling those that were not – the letters from A to I needing one flag each, and the others two. The flags were hoisted to the upper yardarms or the mastheads, wherever they could be seen by the ships they were addressed to; and although the standard phrases needed only a very few flags, an unusual message might need an enormous number. Nelson's frigates, watching Cadiz on the days before Trafalgar, hoisted hundreds of flags to tell him what the enemy was doing.

*

In the American War of Independence, two naval encounters between the British and the colonists are worth recording. One was the curious scene on Lake Champlain, when both sides built ships at opposite ends of the lake, and fought miniature naval battles some hundreds of miles away from the sea. And the other was the exploit of John Paul Jones.

Captain Jones is one of those figures in history whose reality is almost hidden by legend. He was a Scotsman born and bred. His name was John Paul, and he only assumed the name of Jones when he was a man of thirty: and he served his apprenticeship like any other boy of his time, and rose to be a captain of Scottish or English merchant ships in his early twenties. But then he left the sea to live in America; and he reappeared a few years later commanding an American naval ship and harassing the British off the American coast. In 1777 he was sent to France as captain of the *Ranger*, sloop of war; and the following spring he sailed from Brest up the Irish Sea, captured four merchantmen and then attacked the village of Whitehaven in Cumberland, where he had served his apprenticeship. One wonders whether a boyhood grudge made him choose this inoffensive and unimportant place, or whether it was simply that he knew the harbour. To say the attack was a surprise would be an understatement – no hostile landing had been attempted on that coast since the Vikings – but it was not a success. He tried to set the ships in the harbour on fire, but the inhabitants put out the fire before any damage was done. Next he encountered the British sloop *Drake*, which was in as somnolent a condition as the village, with a new crew, only half her officers and only twenty cartridges ready for her twenty guns. When Jones was hailed, he answered 'The American Continental ship *Ranger* – it is time to begin'; and he captured the *Drake* after a fight of a little over an hour. He took her back to Brest, where twenty of the 150 men of her crew enlisted in the American service.

This feat caused enormous consternation in Britain, partly because people thought the *Ranger* had come from America – France was not yet at war – and that the whole country might suffer raids from across the Atlantic. His second expedition, in the following year, was even more alarming.

This time, he sailed from Lorient on the west coast of France, round the west of Ireland and the north of Scotland. His ship was a converted French East Indiaman, which he named the *Bonhomme Richard* (a translation of Benjamin Franklin's Poor Richard), and his officers and crew were a mixture of several nationalities – 23 of them who were British deserted in the ship's boats off the coast of Kerry. He started with seven ships in company, but by the time he rounded Scotland they had all given up except two – or sometimes three, for the captain of one of them, the *Alliance*, was said to be a dangerous madman, and he joined or left the flotilla whenever he felt like it. Between them, they captured seventeen merchant ships, and coming south, off Flamborough Head on the Yorkshire coast, they fell in with a Baltic convoy escorted by the frigate *Serapis* and an armed ship the *Countess of Scarborough*. What followed, in full view of crowds of spectators ashore, was one of the fiercest sea fights in history. In the first broadside, two of the lower deck guns burst in the *Bonhomme Richard*, and the rest were abandoned. That left her much weaker than the *Serapis* in armament; she was hit many times between wind and water and her upper deck guns were gradually disabled. But far from submitting, Captain Jones gave orders to grapple. The jibboom of the *Serapis* caught in the mizzen shrouds of the *Bonhomme Richard*, and Jones lashed it fast himself; it broke, but an anchor caught and held, and the ships lay side by side, bow to stern, with the muzzles of the guns touching. The *Serapis* went on firing her lower deck 18-pounders: they smashed the American's hull to splinters but did no harm to her crew, who had left the lower deck and were fighting with muskets and hand-grenades up above. Both ships were on fire in several places and the *Bonhomme Richard* was certainly going to sink: but at this crucial moment an American seaman climbed out on her main yard, which overhung the deck of the *Serapis*, and dropped a hand-grenade down the main hatch into the gun-room. It exploded the cartridges that were stored there and killed or put out of action nearly forty men. The *Alliance* with her mad captain appeared at this moment and fired a broadside, but apparently at the *Bonhomme Richard*, not at the *Serapis*. There was a call for quarter from the American but it came from a junior officer and the captain put an end to it by hitting him on the head with a pistol. Then somebody released the British prisoners in the hold, who had been taken from merchant ships: they swarmed up on deck and might have taken possession, but Jones firmly told them to man the pumps, and such was his authority or their own bemusement that they did so.

The fight had started after seven o'clock in the evening. Three hours later, when it was almost pitch dark, both crews had fought to a standstill, both ships were burning, the *Bonhomme Richard* was sinking and the main-mast of the *Serapis* was on the point of falling. Both crews had tried to board the other, but neither had succeeded. It had come down to a battle of wills between the captains: somebody had to surrender, or both would go down in the night. And this battle was won by Jones. The *Serapis* struck her flag, just as the mast went overboard. The Americans took possession of her before their own ship sank and succeeded in sailing her to Holland.

John Paul Jones was certainly a fighter of astonishing determination, and there is no knowing what he might have done if he had ever had a proper ship or crew. But it seems a pity that history or romance should have made him too much of a hero. What he did achieve, after all, was no more than hundreds of British captains were achieving all the time off the hostile coasts of France or America. His distinction was that he was the only man, except a few French privateers, who dared to make an attack off the coast of Britain. He gave the British a fright out of all proportion to his strength. That rightly delighted the Americans, and Congress awarded him a gold medal; but he never did anything else worth mentioning and spent most of the rest of his life in France and the Russian navy. His importance in history is that he showed what the French could quite easily have done, with their powerful navy, if they had had the will and the daring to try. But they never followed his example.

*

The naval war began in earnest in 1778, when France and Spain decided to take their revenge on Britain by supporting the colonists. And for a while the two sides were more evenly matched than they had been for a century. Several times, when the British succeeded in bringing the French to a battle, the result was indecisive and only led to arguments at home. It was as if the navy had drifted back to the wars of half a century before. In fact, after the Battle of Chesapeake Bay, which was fought off the coast of Virginia in 1781, the argument was exactly the same as it had been after Mathews' battle off Toulon in 1745. On both occasions, the British commander-in-chief went into battle flying the signal for line ahead, and then hoisted the signal 'Bear down and engage the enemy' without hauling down the formation signal. Again, captains were left to scratch their heads over which of these orders they should obey; and again, they kept in line and did not make any decisive attack because the Admiralty's Fighting Instructions still gave precedence to the formation signal.

But this feeble battle had momentous results. The French fleet had landed reinforcements for Washington, and now by the failure of the British attack it was left in command of Chesapeake Bay itself and the rest of the coast of Virginia: Cornwallis, besieged in Yorktown, was forced to capitulate, and the independence of America was as good as won. And in naval terms, it had another consequence. The rear-admiral was Samuel Hood, who Nelson once said was the greatest sea-officer he ever knew; and the

Nelson boarding a captured ship, 1777, by R. Westall

Sailors carousing, 1817, by Ibbetson
Overleaf. The Mutiny on the *Bounty*

strict adherence to the line ahead frustrated Hood from getting into battle, and left him extremely critical of his commander-in-chief, and of the ancient conventions.

And in the following year at the Battle of the Saints (so called from the small islands off which it was fought in the Caribbean) a break was made at last from the rigid formality. It was only chance that gave the opportunity. The British fleet of 36 ships was commanded by Rodney, and Hood was again rear-admiral; the French had a fleet of 33 commanded by Admiral de Grasse. These great fleets had been in sight of each other, on and off, for several days in calms and variable breezes. But one morning at dawn, with a little more wind, Rodney was in a position from which, if he sailed close hauled, he might get to windward of de Grasse. De Grasse saw what he was trying to do, and formed his own line close hauled on the other tack. So the two fleets were on converging courses, and the first to reach the point of intersection would have the weather gage.

The French got there first. The ships of the British van had to bear away, so that the fleets were passing each other, at very short range, both in line ahead but in opposite directions, and blazing away at each other as they passed. It looked as though another formal battle was going to end with both fleets damaged but neither victorious.

But then the wind shifted abruptly from west to south-west. The French were taken aback, and the British now had the wind on the starboard quarter. Gaps appeared in the French line as ships lost their steerage way. Rodney sailed through one of the gaps, followed by six other ships. But Hood did not slavishly follow, he led his rear division through a gap of his own; and one other ship, ahead of the flagship, went through a gap all alone. As they went through, all of them fired both broadsides at the bows and sterns of the nearest French ships, which could not manœuvre to bring their own guns to bear. In confusion, the French bore away and retreated down-wind, but five of them were taken, including the 102-gun flagship *Ville de Paris*, and de Grasse himself was made a prisoner.

The line ahead remained the normal battle formation all through the days of sail, and indeed it lasted for different reasons well into the age of steam. But at the Saints a considerable dent was made in its sacred reputation. Afterwards, to cut the enemy line was always an accepted and respectable manœuvre. At the Saints, the British ships cut through to the windward side, and so left the French a chance to escape down-wind. But a later refinement was to sacrifice the advantage of the weather gage and cut through the enemy line down-wind, and then come up on the leeward side of the enemy ships so that they could not escape. And this lee position sometimes had a great advantage in a stiff breeze: if the sea was not too heavy when ships were sharply heeled, the lower deck gunports could be opened on the windward side, but on the lee side they were below the waterline.

Nobody had a chance to try this in the American war, because the battle fleets never met again. But when war began against Revolutionary France, Lord Howe brought it off, at least in part, at the battle which came to be known, for want of a better name, as the Glorious First of June. (Naval battles had always taken their names from the nearest point of land, but this was fought five hundred miles out in the Atlantic.)

What happened on that first of June, in 1794, was the culmination of a manœuvre that had been going on since 28th May, when the fleets came in sight of each other. The French were escorting an important convoy, and had either to fight or to draw the British away from it. Howe, of course, was determined to get them into a position where he could attack. This was the kind of sparring which called for all the qualities of a good admiral: ship-handling, seamanship in all its aspects, weather forecasting, the shrewdness to foresee what the enemy admiral would do, and the skill to control a fleet within the limitations of the signal book. Howe scarcely left his quarter-deck for five days and nights, and did not rest at all except in a chair; and he was a man of 68. At dawn on the first, the enemy fleet was six miles away, on the lee bow of the British, and he knew he would get them that day. Soon after seven, he signalled his intentions, and then he signalled the entire fleet to heave to and have breakfast, which also no doubt was an act of good admiralship.

His intention was that each ship should cut through the enemy line, astern of its opposite number, and then fight from the leeward side. And he had prophesied that for every ship that did so he would capture or destroy an enemy. But it was not a thing that a captain could be ordered to do, because it might be impossible, there might simply not be room between the bowsprit of one enemy ship and the stern of the next ahead. So his order allowed each captain, if he could not break through, to 'act as circumstances require'. When it came to the point, only seven ships cut through; the rest, for one reason or another, came to the wind and fought from the windward side; but one French ship was sunk and six were taken, so his prophecy was fulfilled. The shift of wind at the Saints had been the start of an evolution in tactics that continued until Trafalgar.

266

*

Great battles were milestones of naval history, but they were rare events: there were less than a dozen in these 20 years of war. Large numbers of men took part in them, upwards of ten thousand on each side. But each navy by then numbered over a hundred thousand. So a boy who joined the navy, either as an officer or a seaman, was not very likely ever to see the heroic sight of two fleets in action, or hear the formidable roar of two or three thousand guns. The ordinary business of the navy was made up of innumerable uneventful cruises, sightings of distant sails that were lost again, and occasional encounters with one or two ships a side, exciting at the time, especially for the chance of a profitable prize, but not important enough to find a place in any but the most detailed book of history. The sea was a much more constant danger than the enemy, and disease was much more dangerous than either. In the navy, even after the time of Captain Cook and even at the height of war, at least ten times more men died of disease than were killed in battle. Monotony and boredom were the common experience.

It is easy enough to describe a battle of two hundred years ago: there are dispatches, logs, letters and reports, and a legitimate degree of imagination fills the gaps. But it is more difficult now to describe the life of seamen with impartiality: the standards of the eighteenth and twentieth centuries are so widely different, and between them the sentimental and moral judgments of the nineteenth century have clouded the picture. Very few seamen of the time wrote letters or reminiscences of their daily life, because most of them were scarcely literate and none of them had much incentive or opportunity. Not one of them wrote a really informative journal. So, without much direct evidence, two contrary traditions have grown up: at one extreme, the Jolly Jack Tar, brave, patriotic and devil-may-care, and at the other the pitiable victim of a cruel system, press-ganged into a life of misery and oppressed by tyrannical officers. The first had its origin in Victorian romance, and the second in more recent ideas of social justice. Both of them are exaggerations.

It is true that life at sea was still unimaginably hard by modern standards. For the seamen in the last decades of the eighteenth century, nothing had changed since the time of Samuel Pepys – not even their pay, which was still 19 shillings a month for the ordinary seaman and 24 shillings for the able seaman, with deductions of fourpence for the chaplain, twopence for the surgeon and sixpence for the Chatham Chest, which was a pension fund founded by Francis Drake. They still lived in crowded squalor, their hammocks slung fourteen inches apart in the gloom of the lower gundeck. They still ate the same salt meat and weevilly biscuit, and suffered the same ruthless punishments when they got drunk or otherwise misbehaved. And they were still imprisoned in their ships, without shore leave, for as many years as the ships' commissions lasted, and then were discharged ashore to fend for themselves. Yet given half a chance, they still had pride in their ship and their calling.

Some writers seem to enjoy describing the horrors of naval life. But the fact is, of course, that a poor man in the eighteenth century was far more accustomed to hardship and oppression than any normal person in a civilised country now. Seamen did not complain about their living conditions, or in general about their food: they regarded them simply as part of the sailor's life, like the hazard of working aloft, or the endless exposure to the weather. And in fact, nothing much could be done about them. A ship of a hundred guns had to carry something like eight hundred men, not to sail her (eighty men could have done that) but to fight her. And her decks had to be fitted so that they could be cleared from end to end within a few minutes. So there was no room for comfort. And as for the food, while salt was the only known preservative, there was very little scope for innovation.

Nor did seamen object to the punishments, if they were fairly administered; they knew there were men in every crew, drunks and thieves in particular, who needed to be kept in order. And indeed the ceremonial floggings with the cat which were the commonest punishment were probably not so drastic as they appear to us now. Before anaesthetics, men were familiar with pain and were evidently much less apprehensive of it. Few people now would face with equanimity the prospect of having a leg cut off with an ordinary saw and a knife, but they certainly did so then. Presumably an operation like that, or the lash of the cat, were as painful then as they would be now. But the fear of pain has grown since science made it a rarer experience, and perhaps the fear of it may be as bad as the pain itself. The occasional sentences of hundreds of lashes, one must add, were a different matter; they were certainly a barbarous punishment which killed a man or seriously maimed him; but they were only awarded by court-martial, not by the whim of an individual captain.

The press-gang was the most detested institution. It was only used in time of war when the navy had to expand, and it was really only a crude

·form of the conscription every citizen has always been subject to. It was cruel because it was arbitrary, and because it seized men and marched them off to the ships without a chance to say goodbye to their families or lovers. Perhaps its worst acts were taking men off merchant ships in sight of home after voyages lasting years. But it was the moment of losing freedom that hurt; after that, the captives simply had to resign themselves to what had happened and make the best of it, and they usually succeeded. There was not much distinction in a ship between the pressed men and the volunteers. Any of them might dream of desertion, but failing that, they all shook down together to form a close-knit community, cut off from the rest of the world and united for its own survival.

But of course there was a vast distinction between the seamen and the officers, especially the senior officers. Admirals' and captains' cabins were not luxurious but they were elegant, and within them these distant and dignified people succeeded most of the time in living the comfortable life of a gentle-man of the age. But there is no evidence at all that seamen resented the difference in privilege. It was only a reflection of the same distinction ashore. Men were either born gentlemen or they were not, and in Britain at this date they still accepted their station in life as the will of God. Indeed, seamen felt they had a right to be commanded by gentlemen, and usually (with Cook again as an exception) they seem to have felt acutely that they and their ship lost dignity under what was called a tarpaulin captain, one who had worked his way up from humble birth or from the lower deck.

A senior officer in fact was a very different man from his seaman – 'the people', as he would often call them. Most seamen were young: the average age was not much over twenty. Most of them had very little education, and a good many had none at all. As yet, there were no training ships for them: they joined their first ship knowing nothing, and had to learn at sea. But the captain of a line-of-battle ship was a generation older, a man of around forty, a professional who had been at sea since he was a small boy. He came from a squire's family, used to some degree of power and responsi-bility; and he had been educated at home and on board his first ship, so that he could at least write a coherent dispatch and navigate by the sun and stars, and understand the strategy and tactics of the sea. And at any time of crisis, the lives of all the men on board were in his hands.

It was the primitive methods of manning a ship that were the basic cause of the harshness of the discipline a naval captain wielded. Every time a ship was commissioned in wartime, she had to start with a crew who were strangers to each other, always including some men who had never been to sea and some convicted of breaking the law ashore. The captain, or a recruiting officer, began by putting up posters, patriotically worded, calling for volunteers. With luck, he collected most of his petty officers that way, and perhaps half as many seamen as he needed. The rest had to come from the press-gangs, and from the magistrates who sentenced minor offenders, and from the quotas of men demanded by Parliament from counties and boroughs – who also, of course, were men the counties and boroughs were glad to be rid of, the vagrants, beggars, debtors, brawlers and drunks. With this mixed mob of men, he had to put to sea, and might have to join the fleet or even go into action. So they had to be turned into seamen in the shortest possible time. Most of the teaching was done by the petty officers, and few of them had more subtle techniques than threats and curses, and a rope's end or a rattan cane. When the ship settled down, its happiness and efficiency depended on the character of the captain. Seamen liked a captain who was strict and efficient but fair. If he was unfair, he awarded punishments for trivial offences; but if he was lazy and too easy-going it could be worse, because petty tyrannies could flourish among the lieutenants, midshipmen and warrant officers.

There was one thing all captains certainly had in common: they were intensely proud of the navy. It was not only their profession and life, but also for a large proportion it was a family tradition: they were descendants of men who had captained Elizabethan privateers and organised the medieval pirates. Most often, they managed to instil the same pride in their seamen. But then, when the ship was due for a major refit, the crew was paid off and vanished ashore, and the whole process had to begin again.

*

This ancient system had many weaknesses; and one of them was that if a man or a crew had a genuine grievance, they had no way of expressing it. In theory, they could appeal against an unfair or cruel or inefficient captain to the commander-in-chief. But they had nobody to advise them, and they were usually too inarticulate to make a clear case of what they wanted to say; so they were likely to end in more trouble than when they started. Consequently, the navy itself – the Admiralty and the senior officers – had grown out of touch with its own seamen. It simply did not know they had any corporate opinion. And it was shocked, astonished and grieved in 1797, in the middle of the war against France, when quite suddenly the Channel fleet at Spithead refused to put to sea.

This episode gives the only reliable clue to what the eighteenth-century seamen thought of naval life. Of course, to refuse to sail was mutiny, and mutiny was a capital offence; and the requests they risked their lives for are unexpected and pathetic.

The affair was so peaceful and so well organised that it could only technically be called a mutiny. It was more like a strike. It was surprisingly successful, and nobody ever discovered who started it. Die-hards throughout the country put it down to Irish rebels or French gold, but there was no evidence at all of outside influence. What seems to have happened is that the vigorous recruiting during the years of war had brought in a few men who were not the seamen of tradition, but were educated men who had failed in other professions and run into debt, or fallen foul of the magistrates. For men like that, the bounty that was offered to volunteers was sometimes the only possible source of ready money, and the only hope of avoiding a debtor's prison; and so among the seamen in the fleet there were a few ex-lawyers and schoolmasters who could express the feelings of the rest.

They expressed them first in letters to Lord Howe, who was the nominal commander-in-chief of the Channel Fleet. He had been kept in that appointment because he was a heroic figure and popular on the lower deck (they called him Black Jack); but he was 71 and was taking the waters at Bath for his gout, while Lord Bridport was in active command. Howe sent the letters on to Lord Spencer, First Lord of the Admiralty, who was a humane and intelligent man but not a seaman. But nobody answered the letters, because nobody could believe the writers spoke for the fleet as a whole.

Next they wrote to the Lords of the Admiralty and to Members of Parliament. But still nothing happened. And it was because they could not even get an acknowledgment of their requests that the strike was organised. Each ship appointed two delegates to a committee, which met in Lord Howe's cabin and took over command of the fleet.

The first and most important grievance, which the letters placed apart from the rest, was that the pay was too low. The army had recently had an increase, and everything was more expensive than it had been when the rates of pay were fixed, a hundred and twenty years before. They asked for a shilling a day for able-seamen, an increase of 25 per cent. Then came five numbered requests:

1. That provisions should be issued at sixteen ounces to the pound. It may have been news to the Lords of the Admiralty, and it certainly was to

the public, that when provisions were issued to a ship they were reckoned at sixteen ounces to a pound, but when the purser issued them to the men fourteen ounces were taken to be a pound. At some time in the past, the difference had been supposed to allow for shrinkage, but it had become a purser's perquisite.

2. That when a ship was in port, vegetables should be allowed and flour should not be issued instead of meat.

3. That their lordships should seriously look into the state of the sick on board, that they might be better attended and the special necessaries allowed for them should not be embezzled.

4. 'That your lordships will be so kind as to look into this affair, which is nowise unreasonable; . . . that we may in somewise have grant and opportunity to taste the sweets of liberty on shore, when in any harbour, and when we have completed the duty of our ship . . . which is a natural request, and congenial to the heart of man.'

5. That when a man was wounded in action, his pay should continue until he was cured and discharged.

Finally, there was another request, unnumbered: 'If any ship has any real grievances to complain of, we hope your lordships will readily redress them, as far as in your power, to prevent disturbances.' And this, it transpired, meant that if a crew complained about an officer, he should be moved to another ship.

These were all the aims of the mutiny. The letters promised no more grievances would be added – 'We know when to cease to ask, as well as to begin.' For these things the seamen's leaders risked their lives. Having taken the risk, they might just as well have included anything else they felt strongly about, the things that seem so oppressive nowadays. But they did not; on the contrary, the letters were full of expressions of loyalty and pride in the naval service. A cynic might say that was only self-defence; but one has to conclude that every other aspect of naval life was accepted by the seamen of the time.

It was a challenge that very few senior officers had ever dreamed of. But when they came to realise it was not a dream, they behaved on the whole with common sense and charity. They had the usual instinct of men in authority not to surrender. But to balance that, they seem also to have had a feeling of the navy's unity, a wish to protect the seamen against the exaggerated reactions of landsmen. In the result, the Admiralty made concessions bit by bit. The pay claim was reasonable; the pursers' licensed swindle and the surgeons' embezzlements deserved to be ended; and it was a strange injustice that a man's pay was cut off if he was wounded. But shore leave had always scared the naval authorities for fear of mass desertion; and clearly, the Admiralty could not possibly promise to remove any officer a crew complained about.

So the negotiations dragged on for a month; and on board the ships at their moorings off Portsmouth, the committee of delegates kept a discipline as strict as ever. Hangmen's ropes were rove at the yardarms, and people ashore in a kind of delightful horror expected to see captains swinging from them; but in fact they were put there by the delegates to remind the crews that they were still subject to the articles of war. A few men were flogged for getting drunk. Nobody deserted, or no more than usual, although it was a golden opportunity. There were only two notable outbreaks of violence, both caused by a senior officer who lost his temper or misunderstood the temper of the fleet. Some unpopular officers were sent ashore with their baggage, but a majority stayed on board with nothing to do, and the popular ones were treated with extra respect and even affection.

The committee of delegates, negotiating with the Board of Admiralty itself, was extremely suspicious of promises, and in the end Lord Howe was sent down to Portsmouth, in spite of his gout, with power to make a settlement. It was hard on Lord Bridport, who had handled the whole affair with tact. But Howe's reputation was a help. He met the delegates and visited every ship to talk to the crew, and he managed to persuade the seamen they had won every possible concession. The Admiralty would not commit itself to shore leave as a right, and it would not allow a crew any say in appointing officers. But the pay was agreed and the other requests were rather vaguely granted; and the officers who had been put ashore were not sent back to their ships. Among them were three of the sixteen captains whose ships had mutinied. Howe brought with him the King's pardon for the mutineers, and when everything was settled he invited all the delegates to dine with him and his wife, which was certainly a gesture no admiral had ever made before. Portsmouth had a day of celebration.

For a moment it seemed as if the navy was itself again, and that nothing but good had come of the whole affair. But its sequel was much less fortunate. Just as the Spithead mutiny was coming to an end, the fleet at the Nore began another. It had no declared object except to support the fleet at Spithead, and within a couple of days its leaders learned that the Spithead affair was settled and their support was unnecessary. Common-sense would have ended their mutiny straight away; but having made the effort to start, they could not bring themselves to stop. So they embarked on a course that was certain to end in failure and disaster. To justify themselves in carrying on, they had to make new requests: and it was perfectly certain that the Admiralty, having pardoned one mutiny and granted one set of demands, could not possibly contemplate a series of mutinies with a series of new demands. To have led a mutiny and ended by dining with the commander-in-chief was a great achievement all round, but it was the sort of thing that could not happen twice.

And throughout, the mutiny at the Nore was a clumsy copy of what had been done at Spithead. The anonymous men at Spithead had always seemed loyal, respectful and reasonable. But the letters and proclamations at the Nore were pompous and truculent. And they were not anonymous. The delegates chose Richard Parker as president, a literate but sometimes unbalanced man who had once been degraded from the rank of midshipman and then had left the service, but had rejoined for the sake of a bounty of £25. Parker presumably wrote the letters, and he signed them, which in itself was a tactical mistake.

Of the eight demands he made, the first was simply that the Spithead concessions should also apply at the Nore. This went without saying; the concessions applied to the navy as a whole, and nobody could really have been so foolish as to doubt it. Two more of the demands repeated those the Spithead men had failed to win, the right to shore leave and the right to reject individual officers. Two were concerned with back pay. The most notable new ones were for more equal shares of prize money, and for pardons for men who had deserted and then rejoined the service. The last was for unspecified changes in the Articles of War.

Looking back at this deeply emotional episode, one longs to have been there, to have had a chance to try to tell Parker he could not possibly win, to try to persuade the delegates not to put their heads in nooses, but to call it all off while they could. The Admiralty promptly answered the demands: some had already been granted, some could not and would not be granted; the mutineers would be pardoned if they went back to work. But Parker refused repeated offers of pardon. For a while, he seemed to flatter himself he could make the Admiralty change its mind by threats. Under his rule, the mutineers forced other unwilling crews to join them. They alarmed the people of Sheerness by marching about the town with flags and bands, and later they tried to blockade London by stopping all the shipping in the river. All this only lost them sympathy and set everyone against them. For quite a long time, Parker and the delegates must have known they had lost, but did not dare admit it to the men who had elected them. At last, it simply became a question of whether they could escape. There was grandiose talk of taking the fleet to Holland. But by then the Admiralty had sunk or removed the buoys and beacons in the estuary, and only a local pilot with luck could have taken the ships to sea. And by then also, the mutiny was breaking up. Some ships left the fleet, and were fired on as they went. On others, there were fights between different factions. One by one they surrendered.

Parker was hanged, of course, and he died with dignity, admitting his trial was fair and his sentence just. So were some of the other delegates. One killed himself, some were imprisoned, and some suffered the dreadful penalty of flogging round the fleet. Yet three months later, four of the major ships that had mutinied fought as well as ever at the Battle of Camperdown.

*

That was a mutiny that never should have happened; it could not have ended in any other way, and it only tended to undermine the mutual respect that had started at Spithead. And it was not the last. Within the next year, there were several more attempts in individual ships, which were ruthlessly put down.

Yet in the long run, they seem to have done some good. The basic grievance, at the bottom of all the others, had probably been the feeling of impotence and frustration at having nobody in authority who would listen. Spithead had made the authorities listen, and they were never quite so deaf again. And the attitude of officers had been given a thorough shaking. All the evidence is that cruel or inefficient or otherwise unpopular officers, for many generations past, had been a fairly small minority. Probably the three out of sixteen captains sent ashore at Spithead was a representative proportion. Henceforth, at least until the end of the Napoleonic War, the proportion grew smaller. In general, officers felt that British seamen ought not to have been pushed so far as to mutiny, and they were more alert in future to each other's failings. An officer's lower deck reputation was pretty generally known, and by the time of Trafalgar, eight years later, not one of the active commanders-in-chief would have tolerated oppression that was beyond the bounds of naval law and custom.

Within those eight years, of course, there was another influence:

Nelson's. When the mutinies happened, Nelson was on the verge of his short term of high command. He was blockading Cadiz, and had just been promoted rear-admiral. The Battle of Cape St Vincent had been won two months earlier, and it was there, when he boarded two enemy ships, that he first became a hero in the eyes of every seaman. Perhaps the navy needed a hero at that moment, a man to personify the pride which held it together in spite of everything, and made it a better navy than any other. Nelson perfectly satisfied that need: the kindest of men, and the most successful of admirals. In his ships, and in his fleets when he was commander-in-chief, men were unquestionably proud and happy. By the time he died, every officer and seaman had seen it proved that kindness and good discipline could go together, and that when they did the navy was unbeatable.

*

Nelson's early career was very much like any other officer's. As the son of a country parson, he came from the lower edge of the narrow stratum of society that ran the navy. But when he decided to go to sea, at the age of 11, it was easily arranged, because his uncle, Maurice Suckling, was a naval captain. In 1770, while Cook was away on his first expedition, Captain Suckling took Nelson as a servant aboard his ship which was moored in the Medway. There he learned to sail a boat; it was the same place where Drake had learned when he was a boy, and it is still a good place to learn, with strong tidal streams and extensive mudbanks as teachers. At 13, he was sent to the West Indies in a merchant ship to give him more experience; 'If I did not improve my education,' he wrote long afterwards, 'I returned a practical seaman.' And at 15, when he was a midshipman, he volunteered for an exploring expedition, not to the glamour of the South Sea, but to the arctic ice, which still held its fascination for the British. It was on that voyage that he attacked a polar bear, a story made famous by a later romantic painting which showed him all alone, hitting the animal with the butt of a musket. In the original story, told by his captain, it was not such a close encounter, but it was perhaps an early example of a physical courage that often went beyond the mundane limits of common sense.

Nelson showed the qualities of a good officer from the very beginning: he was acting lieutenant at 17, and at 20 he was promoted captain, first of the *Badger* brig and then of the frigate *Hinchingbrooke*, 32 guns – a ship with a crew of over 200 men. That was in the West Indies again, in the final stages of the War of Independence. He was tremendously active, mostly in solitary voyages that took him up to New York and Boston and down to the coast of South America. But his most notable exploit in that period was ashore, an expedition up the River San Juan in Nicaragua, the river that Drake had hopelessly planned to attack in the last few weeks of his life. It was only a partial success. Some forts were captured, but three-quarters of his crew died of tropical diseases, and he himself was sent home as an invalid.

And from the beginning also, he had begun to show the genius for making friends which was his most endearing distinction and the foundation of his eminence. Many much older men, who were his senior officers on his early voyages, remained his devoted friends for the rest of his life, or theirs. As for the seamen, after his next commission his entire ship's company volunteered to serve with him again; and that, to say the least, was a remarkable event in an era when so many seamen only longed for their freedom.

But then that war ended. Service in peacetime did not suit him well. In the Indies, there were too many social functions where he was gauche and ill at ease. And he made himself unpopular among the colonists by being too conscientious. By winning their independence, the Americans had become foreigners, and foreigners were forbidden by law to trade with the colonies. The colonists wanted their trade, and the local governors and customs officials were happy to look the other way. But Nelson would not. The law was the law, good or bad, and his duty was to enforce it; and it was simply not in his nature to compromise with any naval duty. So he harassed the American traders, and made himself unwelcome in most of the British islands.

It was during that unhappy peacetime service, when he was 27, that he married Fanny Nisbet, a widow a year or two older than he was. It was not a romantic affair. There were not many marriageable English women in the Indies, and perhaps he was more attracted by the idea of being married than he was by his bride herself. His letters to her spoke only of respect, not love – quite different from the passionate letters he wrote to Emma Hamilton when he was older. But he brought her home to Norfolk, and for five years he lived as the minor country gentleman he had been born. It was pleasant but after a while it bored him, and he pestered the Admiralty for another ship.

He did not get one until 1793, when he was 34; but then it was a ship worth waiting for, the *Agamemnon*, 64 guns, which always remained his favourite among all the ships he commanded. A month after his appointment, war with France began again. And he began twelve years of constant action, and growing influence, success and fame.

*

In spite of the Glorious First of June, the years from 1793 to 1797 were un-happy for the navy. It always beat the French whenever it found them at sea, but it seldom did; and the advance of French armies slowly drove it out of all possible bases in the Mediterranean. Nelson and the *Agamemnon* were in the thick of it, first under Lord Hood as commander-in-chief, although he was nearly 70, and then under Sir John Jervis. The navy captured the islands of Corsica and Elba; and Nelson, who always liked actions ashore, was besieg-ing the citadel of Calvi in Corsica when he was blinded in his right eye by gravel thrown up by a cannon shot – the first of his wounds. But in 1795, Spain made a treaty with France and then declared war on Britain. The hostility of Spanish ports and the advance of Napoleon through Italy forced the navy to abandon its presence in the Mediterranean and retreat to Gibraltar. Nelson's final duty as the last man out was to bring off British troops and stores from Bastia in Corsica and then from Porto Ferraio in Elba.

Four years of his energetic sailing had worn out the *Agamemnon*, and he was promoted commodore and transferred to a ship named the *Captain*; and in the *Captain* in the winter of 1797 he rejoined Jervis off Cape St Vincent, the strategic headland in the south of Portugal where Prince Henry the Navigator had founded his school and English fleets ever since Drake had lain in wait for their enemies. There in February, Jervis with 15 ships of the line sighted a Spanish fleet which outnumbered him almost two to one and included the monstrous *Santisima Trinidad*, 132 guns, the largest man-of-war in the world.

The Spaniards had ventured out of their ports to escort a convoy. They had been driven far out into the Atlantic by easterly winds, and were beating back for the land without any strict formation. Jervis led his line close-hauled through a gap in their fleet, and then came about on the opposite tack to approach them from the lee. By all the rules, his ships were obliged to follow him and tack where he had tacked to preserve the line ahead. But Nelson in the *Captain* was third from the rear and he saw what Jervis could not see: that the rearmost ships, if they followed his course, would fall astern of the Spaniards and arrive too late for action. He wore out of line, at first away from the enemy, and then came round and headed straight for the Spanish van alone. He was soon supported by other captains, including Collingwood and Troubridge who were both old friends of his. But before they arrived the *Captain* took on seven enemy ships in succession. When she lost her sails and rigging and was losing her steerage way, he told the captain to put the helm a-starboard and lay her alongside the nearest enemy. In a madly un-orthodox act for a commodore, he led the boarding-party and forced the Spaniard to surrender. Another ship, a first-rate of 100 guns, was aboard her on the other side. He jumped across into her main chains and she sur-rendered too: on her quarter-deck he received the swords of the captain and his officers, 'which as I received,' he wrote in his account, 'I gave to William Fearney, one of my bargemen, who placed them, with the greatest sang-froid, under his arm.' And the same account ended: 'There is a saying in the fleet too flattering for me to omit telling – viz., "Nelson's Patent Bridge for boarding First-rates", alluding to my passing over an Enemy's 80-gun ship.'

This action was the first that made him a hero in the navy's eyes. Officers were amazed at his audacity in leaving the line without orders: nobody had ever done it before, it looked at first like cowardice and he certainly risked his reputation and career. But it succeeded, and Jervis gave honour where it was due. As for the seamen, a commodore who led a boarding-party was just the kind of officer they liked, and the Patent Bridge delighted everyone.

Howe had decisively beaten the French at the First of June, Jervis (who became Lord St Vincent) had decisively beaten the Spaniards, and later that year Admiral Duncan, with the ships that had lately mutinied, decisively beat the Dutch at Camperdown, off the coast of Holland. At sea, Britain was in command. But on land, French domination was spreading wider. By 1798, Napoleon believed and said that Europe was too small to provide enough glory for him: he must seek it in the east. Soon France's Mediter-ranean ports were busy with preparations, and the news reached England that something big was coming. The only way to find out what it was was to make a foray into the sea the British had had to abandon.

Nelson was chosen to lead it. It was a choice made on merit, and it caused some jealousy at the time; he was only 39, and had only just been appointed rear-admiral. And he had hardly recovered from losing his arm in an ill-conceived attack on the island of Teneriffe, where again, in spite of his rank, he had not been able to resist the physical danger that always excited him. But in May 1798 he passed through the Straits of Gibraltar in the *Vanguard* (there had been *Vanguards* in the navy since the Armada), with two other ships of the line and two frigates in company, into the totally hostile Mediterranean. For the first time, on this voyage, his wits were to be matched against Napoleon's.

On this voyage also, his first in independent command of a fleet, naval history has to take account of Nelson's other quality, beyond his courage and his tactical skill: the way men loved him. Nobody perhaps at second hand has ever quite defined the reason for it. In letters that other men wrote, one can find his innumerable acts of thoughtfulness and kindness, great and small; one can see that however busy he was, tired, weighed down by responsibility, worry and ill-health, he never neglected old friendships or failed by some instinctive touch to make new ones. Yet one cannot hope to recall the irresistible charm his presence certainly had; one can only imagine it from the way that hard-bitten sailors of every rank took pens and paper and more or less laboriously wrote about their love of him – love, not respect or admiration, was the word that all of them used – and from the amazing outburst of grief throughout the navy when he died. 'Men adored him,' as the sailor wrote at Trafalgar, 'and in fighting under him, every man thought himself sure of success.' Historically, that was the salient fact: no commander was ever more loved, and love bred confidence. Fleets under Nelson's command had a loyalty and coherence no other had ever equalled.

It happened in the Mediterranean. When another ten captains were sent to join him – men Lord St Vincent described as 'some choice fellows' – Nelson first used a phrase that became well known to describe himself and them, a 'band of brothers'. He made them so by his mixture of authority and friendship, by telling them exactly what he planned to do, and by show-ing them he had perfect confidence in them to use their own discretion in doing it. The same confidence, reinforced by constant battle practice, spread down through all ranks in the fleet.

He was thwarted at first because he lost touch with his frigates. The *Vanguard* was dismasted in a sudden storm and only saved from being wrecked by Captain Ball of the *Orion*, who took her in tow within sight of the breakers on a lee shore. The frigate captains, separated by the storm, believed she was either wrecked or would have to go back to Gibraltar for repairs. So they went there. In fact, the fleet's carpenters remasted her at sea. But Nelson was left without frigates for scouting – what he called the eyes of the fleet. So he missed the enormous convoy Napoleon was taking to Egypt. He guessed it had gone to Alexandria, sailed there but arrived too soon and found nothing, sailed back to Sicily, passing the French without sighting them on a thick night. He revictualled, and made another cast to

Nelson, by L. F. Abbott
Overleaf: Battle of Trafalgar, by C. Stanfield

Naval uniforms in 1837

the south of Greece – and there he had news from a French brig he captured that Napoleon's fleet had been seen off Crete, steering south-eastward. So down to Alexandria again, and at last in the afternoon of 1st August, the sight of the masts of a fleet at anchor in Aboukir Bay off the delta of the Nile. He hoisted the signal to prepare for action, ordered dinner and predicted for himself, before that time the next day, 'a Peerage or Westminster Abbey.'

The French admiral, with a stronger fleet than Nelson's, is said to have felt secure, protected by shoals, shore batteries and gunboats, and to have told his officers Nelson could not attack that evening because he had no charts. And in fact neither Nelson nor anybody else could have done it without the understanding he had had with his captains. He had already foreseen this possible situation and told them what he proposed to do about it, and he trusted each one of them to do it even in the dark. No more orders were needed, nor any pause to make a formal line. 'I was sure each would feel for a French ship,' he wrote afterwards; later, he put it that he was sure 'each would find a hole to creep in at'. So they all did, except Thomas Troubridge in the *Culloden*, who grounded on a shoal and had the mortification of only acting as a warning to the others. As dusk was falling, the three leading ships on their own initiative passed inshore of the head of the anchored line, reasoning simply that if there was room for a French ship to swing, there was room to sail round it; and they themselves anchored by the stern between the French and the shore, with springs on their cables so that the ships could be swung to train the guns. Nelson and the others anchored outside the line, each choosing his own opponent: the French were between two fires.

The battle went on most of the night, lit by the flashes of guns and by the French flagship *l'Orient* which caught fire during the evening and blew up about ten o'clock with a devastating explosion that scattered debris all over the combatants. Nelson was wounded in the forehead and temporarily blinded in the other eye: characteristically, he thought he was dying until the surgeon reassured him. Both sides fought to exhaustion. At dawn, the entire French fleet, excepting two ships and two frigates, was seen to be burnt or sunk or flying British colours in surrender. The two survivors cut their cables and stood out to sea. In one of them was Admiral Villeneuve, who was Nelson's opponent at Trafalgar, and in the other Admiral Decrès, who later was Napoleon's Minister of Marine. No British ship had been lost, but nobody was in a condition to chase them. Napoleon and his army were marooned in Egypt. Napoleon himself escaped a few weeks later in a fast Venetian ship, but he left his army to surrender.

This Battle of the Nile, the first under Nelson's command, set a standard entirely new in naval affairs, both as a tactical masterpiece and as a total victory: it was the greatest setback Napoleon or the French navy had ever had. In the next few months, Nelson blotted his reputation at the Admiralty by falling in love with Lady Hamilton at Naples, involving himself in abortive Neapolitan battles ashore, and refusing an order from his commander-in-chief which he thought was mistaken. He was recalled to England. But none of this changed the opinion of ordinary English men and women: his reputation had spread beyond the navy and throughout the country: whatever he did, he was the hero of the nation.

And whatever the Admiralty thought, they had to make use of his skill. Very soon, he was sent to the Baltic to subjugate the Danish fleet – not as commander-in-chief, but under the orders of a very much older admiral, Sir Hyde Parker.

This was something of a side-issue in the war. Nobody British wanted to fight the Danes: it was only that they had been dragged into the periphery of Napoleon's empire and had put a stop to British trade in the Baltic – an especially nautical trade in materials which the navy had to have, spars, flax and Stockholm tar. But it provided Nelson with the second and the hardest of his famous victories, the Battle of Copenhagen, and provided posterity with the most enduring of Nelson stories. 'Leave off action?' were his actual words when Parker, who was not in action, flew that signal at the hottest moment of the battle. 'Now damn me if I do!' And to his flag captain he added, 'You know, Foley, I have only one eye – I have a right to be blind sometimes.' And to make a joke of it, put his telescope to his blind eye and said, 'I really do not see the signal.'

*

By this time, people at home were living under a constant threat of invasion. With a telescope and a good eye from the cliffs of Dover, the encampments of Napoleon's Grand Army could be seen on the hills across the Channel, and Boulogne and the neighbouring smaller harbours were packed almost solid with boats designed and built for the crossing. After Napoleon had to abandon his plans to conquer Britain, he claimed he had never really meant to try, it had only been a feint, and some of his devoted followers believed him. But that was only to save his self-esteem. His papers reveal not only that the threat was genuine, but that the greatest ambition he ever had was to invade and humiliate Britain.

At the turn of the century, the Straits of Dover had therefore become the crux of the war for Britain, and accordingly Nelson was sent there, to reorganise the inshore defences. Dissatisfied with that, he also organised a strong attack across the Channel to destroy the boats in their ports. But it was a terrible failure. Part of the plan had been to cut the cables of the boats, but they turned out to be moored with chains, which was a novel practice; and in the repulse a great many British sailors were killed.

It only proved that that was not the way to stop Napoleon. There was another. His army could not cross unless it was protected by his navy. He needed control of the Channel, if only for a short time – sometimes he said two days, and sometimes six hours. But his fleets were scattered in French and Spanish ports from Toulon in the Mediterranean to Brest in the Bay of Biscay. It became the Royal Navy's duty to keep them there. And in doing so, it achieved the greatest feat of seamanship there has ever been or ever will be, the great blockade: if the British had never done anything else at sea, the blockade of Napoleon's ports would have stamped them as incomparable seamen.

After the Peace of Amiens early in 1803, the invasion threat was intensified. So was the blockade. Nelson was appointed to command it in the Mediterranean, and Sir William Cornwallis in the Bay of Biscay.

Cornwallis was a much older man than Nelson: he was 60, and like most officers, he had served in the navy since he was 11. His career was distinguished, but had somehow always fallen short of fame. The most memorable thing about it was perhaps the number of nicknames he had on the lower deck, which was a sign at least of popularity: Billy Blue, Billy-go-tight, Coachee and Mr Whip were some of them.

But he was a seaman. Of the two commands, his was certainly more difficult and dangerous than Nelson's. Brest, where the principal fleet of the French was lying, commanded by Admiral Ganteaume, is in the north-east corner of the Bay. Outside it is a rocky coast and a wicked stretch of sea, foggy, cold and stormy. Strong tides set through the narrow sounds inside the Isle of Ushant, and the prevailing wind, southwesterly, blows onshore with the whole of the open Atlantic behind it to build up a sea and swell. Even the sailing ships of modern times, such as they are, are advised to keep well offshore. Collingwood, who commanded the blockade in the '90s, had said that this coast was more dangerous than a battle once a week.

Yet to keep the approaches to Brest under observation, Cornwallis had to be close. Ships of the line in those days were unhandy vessels, slow to windward and slow to go about. Embayed on a lee shore with an incoming swell, they could never be sure of clawing off again. Caught in a calm, they were helpless against a tide that might set them into unnavigable sounds. Yet night and day, summer and winter, Cornwallis and his captains stood off and on that shore, estimating the tidal streams and currents, constantly solving the problems of navigation and ship-handling – and not merely in a single ship, but in a whole fleet of them. No modern sailor would dare to explain how they did it; the art of sailing such ships is long forgotten. Even then, the achievement amazed the French, who looked out in every dawn and saw the sails still there. There was only a single exception. In heavy westerly gales, they ran for shelter in Plymouth Sound, a hundred and fifty miles across the Channel – because in a westerly gale, the French could not possibly beat out of harbour. But whenever the wind showed signs of moderating, they were back on station before the French could stir.

In that one respect, Cornwallis's fleet was better off than Nelson's: once in a while they did see a friendly port, and even if they were never allowed ashore, they could land their sick, ask for help in repairs from the dockyard, and perhaps hear some news of home. Nelson's had no such luck. They had less trouble with the weather: the Gulf of Lyons, with Toulon in the middle of it, is also a stormy sea, but its worst wind is the mistral, which blows off-shore. But their nearest ports under British control were Malta and Gibraltar, each between six and seven hundred miles away, much too far to be any use as bases. So they had to rely entirely on themselves, cure their own sick, repair their own ships, and find their own provisions where they could. The only anchorage they used was at the northern end of Sardinia, a beautiful but barren and empty place with nobody ashore except a few peasants and fishermen.

Nelson's achievement in seamanship was different: in these conditions, he managed, like Cook, to keep his men healthy and contented. He spent an enormous amount of his time and energy in the search for healthy food – cattle from Africa, lemon juice from Italy, onions, fish and fruit wherever they could get them. For two years, through his exertions, they lived off the country, and most of them, including Nelson, never set foot ashore. Men died of the ills they would have died of anywhere, but at the end of it the survivors were as healthy as when they started: there was only one man sick in the *Victory*, which was now the flagship. What was more, they were perfectly trained. Every man and boy had his action station and knew exactly what he had to do in battle. And they longed for a chance to do it, and to end the dreary business with a single fight, which they knew they would win, and so to go home.

Nelson's policy also was different from Cornwallis's. Cornwallis, almost in the mouth of the English Channel, was under orders to keep the French in port, and he succeeded. But Nelson, sharing the longing of his crews, did everything he could to lure them out. He cruised well out of sight of Toulon, watched it with frigates, and sometimes sent a squadron, deliberately weak, to tempt the French to fight. They refused, and British seamen despised them for it.

But it was in Toulon that the deadlock began to crack. At the end of March 1805, the French under Villeneuve came out of harbour, and the long blockade dissolved into the chase that finally, six months later, brought the fleets together off Cape Trafalgar.

*

At this moment, approaching the ultimate climax of so many centuries of rivalry at sea, one must spare a sympathetic glance at the French and Spanish navies. Both in their time had been superb. Now both had the awful misfortune to be serving an autocrat who was a soldier, not a sailor. Napoleon, all through the blockade, believed that the British were wearing themselves out at sea while his own navies were conserving themselves in harbour. The opposite was true. The British were hardening themselves and perfecting their training, especially in gunnery, while the French and Spanish were rotting through lack of experience at sea. By the blockade, the British almost destroyed those two proud navies without a chance to fire a shot at them.

And when the time came for his grand design, the invasion of England, Napoleon gave his admirals orders which were impossible to execute – and every one of them knew they were but did not dare to say so. Ganteaume in Brest was ordered not only to break out of port, but to break out unseen without a battle, which was inconceivable. All the fleets were ordered to assemble in the West Indies, and then come back together and force their way up Channel. But few of the crews by then had ever been to sea in the ships they manned; a large proportion of the men had never been to sea at all, or wanted to, and the gunners had only fired their guns on land; not one of the ships was competent, after all those years in port, to cross the Atlantic twice and still remain ready for a fight. And ultimately, the

Emperor's orders were futile because he judged naval strength by simple arithmetic. Villeneuve, he observed, would come back from the Indies with sixty or seventy ships and at least a dozen frigates, far more than the British could assemble to stop him. But he did not observe that nobody had ever successfully manœuvred such a fleet, even under the best of conditions. And the conditions could not have been worse. Villeneuve did not even know the names of the Spanish admirals he was supposed to take under command, and the Spanish ships would have no language in common with his own, no signal book, no training, no tactical practices and no tradition. It was not surprising he hesitated to see his ships destroyed and his crews slaughtered in an enterprise he knew was perfectly hopeless. Pursued by contradictory orders, and with Nelson on his heels, he finished up off Cadiz, where Admiral Collingwood, who was watching the port with two or three ships, withdrew to let him in, and then closed in again to keep him there. And slowly, during the autumn of that year, the British fleets assembled off the port that Drake had seized two centuries before.

*

In those British ships off Cadiz, morale was low. It looked as if the whole tedious business of blockade was going on for another winter, and officers and men were bored almost beyond endurance by the prospect of it. The growing forces came under Collingwood's command. Like most other officers of his generation he was a friend of Nelson's: he had many good qualities, and in particular was a brilliant strategist who always seemed to know what the French were going to do. But he had a puritan turn of mind; he busied himself with all the details of administering a fleet, and had no time for what he might have thought was sociable frivolity. The captains who joined him found to their chagrin that they were not invited aboard the flagship to visit him; and what was worse, he discouraged them from visiting each other. The weather was fine, nothing was happening, the ships lay almost motionless under the hot September sun. All the captains would have liked to invite their old friends to be rowed across for a drink and some dinner together, and more seriously to discuss what they were going to do. But no invitations and no orders came from Collingwood. It was a life of misery, one of them wrote to his wife. A second wrote: 'We have got into the clutches of another stay-on-board admiral.' And a third: 'For charity's sake, send us Lord Nelson, oh ye men of power!' But the *Victory* was in Portsmouth, and Nelson after two years at sea was at his home in Merton, happy in the company of Emma Hamilton, and openly enjoying the hero-worship of the London crowds.

The fast frigate *Euryalus* had been sent to Portsmouth with the news that Villeneuve was trapped. Her captain, Thomas Blackwood – another close friend – stopped at Merton at five o'clock in the morning on his way to the Admiralty. Nelson was up and dressed. 'I am sure you bring me news of the French and Spanish fleets,' he said before Blackwood could speak, 'and I think I shall yet have to beat them.' And so it was: the Admiralty ordered him to sea again, and after three weeks at home he drove away from 'dear, dear Merton, where I left all which I hold dear in this world.' At Portsmouth, he tried to avoid the crowds by embarking from an unusual stretch of shore, but they followed him and people knelt down to bless him as he passed.

Off Cadiz, the *Victory*, wearing his flag, was sighted on 28th September, approaching from the westward. 'Lord Nelson is arrived!' wrote the captain who had asked it for charity's sake. 'A sort of general joy has been the consequence.' At once he wrought his miracle of command. In the next few days, he invited all the captains to dinner, brought them personal messages from home, attended meticulously to their private worries, exerted his utmost tact to soothe any hurt that Collingwood might have felt – and above all explained to them exactly the revolutionary tactics he had devised to 'annihilate' the enemy fleets as soon as they dared to leave port. Boredom vanished, and pride spread through the fleet. In the next few days, all the ships that had not served with him before had men overside in bosun's chairs, repainting in the colours that had been an emblem of his Mediterranean fleet, yellow bands with the gunports black, so that the hulls looked chequered.

In the next few days, Nelson wrote the famous memorandum which confirmed the tactics he had explained to the captains. Not long before, he had written another paper, and the preamble of it applied to both, and expressed the uncompromising confidence he felt and inspired in the navy: 'The business of an English Commander-in-Chief being first to bring an enemy's fleet to battle on the most advantageous terms to himself, (I mean that of laying his ships close on board the Enemy, as expeditiously as possible;) and secondly to continue them there, without separating, until the business is decided – ' And the Trafalgar memorandum went on to say how this would be done. He expected to have a fleet of forty sail, and yet to be outnumbered; and no day was long enough, he believed, to form so many into the customary line of battle. They would attack in three separate divisions. One, which he would command, would cut the enemy's line in the centre. The second, under Collingwood, would cut it twelve ships from its rear. The third, a squadron of eight of the fastest sailers, would be engaged where it was needed. The enemy's van would be left alone. So, although the British might be outnumbered, each division in their simultaneous battles would have the advantage of numbers. 'Something must be left to chance; nothing is sure in a sea fight beyond all others. Shot will carry away the masts and yards of friends as well as foes; but I look with confidence to a Victory before the Van of the Enemy could succour their Rear, and then that the British Fleet would most of them be ready to receive their twenty Sail of the Line, or to pursue them, should they endeavour to make off . . . In case Signals can neither be seen or perfectly understood, no Captain can do very wrong if he places his ship alongside that of an Enemy.' When the day came, he omitted the third squadron because both fleets were smaller than he expected, and because the urgency of getting into battle was even greater. But it was on this memorandum, a complete departure from ancient naval practice, that Trafalgar was fought and won.

*

It never should have been fought. The French and Spanish navies were hopelessly unfit to put to sea, let alone to fight, and all their senior officers knew they were: the French had 1500 men on the sick list, and the magnificent Spanish ships were manned by soldiers and beggars off the streets. But when Napoleon had to abandon his invasion plan he was furious with the navy, which he blamed for his failure, and with Villeneuve in particular. Villeneuve, indeed, had been dismissed: rumours of it had reached Cadiz, and he had heard them from his officers, but he had had no letter confirming it. All he had had was a mandatory order from the Emperor, not only to sail from Cadiz on an insultingly useless voyage to the Mediterranean, but to fight the British whatever the odds against him. 'His Majesty counts for nothing the loss of his ships,' the order had said, 'provided they are lost with glory.' And with that expression of anger and contempt, Napoleon had put the navy out of his mind and left for Austria to begin an army campaign which he enjoyed and understood, the campaign which led to the triumph of Austerlitz. After all the centuries of gallant rivalry, the French and Spanish navies were destroyed – the former for a hundred years and the latter for ever – through the Emperor's injured pride.

At dawn on 21st October they were sighted, 33 of them and frigates among them, ten miles away against the eastern sky. As soon as it was light enough for flags to be seen, the *Victory* hoisted the first of Nelson's signals that day, to prepare for battle, and to bear up and sail large on the course set by the admiral. She swung slowly into the path of the rising sun, and one by one the 25 ships of his fleet altered course to form the two divisions he had ordered. The breeze from the west-north-west was hardly enough to ruffle the water, but a heavy swell was coming in from the ocean.

It was the end of 48 hours of intense anxiety. When the French and Spanish ships had started to straggle clumsily out of the harbour of Cadiz, Nelson had no means of knowing whether they meant to go west and north, for the English Channel, or south for the Mediterranean. But the frigates under Blackwood, by a masterpiece of audacity, had dogged them and signalled every move they made throughout those days and nights.

The approach was a long ordeal. Villeneuve, seeing he was detected, wore and stood back towards Cadiz; but in the meagre breeze and the swell, his ships made scarcely any headway. The British, even with their studding-sails set, bore down on them at about two knots. The ships were soon cleared for action – it only took six minutes in an efficient ship – but six hours passed before the fleets were in range. Nobody had anything to do. Bands on the poops of several ships played cheerful tunes, and could clearly be heard in the ships that could not muster a band. Down on the gundecks, men chalked defiant slogans on their guns and leaned out of the ports for a glimpse of the enemy. Boats rowed from ship to ship, and captains hailed each other and wished each other a prize in tow before the night; for as usual, there was not much talk about the victory England needed, but plenty about the money that might be won.

In the *Victory*, Nelson was surrounded by friends who knew him well – Captain Hardy, his two secretaries, both named Scott, the surgeon, Dr Beatty, Captain Blackwood of the frigates, and many others. All of them worried about his safety; for the *Victory*, leading the line, was sure to have a conspicuous part in the fight, and he was the most conspicuous figure on her quarter-deck. Blackwood tried to persuade him to move his flag to a frigate, or to let another ship take the lead; but Nelson said it would only set a bad example. He knew the danger too, and seemed to expect to die; but that was nothing new, he had always entered battle prepared for death, and the danger, as usual, merely made him happy and excited. During the morning he wrote a codicil to his will, in which he commended Emma Hamilton and his daughter Horatia to the country's care; and kneeling in his cabin, he wrote in his journal the prayer which resigned his own life to God.

At 11.30 the fleets were a mile apart: Nelson called his flag lieutenants. 'I will now amuse the fleet with a signal,' he said with an air of boyish gaiety. 'Suppose we telegraph "Nelson confides that every man will do his duty."' Other people suggested 'England expects', because it was easier to signal, and at 11.35 the most famous battle signal ever made was hoisted to the yards and mastheads of the *Victory*. It inspired generations of Englishmen, but it was not received with unanimous joy in the fleet. Nelson's first version would have pleased them better, for England seemed far away, but Nelson was with them, the embodiment of their pride: his confidence would have meant more to them than England's expectation.

When the flags were hauled down, his last signal was hoisted: 'Engage the enemy more closely.' It flew at the masthead until it was shot away.

Ten minutes to noon: a burst of smoke was seen from the French ship *Fougeaux*, and the sound of her guns came rolling across the sea. With a range of a thousand yards, she had fired a full broadside at Collingwood's *Royal Sovereign*, leading the second line. Five other French and Spanish ships began to fire; the rest of the fleet watched the *Royal Sovereign* standing on towards the enemy line, unable yet to bring her own broadside to bear. She reached it, passed close under the stern of the Spanish flagship *Santa Ana*, firing all her port guns as she passed, and then hauled up alongside the Spaniard. Their rigging entangled and locked together, and to the watchers in the fleet both ships disappeared in the cloud of their own gunsmoke.

The *Victory*'s ordeal came a few minutes later. One of the first shots that hit her killed Mr Scott, the admiral's secretary. Another passed between Nelson and Hardy, walking up and down, as custom demanded, on the quarter-deck. Her steering wheel was shattered, and she had to be steered by forty men on the tiller, down on the lower gundeck. But she also reached the enemy line, and cut through it astern of Villeneuve's flagship the *Bucentaure*, so close that with a gust of wind men could have seized the French ensign. At point-blank range she fired the port carronade on her forecastle, loaded with its 64-pound shot and a keg of musket balls, and then the whole of her broadside. From the *Bucentaure*, the dust of shattered woodwork drifted across her deck. Then she rammed the French *Redoutable*, Captain Lucas, and two more ships were locked together. Close behind her, the *Temeraire*, *Neptune* and *Leviathan* came through the gap she had made.

Nelson had said he wanted to bring about 'a pell-mell battle', and that was what happened. Nothing quite like it had been seen before, and nothing remotely like it since. The formal lines of battle disappeared. In one square mile of sea, some sixty ships were moving independently, and each of them, all the time, was in range of several enemies. For the captains, it was like a deadly game, a mixture of luck and skill. The skill was to bring one's own broadside to bear, and avoid the enemy's. The luck was in the clouds of smoke that often hid everything, so that the ships, friend or foe, loomed through it at the range of a pistol shot. Yet the game was played, as it were, in slow motion: probably, once battle was joined, no ship moved at more than one mile an hour, and to turn them took many minutes.

In this unique situation, the gunners blazed away at any enemy ship that crossed their line of sight, and they were seldom without a target. And all the firing was at very close range – a maximum perhaps of one or two hundred yards, and a minimum of a foot or two. For many ships drove their bowsprits into an enemy's rigging and swung until their sides were grinding together. The *Victory* and the *Redoutable*, already entangled, drifted down on the *Temeraire*, and then all three fell aboard of the French *Fougeaux* – four ships side by side, all facing the same direction as if they were moored at a quay.

Below, on the gundecks, such close encounters were hellish. They were a hell of noise, the concussion of guns that sometimes deafened men for life, the shouts and yells, occasionally cheers, of hundreds of men as they loaded, rammed, and fired, the rending crashes as enemy shot smashed through the wooden sides, and the screams of the wounded. A hell of vision too: through the blinding smoke, the dim squares of light from the nearest gunports, the flashes of fire, the surgeon's men heaving up the wounded who could not walk, men shoving their dead and dying companions through the ports and overboard into the sea; the powder monkeys, small boys running through the horrors carrying cartridges, and the blood that flowed from side to side with the rolling of the ship.

On the upper decks, the dangers were different – from musketry, stray cannon shot, and falling masts and spars. Most men on deck and in the rigging were there to sail the ship, not mainly to fight – to make or shorten sail, to tack or wear on the captain's orders – and they carried on with their jobs and let the enemy, perhaps a few yards away, carry on with theirs. The British rather despised the use of muskets, which they believed correctly could never capture a ship; but some French captains had faith in them and stationed musketeers in the tops, fifty feet up their masts, to harass the enemy decks. And sometimes there was a shout for boarders or for repelling boarders, and everyone snatched weapons stowed at the feet of the masts, and furious hand to hand fighting flared up and died away again.

*

Captain Lucas of the *Redoutable*, alongside the *Victory*, was a brave and efficient man: stuck in harbour, he had been unable to train his crew in naval gunnery, but he had trained them instead in musketry, small-arms fighting and throwing grappling irons, and had promised them a chance to board an enemy. When the *Victory* rammed him, the British were amazed to see his crew slam shut their gunports, and so cut off their main armament. But that was his plan. On his upper decks he had hundreds of men with muskets, bayonets, cutlasses, pistols and hand-grenades.

If Nelson's friends could have foreseen that chance would bring them alongside a man with such ideas, their anxiety for his safety would have been despair. After close action had been joined, his work was done, and so was Hardy's. And therefore they did what they had always done when they had no pressing business: they paced up and down the quarter-deck together. Of course they could see the French musketeers: some of them were only fifty feet away. And they could see their own people falling round them, hit by Lucas's unprecedented fire. Perhaps they were both too absorbed in great events to think of immediate danger; but it was unthinkable that a commander-in-chief or a captain should take cover. Neither of them, in deference to the enemy, would have changed a single step.

It was after half an hour of battle that Nelson was shot and fell. 'They have done for me at last,' he said to Hardy. 'My backbone is shot through.' They carried him below.

By that time, the difference in training between the two fleets had already begun to tell. The British were far better at ship-handling – and in gunnery, they could fire three times as fast as the French, and with better aim. In consequence, casualties in the French and Spanish ships were five or sometimes even ten times as many as in their British opponents. But as Nelson had said, masts and yards were carried away by shot on every side. The British *Belleisle*, which followed the *Royal Sovereign* into battle, soon lost all her masts. The *Mars*, which came behind her, was left with her masts still standing but every bit of her rigging shot away: she drifted through the battle unable to set a sail.

But here, the difference in determination showed. Most of the French and all the Spanish who were dismasted began at once to think of striking their colours in surrender. But it simply never crossed the minds of the British to do so. Some, by prodigious efforts in the heat of battle, got under way again with jury rigs. Some got other ships to tow them, and fought on. Of all, perhaps the *Belleisle* showed the greatest coolness. When she could not move, and her gunports were masked by the sails and rigging that had fallen over her sides, her crew lashed a pike to the stump of a mast and flew her ensign from that, and they moved some guns and fired them from the sternports. Her captain, in the midst of it all, was seen to be standing on deck and eating a bunch of grapes. 'The ship is doing nobly,' he said to the captain of Marines, and offered him some grapes; and then sent him in a boat to accept the surrender of a Spaniard.

It was this that made Trafalgar a total victory: first Nelson's tactical plan, and then the unquestioning confidence he had inspired. While he lay dying, down in the dark cockpit of the *Victory* among the other wounded, eighteen enemy ships hauled down their flags. One other was burning out of control. By four o'clock it was all over. An unknown hand wrote with a pencil in the *Victory*'s log: 'Partial firing continued until 4.30, when a victory having been reported to the Right Hon. Lord Viscount Nelson, K.B., and Commander-in-Chief he died of his wound.'

*

'On such terms, it was a victory I never wish to have witnessed.' So Captain Blackwood wrote to his wife that night; and as the news of Nelson's death spread through the fleet, men of all ranks expressed the same feeling: the elation of victory vanished in genuine sorrow, the commander they lost seemed more important than the battle they won. And the next day, oppressed by this news and exhausted by the fight, they were faced by a worse ordeal: a storm which blew straight towards the enemy coast.

Many veterans said they had never seen such a wind and sea as they saw the week after Trafalgar. And no sailing fleet in history was ever in such a perilous position: nearly fifty ships on a lee shore, including the prizes, about half of them dismasted, and each with scores and some with hundreds of wounded and dying men down on their orlop decks. At first, the British tried to tow the crippled ships away from the coast. Waves swept the decks, guns broke adrift, men worked aloft by day and night on swaying masts and yards, supported by rigging already weakened and hastily knotted or spliced. Seamanship was stretched to its limit. Both fleets were united against this common danger; men who had fought each other struggled now to save each others' lives. But after three days it became impossible. Collingwood, now the commander again, signalled the fleet to abandon the prizes, take the men out of them and sink them or let them drive ashore. So a new struggle began: to drag the wounded up from the orlop decks of the French and Spanish ships, lower them into heaving boats, and row them to British ships that were under control. Hundreds were saved, and many men were drowned in trying to save them; but many hundreds still lay helpless down below and died when their ships went down or were pounded to wreckage on the shoals and rocks.

Not one of the British ships was lost, and that was an astonishing achievement. But only four of the prizes could be saved – and that, to the fleet, was a bitter disappointment which took the glory out of the victory. The prize money they had fairly won was gone, they felt they had nothing to show for their success. One by one, in the following fortnight, the ships limped into Gibraltar to look for repairs for the voyage back to England. Their crews were dead weary, and already the battle seemed long ago.

CHAPTER 21

Pax Britannica I

NEARLY ten years later, on 15th July, 1815, Napoleon climbed up the side of the British ship *Bellerophon* lying at anchor off the French port of La Rochelle, close to the historic Isle of Oléron; and the crew leaned out of the gunports or stared in awe from their stations on deck at the stout little man who had ruled over Europe and threatened England for longer than most of them could remember. A fortnight before, they had heard from a French ship they captured that he had been beaten by Wellington. But it seemed incredible, as he smiled and bowed to the officers, that this was the ogre who had frightened them as children. He pulled off his small cocked hat and said to the captain, 'I have come to throw myself on the protection of your Prince and laws.'

That moment on the deck of a British ship was the start of a century unique in the history of the sea – ninety-nine years, to be precise, when the prestige of the Royal Navy stood so high that sea warfare practically ceased. 'If it had not been for you English,' Napoleon said to the captain at dinner that day, 'I would have been Emperor of the East; but wherever there is water to float a ship, we are sure to find you in our way.'* It was true. The navy felt it was only just and proper that he had surrendered on board a ship – and especially the *Bellerophon*, which had fought under Nelson at the Nile and at Trafalgar. Wellington's army, of course, had been his final downfall. But it was the navy, all those years, that had circumscribed his empire and confined his ambition to the mainland of Europe and the edge of Asia.

And that was all the navy had set out to do: to keep Napoleon in, to stop him invading England or expanding to the east, or strangling British trade. It had never consciously fought to make itself the sole authority on the seas. But all the historic rivals of Britain on the seas had been Napoleon's

---

* He is also said to have used the same phrase later in St Helena.

allies, willingly or not, and when he fell he dragged them all down with him – the French themselves, the Spanish and the Dutch, even the Scandinavians with their traces of the Viking tradition – all except the United States of America, which so far had no wish to rule at sea. So, by a curious irony, it was Napoleon who cleared the way for the British to dominate all the seas of the world. Suddenly, the British found themselves with a strong and efficient navy, and nobody in the world to fight. It was a situation they had not sought, or even clearly imagined since the time of Cook; but there it was, and if there was to be any law or peaceful custom on the seas, the British were the only people left who could organise it.

It was Napoleon also, in his cataclysmic fall, who left the British free to expand and cement their empire; for that, of course, was one use they made of their century of unchallengeable power. But it was not the only one. They also used it to make the sea safe and free for the trade of every nation, including their recent enemies. The Royal Society was active again in research and exploration, and the British merchant navy prospered until it was far bigger than anyone else's. On the day Napoleon surrendered, the role of the navy itself abruptly began to change, from fighting to keeping the peace, from conqueror to policeman and scientist. This is an era the British have some reason to be proud of. After all, it is honourable for a navy to win its battles, but more so to make a wise use of the peace it wins.

The navy's new work needed far fewer ships and men than the war that had ended. In 1815, there were over 700 ships in commission, and 140,000 men: three years later, there were only 130 ships and 19,000 men. The men, as ever, were simply discharged ashore, with most of their pay if they were lucky, when their ship's commission ended, and on the whole they were delighted to be free. If they were still in good health they spent their pay and drifted back to their jobs. But if they were sick or wounded, very little was done to help them, and in all the seaports of Britain, after the war, there were naval seamen reduced to beggary.

All those who remained in the navy were volunteers, and that made a basic difference in the sailor's life. The press-gangs came to an end in 1815 and were never used again; so did the system of sending civil offenders to the ships instead of prison. The unwilling men those methods had put into ships had always been something of a nuisance, dirty, dishonest and ignorant of the traditions seamen valued. But now, a man knew all his shipmates were there because, for one reason or another, they wanted to be. The esoteric comradeship of sailors began anew.

It would be pleasant to say that the navy's tradition of drastic punishments vanished as soon as the pressed men had gone. It could have, but it only happened slowly. Already, violent punishments had declined through the influence of Nelson and his contemporaries in the navy's high command, who firmly believed in ruling by respect and loyalty. But there were still a few captains who had men flogged for very little reason. Strictly speaking, indeed, flogging has never been abolished in the navy; it was only 'suspended' in the 1870s. But in the first half of the century, a series of regulations brought it under control, and crews were no longer left to the whims of their captains.

Shore leave was another benefit that slowly came into the seamen's lives. Even after the peace, no man was entitled ever to set a foot on land, but more captains began to grant them leave, and to find that if most of them came back dead drunk, they did at least come back. Increasing numbers of trusted men were allowed to take their wives to sea; an Admiralty Order merely said, with a charming turn of phrase, that no ship was to be 'too much pestered' with wives. And food very slowly improved. In the mutinies of 1797, the men had asked for fresh vegetables in port, and about twenty-five years later they began to get them. And the greatest of all innovations in seamen's food came at the same time, the invention of bully beef in tins. This, like so many other good things, was a French idea, and its name is supposed to be the British sailors' version of Boeuf bouilli. It was made in England, oddly enough, at the Dartford Iron Works, and began to appear in ships in 1813.

Another benefit to seamen after the war was a deprivation. For generations they had had almost unlimited beer – until it went sour – and a daily issue of half a pint of rum diluted with half a pint of water. It was an enormous amount of alcohol, and everyone knew it was far too much; it turned seamen into alcoholics. Drunkenness was the cause of most of the punishment at sea, and probably of most of the destitution when seamen were discharged. Grog had come to be regarded as a sacred right, and during the war the Admiralty had not dared to cut it down. But in 1824 the rum ration was suddenly halved, and tea and cocoa were issued instead; and to everyone's astonishment, the seamen only grumbled for a little while, and then began to admit they felt much better for it. In 1850, it was halved again.

But none of this was the central part of naval life; the central part of it was still the working of the ship, and that was as tough as it had always been. The only thing that had gone with the war was the chance of battle, and life was duller without it. For battles, in a successful navy, had never been so dangerous as they looked; Trafalgar was the greatest and fiercest of them all, but among the British, less than three men in a hundred lost their lives – it was far worse, of course, among their enemies. And battle had always brought with it the glorious gamble of prize money, the excitement, however remote, of winning a fortune. Seamen never forgot the historic parties there had occasionally been in Portsmouth and Plymouth after a prize, when men expressed the feeling of being incredibly rich by such exploits as buying gold watches and frying them. Nothing quite so good could ever happen in peace.

Yet if life in peacetime was dull for the seamen, it was far duller still for the officers. Seamen were simply paid off at the end of the war and signed on again if they wanted to. But officers had made a life's career of the navy; not many of them wanted to retire, and there was no way of making them do so. When the navy was down to 130 ships, it still had nearly 6000 commissioned officers. Four out of five of them were living ashore on half-pay with nothing to do, and very little chance of ever getting a ship again. A few, fed up with waiting, joined foreign navies, especially the Greeks in their War of Independence, and made names for themselves abroad. And some captains went to the merchant service. Owners liked naval captains for passenger ships, where they presided with social ease in the first class dining saloons.

Naval wardrooms have always had toasts of their own, and one of them is, or was, 'Bloody war or a sickly season'. In the thirty years after Napoleon's war, naval officers suffered acutely from the opposite; no war and not much sickness – and therefore no promotion. The higher ranks became blocked by ageing men. It was a situation that grew depressing, inefficient and finally fantastic. Unless an officer had exceptional private influence, promotion was entirely a matter of seniority, of waiting for older men to die; and in peacetime, they stubbornly failed to do so. Halfway through the century, there were lieutenants over 60 years old in the navy, and a man could suddenly find himself promoted captain or admiral when he had not been to sea for most of a lifetime.

When the Crimean War began in 1854, more ships were brought into commission, and the thing became farcical. The C.-in-C. Plymouth was 81, the C.-in-C. West Indies was 79, and applied for the more active war command of the Baltic. But that command was given to Sir Charles Napier who was only 68, while Sir James Dundas in the Black Sea was 69. The C.-in-C.

appointed to the China Station at the same time had been 'on the beach' for thirty-one years: he started by cancelling all shore leave – there had been none in his day – and trying to quell the resulting mutiny by sending his officers below with drawn swords.

But the navy as a whole was much less moribund than its senior admirals. It had its stations all over the world, and patrolled every ocean as of right. And the very moment Napoleon's war was finished, it also went back to exploring, as if the war had been only an unwelcome interruption. No habitable coast of the world remained entirely unknown, so the true explorer's instinct had to be turned to the Arctic and Antarctic. The old hope of a North-West Passage rose again, and captains began again to put names on barren stretches of rock and ice. Among and beyond the Elizabethan names on the arctic map are now the Georgian and early Victorian names, mixed up with those of other nations, Scandinavians, Russians, Prussians, French and Americans, who all entered into the game in the later nineteenth century. They are not only names of naval officers and ships, but also of whaling and sealing captains, and of royalty, statesmen, friends and sponsors, and even one or two wives and other ladies the travellers hoped to impress. Some people may have been disappointed in this kind of immortalisation: Admiral Sir John Ross, who began to name islands after members of the royal family, was suspected of inventing extra islands because he could not discover enough to go round. And among the surprising names is one with a better claim to immortality in English pubs: the desolate peninsula of Boothia, west of Hudson Bay, was named after Felix Booth, a distiller of London gin, who had made a lot of money and financed an expedition. Among the explorers' names, the most enduring are Parry, Ross and Franklin; and among the ships, the *Erebus* and *Terror*.

By 1818, the first two expeditions were ready to embark, both for the Arctic. For the next forty years, sea explorations were made by quite a small band of enthusiasts, as they had been in the previous century; once started, men tended to want to go on for the rest of their lives. Junior officers commanded later voyages, and all of them were served by naval ratings who made a career of it. Of the expeditions of 1817, one was commanded by John Ross, and two of his juniors, William Parry and his nephew James Ross, went on to make names for themselves. On the other expedition one ship was commanded by John Franklin, a link with the century before; it was he who had sailed with Matthew Flinders in Australia. He had also, in the pauses of exploration, fought twice under Nelson, first at Copenhagen, when he was 13, and then at Trafalgar, when he was partially deafened for life by the concussion of the guns.

All through the 1820s, the greatest effort was made in the North-West Passage. There was no real reason for it. Nobody believed by then, as they had in Elizabethan times, that the passage, if there was one, would have any practical use. It was simply that it remained a fascinating problem, and an especially British problem. British sailors had searched for it so long that it would have seemed a shame to give it up and let somebody else discover it. An award of £10,000 was offered to the captain and crew who succeeded.

The Victorians, like the Elizabethans, were always lured by the hope of a sudden opening in the ice among the islands and a triumphant emergence in the Pacific Ocean. But they only unravelled the mystery very slowly. Their navigating equipment, of course, was far better than the Elizabethans', so that they always knew where they were. But their ships were not much improved – a little more weatherly perhaps, but still essentially the same kind of wooden ships with the same square rig – and those the Admiralty allotted to exploration were small. However, experience had taught explorers how to winter in the Arctic, and some of this new generation spent two or even three consecutive winters frozen in. So they had more time to explore than their forebears, and one by one they pressed a little farther westward.

And in this era, the navy took to exploring overland. It was a strange extension of a navy's function. From ships that were fast in the ice, it was natural enough to think of buying dogs and sledges from the Eskimos and using them for reconnaissance. But there was more to it than that – the feeling perhaps that the navy did almost anything better than anyone else, and that no one else could really be trusted to help in a naval problem, even if solving it had nothing to do with ships. Thus the Admiralty sent Franklin with naval parties on two prodigious journeys through northern Canada, by canoe and on snow-shoes and sledges, to survey the coast and link up, if he could, with the expeditions by sea. And in the course of the century, polar exploration overland became a naval speciality, which reached its culmination in the journeys of Shackleton and Scott.

John Franklin seems the most admirable of the Georgians and early Victorians. As a young man, he was perhaps too serious and puritan to make a comfortable friend, but when he grew older and more famous he was modest, gentle and infallibly kind to his subordinates, who were always fond of him. The first overland expedition was successful, in so far as he charted several hundred miles of the arctic coast, but the return to civilised outposts was a series of dreadful disasters. He had only four naval companions, a surgeon, a seaman and two midshipmen. For porters and hunters, he had been told to rely on the Indians and the native Canadian trappers. The mixture was a calamity – the naval men disciplined and devoted to duty for its own sake, and the others wildly independent and wholly unconcerned with what seemed to them a pointless enterprise. All of them were reduced to living on lichen they scraped from rocks, and bones left over by wolves, and they ate their own shoes; and when one of the hunters came in with some frozen lumps of meat, they devoured them before they discovered he had murdered another Canadian and one of the midshipmen. Men died of starvation and exhaustion; the party was separated into twos and threes, and there was one macabre journey when the surgeon and the seaman, struggling through the snow along with an Indian, came to believe the Indian, crazy with hunger, had already killed several others and intended to kill them too. The surgeon shot him dead with a pistol.

Yet the three naval survivors all wrote of the affection they had for their leader, and when he went back for another similar journey two years later, all three of them volunteered to go again. One more lesson of exploration had been learned; this time, Franklin took a crew of a dozen naval ratings. The whole thing became a naval occasion, run like a ship at sea, and the result was a much less harrowing experience.

It very nearly solved the old mystery. While Franklin was tramping overland, and sailing along the sea coast in canoes, Parry entered the Passage by sea from the east, and another naval captain named Beechey attempted it from the Pacific. The hope was that two at least of these expeditions would meet, and especially that Franklin would somehow sight Beechey, which would have completed a tenuous line of survey right through from one ocean to the other. They only just missed. Franklin was driven back by ice and fog, with winter coming on, when he had covered altogether 1200 miles of the north Canadian coast. At the same moment a boat sent ahead by Beechey was only 160 miles away; but neither of them, of course, had any means of knowing the other was there.

When they did know, the gap seemed very small. Franklin certainly spoke for all the explorers when he wrote his report. 'It is sincerely to be hoped,' he ended, 'that Great Britain will not relax her efforts until the question of the north-west passage has been satisfactorily set at rest.' But the Lord High Admiral at the time was the Duke of Clarence, the future King

William IV, a capricious and troublesome man. He ordered Franklin to draft a scheme for a new attempt. Franklin put a great deal of time and thought into it, and submitted his proposals. The next day, he had a curt acknowledgment from a junior official: His Grace did not intend to recommend any further northern expeditions. And that was that.

So explorers turned south, which for some unaccountable reason the Duke did not discourage. Franklin had a long spell ashore as Governor of Tasmania, which was not entirely happy; but James Ross went down to the Antarctic, where he entered and named the Ross Sea and found, for the first time, the great ice barrier and the edge of the continent. Cape Crozier commemorates his second in command, and the twin volcanoes Erebus and Terror bear the names of his ships. British whaling captains were also pressing south: the Weddell Sea is named for one of them.

Yet still the North-West Passage enticed them all. In 1845, when King William was dead and the Queen was on the throne, all the veteran explorers combined to persuade the Admiralty. They won over the Hydrographer, Admiral Sir Francis Beaufort (the originator of the Beaufort Scale of wind), and induced the Secretary of the Admiralty to write to the First Sea Lord. There was a general feeling, he said, in the navy and the scientific societies that the search should not be abandoned. 'If the completion of the passage be left to be performed by some other power,' he wrote, with a little exaggeration, 'England by her neglect of it, after having opened the East and West doors, would be laughed at by all the world for having hesitated to cross the threshold.' The appeal to national pride, and perhaps the mere hint of being laughed at, brought the Admiralty's consent. The *Erebus* and *Terror* were still fit for another expedition. As commander, John Ross was certainly too old, and Parry felt he was. James Ross had just got married after sixteen years of polar exploring, and he wanted to stay at home. So the choice fell on Franklin, who was 59.

James Ross became head of a new naval Department of Steam Machinery, and that may have helped to extract another concession from the Admiralty. The *Erebus* and *Terror* were fitted with emergency engines, which the explorers believed would be useful in the ice. Each was given a retractable propeller which could be lowered through a well in the stern. The boilers were designed to provide a kind of central heating, the first time such a luxury had been taken to the Arctic. But the engines were not designed for the service at all; they were second-hand railway engines.

In these two veteran ships, Franklin sailed in May 1845 with 128 officers and men who were carefully picked from the navy's volunteers. Many wrote letters home from Greenland, recording the happiness on board; and none of them was ever seen again.

The disappearance of Franklin did more than anything else to open up the far north-west. It added a human mystery to the ancient mystery of the Passage. The search for the Passage became a desperate search for Franklin which continued for fifteen years, long after all hope was lost of finding anyone alive. The Admiralty sent out large co-ordinated expeditions, many individual captains sailed with more or less whimsical theories of their own, and Lady Franklin organised searches long after everyone else had given up. Naval officers and men made sledge journeys over a thousand miles in length, and it was said that 7000 miles of coast were newly explored. In the course of it all, one man and his crew at last made their way through the Passage, from Pacific to Atlantic, after spending three winters on the way. This was Captain Robert McClure, and he won the award of £10,000. But he did not take his ship through. She was hopelessly beset by ice in a place he called the Bay of God's Mercy. He was preparing to abandon her when he was found, through what did indeed seem a miraculously slender chance, by a sledge party which had come from the opposite direction.

Yet the mystery of Franklin's disappearance was never solved, except by inference; it will always remain a sea disaster without a complete explanation. A few skeletons were found, widely scattered; two of them were in a boat which seemed to have been hauled overland and contained an inexplicable variety of goods, including 40 pounds of chocolate and two rolls of sheet lead. Eskimos all over a wide area had things like spoons and forks, and even telescopes, that could only have come from the *Erebus* and *Terror*, and they told stories of large parties of strange men – but always at second hand. An enigmatic and self-contradictory message was found in a cairn, and in 1851 a brig off Newfoundland sighted two ships high up on a drifting iceberg, but did not go near enough to make certain what they were. All the discoveries still left room for speculation which has gone on ever since.

It is often the fate of pioneers that someone else steps in and wins the goals they aimed for; and if one took a narrowly nationalistic view, one might say that happened to British polar exploration. The British searched for the North-West Passage for three hundred years, beginning with Martin Frobisher. But it was the Norwegian Roald Amundsen who first sailed through it, from 1903 to 1906, in what must have been the smallest ship on such an enterprise since Stephen Borough's pinnace in 1557. Amundsen, of course, beat Scott's naval party to the South Pole in 1911. The American Robert E. Peary was first at the North Pole in 1909 after a longer life as a polar explorer than anyone else; and another Norwegian, A. E. Nordenskjold, in 1878 and 1879, passed through the North-East Passage that the Elizabethans had imagined and Willoughby had attempted in 1553. But no British explorer would much have resented these attainments; the polar regions are the only places on earth where national rivalries have almost always been forgotten.

CHAPTER 22

Steam

For almost half a century after Trafalgar, the navy had patrolled the world in exactly the same kind of ships that Nelson used. Yet in the same half-century, the greatest of all changes had come in merchant ships: steam engines and iron hulls.

It was only chance, of course, that steam was beginning at the moment when Pax Britannica began. But it was a moment when the merchant navy had competition and the fighting navy had none; a moment also when merchant ships were controlled by young men, and fighting ships by old ones. So the merchant navy rushed enthusiastically into all kinds of experiments, while the Admiralty watched and did nothing with an air of superior disdain which seems to have hidden unhappy bewilderment. When the Admiralty, as a special concession, put second-hand railway engines into Franklin's ships in 1845, it was most of thirty years behind the times: the merchant navy already was running regular passenger steamers across the Atlantic.

The two navies had always been rivals, ever since they grew into separate services in Stuart times – and not always friendly rivals, especially when naval press-gangs took men off merchant ships. Their two kinds of seaman-ship appealed to men of different temperaments. The fighting navy sailed its ships by drill, because it had to handle enormous crews: the merchant navy worked a ship with a tenth of the number of men or even less, and so it depended on them more as individuals. Some people like drilling, or even being drilled, and some detest it; so a naval crew could always look down on a merchant crew for what seemed to be slovenly ways, and a merchant crew could pity a naval crew for excessive discipline.

But among the diversity of merchant ships that existed when steam began, there was one class that bridged the gap: the East Indiamen. The East India Company which Queen Elizabeth chartered in 1600 remained a monopoly, through many vicissitudes, until 1834. Since the early days when it could not always scrape up the cash to pay its crews, it had made pro-digious profits, and at sea it created a style and standard which were unique. It did not own all its ships; more than half of them were chartered from private owners, who used to be called ships' husbands. But whether it owned them or not, it could afford to see they were built with an eye to perfection, and to insist that every plank and bolt and coil of cordage was the best that money could buy. And it attracted a special quality of officers and seamen, by paying them very little but allowing them to trade on their own account. Late in the eighteenth century, the pay of captains in the company's service was £10 a month, but they expected to make £5000 by trading on a single voyage, and hoped for twice as much; and even a seaman with a little capital and a trading instinct could do very well for himself. Among the things they brought home, in small packets at first, was tea; and so they started a well-known British craving which in the end demanded ships of its own, like pepper in earlier times.

The sense of monopoly ran through everything the company did. There were fortunes to be made by ships' husbands, so many directors of the company became ships' husbands too. What was more, they evolved a kind of hereditary right to supply the company's ships. When a ship was worn out in the service, its successor was said to be built on the old ship's bottom, and the same husband could claim to replace a worn-out bottom. And the best known of the ships' husbands, Robert Wigram, also had a controlling interest in the famous yard where most of the ships were built, the Blackwall Yard, close by the East India Docks on the Thames downstream from Greenwich.

It was a tangled skein of privilege, and in the end it led to scandalous corruption in the East. But it did produce magnificent ships, and crews with a pride and social status equal at least to the navy's. The ships were built for reliability, elegance and comfort, but not for speed; speed was not much of an asset on the eastern run which depended on the seasonal monsoons, and the company always allowed eighteen months for the round voyage. So service on company ships was seldom hurried. It became a kind of seafaring distinct from any other, leisurely, dignified and wealthy, a life for gentlemen.

At the other extreme perhaps of the British merchant service at this crucial moment were the whalers in polar seas. That also was a paying trade, and its seamen could make good money. But it needed and got the toughest of captains and crews, who lived lives of sordid discomfort and danger. Or the slavers, mostly Liverpool ships, which still followed John Hawkins's triangular route until the law put a stop to it in 1807; down to the coast of Guinea with cheap trade goods, across to the Americas with slaves, and back with a cargo of sugar. And between these extremes, the elegant and the sordid, was the North American and Caribbean trade, and the tide of immigrants which was just beginning to America and Australia, and the vast numbers of smaller ships that coasted round Europe, wherever and whenever wars allowed them, very much as they had in the middle ages. When trade was spreading and ships were small and slow, enormous numbers of them were needed, and probably more merchant ships were afloat in the eighteenth and early nineteenth centuries than in any other age. In the year after Trafalgar, in spite of the war, there were nearly six thousand sailings of British merchant ships to foreign ports.

*

These crowds of ships, on the verge of the century of peace, were protected by another British institution which was already revered and ancient: Lloyd's. In England, the idea of spreading a shipowner's risk went back to the sixteenth century, and an Act of Parliament in 1601 put the whole idea of insurance in a nutshell: 'By means of . . . Policies of Assurance it comethe to passe, upon the losse or perishings of any Shippe there followethe not the undoings of any Man, but the losse lightethe rather easilie upon many, than heavilie upon fewe.' By 1688, men in this line of business had drifted to-gether as customers of the coffee-house in Tower Street which belonged to Edward Lloyd. In the early days, shipowners took a slip of paper to the coffee-house, showing the name of their ship, its captain and destination and the value of ship and cargo. One customer offered a rate for the voyage and underwrote the slip with his initials and the percentage of the risk he would take; and then the owner collected initials until the whole sum was covered. It has worked the same way ever since; and even now, with a premium income of hundreds of millions of pounds, and computers installed out of sight, Lloyd's underwriters or their agents sit in apparent discomfort in boxes derived from the coffee-house seats, and merely initial the slips that brokers bring them. Lloyd's survived and grew colossal through personal integrity, and through the competition that was inherent in its system. It is not Lloyd's that insures a risk, it is individual underwriters, or syndicates of them; a broker can go from box to box until he gets the best rate, and each underwriter has always been responsible with all his possessions for the risks he initials. There have been a few traumatic occasions when individuals have come to grief, but the system itself has never failed, and could never conceivably dishonour its members' agreements. And through the years it has had offshoots. Very early, it began to collect intelligence of shipping and publish it daily in Lloyd's List; and in the 1760s Lloyd's Register was started, a separate society which surveys and classifies ships and upholds the standards of seaworthiness. By the nineteenth century, all these operations were world-wide, and Lloyd's members already had the reputation of insuring anything on the sea. The coming of steam was something they took in their stride.

*

With a respectable tradition, protected by the prestige of the navy and the solid honesty of Lloyd's – and by Navigation Acts which restricted foreign ships in British ports – the merchant service could hardly have failed to grow. But the first decades of Pax Britannica were mainly marked by American competition. On the Atlantic crossing, Americans were the first to organise shipping lines and offer a more or less regular service under sail. For a while, they beat the British in the design of fast sailing ships, and in the 1820s and '30s the two nations ran neck and neck in building steamers. But America's early efforts in steam were put mainly into river boats like the great stern-wheelers of the Mississippi. Britain, without interior water-ways, was obliged to build steamers which could go to sea; and perhaps for that reason took the lead with ocean-going steamers in the 1840s. And the competition might have gone on; but the Civil War, and the Americans' preoccupation with expansion to the west, made them lag behind at sea and left Britain to lead alone with merchant shipping in the second half of the century.

Those first decades must have been exciting times for anyone on the sea who did not hate machinery. The first successful steamship in the world was the *Charlotte Dundas*, which towed barges on the Forth and Clyde Canal in 1801. The war held things up, but before the end of it there were new achievements every year. In 1812, the year of Napoleon's retreat from Moscow, the *Comet* began a steamship service for passengers on the Clyde. In 1814 the *Margery*, which also was built on the Clyde, was taken through the canal and down the east coast to London, to start a service on the Thames. In 1816, as soon as the war was over, the first passenger steamer ran across the Channel, from Brighton to Le Havre, and two years later a regular crossing began from Greenock to Belfast. In 1819 the American ship

Savannah turned up in Cork with a claim to be the first steamer to cross the Atlantic; but to tell the truth, it was not an inspiring claim, because she was only a sailing ship with detachable paddle wheels which were stowed on deck for nine-tenths of the crossing, and she was only sent across because her owners hoped to sell her to the British. In 1825 the *Enterprize*, 470 tons and 120 horse-power, reached Calcutta in 113 days, using steam for two-thirds of the distance: she must have burned whatever fuel she found at ports on the way. And in 1827 the *Curaçao*, built in Dover and sold to the Dutch as a warship, began a series of crossings from Holland to the West Indies.

The navy took no part in any of this excitement, except that it chartered a few steam tugs in the early '20s to tow ships out of harbour in contrary winds.* The thought of using steam in a warship appalled and disgusted its senior officers, and in 1828 the First Lord of the Admiralty, Lord Melville, made a memorable statement: 'Their Lordships feel it their bounden duty to discourage to the utmost of their ability the employment of steam vessels, as they consider the introduction of Steam is calculated to strike a fatal blow at the supremacy of the Empire.'

It was not quite so absurdly short-sighted as it seems. The ships of Nelson's time had been evolved for fighting through so many centuries: it was not unnatural to think that the ships that had won so many wars were the best to keep the peace. And for the navy, there were some plausible arguments against the use of steam. First, it was less reliable in the long run than the wind. Secondly, paddle wheels were vulnerable and would get in the way of the broadside of a warship. Thirdly, if the navy with its world-wide mission relied on steam, it would have to set up world-wide coaling stations, and defend them. And finally (an illogical argument) the navy had a fleet of sailing ships far stronger than anyone else's, so why should it encourage a new idea that might make its own ships obsolete?

In the merchant service, steam had its opponents too. Probably no new kind of ship since history began has ever been launched without a crowd of conservative old seamen standing around and prophesying disaster for it. But the most famous and influential critic of steam was not a seaman at all; he was the Rev. Dr Dionysius Lardner, an Irishman, professor of natural philosophy and astronomy at University College, London. At meetings in

---

* It did build a steamer in 1815, which was named the *Congo* and destined for Africa; but leaving London on its maiden voyage it only reached Greenwich under steam, and then the engine, in despair, was taken out and the ship sailed on without it.

the early 1830s he proved by a totally false projection of statistics that a ship could only steam for fifteen days, or 2080 miles, before it had burned all the coal it could carry; and therefore the voyage from New York to Liverpool was 'perfectly chimerical', and one might as well talk of a voyage to the moon. Another speaker in reply called him 'an impudent and ignorant empiric', for it was a subject that roused everyone's emotions. Very soon after his announcement, the Atlantic crossing was almost a commonplace and he was discredited; but then he won another kind of fame by eloping with a lady called Mrs Heaviside, whose husband was a cavalry officer and successfully sued him for £8000. He was forced to leave the country, crossed the Atlantic himself, made £40,000 on a lecture tour of the United States, and retired to Paris. But of course it is wrong to laugh at the opposition to steam. Nowadays, nothing could have quite the daunting novelty of steam, or its half-religious implications – the first and only source of power that did not derive from muscles or the wind or falling water. Nowadays also, everybody is used to the constant advance of science, and nobody would dare to predict that anything is impossible. But then, it was far from obvious that a continual process of discovery was beginning, and that if ships could not steam to New York, inventors would certainly improve them until they could.

It is appropriate that the very first successful steamer was built in Scotland, for with steam the Scots found a place of their own in seafaring. Hitherto, one has to admit, most of the history of the British and the sea had been English. In the navy at Trafalgar, the Scotsmen, Welsh and Irish put together were outnumbered two to one by Englishmen, and the same had probably always been true of merchant ships. But in steam, a latent genius of the Scots was suddenly released. They took a leading part in designing and building engines, and a little later in shipbuilding too; and as engineers they went to sea, to such an extent that anyone meeting a steamer anywhere on the seven seas expected to find a Scotsman down below, alone, as Kipling said, with God and his engines, grumbling perhaps at the foreigners up on the bridge, but enslaved by his love of machinery.

But the two outstanding men about 1840 were an Englishman and a colonist, Isambard Kingdom Brunel and Samuel Cunard, who were both distinguished at their jobs before they were 30 years old. Both of them, one might say, had narrowly escaped being foreigners. Brunel's father was a French royalist, which no doubt was the cause of the names he gave his son; he fled to America at the time of the revolution, and only came to England shortly before the son was born. Cunard's father was a Quaker of Philadelphia, an anglophile who left in disgust at the Declaration of Independence and settled in Halifax, Nova Scotia. But both the sons grew up to be emphatically British, each typical of his class, the engineer and the merchant shipowner.

Brunel's father was the inventor of machines which made, among many other things, blocks for the navy's rigging and boots for the army; and as early as 1814 he had a brush with the Admiralty over steam. He was the first to persuade them, ten years too soon, to try a steam tug for towing ships out of harbour; and in the end he had to pay for the experiments himself, because the Admiralty said they were 'too chimerical to be seriously entertained'. But Brunel the son had no upbringing to the sea: he was a railway engineer. He was a very small man, and photographs show him in baggy trousers, a shapeless cutaway coat and a stovepipe hat that seems unbelievably big. It makes him look old. But in fact he was 27 when he was appointed engineer, in 1833, of the projected Great Western Railway from London to Bristol. At a board meeting that same year, before the line was begun, he is said to have suggested they should make it longer, and have a steamboat to go from Bristol to New York, and call it the *Great Western*. It seems just the sort of thing a young man might have said at a boring meeting, but the directors took it seriously and told him to go ahead and design the steamboat. And so among the drawings of the elegant bridges and tunnels that still decorate the west of England, he drew a ship – the first of his three great ships.

The *Great Western* was much the largest steamer that had yet been built: she was longer than any warship the navy possessed. Brunel had wanted to make her larger still, but the directors were more cautious. Her size was not just a matter of prestige and grandeur: it was engineering logic. The overall efficiency of early engines, in terms of horse-power-hours per ton of coal, was very low. This was partly because the engines themselves were inefficient, and partly because boilers, of riveted iron plates, could only be built to stand low pressures – there were disasters with boilers that burst all through the early years. The efficiency, of course, was slowly improved, and the improvement led in the end to triple expansion engines and turbines; but in the beginning, steamers burned an enormous amount of coal per mile.

For long voyages, size was the only answer. Brunel pointed out, in arguments against Dr Lardner, that the horse-power needed to drive a ship increased roughly as the square of its main dimensions, but the amount of coal it could carry increased as the cube; and therefore, the bigger it was the farther it could steam, and still have spare capacity for passengers and cargo. The only problem was to build a hull that was strong enough, and that, in his eyes, was just a matter of structural engineering. The *Great Western* was built of wood, but he used diagonal iron braces to give her strength, and she showed her railway origin in being largely fastened with nuts and bolts. It was lucky for the company that Bristol had a forward-looking shipwright. His name was William Paterson, and he was said to be 'not prejudiced in favour of either quaint or old-fashioned notions'. He laid the keel in 1836 – it was oak, and 206 feet long; and the next year, when Brunel was 31, the masterpiece was launched. Three weeks later, she sailed to the Thames under her schooner rig to have her engines fitted.

Rivals in the nineteenth century enjoyed dramatic competitions, and steam on the Atlantic really began with one in 1838. The rivalry was not only between shipowners, but between the ports that hoped to become the terminals of transatlantic shipping, which at that time were Bristol, Liverpool and London. Bristol was a jump ahead with the *Great Western*. London was building a ship that was slightly bigger, to be called the *British Queen*, but her engine-makers went bankrupt and a much smaller steamer, the *Sirius*, was chartered to try to beat the *Great Western* to New York. Liverpool had a ship on order too, but it was not ready, and they chartered the *Royal William*, a cross-channel packet built for the Dublin run. In March 1838 the *Great Western* was running her engine trials on the Thames and her first sailing was advertised for April. But the *Sirius* got away on 28th March, and passed the *Great Western* off Gravesend. She put in to Cork for coal, and left there with forty passengers on 4th April, bound for New York.

The *Great Western* steamed down the Thames three days astern of her. When she worked up to full speed in the estuary, the lagging of her boilers caught on fire. The stokehold crew was driven out by the smoke; four of them in a panic took to a boat and rowed ashore. The ship was beached on the Nore sands and lay there for an hour with her engine running, because nobody could get at it to stop it; and Brunel fell fifteen feet into the boiler room and was so badly hurt he had to be taken ashore. No serious damage was done to the ship; she floated off with the tide and churned on to Bristol at an average speed of nearly thirteen knots. But almost fifty passengers who had tickets for the maiden voyage asked for their money back. It was really no wonder. Since the earliest times, fire in wooden ships had been a terror, and the whole idea of installing a furnace on board seemed a denial of all

Isambard Kingdom Brunel, 1857

Launch of the *Great Eastern*, Millwall, 1858

Trade: British ships in an African river, *c.* 1860

Send a Gunboat: Sudan, 1880s

the precautions seamen had always taken. So she left Bristol to chase the *Sirius* with only seven intrepid passengers left: one of them was a woman.

The *Sirius* was first in New York, but only just: she took eighteen days from Cork, and the *Great Western* took fifteen days from Bristol, and came in 3½ hours behind her. The *Royal William* from Liverpool also ran, but not until two months later. And the three voyages demonstrated the point Brunel had made about size. His ship reached New York with 100 tons of coal in reserve. The smaller *Sirius* had only 15 tons, and some reports said she had burned her cabin furniture. The *Royal William* only just made it, although she left Liverpool so laden with coal that her paddles were buried six feet in the water and her crew could lean over the bulwarks and put their hands in the sea.

So it could be done; and the *Great Western* carried on to cross the Atlantic ninety times. Whether it was worth it was a more difficult question. Steamers cost far more to run than sailing ships, and had far less cargo capacity. And paddle steamers were really unsuited to the open sea. Sometimes when they pitched, both paddles came out of the water and let the engine race, and then sank up to their axles and almost brought it to a stop. When they rolled, one wheel was too deep in the water and the other too shallow; and they rolled excessively, because the paddle shaft and most of the weight of the engine was above the waterline. But the problem of making them pay was solved by Samuel Cunard, and the problem of making them seaworthy by the designers of the screw propeller.

Cunard's achievement seems in retrospect a simple piece of logic, but it needed something of a genius to perceive it in advance. First, a steamer with its limited cargo space could pay best as a passenger ship, because passengers paid more in proportion to the space they occupied than any other cargo. And to passengers, steam could offer not only speed but something more novel and attractive: punctuality. Since the beginning of time, anyone who made an ocean voyage had had to wait for a favourable wind; he could not know when he would start, much less when he would arrive. With steam, sailings could be predictable and regular, except in the dirtiest weather. But on the Atlantic run, one steamer was not enough, even for a monthly sailing, and even if it never broke down. A regular service needed several identical ships; and that was what Cunard provided.

He was a man of nearly 50 when he arrived in Britain in the year the *Great Western* sailed; since he was 27, he had been a well-known owner on the north American coast, running a mail service from Newfoundland down to Boston and Bermuda. On the Clyde, he fell in with three of the Scotsmen who had started young in shipping: George Burns and David MacIver, who had each been running coastal steamers, and Robert Napier of Dumbarton, who had served his time in a smithy and worked his way up to be a leading engine builder.

It was a powerful partnership. What it needed to get it started was the Government's mail contract, a prize that every shipping line was hoping for. The Post Office hitherto had run its own brigs across the Atlantic, manned by naval crews. The idea of sending the mails by steamer was given some impetus when the *Sirius*, homeward bound, overhauled a Post Office brig far out at sea, took over the mails she was carrying and reached England long before her. The Great Western company asked for a contract and offered to build enough ships to keep up a regular service. But Cunard, up in Glasgow, heard what was happening, hurried to London and managed to talk the Government into giving the contract to him. At the time, he possessed no ships at all, and the Great Western company thought he had used some sinister influence; but try as they did, they never managed to prove his influence was more than a charming manner and a power of persuasion. At all events, he went back to Glasgow with a guaranteed income from mails, and he and his partners set to work on the Clyde to build their first four identical Cunarders, paddle steamers with no special distinction except that they were all the same. The only small snag was a bit of bureaucracy typical of Britain. The Admiralty had been responsible for the safety of mails at sea, and it would not give up the privilege. So each of the early Cunarders had to carry a naval officer to look after the mails. At sea, these gentlemen had nothing whatever to do except eat and drink, and they were a constant annoyance to the merchant navy officers who were doing all the work.

So Cunard took the bread and butter of the Atlantic service. Other great shipping lines grew, with routes all over the world, but the earlier owners in London and Liverpool were put out of business. The fate of the Great Western company, because it had Brunel, was to carry on with ships that were years ahead of their time, and to bankrupt itself in doing so. Its second ship, the *Great Britain*, was built of iron and driven by a propeller.

Of all ships that had ever been built, the *Great Britain* was the most revolutionary, much more so in her way than the *Henri Grace a Dieu* or the *Sovereign of the Seas*. She represented the invasion by a structural engineer of the ancient and esoteric craft of the shipwright. She upset every preconceived idea. And no ship ever had a more extraordinary life, for she still exists.

She was not the first iron ship; the first, apart from barges, was probably the *Aaron Manby*, which was built in a Staffordshire ironworks in 1820, assembled in London and used on a direct run from London to Paris up the Seine. And there had been others. But the *Great Britain* was 322 feet long, almost half as long again as the largest man-of-war. She was launched in Bristol on 19th July, 1843, and that could be called the day when modern shipbuilding began.

The company started to build her in its brief moment of prosperity when the *Great Western* was doing well and Cunard had not yet started. By the time she was launched, its board was far less optimistic and its shareholders were showing signs of panic. Everything about her was so novel and so big that no established shipyard was willing to try to build her, and no firm of engineers had the plant to make the engine Brunel specified, a thousand horse-power, with a cylinder over four feet in diameter and a stroke of seven feet. So the company had to dig out a graving dock of its own, employ its own labour and set up its own workshops. And the building of the hull had already begun, and the engine had been designed for paddle wheels, when Brunel began to think about a screw propeller.

Again, it was nothing new in theory. Brunel was not an inventor: he was a genius at taking an idea and scaling it up to a size that nobody else had dreamed of. The propeller derived from the screw Archimedes invented for raising water in about 200 BC, and several people in Britain and America had made experiments with it for driving ships. The first demonstration which looked commercially hopeful was made by a Swedish engineer in practice in London and an English amateur called Francis Pettit Smith. Both of them had patents for propellers, and in 1838 they combined to build a small propeller-driven steamer which they named the *Archimedes*. She was the ship that caught Brunel's attention. He chartered her and tested her at sea, and convinced himself and the company that propellers were the thing of the future. For the *Great Britain* he made several of different design and pitch, and all of unprecedented size. But there was nothing much he could do about the engine. He mounted it lower in the ship and turned it round, fore-and-aft instead of athwartships. But it was still the slow-running kind of machine that worked with paddles: it ran at $16\frac{1}{2}$ revolutions a minute, and to drive the propeller it had to be geared up by chains which ran on a monstrous wooden sprocket.

The great ship was launched, or rather undocked, by the Prince Regent, watched by enormous crowds. But it was a disappointing ceremony, not only because the lady who threw the bottle missed the ship, but also because the ship was too broad in the beam to go out through the locks to the river. The Bristol Harbour Company had been asked before she was built to widen the locks, but they had put it off; and they went on arguing about it for another six months while the ship lay land-locked and the owners lost the revenue she might have been earning. In the end, one night in December, there was a dramatic scene by the light of burning tar-barrels, when Brunel recruited a huge gang of men and tore down the walls of the outer lock and a bridge that ran over it, and hauled the ship out and grounded her in the river. Next day, they took her down-river, started her engine and ran her up to a speed of eleven knots. But they left the Harbour Company to put the lock together again and took the ship to Liverpool; and Bristol for ever lost its chance to become the terminal for Atlantic passenger traffic.

She made four trips to New York. Her first propeller broke up, and she had all the other teething troubles one might expect. The company was desperate for money. There were times when they seemed to be too hard-up to put her in commission, and laid her up and charged admission fees to sightseers. But by September 1846 it began to seem that the troubles were over. She left Liverpool with 180 passengers, a record number for a transatlantic steamer: and her captain mistook a lighthouse in Ireland for one on the Isle of Man and ran her ashore at full speed on the Irish coast at high water springs. Nobody was hurt, one man slept through it all, and when the tide ebbed the passengers walked ashore or were carried by the local peasants. But the company was bankrupt.

The ship lay there for eleven months before she was floated again, and demonstrated that iron could take a pounding that would have broken up any wooden ship. She was towed back to Liverpool and sold for a fraction of her cost. Six years after she stranded she was ready for sea again, and she made one run to America. In 1852 there was a gold rush in Australia, and her owners put her on the Australian run. Not even she could steam so far as that, and she was fitted for sailing with a retractable propeller which could be hauled out of the water by an enormous capstan. She remained a successful Australia packet up to 1876, with interludes as a troopship in the Crimean War and the Indian Mutiny. When she was forty years old, her engine was taken out, and she became a sailing ship in a bulk cargo trade to Peru and San Francisco. In 1886 she was dismasted off the Horn and put back in distress to the Falkland Islands. The islands had become a somewhat notorious trap for disabled ships: a blacksmith there earned as much in a day as a seaman in a fortnight, and repairs were so expensive that many ships were abandoned by their owners and fell into the hands of the company that ran the place. That was the *Great Britain*'s fate. She was moored, her cargo was sold, and she became a hulk for storing the islands' produce of wool and tallow. So she remained for fifty years. In 1937 she was beached in a cove and left to disintegrate. But still Brunel's ironwork refused to fall to pieces; and in 1970 she was floated again, put on a pontoon and towed back to the dock in Bristol where she was built, to be cared for as a relic of her age.

*

Brunel was unlucky in the use that was made of his ships. They expressed in the terms of the industrial revolution the same kind of maritime pride as the ships that were built by the Petts for the Stuart kings. But he was too far ahead: the economic structure of the merchant navy was not ready for him. As ships, they were all magnificent and totally original, but as investments they were all disastrous. His third and last and greatest was financially the worst.

This was the *Great Eastern*. She was built on the Thames, broadside to the riverbank almost opposite the observatory at Greenwich, and he launched her after a struggle that lasted three months in the winter of 1857. In tonnage, she was three times the size of any ship that had ever been built – except Noah's Ark, some Biblical scholars said. She was 692 feet long and 120 feet wide, designed to carry 4000 passengers; she had six masts, 58 thousand square feet of sail, five funnels and two sets of engines which drove paddle-wheels 58 feet in diameter and also a 24-foot propeller. No other ship so big was built until the *Lusitania* in 1906, and no propeller so big has ever been used again. She would have been far too wide for the Panama Canal, which is still wide enough for most of the shipping in the world.

Her size was a logical evolution of Brunel's ideas. She was designed for the round trip to Trincomalee in Ceylon, which was already a British naval base. The idea was that most of the passengers and freight from the whole of the far east would converge on Ceylon and make use of her safety, speed and comfort for the voyage to England. No other ship, with the inefficient engines of the time, could do anything like the distance on steam alone, and she needed a coal capacity of 15,000 tons. Brunel rather blandly explained that 'nothing is proposed but to build a vessel of the size required to carry her own coals on the voyage'.

But she was never sent to Ceylon. Her first owners ran out of money before she was finished, and they sold her to another company which put her on the north Atlantic run, where her size and range were no advantage to her. She brought down the time to ten days from Liverpool to New York, and at her best she carried 1500 passengers. But she was the antithesis of the Cunarders: when she was delayed for repairs, as she often was, the owners had nothing else to offer their passengers. She was sold again and again at dwindling prices until she came into the hands of a cable company. Her greatest achievement was to lay the first Atlantic cable in 1866, but she had to be gutted to do it. She lay for ten years in Milford Haven, accumulating debts, because nobody could think of any more use for her, and when she was 30 years old she finished up as a fun-fair in the Mersey. It was said the only people who made a profit out of her were the shipbreakers, who sold innumerable bits of her as souvenirs.

But Brunel saw none of her downfall. Two days before her maiden voyage began, when he was 53, he had a stroke, and he died a few days after. Looking back, one can see that his will to experiment achieved far more than the building of three ships. It was a prototype of Victorian enterprise, and it set a target for British shipbuilders which lasted long after his death – until the British, before the end of the century, owned well over half the merchant ships in the world, and built even more than that.

*

Brunel also played a part in dragging the Royal Navy into the age of steam. In 1840, when the *Great Western* had started her regular service and the first Cunarders were building on the Clyde, Lloyd's Register listed 720 steamers owned in Britain; yet the navy still did not possess, or want to possess, a single major warship with an engine. The Admiralty was still observing Lord Melville's dictum that steam would be fatal to the Empire; it seemed to think steam was a fashion that would pass.

But Brunel's report on propellers, when the *Great Britain* was already on the stocks, did penetrate the navy's self-satisfaction. A propeller, if it could be proved to work, would remove one objection to steam – that paddle wheels would get in the way of a broadside; and quite likely the navy saw in this a chance to take to steam, after all they had said against it, without a loss of face. It was typical of the navy in any age that it would not accept the tests Brunel had made with the *Archimedes*: it had to build an experimental ship of its own. However, it did invite Brunel to give some advice; and the result was the small steam sloop *Rattler*, which made a famous and dramatic test in 1845. She was matched against a paddle steamer of similar size and power, ending the test by a tug-of-war with the ships lashed stern to stern. The *Rattler* won, and towed the paddler backwards. By 1851, when successful steamers had existed for exactly fifty years, the navy, still with reluctance, was giving up the fight. New warships after that were designed with engines and propellers, and some of the old ones were fitted with them too. But still they were sailing ships; most of the engines were only small auxiliaries, to be used in leaving harbour or as a last resort when the ships were becalmed.

Even when steam had inevitably come, most naval officers, especially the older men, detested it. They had fought it with practical arguments, but at the back of it all was the thought that steam was dirty, smelly, ugly and inartistic. Since the peace began, much of the navy's energy had been put into what the army called spit-and-polish. Some captains took it too far – it was said some had their cannon-balls polished – and some landsmen made fun of it, like Gilbert some years later in HMS *Pinafore*, whose admiral had started life polishing the door-handle of an attorney's office:

> '*I polished up that handle so carefullee*
> *That now I am the Ruler of the Queen's Navee!*'

Nevertheless, it has always been part of a sailor's pride to have things ship-shape, and the navy's sailing ships had been beautiful in the eyes of their crews – decks scrubbed, brightwork gleaming, and sails snow-white. And another part of their pride was to handle their ships with perfect artistry. Napoleon had noticed it, on board the *Bellerophon*. In a French ship getting under way, he said, everyone shouted at once. But in the *Bellerophon*, or any good British ship, the whole operation needed only two words, 'Make Sail', and the mooring was dropped and the sails were set in silence, because everyone knew exactly what to do. And that precision and artistry were almost more important in peace than they were in war; for the navy's task was not to fight other nations, but simply to impress and even entertain them in ports all over the world – to 'show the flag'. It was the primary business of a naval ship in a foreign port to look immaculate, seamanlike and utterly confident, and the navy was extremely good at it.

And what place had steam in this? the naval officers asked. What elegance would remain in ships that smelled of oil, with machinery down below that covered the decks with coal dust (of all things) and the snowy sails with smuts? What beauty or artistry could there ever be in getting a steamship under way, or bringing her up to a mooring? Sailing people have the same feeling still.

*

The navy was behind the times, but it was not alone in believing that something fundamentally good was vanishing with sail. And strangely enough, the industrial revolution which put steam on the seas also gave a new lease of life to sailing ships. Speed was the new fetish. Hitherto, nobody on the sea had worried much about it, except in naval frigates. Seamen had always accepted the winds as heaven-sent, and so had their passengers; they thanked God for a safe passage, and did not care very much how long it had taken. But now, the habit of hurry on shore infected life at sea. Owners and captains of steamers, especially on the Atlantic, were caught up in a hectic competition to knock a few minutes off the record run. And in the same decades, the age-old craft of building sailing ships was invaded by science, with the undisputed aim of making them faster.

So it came about that sailing ships only reached their ultimate grandeur after they were obsolete. The ancient rule-of-thumb in hull design, with its circular arcs and ellipses, was certainly due for a change: it had lasted for centuries. Engineers began with steamer hulls, to do their best to make them easier to drive, and so to achieve a little more speed and range; but most of the calculations they made were valid for sailing ships. New ships began to appear with altogether finer lines than any had had before, and a ratio of length to beam that had not been seen since the Viking ships and the Mediterranean galleys.

Moreover, steam tugs gave sailing ships new freedom. In the past, they had had to be handy enough to enter harbours and docks without any help, except from rowing boats when the wind fell away. Now, they could be built with much less limitation of size and rig, to show their ability only when the land was astern of them. In the cult of speed, sail plans and rigging were elaborated until a crack ship could set thirty square sails and fifteen fore-and-afters. It was the biggest change there had been since the British moved from a single mast to three in the fifteenth century.

The Blackwall Yard which had built East Indiamen began a new dynasty of ships in the nineteenth century, the Blackwall Frigates, which could out-sail any merchant ship that had been on the sea before. But this was something the Americans excelled in, and for a while the New England clippers could beat all-comers on the long sea-routes. About 1850, the Scots began to build sailing ships that could hold their own with anyone, and later in the century the Germans had some that were huge and famous in their day. Fast sailing became a cult, a mixture of sport and commerce; the rival nations claimed records for a day's run – some, rather suspect, were well over 400 miles – and they ran races to Australia and the east and back again.

The most publicised of all the races were in the tea trade – to be the first to reach England with the new season's China tea. They began as an Anglo-American competition, but when the Americans' interest started to wane at the time of the civil war, the British clippers fought against each other. The most memorable race was in 1866, when the clippers *Ariel*, *Serica* and *Taeping* all left port in China on the same day. They separated, and did not sight each other again until they were in the approaches to the Channel. The *Ariel* and *Taeping* were actually abreast, and they raced up-Channel with the *Serica* an hour or two behind them; and the *Ariel* won by ten minutes in a voyage of ninety-nine days. But that was not a record time. The American *Witch of the Wave* set a record of ninety days in 1852, and the British did not beat it until *Sir Lancelot* took a day off it in 1869.

Nowadays, an addict of tea may wonder what it was all about: could the British in those days really tell the difference between one season's tea and another, or was it all a salesman's stunt? Certainly the drama of the annual race half round the world was an excellent advertisement for tea, and the cargo of the ship that won was sold at exalted prices. And it had a reciprocal advantage: it kept the sailing ships alive. But of course it had to end. The Suez Canal was opened in 1869, the year of *Sir Lancelot*'s record, and that was the death of it. Steam engines by then were more economical in coal. Steamers could reach any port in the world, without the monstrous size that Brunel gave them; and through the canal they could bring home an eastern cargo far faster than any sailing ship. From that date on, sailing ships were driven to end their days in ignominious trades where speed did not matter much. The last in British trade was the *Garthpool*, which ran ashore in the Cape Verde Islands in 1929. A few in foreign possession, forlornly beautiful, lasted until the 1930s, carrying fertilisers from South America.

People still look back on the era of clippers as a time of high romance, and of course people still run races under sail, and always will. But perhaps the truest virtue and delight of sailing ships is something older than the cult of speed: not always to try to go faster than anyone else, but to go slowly, at the pace that people always used to go.

CHAPTER 23

Pax Britannica II

In the navy, the last arguments against the use of steam were demolished by the Crimean War in the 1850s. There was no naval opposition worth mentioning, but the ships with engines were more useful, in the Black Sea and the Baltic, than the ones without: in supporting armies, they could keep out of the way of shore batteries while the sailors were caught by their fire. And the same war taught another unwelcome lesson: that great ships of the line, impressive though they were, were not much tactical use unless they were opposed by others equally large. For one thing, their draught was too deep. There were too many shores and harbours they could not approach, and small vessels could escape them by making for shoal water. From the problems of that war, a new naval concept began: the small steam gunboat. And for the next fifty years, 'Send a gunboat' was a well-worn phrase in British diplomatic files.

In the Victorian navy, the kind of officer who prefers small ships was given his chance by the gunboat. At last, after forty years when young men had had to wait for older men to die, a new generation had a prospect of command. And they made the most of it.

Gunboats evolved like everything else, but all of them were 100 to 120 feet in length overall, with engines from 20 to 60 horse-power, and a full rig of sail. Another type, known as a gunvessel, was rather bigger. The idea was to put the largest possible gun in the smallest possible ship, and the early ones carried a 68-pounder forward, a 32-pounder aft, and two 24-pounders amidships. There were thirty to forty men in the crew, and when they went into action all the officers and men, except the lieutenant in command and the stokers shovelling coal, were either manning the guns or passing up ammunition. Even so, they could not use all their guns at once. Most of the space below was filled by the engine, bunkers, boiler and magazines, and accommodation was minimal: a tall officer, it was said, had to shave with his head sticking out of a skylight and the mirror propped on deck. Nearly two hundred of these ships were built in 1855 and 1856, in the rush of the

Crimean War, and they were still being built in 1900. All that time, they were an essential part of the structure of the Empire.

Gunboats were not very often used as offensive weapons, although they sometimes supported the army on its campaigns – up the Nile, for example, or up the rivers of China. For the most part, all over the world, they were the equivalent of the policeman on his beat; and all over the world, people in any alarming situation asked for their help and protection. British traders especially, caught up in riots or revolutions in distant countries, sent urgent requests for gunboats; so did colonial governors, consuls, chargés d'affairs, and even foreign rulers. In one year, for example, 1858, such requests came (among other places) from New Zealand, Jamaica, Panama, the Kooria Mooria Islands (to protect the guano trade), Honduras, Siam, Brazil, Sarawak, Alexandria, Vancouver (because of the excitement of a gold rush), Vera Cruz, Morocco and the fishing grounds off Newfoundland; and every one of these far-flung demands was granted. More specific errands were to investigate a murder in the New Hebrides, to help Dr Livingstone on the Zambezi, to demand the release of British prisoners in Sierra Leone and in Formosa, and to visit Jeddah 'on account of an outrage'. Even the British Museum and the Archbishop of Canterbury asked for gunboats – the first to protect an archeological dig in Cyrene, and the second to look after missionaries who were in trouble in Borneo.

The older men of the navy may have been scornful of seamanship under steam, but it was no small feat to take these clumsy little steamers all over the world: with their shallow draught and the heavy guns on deck, they had lost the seaworthiness sailing ships had had since long before Tudor times. And in spite of their sails, stories were often told of scraping the last lumps of coal from the bunkers, and breaking up the wardroom furniture to keep the boilers going. But that feat of seamanship was the cause of their success: they were effective simply because they could and did turn up wherever there was any sign of trouble. They did not often fire their monster guns. The sight of the ship, the guns and the British ensign, steaming into a roadstead or a river mouth with a conscious air of nonchalant rectitude, was enough to discourage most trouble-makers. It was a threat, or a promise, of invincible power, a reminder that Britain was keeping an eye on things.

The young men who commanded the gunboats were often thousands of miles away from their senior officers, and British policy put a big responsibility on them. Single-handed, they were expected to weigh up a local situation, judge who was right and who was wrong, and decide whether tact or a salvo of shells was the better solution. Here, for example, was the gunboat *Lynx*, 400 miles up the River Niger to settle a quarrel among the traders in palm oil, with the whole of her crew down with fever and only four men on their feet. Or the *Lee* and the *Dove*, 500 miles up the Yangtse, being shot at by rebels who were supposed to be friendly, and trying to understand the mysterious politics of the Manchu dynasty. Or others in Panama or the River Plate, suddenly finding themselves the arbiters in Spanish American revolutions. The power they carried did not seem to worry the young lieutenants, but it did worry the Admiralty and the Foreign Office, and gunboat commanders were often told not to exceed their orders, and not to involve themselves in politics – which was easier ordered than done. Very occasionally, things went badly wrong; for example, in Jamaica in 1865, when the British governor declared martial law in a riot and appointed a gunboat commander named Herbert Brand as president of a court martial. Brand was only 26, he had no relevant books of law on board and nobody to advise him; and he broke all the rules of the administration of justice and condemned 177 civilian Negroes to be hanged.

But that was an exception, and it caused an outcry in Britain. Gunboat diplomacy on the whole, in its fifty years of life, unquestionably did more good than harm. Of course it put British interests first – not mainly British conquest, but British trade. But it often went far beyond that, to sort out troubles where Britain was scarcely involved at all – to support a local ruler whose regime was peaceful, to oppose a movement that offended British ideas of law or morality, to protect a lawful person against lawlessness, whatever his nationality. Perhaps it was arrogant – some Victorians said so – but to most British people at the time it seemed a duty, one of the obligations of wealth and power. Some other people of other nations sometimes resented it, especially perhaps in France and the United States; but most of the world appeared to be quite content, for most of the time, to let the British navy carry on with its laborious and almost thankless chore, and to reap the benefits of it.

*

The benefits were no less than the freedom and safety of the sea. That was the primary interest of Britain, and equally of all seafaring nations. To achieve it, the British navy put an end to piracy. Pirates had existed ever since men went to sea; the last of them, at least of the organised kinds, were hunted out of their lairs by British gunboats in the 1860s. It also put an end to the slave trade at sea, by years of patient and dangerous patrols off both the coasts of Africa and in the Persian Gulf and Caribbean. Critics of Britain, of course, could call this hypocrisy, because sometimes in the past the British had been the most competent of pirates and slavers. But it must be admitted that the character of nations can mature, and British ideas of what was right and wrong had risen to a somewhat higher plane.

And the policy that the sea should be safe and free meant more than suppressing human malefactors: it also meant helping ships to avoid its natural hazards. British naval ships in the nineteenth century surveyed every coast in the world, except those of the United States, with a patience and meticulous care that are hard to imagine; and successive hydrographers issued charts and *Pilots* – the volumes of sailing directions – which were far better than any others, even where others existed. It was a huge and romantic undertaking, so expensive in time and money and ships that nobody else could possibly have done it, and the fund of information it collected might well have been treated as a naval secret. In war it would have been priceless. But war seemed inconceivable, and the charts and *Pilots* were published for any seafarer to use. They still are. Some other nations since then have made their own, at least of their home waters, but the original British surveys are hard to beat. They are kept up to date by all the electronic gadgets of modern surveying; but many of them still are based on the charts that were drawn by Victorian officers who crossed and recrossed every ocean, under sail or in the early steamships, observing the sun and stars and sounding with lead and line – who landed with infinite patience on every rock and reef and were rowed into every creek and harbour. Even in such a civilised sea as the Mediterranean, a navigator at the present day uses British charts dated back to the 1830s, inscribed with the names of the captains and ships that made them, and corrected for every change that has happened since.

The Royal Society, which had sponsored the explorations of the eighteenth century, made use of these world-wide expeditions by sending scientists on the surveying ships. So the surveys produced a by-product of knowledge of the natural sciences. The most famous by-product of all was on the voyage of the *Beagle*, which was sent on a five-year routine survey of the coast of South America in 1831; for the young scientist on board, of course, was Charles Darwin, and the result was his life's work on the origin of species.

But the greatest of purely scientific naval voyages was the *Challenger*

Expedition. The *Challenger* was a wooden steam corvette, and in 1872 she was put at the Royal Society's disposal. The Society sent her out with her naval crew and a bevy of distinguished naturalists. For four and a half years, she sailed again and again across the Atlantic and Pacific, and incidentally became the first steamer to cross the Antarctic Circle; and all the way, the passengers made zoological, botanical and geological collections, took deep-sea soundings and samples of the bottom of the ocean, made meteorological and magnetic observations and measured the temperature and chemical content of the sea. The report of the voyage was published in fifty volumes, a solid monument to the patience of the navy and the Victorian passion for accumulating knowledge.

*

But the real essence of Pax Britannica on the seas was law. For hundreds of years the ancient Black Book of the Admiralty had been a sufficient summary of British maritime law. But the expansion of shipping demanded a new and enormous mass of legislation in a series of Merchant Shipping Acts.

These acts were not meant to extend the British rule, or to bring foreign ships under British jurisdiction: Britain never claimed any legal authority over anyone else on the high seas, excepting the pirates and slavers. On the contrary, the last of the restricting Navigation Acts was repealed in the middle of the century, and the new Merchant Shipping Acts – or at least the first of them – were designed to protect sea-passengers and seamen against the possible wickedness of British shipowners. Like so much of the best of Victorian progress, the spate of new law was begun by a single passionate reformer. He was Samuel Plimsoll, a rather insignificant coal merchant who became a Member of Parliament in 1868. His passion was the suffering of seamen in what he called coffin-ships, unseaworthy or overloaded ships sent out by unscrupulous owners and heavily insured. He wrote a book about it and managed to get a royal commission appointed, and a Bill was introduced to bring the shipowners under control. But before the Bill was passed, Disraeli, who was Prime Minister at the time, announced that the Government had decided to drop it. At that, Plimsoll lost his temper in the House, called members of it villains, and shook his fist in the Speaker's face – and by that scandalous outburst did more for seamen than he could have done by a lifetime of patient argument. He had to apologise, but the uproar he had made roused public opinion on his side; the Bill was revived, and in 1875 it became law. It gave power to the Board of Trade, as the government

agency, to survey ships and pass them as fit for sea, and to have them marked
with the load line which has been known ever since as the Plimsoll line.

In the next thirty years this original Act was extended until every con-
ceivable aspect of shipping was controlled by law, and a merchant service
captain had to become not only a seaman but something of a legal expert too.
A modern manual of law for owners and masters admits rather ruefully that
'the misdemeanours created by the several Merchant Shipping Acts are
numerous enough to test even an excellent memory.'

Most of this British legislation was adopted with very little change by
other seafaring countries. It would be difficult now to analyse exactly how
this came about. Some regulations had to be international to be any use –
the rules for avoiding collisions, for example, which were first put into legal
form with the authority of Parliament in 1863 – and these were adopted by
international conventions. Some, like the regulations of safety and seaworthiness, spread mainly because such a large proportion of foreign ships were
built in Britain and insured at Lloyd's. And in general, British law was
probably used as a model because it was the first to exist and was proved in
practice to be workable and just.

It would be foolish to claim that Pax Britannica at sea was philanthropic:
national motives are never quite so simple. Britain stood to gain more than
anyone else through freedom and the rule of law at sea, simply because the
British merchant service, and the shipbuilding industry, were much bigger
than anyone else's. But on the other hand, it was not entirely selfish, and that
was the remarkable thing about it. Britain did most of the work of ensuring
the safety of the sea, and claimed no privilege in return. Perhaps even that
suggests a national virtue that could never really have existed. It is often said
the British acquired an empire without intending to, and the same might be
said of the freedom under law that they established on the sea. They may
never quite have been conscious of what they were doing. Nevertheless, the
sea now is safe from pirates, slavers, uncharted rocks and unpredicted
currents. Everyone takes it for granted that ships of every nation, in times of
peace, can go unmolested on it wherever they wish. But that is certainly
not an ancient freedom. It is only a legacy of the hundred years when Britain
controlled the seas, and conceived that this was how things ought to be.

*

In the second half of the century, the British began again to take a romantic
pride in the Royal Navy, a pride that had rather lapsed since the end of

Napoleon's war. It was a great age for naval songs and verses – not sailors' songs, which might have been thought to be coarse, but songs that glorified sailors. 'The Old Superb', 'Drake's Drum', 'Admirals All', 'Land of Hope and Glory', 'Rule Britannia': gentlemen sang them at musical evenings in ladies' drawing-rooms, and humbler men in pubs, and everyone joined in the choruses, which could bring tears to their eyes. In sober fact, the British were beginning to delude themselves about the navy. Britannia seemed to have ruled the waves so long that they could persuade themselves she always had and always would. Historically, of course, it was nonsense; and as to the future, it was rather dangerous nonsense. People began to have blind faith in the navy's invincibility, and the blind faith infected the navy too. But as the century passed, the navy's supremacy was resting more and more on past prestige, and less on present power.

Meanwhile, popular admiration improved the sailor's lot. People outside the navy began to take an interest in how it was run. No sailor likes to be told what to do by landlubbers, and the Admiralty was as touchy as ever at anything that looked like criticism; but the public interest made it take a fresh look at its own administration. To begin with, it started training ships. A young volunteer no longer had to learn the ropes at sea in an active ship, and risk the wrath of the petty officers if he was slow to learn; he was taught some seamanship and gunnery, and given some general education, before he went to sea. And the navy began at last to offer its seamen a steady career, with a pension at the end of it. Seamen no longer signed on in a specific ship, to be paid off ashore when its commission ended. They signed on in the navy, and a ship was always found for them. New ratings with extra pay were created, so that a competent seaman could become reasonably prosperous.

All this gave a new kind of dignity to the naval seaman's job: so did another thing, the introduction of uniforms in 1857. It is a mystery why the navy resisted the use of uniforms so long, except that it resisted so many things that looked like innovations. Soldiers had had them for centuries, and naval officers for over a hundred years. They had been recommended for seamen for at least as long, especially by naval doctors who knew that men brought aboard in their own dirty clothes brought vermin and diseases that flourished in the confines of a ship. Pursers, sold clothes to seamen from their slop-chests, and they were more or less standardised; but men had to pay for them, and when they were broke they wore what rags they had.

The Great Eastern

The *Cutty Sark's* win over *S.S. Britannia*, 25th July, 1888 by David Cobb

The Naval Review, Spithead 1897, by C. Dixon

King George V in full-dress uniform of
Admiral of the Fleet

The new uniform was designed by an Admiralty committee, but it followed the fashion that seamen had made for themselves. It was much the same as it is today, except that it had a straw hat. The navy has always liked to believe the black scarf was a sign of mourning for Nelson, and that the three rows of tape on the collar represented his three famous victories. But the committee did not have that romantic idea. The scarfs had been in fashion long before Nelson's time; men tied them round their heads on the gundecks in battle to protect their ears and keep the sweat out of their eyes. As for the tapes, the committee seems to have decided on three rows because some members wanted two and some wanted four. But still, generations of seamen have worn these things as emblems of Nelson, and the tribute is all the more sincere for being unofficial.

The uniform had none of the army's garish colours; it still stuck to the sober blue of the Duchess of Bedford's riding habit. But it was certainly distinctive, something the seaman at last could 'cut a dash' in. Any man who swaggered into town in it was assumed to have a character to match – intrepid at sea and disarmingly wicked ashore. By the end of the century, the music-halls added their songs to the seaman's new reputation. 'All the nice girls love a sailor': everyone sang it, and that at least was an image a seaman was glad to live up to.

*

It was not in the quality of its seamen or officers that the navy began to lag behind, it was in the design of its ships and armament. The French were again the nation which began to show signs of rivalry. As early as 1848, they launched the first line-of-battle ship that was designed for steam: it was named the *Napoleon*. The British did the same two years later, choosing to revive the name of Nelson's favourite ship, the *Agamemnon*. But the *Napoleon* could and did make voyages under steam alone, and achieved the remarkable speed of fourteen knots; the *Agamemnon* was only a sailing ship with a small auxiliary engine, and she looked very much like her predecessor except for the narrow funnel between her main and mizzen masts. A more direct reply to the French *Napoleon*, and more aptly named, was the British *Duke of Wellington*, completed in 1853. She also was much the same in appearance, but she had an engine of 2000 horse-power.

The next move was in the late 1850s, when the French introduced explosive shells for naval guns, instead of cannon-balls, and also built the obvious corollary, an armour-plated ship that could withstand them. As it happened, this was again the *Napoleon*, which was fitted with a belt of 5-inch iron plates and renamed *La Gloire* in 1859. The British replied with their first iron-clad, the *Warrior*, which had 4½ inches of wrought iron on a backing of 18 inches of teak. Then breech-loading guns: both navies started them at about the same time, but the French mechanism worked, while the British one so often burst and killed its crew that the navy went back to muzzle-loading for another twenty years.

Larger guns had longer range and far more hitting power, so that a few large guns became better than a mass of small ones. That meant putting them in revolving turrets on the centre-line of the ship, instead of the broad-side gunports that went back to Henry VIII. And that in turn meant that masts and rigging restricted the arcs of fire. The daring answer was to abandon the sailing rig and rely on steam alone. The United States took this step with the *Monitor* of 1862. But she was not an ocean-going ship, and the British could claim, with the *Devastation* of 1873, the first battleship in the world that was designed without a sail. She was a product of fierce contro-versy, and a rather more orthodox rival was launched the same year, reviving another of Nelson's names, the *Captain*. She had everything, armour, steam, guns in centre-line turrets and a full rig of sail. But she also had the low freeboard which the heavy guns demanded, and she overturned and sank in the Bay of Biscay, and took her designer down with her. That disaster, after so many centuries, was the final end of the battleship under sail.

The trouble was not, as it might have appeared, that the British were lacking in inventiveness: on the contrary, they were leading the world in invention at sea. But it was always the merchant navy that used the inven-tions first: the Admiralty still behaved, with every new idea, just as it had with steam. It seemed to want to shut its eyes as long as it could to anything that threatened to make the ships it cherished obsolete.

The history of submarines was a case in point. The earliest submarines were American, and they began, under man-power, a surprisingly long time ago. One at least was used in the War of Independence, and in 1804 another was offered to the British by Robert Fulton, the American inventor who built some of the earliest steamboats. The First Lord of the time, the great St Vincent himself, rejected it – not because it would not work, but because it might. The Prime Minister, he wrote, was 'the greatest fool that ever existed to encourage a mode of warfare which those who commanded the seas did not want and which, if successful, would deprive them of it.' The grammar was extraordinary, but the thought was perfectly typical of the

Admiralty for generations to come. Submarines continued to exist, but the navy continued to behave as if they did not until 1899, when the French built one that was capable of making ocean passages; and even then, not many people in Britain saw the significance of it.

Torpedoes were another invention the British would gladly have done without. In elementary forms, they also dated back to the War of Independence, but the first that could steer itself under its own power was invented by Robert Whitehead in 1867. Whitehead was a Scotsman, but his invention was inopportune. It could be fired by a very small ship and sink a very big one; and Britain, of course, owned most of the very big ships in the world. France, Germany, Russia and Japan all equipped themselves with fast torpedo boats; the British once more were obliged to defend the status quo – this time by fitting their battleships with anti-torpedo-boat guns, and with cumbersome nets which were rigged round the ships at anchor.

In the 1880s and '90s, new ideas and inventions were coming so fast that a new naval ship could be obsolete before it was launched. Britain had formed a policy of keeping a navy larger than any other two navies in the world. It was perhaps a policy that gave too much importance to size, and not enough to quality. Other navies grew, and a race in sheer numbers began. British yards turned out new warships at an astonishing speed; but the navy became reluctant to scrap its older ships – there was always a use for them in showing the flag, long after they were out of date as warships. So the navy, which looked so invincibly strong, began to have a hidden inherent weakness: its ships were not designed to form a coherent fleet, or to fit a strategic plan for a naval war. And there were so many different kinds of ships of assorted ages, and of machinery, guns and ammunition, that training, store-keeping and maintenance could hardly keep pace.

The navy itself, on the whole, was not aware of this weakness; there was no other navy fit for comparison. And the peace-keeping navy reached a kind of apotheosis in 1897. The occasion was the Diamond Jubilee of the Queen: seven miles of ships were assembled at Spithead in review. No other display in any single place could so directly have symbolised the integrity of imperial power; for the navy was the chain that bound together all the scattered lands of the British Empire, and its mastery at sea was their protection. Ordinary British people were not particularly proud to have an empire: it was something too far away to be easily imagined. But they were still intensely proud to have such a navy, which was visible and splendid.

And the navy still reflected this national pride with a pride of its own. It still thought of itself as Nelson's navy, or even Drake's, incomparably the finest navy the world had ever seen. Other nations might have minor navies; but to a British officer or rating at the end of that century, it was inconceivable that any foreigner could come near the elegance, precision, confidence and efficiency of British naval seamanship. It was something only the British could do to perfection; or at least, they thought it was. The navy there at Spithead, stately and dignified, was prepared to be admired, loved, cheered, painted and photographed – one hundred and seventy ships dressed overall, immaculate in appearance and faultless in ceremonial. It was the largest assembly of warships there had ever been, unless one re-membered the masses of little ships of early kings, like the fleet that put out from this same roadstead to take the army to Agincourt. And yet it was only a fraction of British strength at sea: even on that day, the navy was at its usual stations and on its routine patrols in every sea in the world. The royal yacht cruised down the glittering lines, followed by steamers carrying royal guests. The Prince of Wales, who of course was an admiral, took the salute of the ships: the Queen had not felt up to the strain of it. The crews manned ship and raised their caps and cheered, and on the shores and in innumerable boats, more ordinary people waved and cheered among the gunfire and the music, and enjoyed the reflected glory.

*

That Jubilee year marked a climax also in Britain's trade at sea. The mer-chants since Norman times had steadily pushed out their routes at sea, taking as little notice as possible of wars and the whims of kings and governments; and at the end of the nineteenth century they came to a peak of power not even they could ever have excelled. Fifty-two per cent of all the shipping in the world was owned in Britain; the next competitor was the United States, with only 8 per cent. Shipbuilding was even stronger: 64 per cent of all the tonnage afloat had been built in British yards. And these figures had not been achieved by repressing anyone else; they had been won in straight-forward competition, simply because the British in those single-minded days built better ships and ran them more efficiently than anyone.

It was half a century since the death of Brunel, the pioneer. Those had been years of growth so quick that it was bewildering. Ships had increased beyond belief in size and diversity. Up to the seventeenth century, there had roughly speaking been one kind of ship which was used for everything. Up to the early nineteenth century there had been two, the merchant ship and the warship. But now there were dozens, each with a special purpose of its own: the passenger liners, cross-channel packets, ferry boats, coasters, refrigerator ships, ore carriers, the first oil tankers, tramps which picked up cargoes wherever they could, and the colliers which filled the coaling stations all over the world that kept the others going. Looking back, there is tragedy in the thought of the armies of craftsmen and labourers in Scotland and the northern estuaries of England, who built this multitude of ships to roam the world but spent every night of their lives in dreadful tenements, or the clerks on the stools in the magnates' offices, writing out lists of cargo for exotic ports they could never hope to see. But the poets of Empire could find romance in it all: 'Yes, weekly from Southampton, Great steamers white and gold Go rolling down to Rio – '; or at another extreme, the 'Dirty British coaster with a salt-caked smoke-stack, Butting through the Channel in the mad March days.' Britain had never before been a nation so sea-minded.

There was another source of romance in the shipping lines that were founded, grew to commercial empires, bought and sold each other and often died. Each of the great survivors of those lines had a character of its own, a pride in its flag and a jealous regard for its routes. The Atlantic crossing remained a desperate competition in speed and comfort, Cunard and White Star building ship after ship, each bigger and faster and more elegant than the last. In the 1850s – to pick out a few – the Cunarder *Asia* had a displacement of 3600 tons and a speed of twelve knots; in the '70s, the *Britannic*, 9600 tons and sixteen knots; in the '90s, the *Campania*, 21,000 tons and twenty-two knots; and beyond the turn of the century the Cunarders *Lusitania* and *Mauretania*, and the White Star's unfortunate *Titanic*, took the record of size beyond 50,000 tons and of speed beyond twenty-five knots. Other passenger lines were less hectic. The Union-Castle, from Southampton to South Africa; Shaw Savill and Albion, going regularly round the world, out to New Zealand by the Cape of Good Hope and home by Cape Horn; the Pacific and Royal Mail to South America and Australia; the British India Line among the Spice Islands that seamen had sought so long – all these gave hundreds of thousands of British people a glimpse once or twice in a lifetime of tropical seas. Of them all, the P. & O. had the most individual air, because it was the home-link for all the British in India; on its long leisurely voyages through the Mediterranean, the Suez Canal and the Indian Ocean, ship-board romances were planned and flowered or faded, the distinctions of class and rank were most rigidly observed, and the whole esoteric world of the Raj was displayed in a microcosm.

And whenever any of this host of passengers, anywhere on the oceans, were idly watching the horizon and sighted another ship, more likely than not it was flying the same red ensign as their own. It is really no wonder they felt the seas were theirs.

Yet at the core of all the skill and grandeur was that undetected flaw: the huge variety of unco-ordinated ships that formed the Royal Navy. In the Jubilee year itself, there was a shock: a foreign liner – and not even American – suddenly seized the Blue Riband of the Atlantic, a ship that was bigger and faster than the latest of all the Cunarders. Her name was *Kaiser Wilhelm der Grosse*, and perhaps a few people in Britain saw an omen. But very few saw the truth: that if another industrial nation chose to ignore the accepted status of Britain, and to build a smaller, modern, cohesive fighting fleet, British tradition and most of the British ships would be powerless; for the finest of seamanship could not do much, after all, against faster ships and guns of longer range. And within a year of the great review, another nation made that deliberate choice – not one of Britain's rivals of the past, but an upstart in naval affairs that had never had any power at sea since the middle ages: Germany.

*

In modern times historians, especially British historians, have often said the navy had grown complacent, and have blamed it for the dangerous state it was in. Certainly, the Admiralty had sometimes been absurd, but there is another side to the picture. A hundred years is a long time, and all that time the policy of Britain had demanded a peace-keeping strength from the navy, not a strength for war, which was quite a different quality. And all that time, the navy had done extremely well the duty the nation gave it. It was really the job of the politicians, not the admirals, to foresee that the policy might be challenged and might be forced to change.

Luckily, the navy produced one officer at the end of the century who saw that the challenge was coming, and that the navy, to meet it, needed different ships and training and strategy, and a different attitude of mind – that it needed, as he put it, reform from top to bottom or else (it was one of his favourite phrases) it would be caught with its breeches down.

This was Admiral Sir John Fisher: Jacky Fisher, as he was known throughout the navy. In 1898 he was C.-in-C. Mediterranean, an efficient, energetic, rude and outspoken little man whose naval career went right back to the sailing battleships of the Crimean War. He adored the navy, and was extremely worried about the state it was in.

There was nothing he could do about it until 1901. Then he was appointed Second Sea Lord, which put him in charge of personnel and training; and the navy found it had something like a hurricane on its hands. He only held the post two years, but in that time he swept away the whole of the system of training the navy had relied on for half a century, and ruthlessly trampled on all the opposition: 'Get on or get out' was another of his phrases. He scrapped the ancient training ships, founded the colleges for officers at Dartmouth and at Osborne in the Isle of Wight, extended officer training from one and a half to four years, and built schools ashore for seamen in the dockyard towns.

After that, he had a year as C.-in-C. Portsmouth. Then he came back to the Admiralty as First Sea Lord, which gave him the chance to be equally ruthless about the navy's ships. 'Scrap the lot' was the phrase of this period: he wrote it across a list of 154 ships, including seventeen battleships, which he said were only devices for wasting men. He insisted that only four types of ship were needed for the kind of war that might be fought in the future: battleships of twenty-one knots, driven by turbines (a new British invention) and armed entirely with 12-inch guns; armoured cruisers of twenty-five-and-a-half knots; destroyers of thirty-six knots; and submarines. Through his threats and persuasion, the first of the battleships was ready for trials at sea a year and a day from the laying of her keel – the same vaguely mystical length of time that the Scots took to build the *Great Michael* in 1506. She was the famous *Dreadnought*, a masterpiece among warships. By 1908, the navy had seven Dreadnoughts in commission or building, and a corresponding number of new ships of the other classes, all as up-to-date as science could make them.

And Fisher also scrapped the navy's world-wide strategy. No navy, he said, however large, could police the whole world and also be ready in European waters for a major war. So he progressively brought it home and disposed it to meet the threat from Germany; oceans that had known the British presence for a hundred years were now left empty. Plenty of people saw in this the downfall of the empire; and perhaps they were right, in so far as it was the beginning of its end. But Fisher insisted downfall was coming certainly and soon unless the navy were concentrated for the defence of Britain.

To achieve all this, he was cruel and intolerant, and mercilessly wrecked the careers of men who got in his way. Opposition made him more and more angry, impatient and dictatorial. Some of the opposition, one has to admit, looks stupid in retrospect. People criticised the *Dreadnought* with the same old illogical argument the navy had used against steam and submarines, and almost every other innovation: they agreed she was a splendid ship and made all foreign battleships obsolete, but they opposed her because she also made all British battleships obsolete. And on another of Fisher's proposals, the First Lord (the civil head of the navy) brought forth a final example of reactionary blindness. Fisher believed in oil, not coal, as the fuel for warships. And the First Lord replied that 'the substitution of oil for coal is impossible, because the oil does not exist in this world in sufficient quantities.' Luckily, Fisher had his way again: oil-fired boilers were fitted first in the smaller ships and then in destroyers and cruisers, and soon were followed by diesel engines; and of course, the more oil the navy needed, the more it found.

In the end, power quite turned the head of this extraordinary man. He came to believe he was always right, and everyone else was almost always wrong. He had favourite names for people who disagreed with him – the Yellow Admirals, the Syndicate of Discontent, the Bathchair Harriers. In his early days, he had often said he would break any man for the good of the navy; later, he openly said he would break any man who opposed him. The two things probably meant the same to him, but they sounded very different to other people.

At last, the navy rebelled. On the whole, it understood his reforms, but it could not stand his methods or his manners. He had such a disastrous quarrel with the C.-in-C. Channel Fleet, Lord Charles Beresford, that the Prime Minister had to appoint a Cabinet committee to investigate it. Among other things, the committee proposed there should be a Naval War Staff to advise the members of the Board of Admiralty, and the Commanders-in-Chief at sea, on naval strategy and tactics. That idea drove Fisher to his final fury: there was only one opinion on strategy and tactics, he believed, and that was his. The proposal was a rebuke of his single-handed rule. A War Staff, he wrote, was 'a very excellent organisation for cutting out and arranging foreign newspaper clippings.' It would 'make excellent sea officers into very indifferent clerks.' So he had to go. His office had lasted just over five years: not long, but the terrible storms he raised had blown away a century's dust and cobwebs. That was in 1910: it was only just in time.

CHAPTER 24

The Climax of Power

IN the long history of the British and the sea, the present century shows an ultimate peak of power and an ultimate decline. To put a date on the peak would be a matter of opinion. Perhaps the greatest achievement of the British at sea was the century of peace which ended in 1914; or perhaps, by more martial values, it was the fighting of the early 1940s, when seamanship was put to as hard a test as any in all the centuries before.

The decline, when it came, was not due to any lapse of seamanship, it was caused by poverty, the economic exhaustion of the two world wars. And it was not simply a decline of the power at sea of one nation. It was a passage into an era when power at sea, whoever possesses it, is no longer self-sufficient or all-important: the era when ships on the surface in war are outmatched by aircraft above and submarines below, and oceans are spanned by missiles, and everything is overshadowed by atomic weapons – the era also when most of the ancient arts of seamanship, in war or peace, can be outdated by electronics. Britain has lost her supreme power, but the same kind of power could not exist in the modern world, or ever exist in isolation again.

The Germans in 1914 were the only people who ever actively coveted the costly and thankless privilege of ruling the seas. But the fleet they were building was still a long way from equality with Britain's when the First World War began. They had twenty new battleships and battle-cruisers, and seven building; Britain, thanks to Fisher's push, had twenty-seven, and twenty building. And Britain still had a vast number of older battleships and cruisers scattered round the seas. France, the old naval enemy, was Britain's ally, but after setting the pace in the earlier days of steam, the French navy had lagged behind, and it had very few big modern ships.

Yet counting up capital ships was not a good measure of strength for the wars that were coming. The great battlefleet under steam was still the principal pride of the navy, and still the principal emblem of power at sea; but a long period was just beginning – a period of forty years – in which the proudest and most splendid fleet was slowly proved to be an illusory weapon which could hardly ever fight the battles it was designed for. The British had to have a battlefleet in 1914 because the Germans had one: the Germans built one because the British had one. And the British still had one, with much less reason, when the second war began in 1939. But even in the first war, sixty years ago, it was a puzzle to find enough positive use for it to justify its enormous cost. Its main function was the same as Cornwallis's in 1804, the dull and inglorious chore of simply existing, in order to keep the enemy fleet in port.

In both the wars the British had more than enough of the greatest ships, the visible symbols of strength. It was not only the navy that took a pride in them: everyone did, and many people in retrospect still do. But they took too much of the navy's money, manpower, shipyard and dockyard space; and Britain came near to losing both the wars through lack of the smaller, humbler ships which could do the work that battleships could not do.

That was not the only resemblance between the two world wars. On land, they were entirely different: the first fought in trenches on static fronts, the second in fast thrusts of armoured troops. But at sea they were remarkably alike, in spite of the quarter-century between them – two variations on a single theme. The navy's role was the same in each of them: to defend the country against invasion or sea-attack, to blockade a continental enemy, to prevent a blockade of Britain, and to carry armies overseas and land them on hostile shores. And indeed this role was exactly the same as it had been in Nelson's time, or Drake's.

It took some weeks of war, at the end of the hundred years of peace, for the navy to regain the Nelson outlook. Perhaps it was helped by a sad coincidence. In August 1914, two German cruisers were at large in the Mediterranean, and the Admiralty ordered the C.-in-C. Mediterranean not to engage superior enemy forces. That was a signal any officer would have scorned in Nelson's time. But two days after war was declared, a force of British cruisers met the Germans. The British admiral knew the Germans could outrange his guns, and against his own inclination he observed the order and withdrew. As it happened, he was Rear-Admiral Troubridge, a direct descendant of Nelson's famous captain. He was court martialled and acquitted, but never given another command at sea. The incident shocked the navy, and his name reminded it of better-spirited actions. It was not very long before it began again to think and act as it had under Nelson's command – to observe, whatever the situation, the last signal he hoisted at Trafalgar: engage the enemy more closely.

Both wars began with isolated German warships stationed far out in the oceans, ready to raid merchant ships; in both wars, the first naval battles were fought far from home off the coasts of South America. On a November evening in 1914, in rough seas off the port of Coronel in Chile, three British cruisers and an armed merchantman encountered five German cruisers. Both sides, like the eighteenth-century fleets, formed line ahead and set converging courses to attack. But the British were to the eastward, and the German admiral, the famous Graf von Spee, held off until the sun went down. The British were then silhouetted against the sunset sky, the Germans almost invisible. In half an hour of long-range shooting one British cruiser, the *Monmouth*, was set on fire and out of control. Soon after, the flagship *Good Hope* exploded and the whole of her company was lost. The two surviving ships drew off to the southward, where an ancient battleship, the *Canopus*, was striving at eleven knots to reach the scene; and von Spee lost touch in the darkness and withdrew to the north.

At that time, the First Lord of the Admiralty was Winston Churchill, and at his insistence Admiral Fisher had been recalled as First Sea Lord. These two determined men had always had a somewhat uneasy respect for each other's talents. Fisher came back into office the day before news reached London of the Coronel disaster, and his reaction was characteristic. He instantly ordered two of the new battle-cruisers built under his regime to sail from Plymouth full speed for the Falkland Islands in case the Germans tried to come round Cape Horn. The dockyard said the ships were not ready for such a long voyage: he gave them three days to get ready. Then he was told the firebricks in their boilers were being rebuilt and could not possibly be finished so soon. He answered that all the bricklayers in the dockyard would have to go with the ships and finish the job on the way.

Of course they sailed within three days; Fisher on his mettle was still not a man to admit impossibility. They reached the Falkland Islands on 7th December and began to refuel; for this was one of the scores of coaling stations the navy maintained all over the world. The very next day the German squadron was sighted. Outmatched, it made off towards the south Atlantic, but the battle-cruisers overhauled it and took revenge for Coronel. Four of the five German cruisers were sunk the same evening. One escaped, back round the Horn, and later was found at anchor off Masafuego, the little island near Juan Fernandez where Philip Carteret took refuge, in his crazy sloop the *Swallow*, at the beginning of the eighteenth-century age of exploration. As soon as she came under fire, her captain scuttled her.

That was the last of the Germans' surface ships on the high seas. Their merchant ships had all disappeared. Of their other warships, the two in the Mediterranean had entered the Black Sea and would certainly never get out; one, the *Emden*, had been sunk off the Cocos Islands after a short but successful and daring career; one had exploded in the Caribbean, and one had been driven into a mangrove swamp on the east coast of Africa. The German High Seas Fleet itself was in its home ports, and the British Home Fleet was confident of keeping it there. On the face of it, within four months of the war's beginning, the navy had beaten the challenge and kept its total command of the oceans. But Germany was working on new weapons designed to destroy sea-power in its traditional form.

Before those weapons were thoroughly in action, the navy involved itself in a task it ought not to have started, and became a victim of its own tradition of refusing to admit there was anything on the sea it could not do. This was the Dardanelles campaign. It was Churchill's idea to send a fleet through the Dardanelles to Constantinople and the Black Sea. The political aims were to force the Turks out of the war, which they had joined on the side of the Germans, and to open a supply route to Russia – the latter a problem which arose again in the second war and then was partly solved in a different way, and with almost equal suffering.

It started in January 1915 when Churchill signalled the admiral who was watching the Dardanelles in case the two German cruisers tried to come out: 'Do you think it is practicable to force the Dardanelles by ships alone?' The admiral, in duty bound, produced a plan to do it. Fisher disliked the idea, but mainly because he thought it would take too many ships away from home waters: he could not bring himself to say that the navy could not do it.

It has been argued ever since, but the fact seems clear: it was not and could never have been a proper use for warships to fight through a narrow strait which was held on both sides by an enemy and defended by land artillery and mines. Ships were designed to fight ships, with sea-room to manœuvre. In waters where there was scarcely room to turn, in point-blank range of shore emplacements, no amount of naval skill could make them anything but sitting targets.

During February and March, the navy made three attempts at this desperate enterprise, supported by the French. In the third of them, six battleships and battle-cruisers were sunk or put out of action. They were ready to go on trying, but at that point Churchill persuaded Lord Kitchener, the Secretary of State for War, to provide a large army for support. There was a long pause while the army was assembled. At the end of April, the navy began to put it ashore. But the Turks by then were well prepared to resist it, and in another eight months, with terrible mortality, the soldiers never gained more than a foothold on the fateful peninsula of Gallipoli. In December, the disastrous affair was abandoned, and the navy took the last survivors off.

Perhaps it was right to try. No doubt success would have shortened the war and saved other lives. But it cannot have been right to try with ships alone and then, three months later, when the defence was fully alerted and prepared, to land an army. As things went from bad to worse, Fisher quarrelled disastrously with Churchill and resigned; and when it was proved impossible after all, Churchill also lost office as First Lord.

While that violent action was going on in the eastern Mediterranean, the Grand Fleet in home waters, like Nelson's fleet before Trafalgar, was suffering the boredom of blockade. Tradition demanded a close blockade of the enemy's ports – tradition that went back far beyond Nelson's time, to the strategy Drake had preached when England awaited the Armada. But close blockade was something a sailing fleet could achieve and a fleet under steam could not; for a sailing fleet, of course, could stay out at sea for years, but a fleet under steam had to come back to port for coal. And something else kept the fleet of 1915 at a distance from German ports, the hidden weapons Germany relied on, the submarine and the mine. A deep minefield had been laid off the whole of the German North Sea coast, with only three guarded channels through it. And outside it, any ship ran the risk of torpedoes from the submarines, against which there was no defence more practical than luck – and the larger the ship, on the whole, the larger the risk. So the Grand Fleet was obliged to block the northern exits of the North Sea, to patrol in cold and stormy seas and shelter in the bleak anchorage of Scapa Flow or the wild sea lochs of the west coast of Scotland. The blockade was perfectly successful and it rendered useless the German High Seas Fleet; but the British longed for the more resounding victory their great ships had been designed for, while the Germans equally longed for the open sea.

For nearly two years, the fleets faced each other across the North Sea and never met. Both sides made sorties with cruisers and destroyers, and sometimes with battle-cruisers. Both tried to lay traps, by using a weak force to lure a major fleet towards one even stronger, or towards a pack of submarines. There were several minor battles, and from time to time the Germans in hit-and-run raids shelled seaside towns on the east coast of England, which made the inhabitants ask angrily what the navy was doing.

Ships of both sides were often out together in the no-man's-land of the North Sea without sighting each other. The ships of that war, in spite of their power and speed, had no better means of detection than Nelson's fleet: the human eye. Senior officers, and officers of the watch, not only carried telescopes under their arms, they still used them; and masts were still manned by lookouts who watched the horizon no longer for sails but for smoke. Radio was used for sending orders in morse from shore to ship, and less often between the flagships of separate squadrons; but signals within a squadron were made by flags or lamps. There was only one omen of things to come in these North Sea skirmishes: the Germans sometimes used Zeppelins, their airships or dirigibles, to search for the British fleet.

The great encounter came at last on 31st May, 1916. Very early that morning, the German fleet put to sea in force towards the coast of Norway. The reason for their change of strategy, when nothing else had changed, may have been that they had a new and aggressive commander-in-chief, Admiral von Scheer, who evidently hoped for battle.

The Admiralty had broken a German naval code and had intercepted radio signals which warned it of the German intention. So it was able to order the Grand Fleet out before the Germans sailed. From Scapa Flow, the Cromarty Firth and the Firth of Forth, the Fleet emerged with the splendour that distinguished this weapon of war: twenty-eight modern battleships, nine battle-cruisers, eight armoured cruisers, twenty-six light cruisers, seventy-seven destroyers and torpedo boats.

It was by far the most powerful fleet ever sent to sea in war under one man's command, and the man was Admiral Sir John Jellicoe, flying his flag in the *Iron Duke*. Jellicoe was a man of 57, who had entered the navy in the traditional way when he was 13; he was highly respected as an organiser and a strategist, and he had been a member of Fisher's committee which designed the new ships that formed his fleet. Among the nine Admirals serving under him, the best known at the time was David Beatty, commanding the First Battle-cruiser Squadron, a dashing, flamboyant fighter whose bulldog expression, enhanced by his habit of wearing his cap on one side, epitomised the British concept of a sea-dog. Beatty's first command had been a gunboat on the River Nile, and he fought in it at the Battle of Omdurman in 1898; his last a battleship on the China station. He was a protégé of Churchill's.

In their function as scouts, fast and well armed enough to take care of themselves, the battle-cruisers were largely independent of the battle fleet, and Beatty led them in the *Lion* that night, across the North Sea to the exit of the channel through the German minefield, supported by four battleships and a large number of cruisers and destroyers. Early the next afternoon he was 100 miles north of the minefield and about the same distance off the Danish coast of Jutland, when the Admiralty intercepted another German radio message. But they misread it and signalled him and Jellicoe that the German fleet was still in port. So he turned north to meet Jellicoe.

It was a misty afternoon, and by a pure chance one of his outlying cruisers sighted a German cruiser. He turned back to investigate. But the supporting battleships did not see the flag signal he hoisted, and it had to be repeated to them by a searchlight in morse. They were ten miles away before they read it and followed his turn. This was the second of the failures in signals that were to have a cumulative effect on the impending battle.

At half past three, Beatty sighted four German battle-cruisers which turned away to the southward. He signalled Chase, and at 3.45 both sides opened fire at a range of nearly nine miles.

These opening shots were an astonishing disaster. The *Lion* was hit on one of her midship turrets, a fire was started below, and the ship was saved only by flooding the midships magazines. A few minutes later the *Indefatigable*, another of the new Dreadnought battle-cruisers, blew up and immediately sank. Only two of her crew were saved. Within half an hour another, the *Queen Mary*, had the same dramatic end. 'There seems to be something wrong with our bloody ships today,' Beatty is said to have said; and indeed there was something wrong, but nobody knew what it was. He merely gave the order to engage more closely. The supporting battleships came up and also went into action.

But the German admiral was not in flight. He was leading Beatty towards the German battlefleet which, far from being in port, was almost in range to the southward. Soon after 4.30, a light cruiser made the signal everyone had awaited for two years: Enemy battlefleet in sight. The signal was repeated by radio to Jellicoe.

That made it Beatty's turn to try to lead the German battlefleet into contact with Jellicoe's, and to do it without allowing their cruisers to sight the British first and give a warning. He reversed his course; but the battle-ships missed the signal again and carried on until they were in range of the German battlefleet. They survived, and did more damage as they went.

The two great fleets were approaching each other at an aggregate speed of over forty knots. All in all, 246 ships were steaming at top speed in a small area of sea, and gun and funnel smoke were being added to the North Sea mist. Visibility fell to less than the range of the big guns of either side, and so any squadron was likely to find itself suddenly under fire. Soon after six o'clock, yet another battle-cruiser, the *Invincible*, was split in two by an explosion: she sank with her midships section on the bottom of the shallow sea, and her bow and stern both sticking out of the water. Admiral von Scheer, leading his fleet in line ahead, did not know the British fleet was anywhere near until 6.15, when he sighted it crossing his bows, well within range, and his three leading ships were hit. By a last minute deployment, Jellicoe had put his fleet in the position of advantage the French had held at Trafalgar. The Germans altered course 180 degrees, and in twenty-five minutes they were out of sight again.

It was a standard belief that a retreating enemy fleet would sow mines in its wake and use its destroyers in torpedo attacks; so Jellicoe did not follow immediately. But soon after, Scheer came back to the attack, hoping perhaps for a better tactical position. Cruisers saw him and signalled to Jellicoe; and Jellicoe again succeeded in 'crossing the T' of the German line. Again, the leading German battleships were hit – two of them sank in the night – and again Scheer was forced to reverse his course. This engagement was even shorter than the first. To cover his second retreat, Scheer's destroy-ers laid a smoke screen and fired a large number of torpedoes.

Against torpedoes, when he knew they were coming, a commander could either turn away and retreat at high speed beyond their range or, at greater risk, he could turn towards them and meet them bow on. Jellicoe made the signal to turn away. So he avoided the danger, but lost sight again of his enemies; and he never found them again. During the night, Scheer's fleet crossed Jellicoe's track astern of him. It was attacked by destroyers, and sighted by some of the cruisers in the rear of his line. Its radio signals, indicating what it was doing, were intercepted by the Admiralty. But neither the Admiralty nor his own captains told Jellicoe where it was, and by dawn its survivors had retreated safely into the main channel through the German minefield.

Admiral Fisher by A. S. Cope

H.M.S. *Dreadnought* 1907

Arctic Convoy to Russia in the
Second World War, by C. Pears

Sinking of the *Bismarck* 1941,
by C. E. Turner

Aircraft Carrier *Ocean*
on way to Korea in 1952

H.M.S. *Prince of Wales*
at Singapore

Officially, both sides claimed to have won. The Germans were able to say with truth that the British had lost more men and ships, and the British to say that the Germans had been driven off the sea. But both fleets felt they had failed. The British had always hoped for another Trafalgar if they met the German fleet – to sink a large part of it, not merely force it back to port. Many things had combined to stop it working out like that: the mist and smoke, the series of failures in signalling, Jellicoe's two decisions not to chase, and Scheer's precipitate flight. An inquest on the battle began at once in naval circles, and it has never really stopped.

The immediate lesson was the fatal flaw in the design of the Dreadnought battle-cruisers, which had destroyed three ships and almost the whole of their crews. Their gun turrets could be penetrated by a single shell, and if they were, the flash could pass down to the magazines below. All the surviving battle-cruisers had to go to the dockyards to be altered.

The long-term lesson was not so apparent at the time. The British like to believe, or at least to say, that their army and navy in peacetime are always preparing to win the last war, not the next one: and even Fisher, far-sighted though he was, had prepared in some degree for a war that could never happen. Back at the turn of the century he had foreseen great battles of high-speed manœuvre and long-range gunnery in which whole fleets would be engaged. But as it turned out, great formal battles at sea were things of the distant past.

The fact was that battleships had never been very much use except to fight other battleships: the British had noted this in the Crimean War, but lost sight of it again when steam and explosive shells developed. And it had always been rare for two battlefleets to put to sea intending to fight each other. It had happened at Trafalgar, but only through Napoleon's fit of temper, and one would have to look far back in the eighteenth century to find another example. It happened again between American and Japanese fleets in the special conditions of war among the Pacific islands in the 1940s. But in the whole of the age of steam, the British battlefleet never fought as a tactical unit except at Jutland, when it was engaged in the work it was built to do for a total of forty minutes.

Indeed, the battlefleet was a splendid monster that had outgrown its use. It was such an immense industrial investment and such a precious source of pride that no nation that owned one could afford to run a serious risk of losing it. In either Britain or Germany, the loss of the fleet, apart from any strategic result, would have been a disastrous shock to the nation's will to win. In any encounter, one side would always feel it was the weaker, in ships or skill or tactical position, and that side would always be under orders to avoid a battle. Other weapons in modern times, gas, disease and atomic bombs, have been unused for fear of reprisal, but the battlefleet under steam was the only weapon that could not fulfil its primary function because it was too grand and too expensive.

Hitherto, the only way to beat a powerful fleet had seemed to be to build one even stronger. The real lesson of Jutland, perhaps, was that somebody soon would think of another way that was cheaper and more certain. The idea that such magnificent fleets might ever be obsolete was far from acceptance in Britain. But Admiral von Scheer had not only a fleet which he could not use; by then, he also had over 300 submarines.

Inevitably, there was at least one British admiral who said submarine warfare was 'underhand, unfair and damned unEnglish'. American opinion was also offended by it when it was used against merchant ships, and especially passenger liners. And it was contrary to international law, for what that was worth, to sink a merchant ship without ensuring the safety of its crew.

In the first year of the war, Germany had defied the law and neutral opinion by sinking ships without warning. Fisher had foreseen the importance of submarines, but the British navy was very badly off balance to deal with them. The big ships, of course, were useless against them: a battleship could scarcely put to sea without a screen of anti-submarine destroyers to protect it. There were nothing like enough small manoeuvrable ships to protect the merchant navy. The Admiralty improvised an Auxiliary Patrol of nearly a thousand ships, from trawlers upwards in size, which had some success in coastal waters. It was manned entirely by reserve officers and conscripts, who on the whole were rather sorry for the regulars, condemned to the formal discipline of the big ships. But in that first year almost a million tons of merchant ships were sunk.

For Britain, the sinking of the great Cunarder *Lusitania* in 1915 was a fortunate tragedy. It started world-wide protests, especially from America, which grew until the Germans felt obliged to restrict their submarines, and the losses of merchant ships fell to a manageable number.

But after Jutland, blockade by submarines was the Germans' only visible hope of winning the war. Von Scheer began unrestricted attacks again in February 1917. By early summer, he had sunk a million and a quarter tons of merchant ships; by autumn, two-and-three-quarter millions. The British merchant fleet was still by far the biggest in the world, but ships were being lost more quickly than they could be built. And the cold statistics leave one to imagine the suffering they represented, the uncounted deaths at sea, some sudden, but many lingering and lonely.

Jellicoe was brought to the Admiralty as First Sea Lord to organise defence against this threat, and Beatty took over the Grand Fleet. The use of convoys was suggested, but Jellicoe opposed it. It seems extraordinary now that this means of defence was neglected for almost three years: it had been used by a kind of instinct all through the eighteenth-century wars, and indeed as far back in history as any records go. Jellicoe's reason was that even if convoys were organised, the navy had not enough destroyers to protect them. It was the most damning confession of lack of foresight the navy has ever made. The navy was still using shipyards and manpower to make its enormous battlefleet even stronger: by the end of that same year it had no less than forty-three Dreadnoughts watching the German fleet, which had only twenty-four. It was short of small ships solely because it spent so much time and money building big ones, though most of the big ones never fired a shot at any enemy. And for that reason Britain was reduced, before the year was out, to six weeks' reserve of food, and the Grand Fleet itself, ironically, had to cut short its exercises for lack of oil.

When the United States entered the war the shortage of escort ships was solved. Even then, Jellicoe was reluctant to start the convoy system. He was dismissed and the convoys were organised; and they worked, as they always had. Losses of merchant ships declined, and losses of German submarines increased. By May 1918, after a desperate fifteen months, it could be said that the Germans' final effort on the sea had failed.

It had been a near-run thing. But at the end, the navy could congratulate itself on having provided the means to win the war; for on land the armies were locked in a ghastly stalemate until the navy's blockade undermined the German will. The downfall of German power began with mutinies in the thwarted crews of their battlefleet; and when the German fleet steamed into Scapa Flow to surrender in November 1918, it seemed a vindication of naval policy. The British still could feel that the navy had never failed them.

*

Historians are famous for being wise after the event, but it is strange that the high command of navies – not only the British navy – has given so many

347

chances for that spurious kind of wisdom. The creation of the race-built ship and the reliance on gunnery in John Hawkins's time under Queen Elizabeth – that was one supreme stroke of imagination and forethought in naval war. Perhaps the creation of the Polaris submarine and its successors was another. But in between, elder seamen have mainly been distinguished for dogged conservatism, whether they are fishermen or admirals.

Looking back on the twentieth-century naval wars, in the light of all the long history before them and the short history since, one is struck by two things about the British navy. At sea it never seriously failed in skill or spirit. But ashore, its plans were distracted time and time again by conservatism, and especially by the romance of its big majestic ships. It almost seemed that admirals cherished battleships, not for their practical utility in war but because they could display the ultimate pageant of naval seamanship. It was not only British admirals; all navies that had battleships clung to them in face of doubt and criticism. And perhaps it would be foolish now to judge the choice too harshly. Affairs of nations are often guided by sentiment rather than logic, and battleships in every age were wonderful creations. They had a fierce feline beauty like a tiger, a 'fearful symmetry'; and even when they proved impractical, their beauty may have had some martial value in itself, to give confidence to a nation that possessed them, and give pause to a nation that did not.

The first war ended at a moment of transition; air power had just begun to influence sea power. The British had pioneered the aircraft-carrier (the first was in service in 1917), and had fitted catapults on battleships for launching seaplanes, which were used for reconnaissance and for spotting the fall of shot for the gunnery officers. But at the end of the war, this growing naval air activity was combined with the Royal Flying Corps to form the Royal Air Force.

A tremendous argument was just beginning, and it raged all through the twenty years between the wars: could a battleship be sunk by bombs from aircraft? Admiral Fisher, who had done more than anyone else to create the battlefleet, was one of the first to say it was out of date. In his old age he wrote innumerable letters to his friends, and to *The Times*, full of ridiculous overstatements, underlinings and exclamation marks; and nobody took any notice of them. But shortly before he died in 1920, his prophetic vision still had moments of astonishing clarity. 'To build battleships,' he wrote, 'so long as cheaper craft can destroy them . . . is merely to breed Kilkenny cats unable to catch rats or mice.' And a little later: 'Why keep any of the present lot? All you want is the present naval side of the air force! – that's the future navy!'

But Beatty had no doubts. He had come out of the war as the personification of the navy that still held the trust and affection of the British people. The big ship was still the essence of sea power, he maintained. It might have to evolve in the future, but to abandon it for visionary schemes of aircraft and submarines would leave the nation unprotected. As First Sea Lord in 1921, he demanded four new battle-cruisers which were to be by far the largest, most powerful and most expensive warships ever built. And the project was approved.

In the United States the same argument broke out, and the partisans of either side, the air and the sea, were even more belligerent and outspoken than in Britain. In 1921 a histrionic display was organised, in which one of the surrendered German battleships was bombed by squadrons of planes. In the end, the battleship sank, and the advocates of the air were jubilant. But the demonstration did not settle anything. The naval party pointed out that the ship was stationary and defenceless. The air party replied that if her magazines had been stocked she would have sunk all the quicker. So the argument went on.

Beyond the sentiment for battleships, there was also a sentimental attachment, at least in Britain, for their weapon, the naval gun. In the first war, the torpedo had been the dominant weapon: it had done far more damage than gunfire. But the guns of the navy had defended Britain for four hundred years, and there was a strong inclination to argue in their favour despite the facts. They still had a far longer range than anything else. To fire a torpedo, you first had to deliver it, well within the range of the enemy's guns. The first means of delivery had been small fast torpedo boats, and they had been countered by putting a secondary anti-torpedo-boat armament on the battleships. The second had been submarines. Against them there were depth-charges, carried by the battlefleet's screen of destroyers, and also a secret device the British developed between the wars. This was asdic, which later changed its name to sonar, a method of locating submarines under water by reflected sound waves. It was efficient, and with depth-charges guided by asdic the British navy came to believe it had the answer to submarines.

A third foreseeable means of delivering torpedoes was to drop them from aircraft. As an idea, this was surprisingly old. A British naval seaplane dropped the first torpedo from the air in 1914. Three were dropped in the

Dardanelles campaign, and sank three Turkish ships. But then the whole project languished, for no apparent reason except that the navy disliked the torpedo as it disliked the submarine. After the war a few enthusiasts kept up a small training unit, always with out-of-date aircraft. But the torpedoes had to be dropped at short range, as slowly as possible, a few feet above the water, and the big ship advocates were content to assume that this would always be so, and that they would always be able to shoot the aircraft down. Battleships were equipped with a great array of new kinds of anti-aircraft guns; and the only people who persevered in secret with torpedo aircraft were the Japanese.

So the great ships survived, and the British people took comfort from their existence, as they always had. But more and more of the strength of each ship was being diverted to its own protection.

During the First World War the era had ended when Britain could police the oceans single-handed. Perhaps in the fight for survival nobody noticed its passing; and indeed at the end of the war, in spite of its losses, the navy was stronger than it had ever been before. But the wealth of the empire had been poured into the fight, and it was impossible ever again to maintain a huge navy in peacetime. Besides, other nations had developed a naval pride of their own. Japan had become a power in eastern seas, and the United States had resolved to have a navy second to none. In 1922, at a conference in Washington, the maritime nations agreed on their naval strength. Britain and the United States were to have navies of equal size, Japan 60 per cent of the same, and France and Italy 35 per cent. To bring their proportions down, Britain and the United States both had to scrap a good many ships, and Beatty's new battle-cruisers were abandoned. For the next fifteen years, the building of new ships for the British navy was limited by treaty, the first time such a thing had ever happened. But still, Britain was able, within the treaty limits, to lay down two new battleships in the 1920s, the *Rodney* and the *Nelson*.

In 1933, when Hitler came to power, the Germans began to build a navy again. Britain, still bound by the treaties, began to modernise old ships, but did not order new ones until 1936, when a second war with Germany was seen to be inevitable. In that year and the next, the Admiralty ordered five new battleships, three aircraft-carriers, twelve cruisers, twenty-five destroyers, eleven submarines and nine escort vessels.

Of all the acts of the Admiralty through the centuries, this is hardest to explain. Of course, to the nation's naval experts, the choice of ships seemed logical at the time: the difficulty now is to discern the logic. Germany was known to be building or planning a few big ships which would have the benefit over any British ship of fourteen years of technical advance – but they could only be few. Italy was likely to fight on the side of Germany and already possessed a fleet – but while the British held Gibraltar the Italians could hardly escape from the Mediterranean. It was more significant that Germany again was building a large fleet of submarines. The British navy once more was being planned with what now seems a superfluity of the biggest ships, and with what was certainly far too few of the smallest, especially of escort vessels for protecting convoys – the same shortage that had almost lost the 1914 war. At least a score of escort vessels could be built for the price of one battleship, and the nine that were ordered were a negligible number. So when war began again in 1939, the navy entered it with the same spirit, the same strength and the same almost fatal weakness as before.

*

The first events were the same. Churchill again became First Lord, and the Admiralty signalled the fleet: 'Winston's back.' German merchant shipping vanished from the high seas, but German raiders were stationed in readiness far out of sight of land. The most powerful of them were two 'pocket battleships', one of which was named *Admiral Graf Spee* after the victor of the Battle of Coronel in 1914; and the first battle again was off the coast of South America.

In October and November, the *Graf Spee* sank a dozen merchant ships in the South Atlantic, and was hunted by about two dozen British warships. In December, by a kind of nautical intuition, three cruisers found her off the mouth of the River Plate: the *Ajax*, *Exeter* and *Achilles*. On the face of things, the *Graf Spee* was stronger than the three other ships combined. She had 11-inch guns against the 8-inch of the *Exeter* and the 6-inch of the other two, she was heavily armoured and, as it turned out, her gunnery was directed by radar, which no British cruiser yet possessed.

Going in to attack, the *Exeter* drew the fire of the *Graf Spee*'s main armament, and the *Ajax* and *Achilles* were able to close the range until they were hitting the battleship, though their 6-inch shells were doing no visible damage. The *Exeter* was hit many times, two of her turrets were put out of action, and she lost speed until she fell out of the fight. Then the *Graf Spee*

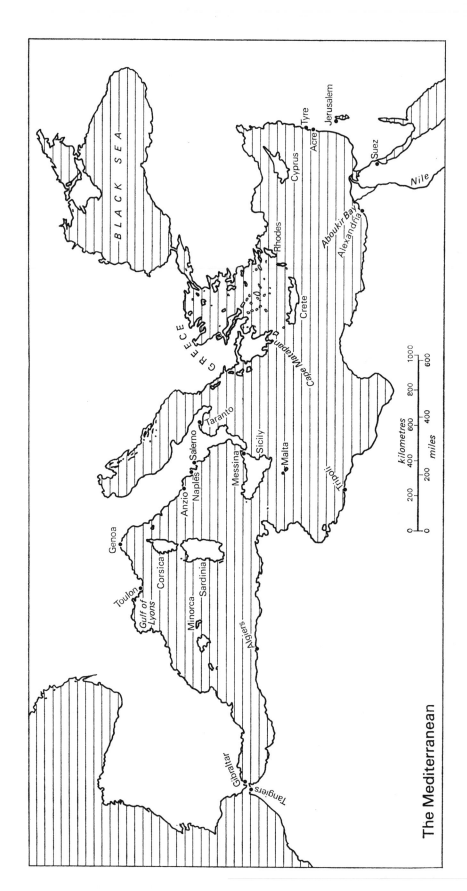

The Mediterranean

turned her big guns on the other two. *Ajax*, which was the flagship, was hit twice and her turrets were destroyed. The *Achilles* could not conceivably beat the *Graf Spee* alone, so the two ships settled down to shadow her and signal for reinforcements. They expected a long chase, but the *Graf Spee* headed for the river mouth and entered the neutral port of Montevideo. They had done her more damage than they thought.

That put the battle into the hands of diplomats and lawyers – to keep the *Graf Spee* in harbour until the reinforcements could arrive. A succession of British merchant ships was sent out of the harbour, because each of them by international law was entitled to a start of twenty-four hours before a belligerent warship was allowed to sail. Rumours were started of overwhelming British forces assembled in the offing, although the nearest in fact were still steaming across from Cape Town. And four days later the German captain took his ship down to the river mouth and scuttled her, and then committed suicide.

It was a victory: the fight of the cruisers had an air about it which assured the British their navy still had its customary flair. But the navy itself was not entirely happy; it did not like the trickery ashore, and it was dismayed by the captain's death. Almost always through history there has been a mutual respect among seamen, even on opposite sides in wars; and while they would fight to the death at sea, it seemed shameful to drive a good seaman to suicide.

There was a sequel to this fight that was altogether more pleasant. The *Graf Spee* had a supply ship called the *Altmark*, and she had honourably put aboard it all the merchant seamen she had captured from ships she had sunk. The *Altmark* was not detected until she was off the coast of Norway two months later, heading for home. She took refuge in a fjord. By law, the Norwegians should have released the prisoners, but they were slow to do it; so the destroyer *Cossack* steamed into the fjord by night, grappled and boarded the *Altmark* like a warship of sailing days, rescued the prisoners, and out of respect for Norwegian neutrality let the ship and her crew go free. About 300 men were found in her hold. It was said the first of them roused the rest with shouts of 'The navy's here.' It sounds perhaps like an afterthought, but it did express something the British never doubted: that when the navy was there, something would always be done, and done effectively.

It was in Norway a few weeks later, in April 1940, that war at sea flared up again on a scale that had not been seen since Jutland. The Germans' invasion of Norway used all the naval ships they possessed which were ready for sea: two battleships, the *Scharnhorst* and *Gneisenau*, the pocket battleship *Lützow*, seven cruisers and fourteen destroyers, besides torpedo boats, auxiliaries and transports. It was a far more ambitious and offensive effort than any they had made at sea in the first of the wars: it showed that under Hitler they would not hesitate to use what ships they had. And the British home fleet was too late to do anything to stop them; for this was the first experience of the speed and efficiency of the new kind of German war, and reaction in London was too slow. By the time the fleet was in action, the Germans had captured Norwegian air bases, and for the first time in history the fleet was in range of land-based enemy bombers, and beyond the range of any fighter escort. It looked as if the argument of battleships and bombers was to be settled soon.

But in fact it was not. As it happened, no battleship was detected by aircraft, and the only major warship sunk by bombs was a German cruiser in harbour at Bergen, which was attacked by naval dive-bombers from Scapa Flow. The fighting was mainly distinguished by destroyer actions. The *Glow-worm*, separated from the fleet, encountered all alone a German cruiser and its escorts, and hopelessly outmatched she rammed the cruiser and sank. Five destroyers went into the fjord at Narvik and attacked ten German destroyers and some armed transports which were inside. And later, when British forces had been landed and taken off again, two destroyers escorting the aircraft-carrier *Glorious* met both the German battleships and attacked them, and hit the *Scharnhorst* with a torpedo before they were sunk. They failed to save the *Glorious*, but they did save troop convoys which were returning from the abandoned operation.

That seaborne invasion, totally successful though it was, cost the Germans a large proportion of their fleet; three out of seven cruisers were sunk, one by Norwegian defences and two by British submarines. More than half their destroyers were wrecked in Narvik, and the *Scharnhorst* and *Lützow* were damaged and out of action for repairs. But of course it cost the Norwegians their freedom, and it vastly increased the British navy's problems: for the Germans had the Norwegian ports and airfields, a sheltered route out of the North Sea towards the Arctic and Atlantic, which they had never possessed in the previous war.

And then France. The French and British armies were overwhelmed because they had prepared for the war they had won in 1918, and had formed no conception of the armoured tactics the Germans had devised. In May, the

British army on the Continent was surrounded and retreating to Dunkirk. This was a situation the navy could not have been expected to provide for: to rescue a large army under air attack from shallow beaches and a single devastated harbour. No ship bigger than a destroyer was any use, and even destroyers by their size were in excessive danger. But it was a situation that stirred some kind of folk-memory among all British seamen. The army was beaten, but the sense of defeat only reached as far as the shore. Beyond, on the sea, the idea of defeat had really not entered anyone's head.

Churchill was one of the people who saw the historical associations of what happened: for this was a small stretch of sea, from the coast of Kent towards the coast of Flanders, that the British had known very well since the Anglo-Saxons rowed across it, the Narrow Seas where King John had claimed his sovereignty at the time of Magna Carta; and the crowds of small ships and boats that began to cross it in 1940 were reminiscent of the fleets the medieval kings assembled to take their armies to France and bring the remnants back.

Perhaps not many seamen thought of things in such a distant past, but certainly when it came to the point they acted on a native instinct. The army was in trouble, so the seamen went to fetch it off – not only naval seamen, but any seamen who happened to be around and could find a boat. The navy began it, of course, and provided what organisation there was. It sent over one anti-aircraft cruiser and thirty-nine destroyers, and few of them escaped any damage. About 300 other small assorted ships were under naval command. Five hundred or so, commanded and manned by civilians, were officially counted, and there were certainly several hundred more which simply went and did what they could without reporting to anyone, including the lifeboats from ships in London docks and the motor yachts laid up in south-east harbours. Almost one third of them all were sunk, mostly by aircraft. Between them, in nine days, they rescued 336,000 men who would otherwise have been killed or taken prisoner. It was an action that astonished everyone except the seamen, to whom it seemed the obvious thing to do. The whole episode, of course, was a catastrophic defeat, but the rescue made it seem like a victory.

There were plenty more grounds for historical reminiscence in that summer of 1940. With the Germans victorious across the Straits of Dover, the British were under imminent threat of invasion again, and they were roused and united by it as they always had been by that particular threat. And the plans of the last two tyrants who made the threat, Napoleon and

Hitler, were remarkably alike. Both of them collected fleets of boats and barges in the harbours across the Straits, and armies which were ready to embark. Both times, the British were absurdly unprepared, but totally defiant and unreasonably sure of themselves. And both times, the defiance made the tyrants hesitate until it was too late; neither of them could quite believe there was no strength behind it.

The British had less reason to be confident in 1940 than they had in 1804. Ashore, the army was largely disarmed, and the citizens were preparing to fight with shotguns, home-made bombs, and ancient rifles which had five or ten rounds each. As for the sea, the navy had understandably given no thought to this situation. Its destroyers and cruisers would have come to fight the invasion if it had started, but they were too big and too few to put up a constant patrol. It had very few smaller ships except minesweepers and converted trawlers; there were at most half a dozen descendants of the nineteenth-century gunboats. To watch for the invasion fleet was the country's first line of defence, and to meet that unforeseen demand the navy had to make the craziest improvisations. Every night that summer, the invasion coast was patrolled by small fishing boats and pleasure cruisers, manned by fishermen, yachtsmen, tugboat skippers, garage mechanics who could keep an engine going, anyone who could say or pretend he knew something about the sea. Each boat was armed with a rifle, a pistol and a rocket; the lucky ones, as summer passed, were given an old machine-gun. The crews were dressed up in naval uniform, but nobody had time for any training. Their orders, if they sighted the German invasion fleet in the dark, were to let off their rocket, which would warn the people ashore, and then of course to engage the enemy with their rifle and their pistol, while the harbours were blocked behind them. Some government department, charged with the nation's morale, had chosen this time to cover the country with posters which showed a battle line of huge warships, with the caption 'Mightier Yet', a phrase quoted from 'Land of Hope and Glory': and that added a note of hilarity to the nightly patrols.

And yet, ridiculous though it seemed soon afterwards, these amateurish sailors had not the slightest doubt they would succeed, for no reason at all except a vague pleasure in seeing themselves as descendants of Drake, and a schoolroom recollection that they were doing exactly what the Sea Fencibles did when Nelson commanded them. Perhaps, just by being there, they added a little to Hitler's hesitation. And perhaps indeed, in the spontaneous actions of Dunkirk and these invasion defences, there was a genuine distant echo of something no great steamship could evoke: the pirates' enterprise, the impertinence of privateers, and the self-dependence of the first explorers.

But between the invasion plans of Napoleon and Hitler there was one significant difference. To put his armies across, Napoleon needed command of the waters of the Channel, and he finally fought for it and lost it at Trafalgar. Hitler needed command of the air above the Channel, and he fought for it and lost it in the Battle of Britain. For the next three years, the Channel was controlled by aircraft. People on the south coast of England for many centuries past had looked out on the busiest shipping lane in the world; now, day after day, they looked out on an empty sea.

The navy was growing again. In ages past, it had been an unpopular service which depended on its press-gangs, but in the twentieth-century wars the nation's affection for it easily gave it all the men it needed. It absorbed them with unstudied psychological skill. Thrust into barracks in the ancient naval towns, Plymouth, Portsmouth and Chatham, they found themselves, still bewildered, eating on mess-decks and sleeping in hammocks in barrack blocks named after naval heroes everyone remembered from their school-days; they discovered they had to respect a sacred stretch of gravel called the quarter-deck, and that if they wanted to walk out of the gates they had to wait for shore leave, when the liberty boat would be alongside. It seemed absurd at first, but it was an attitude of mind that infected everyone, and they soon entered into the seaman's esoteric world and began to regard them-selves, as seamen always have, as people quite distinct from landsmen, and probably superior.

The need for small fighting ships gave young officers an early chance of command, even though their first command might only be a fishing boat with guns. The navy quickly used up its regular reserve of merchant service officers, the RNR, and it began to train a great number of other young men. They were called the RNVR, the volunteer reserve, although most of them had not been reservists or seamen of any kind before the war. They served six months or more on the lower deck, and then had three months' training aboard HMS *King Alfred*, a disused holiday building on the sea-front near Brighton. There also, the navy's psychology was sound. Straight from a seamen's mess, men dined in the wardroom and drank the toasts the navy had drunk for centuries. They were taught by chief petty officers, who are the backbone of any navy, men who knew everything and could shout a stream of naval oaths and attach the word 'Sir' to the end of them with intonations of infinite subtlety; and the young men emerged as sub-lieutenants with perhaps a little knowledge of navigation, seamanship and signals, and certainly a strong conviction that, come what might, they had a high tradition to uphold. They were always distinguished from regular officers by the wavy gold braid on their cuffs, but they rose in rank and experience until they commanded almost all the small ships the navy had begun to build at last, the motor torpedo boats and gunboats, minesweepers, launches and landing craft, the minor escort vessels and even some destroyers. They made a citizen navy.

When France fell, and Italy under Mussolini joined with Hitler, the British navy was harder pressed than it had ever been before. So also was the merchant navy. The Germans had not only Norway, but now the French Atlantic ports, which gave them submarine bases five hundred miles nearer the British convoy routes. In the Mediterranean, the Italians had a modern battlefleet and 105 submarines, with airfields on both the shores which put the whole sea within their range. Geographically, the position was much the same as in the Napoleonic wars, except that Spain was precariously neutral. Strategically, it was much worse, not only because of the difference of sail and power, but also because of the influence of the air. Again, the navy was called on to surround and contain the whole continent of Europe.

The first most urgent need was to stop the Germans getting control of the French navy, which was the fourth biggest in the world. Some French ships were already in English ports, or in the British naval base at Alexandria, and their crews accepted what they could not avoid and came under British command. Some were in Toulon, in the part of France the Germans had not yet occupied, and nothing could be done about them. Some in the West Indies were peacefully immobilised. But those in the French North African ports rejected every alternative the British offered them, and as a last resort the government ordered the navy to destroy them. They began to fight back, but one of their battleships blew up and three more were so damaged that they could not move. Only one major ship escaped and returned to France. That one, and the others in Toulon, remained a worry, but when the Germans occupied the rest of France, the French dutifully scuttled the ships that would have been captured. The whole episode was embarrassing and emotional, but the French people on the whole seemed to understand it had to be done.

The next opponent was the Italian fleet. The British still had their naval bases at each end of the Mediterranean, Gibraltar and Alexandria, and in the middle on the island of Malta. Malta is only one night's steaming from the Italian naval base at Taranto, and here it looked as if the great battles of rival fleets which the navy had always planned might really happen. But they never did, for the same old reason: that one fleet was always willing and the other was not. It is no insult to say the Italians were good shipbuilders but bad fighters; the world, after all, needs people who value common sense more highly than blind courage. They had a splendid fleet, but when it met a comparable enemy it always ran for home. The British only managed to bring it to battle when they could slow it down by air torpedo attacks from carriers. The biggest encounter was off Cape Matapan in Greece in March 1941, when an Italian battleship, eight cruisers and fourteen destroyers were intercepted at a distance. Aircraft from the carrier *Formidable* torpedoed the battleship and one of the cruisers. The battleship still had its speed and it escaped, but the cruiser was stopped. Two other cruisers and two destroyers were ordered to stand by it as dusk was falling, and in a night action the British fleet caught them and sank them all by gunfire without any damage to itself.

What was proved in the Mediterranean was that big ships, as Fisher had foreseen a quarter of a century before, were vulnerable to other much cheaper weapons. At the beginning, the British launched twenty-two aircraft from a carrier to attack the Italian fleet with torpedoes in its harbour at Taranto. They sank three battleships there – one was brand new – at a cost of two aircraft. And a year later, wisely choosing Christmas Eve for their exploit, Italian frogmen riding on two-man submarines got into Alexandria harbour and damaged two British battleships so badly that they settled on the bottom where they lay. At sea, the British fleet was always open to attack by submarines and aircraft from the bases on both shores. The submarines – German, not Italian – sank the aircraft-carriers *Eagle* and *Ark Royal* and the battleship *Barham*; torpedo aircraft damaged the *Nelson* and many lesser ships. But the big ships survived the particular threat that had been argued so hotly between the wars. No capital ship was sunk by bombs from aircraft: they came through thousands of bombing attacks in the course of two years. Merchant ships, on the other hand, could not survive the hordes of aircraft that were sent against them, and from 1941 to 1943 no normal convoys could be run from Gibraltar to Suez. Everything for the Far and Middle East had to go round the Cape of Good Hope.

The principal constant aim of the British naval effort in the Mediterranean was to keep Malta alive and free, and use it as a base to interrupt supplies to the German and Italian armies in North Africa. The navy's fortunes varied with the ebb and flow of the fighting in the desert, but always stupendous efforts were needed to send fuel and food and armament to Malta. Malta is nearly a thousand miles from Gibraltar and over 800 from Alexandria, but only fifty from the Italian shore of Sicily. Convoys over these perilous routes were the most heavily defended there have ever been, and the most heavily attacked: merchant ships were sometimes outnumbered three to one by their escorts, yet sometimes only a third of them got through. When things became desperate, stores were even sent in by submarine, and fighter aircraft for the defence of the island were sent part of the way by carrier, and flown off when they were in range.

In spite of everything, Malta never fell, and the navy never came near being driven out of the Mediterranean, as it had been in the hardest period of the Napoleonic wars. It held its own, and more, until the enemies were driven out of North Africa and it could turn from the defensive to the positive action of putting armies ashore in Europe again. For the British nowadays, the Mediterranean is a holiday resort, and they do not think how many of their ships are lying at the bottom of it, or how many of their seamen were drowned in it in 1941 and 1942; and perhaps it is just as well to forget it.

In those same years, the Battle of the Atlantic reached its climax. The Germans knew that seaborne trade was still the Achilles heel of Britain, and they attacked it with all they had: submarines, aircraft and their remaining warships.

After the invasion of Norway, they had only one major ship in action, but by the end of 1940 they had repaired three more; and they were building one more heavy cruiser, the *Prinz Eugen*, and two super-battleships, the *Bismarck* and the *Tirpitz*. All these, having little other use, either went or tried to go out commerce raiding.

After the *Graf Spee*, the first and the most successful was the pocket battleship *Admiral Scheer*. She escaped from Germany, up the coast of Norway and through the channel north of Iceland, in the winter of 1940, and in the Atlantic she sighted a convoy of thirty-seven ships escorted only by an armed merchant cruiser, the *Jervis Bay*. In a famous action, the captain of the *Jervis Bay* signalled his convoy to scatter and steamed out alone to challenge the battleship, sure of the destruction of his own ship and its

From F. H. Mason's H.M.S. *Superb*
leading the Mediterranean Fleet, 1918

The Quick Turnround: the Merchant Navy in War, by J. E. Platt
Overleaf: The Withdrawal from Dunkirk 1940, by C. Cundall

company. He fought her long enough, before he went down, for all but five of the merchantmen to get away. The *Scheer*, having been reported, went on to hide in the south Atlantic and the Indian Ocean. She stayed at sea uncaught for four months, refuelling from a supply ship, sank sixteen merchant ships in all, and then went back to Germany by the way she had come.

Commerce raiding was never an economical use for big ships: more harm could be done more cheaply by submarines. But it had the advantage for the Germans that one battleship or cruiser out in the ocean could occupy dozens of similar British ships in searching for it. The fate of the *Jervis Bay* also forced the Admiralty to use its older battleships as convoy escorts; and that was the reason why later raiders had less success. They were all under orders to sink merchant ships, not to involve themselves in fighting battleships; so when they sighted battleship escorts they always made off. The cruiser *Admiral Hipper* and the battleships *Scharnhorst* and *Gneisenau* all came out that winter and added to the damage; but then they all retreated to harbour in Brest on the Atlantic coast of France. The RAF bombed them there continually. It did them no mortal damage, but it kept them in harbour for months needing minor repairs. And by May 1941 the *Bismarck* and *Prinz Eugen* were ready for sea, and the Germans decided to use them too for this menial task.

The Germans believed the *Bismarck* was the most powerful warship ever built, a ship that could outfight any other in the world. They were probably right; she was certainly a masterpiece of naval architecture. But she was unlucky. She left German waters on her first operational cruise on 18th May, and nine days later she was a shattered wreck.

The day after she sailed, she was seen off the south coast of Norway, with the *Prinz Eugen*, by a Norwegian patriot, and that was her first bad luck. He knew a man who had a radio transmitter in the attic of his farm, and he sent him a note of what he had seen. The farm was already under suspicion and surrounded by German troops. A girl hid the note in the top of her stocking and carried it through the German ring, and the farmer encoded it and sent it to London that night.

So began the most dramatic sea-hunt of the twentieth century. The Home Fleet was ordered out to cover the channels north and south of Iceland that the Germans might use. By then, the major British ships had effective radar, and on the 23rd two cruisers, the *Suffolk* and the *Norfolk*, reported the *Bismarck* and *Prinz Eugen* in radar contact north of Iceland, close to the arctic ice, and shadowed them southward through the Denmark Straits. South-west of Iceland, the battleship *Prince of Wales* and the battle-cruiser *Hood* received the signal and steamed to intercept.

The British had only two ships which matched the *Bismarck*. The *Prince of Wales* was one of them, and the other was the *King George V*, flagship of the Home Fleet – the first two to be completed of the four new battleships ordered in 1936. But the *Prince of Wales* was so new she had not finished working up, and still had civilian technicians on board who were trying to remedy faults in her gun mechanism. The *Hood* in her day had been the largest warship in the world, and in many men's eyes the most elegant; but she was lightly armoured, designed in the First World War, and launched in 1918.

At dawn on 26th May, these two ships sighted the Germans and confi-dently closed to attack. The *Bismarck* opened fire at a range of fourteen miles and immediately hit the *Hood*. A shell of her next salvo hit her again, and men in the *Prince of Wales* saw the great ship explode and disappear. From her company of some fifteen hundred men, three men survived. The *Prince of Wales* was also hit by four 15-inch shells and half her guns went out of action. She had to retreat out of range and join the cruisers in shadowing. But she had also hit the *Bismarck* and holed a fuel tank. The *Bismarck* was leaving a trail of oil behind her.

The sudden annihilation of the *Hood*, so like the fate of the battle-cruisers a generation earlier at Jutland, was a shock to everyone in the navy; everyone knew her well, and most men had friends aboard her. So was the failure of the *Prince of Wales*. It was already a matter of duty to sink the *Bismarck*: it became a matter of pride and revenge. Ships were diverted from every quarter of the Atlantic to close in on her, a tremendous concentration of sea-power in its traditional form. From Scapa Flow, the flagship *King George V* was out, with the battle-cruiser *Repulse*, the carrier *Victorious*, four cruisers and their destroyer screen. From Gibraltar the carrier *Ark Royal*, with the *Renown*, the *Sheffield* and destroyers; from Halifax the *Revenge*; from convoys at sea the battleships *Rodney* and *Ramillies*, and the heavy cruisers *London* and *Edinburgh*. Even the old 6-inch cruiser *Arethusa*, without armour or radar, was sent alone to the edge of the ice in case the *Bismarck* turned back the way she had come; and it was noticeable on board her that the regular officers passionately hoped the *Bismarck* would come that way, while the reservists, perhaps a little more detached and closer to reality, were inclined to hope she would not.

Men in navies always think of themselves as fighting other ships, not other men; tens of thousands of British seamen were out to get the *Bismarck* whatever it cost, and they gave little thought if any to the lives of her German crew. In every ship a stream of signals was coming in day and night, from the Admiralty and the other ships; and as each was decyphered and movements were plotted on the Atlantic charts, the hunt became intensely exciting: the theoretical problem shown on the tables under the chartroom lights, the practical problem revealed outside by the grey seas, the mist and low cloud, the strong wind and the heavy swell.

All day on the 24th the crippled *Prince of Wales*, with the *Suffolk* and *Norfolk*, remained in contact, steaming south at twenty-five knots. The nearest ships fit to attack were the Home Fleet, coming down from the north-east. By evening, the carrier *Victorious* was just in range with her torpedo aircraft, and she launched them in the dusk and rain.

They were Swordfish, the archaic biplanes more aptly known as String-bags, which were still in use in the fleet although they were years behind land-based aircraft in design. It was on this precarious weapon that the whole action came to depend. They floundered low across the ocean, hit the *Bismarck* with one torpedo, and all succeeded in finding their carrier again and landing in the dark. For a short time, hopes were high. But the *Bismarck* was superbly built, and one torpedo amidships did not even slow her down. During the night, she escaped from the shadowers and disappeared into the wastes of ocean. All the next day and night, she was lost.

That day, the German admiral made one mistake: he sent a long radio signal to report what was happening. Perhaps he did not know the British had lost him. Everywhere, British ships took bearings on his signal and reported them to the flagship and the Admiralty. The position plotted from them showed he had altered course towards the Atlantic ports of France. But by then the Home Fleet was a hundred miles astern and could not hope to catch the *Bismarck*, unless somebody could slow her down.

The only people who possibly could were the pilots of the *Ark Royal*, coming up at speed from Gibraltar through heavy seas that were trying her destroyers to the utmost. In the morning of the 26th the *Bismarck* was sighted by an RAF seaplane on reconnaissance from England. An hour later the *Ark Royal's* reconnaissance also found her, and the admiral of the Gibraltar force detached the cruiser *Sheffield* to shadow her. By afternoon, the *Ark Royal* was in range, and she turned into the wind to fly off her Swordfish. They claimed afterwards that her bow was rising and falling fifty feet and that no other ship in the world could have flown her aircraft off and on in the sea that was running. But she did.

Nobody had warned the pilots about the *Sheffield*. A desperate signal was sent in clear to tell them she was there, but they spotted her on their radar and half of them attacked her through the low cloud before she was recognised. By luck, she escaped, perhaps because the torpedoes had a new magnetic pistol and exploded prematurely in the heavy sea. The aircraft all came back to their ship. An hour and a half had been wasted, there was only one hour left before dark; and by dawn the next morning the *Bismarck* would be under air cover from the shore and unapproachable.

The Swordfish were rearmed, and the torpedoes refitted with contact pistols. They flew off again. One hit the *Bismarck* in the bow, and then another on the one vulnerable spot that any ship must have, the rudders and propellers. The *Sheffield* reported her turning in circles and then steaming north at ten knots.

All that night she was held in action by destroyers. She could only move slowly, and apparently she could not turn her stern to the sea, so that she made no progress towards the sanctuary of air cover close to the coast. At dawn, the *King George V* and *Rodney* and several cruisers were in range, and they all opened fire. The Germans might reasonably have surrendered and scuttled their ship and saved their own lives, but they would not. They fought back, without any effect, perhaps in a hopeless heroic gesture, or perhaps in a final hope of holding out until submarines could assemble to counter-attack the attackers. So their magnificent ship was pounded to ruins, and most of them were killed. But gunfire could not sink her. By mid-morning, both the British battleships were down to the last reserve of fuel they needed to get back to port, and they drew away. The cruiser *Dorsetshire* was sent in to finish her off with torpedoes, and destroyers to rescue the few men who had jumped overboard and were still alive.

That was the end of the German fleet on distant seas. The *Prinz Eugen*, which had separated from the *Bismarck* undetected after the fight with the *Prince of Wales*, went straight to Brest with engine trouble, and joined the *Scharnhorst* and *Gneisenau*. Some months later, to the mortification of the navy and air force, the two battleships succeeded in running the gauntlet of the English Channel and reaching port in Germany. But both were damaged by mines. The *Gneisenau* never went to sea again; the *Scharnhorst* survived to fight the last big-ship battle in European waters, when she was caught off the north coast of Norway by the new battleship

Duke of York and four destroyers, and was sunk in the arctic night.

The raider war had been dramatic, but it had never been decisive. All told, surface raiders sank 237 merchant ships in the whole of the war, which was bad enough; but submarines sank more than ten times as many. The threat that nearly lost the first war came nearer than anything else to losing the second. It was certainly not defeated by any forethought of the Admiralty. What beat it in the end was a native skill in scientific invention, and the stubbornness of naval crews who manned inadequate ships, and perhaps most of all, the courage of merchant seamen.

It is the custom to describe this battle in graphs, which show month by month the tonnage of shipping lost and the number of submarines sunk. Perhaps that is the only way to follow its strategy; but of course graphs do not show weariness, suffering, fear, courage, panic or resignation to approaching death. It was a battle that lasted year after year without ever a single decisive action, an accumulation of thousands of isolated fights, few big enough or important enough to merit a place in history, but each a matter of mortal importance to the men caught up in it. Convoy work, more than most kinds of war, was a life of acute discomfort and long monotony, which might erupt at any second into a savage crisis.

An anti-submarine ship must be quick to alter course and put on speed, and therefore it must be small. Destroyers were the best of convoy escorts, but after the losses of the Norwegian campaign and Dunkirk, there were scarcely enough of them left to protect the battlefleets. In the Atlantic, the navy had to make do with ships that were even smaller, and even less comfortable or sure in winter gales. After a while, the shortage was eased by the loan of fifty ancient American destroyers which had long been laid up in reserve. They did splendid work, but it was a beggar's choice to put to sea in them.

So the navy suffered most of the discomfort – and most of the navy, in this kind of job, was drawn from the volunteer reservists. But it was a kind of war that was harder still for the merchant navy. Even in the most sophisticated age, men in a fighting navy are more or less sustained, as they always have been, by discipline and some hope of martial glory. And what is more, perhaps, they can fight back. But the merchant navy had none of these encouragements, or only the dimmest reflections of them. There cannot ever have been a much harder test of courage than to man a slow merchant ship in a winter convoy – to be stationed on deck with the solitary inefficient gun and see nothing to shoot at, but to see the columns of smoke as ship after ship was torpedoed, or to sweat in the stokehold seeing nothing but only feeling the explosions – and all the time to expect to be blown to bits or slowly drowned in the dark and the numbing sea.

These men were not compelled by any kind of discipline but their own, and nobody can quite explain in retrospect why they went on doing it; it is like the unanswerable question of why the Elizabethan seamen went on volunteering for arctic expeditions when so few of them survived. Some of them might have gone so far as to say the British had always been seamen, and to hell with Hitler if he thought he could stop them. But the British nowadays are embarrassed by heroic attitudes, and their self-confidence at sea was so deep-rooted that nobody needed to put it into words. Nor would they have dreamed of claiming a monopoly of the kind of stubborn courage their work demanded. Men of all the allied nations were still at sea.

The convoys on the arctic route to Russia were the worst of all, because they passed close to the north of Norway where the Germans had air and submarine bases, and anchorages for what remained of their fleet. There is no part of the seas of the world that does not contain a bit of British history, but perhaps it is worth recollecting that the hardest of all tests of modern seamanship was on the very route of the first of all British explorations: the route to Archangel that Richard Chancelor opened up in 1554, when Sir Hugh Willoughby and his crews were lost and froze to death. And having said that, one must add that it was not only British seamen who risked that awful route in the 1940s; there were Americans and Norwegians too.

It was a ten days' voyage to the Russian ports, and of 811 merchant ships that attempted it in forty convoys, ninety-two were sunk on the way: one in nine. Many more, of course, were damaged, and men in them injured or killed. And those that came through had to make the same journey back again unladen. It would have seemed a good chance of survival to Elizabethan explorers or privateers, but in modern life it was a very high risk to face. And the circumstances were not conducive to courage. In summer it was daylight all the time, and the convoys were open to attack all through each twenty-four hours. In winter the darkness gave more protection, but then there was freezing fog and snow, ice on the rigging and the guns, the vigilance needed to keep in station, and always the knowledge that the surrounding sea was so cold that a man could only live a few minutes in it.

And of all Russian convoys the worst was in the mid-summer of 1942. It was escorted by the usual anti-submarine and anti-aircraft ships and also by two American and two British cruisers; and the Home Fleet, with the

USS *Washington* in company, was also ordered out to give distant support, because two German battleships and a heavy cruiser were known to be in northern fjords of Norway.

There has always been argument about what happened; it seemed to be an occasion when not only the Germans but also the British, with the Americans under their orders, refused to risk their immensely expensive warships. The Home Fleet was at a distance partly because it could not afford to be away from Scapa Flow for too long, and partly at least because the neighbourhood of the convoy was sure to be full of enemy aircraft and submarines. While the convoy was passing the north of Norway, Admiralty intelligence reported the big German ships preparing to sail. They could have overwhelmed the close escort before the Home Fleet could come up, and the First Sea Lord ordered the cruisers of the escort to withdraw and the convoy to scatter. The German ships did come out, but did not attack the convoy and soon retreated to their bases, because they wrongly thought the Home Fleet, with the aircraft-carrier *Victorious*, was dangerously close.

So the major ships of each side never met, and did nothing; and the scattered convoy was left among a swarm of aircraft and submarines. Of its thirty-six ships, only thirteen came through to Russia. It had been a terrible experience for the men who had watched the rest go down, and for once the merchant seamen felt, and said, that the navy had abandoned them. It was hard to deny; but the responsibility lay with the First Sea Lord in London, not with the captains of the cruisers at sea who would certainly have stayed, whatever happened, if they had had the choice, and fought it out.

All through those dangerous years, the British view of sea-power had been half-consciously evolving. Big ships could be seen to be playing an ever-decreasing part in the winning of the war: true power at sea, it began to appear, was invested in merchant ships and the smaller naval ships that could protect them, and in the skill and pertinacity to keep them going. It was easy to see that the Germans, as aggressors at sea, would have done better to use their money and time and shipyard space in building a hundred more submarines than in building a few big ships; and also easy to see that if they had, the British big ships would not have had anything to do. It was a most unwelcome thought: the British had trusted big ships so long for their security, and few people had the agility of mind, like Fisher in 1920, suddenly to discard such a long-standing national sentiment.

Most ordinary British people were also too busy with immediate events to see the omens. They did not see them in the air control of the Channel, or the destruction of the Italian ships by aircraft at Taranto, or even in the fate of the American fleet at Pearl Harbor. It was a single event, just after Pearl Harbor, that brought it home at last. The *Prince of Wales* and the battle-cruiser *Renown* were attacked with bombs and torpedoes by Japanese aircraft in daylight at sea off the coast of Malaya, and in ninety minutes both were sunk and 840 men were killed. After that, the British had a chilling knowledge in the backs of their minds that the power of great fighting ships, which had been their support and pride for so many centuries, would have to be surrendered soon to other more novel kinds of martial power. They knew a long era was ending.

But they did not submit to it passively: they used the new weapons too, especially against the remaining German battleship. This was the *Tirpitz*, another and newer super-ship like the *Bismarck*. The *Tirpitz* never reached the high seas at all, and never fought the kind of fight she was designed for. She was sent up the Norwegian coast to menace the arctic convoys, and it was her fate to hide in a series of fjords and slowly be beaten to death by lesser weapons. She was often bombed from the air. In Trondheim, the navy tried an attack with the two-man submarines Italian frogmen had used in Alexandria: a Norwegian fishing boat bluffed its way into the fjord with the submarines and their crews, but then the submarines were lost in bad weather. Farther north, they tried again with a bigger kind of midget submarine, and this time two got through all her elaborate defences and damaged her badly under water. Naval aircraft attacked her from carriers, and air force bombers from bases in Russia. She was always under repair and seldom fit for sea. Towards the end, she could not even go back to Germany for the major refit she needed. Finally, in November 1944, the air force hit her with bombs of twelve thousand pounds, and she capsized at her moorings and sank upside down in shallow water. After twenty-five years, the old argument had been resolved.

Already the Italian fleet had surrendered and was under British command in Malta, and when the *Tirpitz* was gone there was nothing more for the big British ships to do in Europe. The newest and best were sent to the Far East to join the American fleet against the Japanese, where a full-scale naval war was still being fought among the old Spice Islands. The Americans did not seem to need or want any help at first, but by tact and insistence British admirals managed to make themselves and their ships acceptable: and the last actions of British battleships and carriers were fought as a Task Force under supreme American command, before the first atomic bomb went down.

But in 1944 the English Channel itself was the scene of the biggest and most complicated of all operations in naval history: the invasion of Normandy. Five thousand two hundred and ninety-eight ships were assembled for this occasion, by far the largest fleet that ever sailed for any purpose, in any century or on any sea.

Within a few weeks of being thrown out of Europe at Dunkirk, the British had started to make their plans to go back, and since the improvised defences of 1940 they had made gigantic preparations for attack. The navy again was in its ancient role of putting armies ashore; it had done it already in North Africa and Sicily, and on the Italian mainland at Salerno and Anzio.

In all these operations, the British and United States navies worked together, as they did in the east; and while the Americans were much the larger force in the east, the British were much the larger in Europe. For Normandy, the armies were equally divided, and so were the air forces, but 80 per cent of the ships were British; not that it mattered much which navy they belonged to. The co-operation was a healthy experience, certainly for the British and perhaps for the Americans too. The British had many foreign ships and crews among them, French, Dutch, Norwegians and Poles who had escaped from Europe; but never since the early eighteenth century, before the Americans declared their independence, had they fought in such close combination with a navy as strong as their own. Both navies were shocked, or pretended to be, at the customs, manners and equipment of the other. But it was certainly time the British discovered there could be other ways of doing things at sea, which might sometimes seem to them bizarre or inartistic, but undeniably worked. And it was not a bad time to remember that most of the history of the British at sea was American history too.

In this tremendous armada there was every element of naval power, excepting aircraft-carriers. Here were six battleships, two monitors and twenty-three cruisers to bombard the coast of France, seventy-nine destroyers for protection and closer bombardment, 4100 troopships and landing craft, seventy-two old ships to be sunk as breakwaters, tugs towing enormous concrete sections of artificial harbours. The whole fleet was led by two midget submarines to act as markers, and by 350 minesweepers to clear and buoy ten lanes from coast to coast.

It is easy to list the numbers on paper now, but nobody ever saw this fleet as a whole. Some soldiers after a miserable seasick night were inspired, encouraged and astonished to see the strength of the force that was there to support them, but all they could see was only a fraction of it. The most privileged view was again from the headlands of southern England where people had stood to watch the Spanish Armada. But now there were no idle sightseers, as there had been then: only the coastguards who for the past four years had felt they stood on the very edge of the ordered world, looking out on a sea more menacing than it had ever seemed since Anglo-Saxons anxiously watched for Vikings.

From St Albans Head, which had the last glimpse of the *Victory* hull down on her way to Trafalgar, they still saw the cliffs of the Isle of Wight to the eastward, little changed, and to the west the wide sweep of Weymouth Bay and beyond it the distant outline of Portland Bill. The few men who were there that summer of 1944 looked down on a pageant more splendid in English eyes than had ever been seen from this ancient watchpost. The harbour at Portland, empty so long, had slowly filled with ships until the whole surface looked black. Then it overflowed, and the seventeen miles of Weymouth Bay began to fill. Day and night, a screen of destroyers steamed back and forth across the mouth of the bay, while ever more and more ships came to anchor, until their number could not possibly be counted.

And on the morning of the 5th of June, the fleet put to sea. Close under the cliffs of the headland, the landing craft passed by; the men on top could see the troops on board. Beyond them, line after line of tank landing craft were escorted by motor launches. There were armed trawlers and ocean tugs, and far out and ahead the echelons of minesweepers. Destroyers took up their stations out to sea, French, British and American cruisers, tank landing ships and infantry transports carrying small landing craft on davits; and on the horizon, coming up from the west, the battleships and monitors and heavy cruisers. Then in the east, more landing craft and escorts emerged from Poole, and in the far distance another separate fleet steamed out of the Solent and turned south in silhouette against the cliffs of the island. Before evening, the last of the ships had gone, beyond the southern horizon, and the sea was empty again.

The ports where this fleet had grown, the landmarks it passed, the seas it crossed and even the beaches where it put its passengers ashore to fight their way back into Europe, had all been the scenes of previous endeavours of the British on the sea; and this was the climax of them all. The ships had come out from the Clyde where the first Cunarders were built; from the Bristol Channel, where Cabot set out to discover north America; from Plymouth, the home port for more adventure on the sea than any other in the world; from Devon towns where the streets had run red with the pirates' Bordeaux wine; from Poole where the British navy in King Alfred's time had fought its first battle and run all its ships aground; from Southampton where the fleet had been gathered for Agincourt. And the whole host of ships converged at a rendezvous south of the Isle of Wight which was given the code-name of Piccadilly Circus: it was exactly the place where the Spanish Armada lay becalmed and Lord Howard knighted Frobisher and Hawkins.

And across on the other side, the fleets of landing craft let down their ramps on sandy shores the British had known before. Between the beaches the Americans called Omaha and Utah is the mouth of the River Vire, where William the Conqueror's fleet was assembled for the last successful invasion in the opposite direction. On Utah beach itself, when the Americans waded ashore in the dawn of 6th June, it was not the first time it had happened. In July 1346 another British fleet lay off that desolate stretch of dunes, just to the north of the American bridgehead, with an identical purpose. It carried King Edward III, who had fought the Battle of Sluys in his cogs, and his son the Black Prince, his earls and barons, four thousand men of arms and ten thousand archers armed with the English longbow which astonished and routed the French that August when they met at Crecy. Perhaps it was chance, or perhaps a staff officer who knew his history, that sent the British cruiser *Black Prince* with American battleships to bombard that very spot. And perhaps the American infantry, stumbling ashore through the waves, overloaded with their own accoutrements, could have felt a flicker of sympathy across six hundred years for one man in that other invasion who did the same thing in armour. 'The kyng yssued out of his shyppe,' the chronicler Froissart wrote, 'and the first fote that he sette on the grounde, he fell so rudely, that the blode brast out of his nose. The knyghtes that were aboute hym toke hym up and sayde, Sir, for Goddessake entre agayn into your shyppe, and come nat a land this day, for this is but an yvell signe for us. Than the kyng answered quickely and sayd, Wherfore, this is a good token for me, for the land desyreth to have me. Of the whyche answere, all his men were right joyfull. So that day and night the kyng lodged on the sandes, and in the meane tyme dyscharged the shyppes of their horses and other bagages.'

371

It had happened before, but one can hardly imagine it will ever happen again. Looking back from an age when whole cities, or whole fleets, could be destroyed by a single atomic weapon, D-Day and Crecy seem almost equally archaic.

Once more the navy had defended Britain and the ideas the British valued – for fifteen months alone, and then in concert with the navy of the United States. At the end of the war it had grown again, in spite of all its losses, to nearly 3500 fighting ships, including no less than fifty-seven aircraft-carriers, and well over a quarter of a million men. But this time the British were even more impoverished by the effort of the war. Fighting ships were becoming more and more expensive and complicated. And besides, naval power was no longer any use without an equivalent power in aircraft and ballistic missiles, which needed an even bigger reserve of industrial wealth. After the first war, the British had had to accept equality with the United States; after the second they could not think of competing.

And the British had survived with a change of heart. Some of them looked back nostalgically to the centuries of power, but a good many felt they had grown up, beyond the age when power seems desirable; they were tired, too diffident in their opinions to want to impose them any more on other people, and doubtful of the morality of some of the things their ancestors did so proudly.

So, although the merchant navy remained and grew again, ship after ship of the fighting navy was scrapped or sold. The last of the battleships went to the breakers in 1959. The last of the carriers was due to go in the 1970s – the last *Ark Royal*, still bearing the name of Lord Howard's Elizabethan flagship. The long ages of naval grandeur had come to an end. The navy spent its remaining budget on submarines, some nuclear powered and some with Polaris missiles, and on anti-submarine ships and ships for amphibious warfare. It was a logical choice, except perhaps the Polaris submarines, which some people argued could never be more than a small addition to the American deterrent; and that particular choice was political rather than naval. The drastic reduction in size had a compensation: it was a total break with the past. The Admiralty recovered from its old conservatism, and all the inventive skill of the navy was put into new economical designs and new equipment: new frigates, for example, which packed more punch than old battleships. The navy had to be small, and that was all the more reason to make it efficient.

With the British survival, the idea of Pax Britannica also survived. The concept had outlived the power, and was ready to be renewed when the fighting stopped. In 1949, when an American admiral was appointed the first supreme commander of NATO's forces in the Atlantic, there were a few rumblings of outraged pride in Parliament; but all the British could do was contribute a fleet to serve under him, and on the whole they knew they should be glad it was somebody else's turn to take the thankless responsibility of power. Sovereignty of the seas, for what it now was worth, had been inherited by the United States.

It was not a bad inheritance. It is the fashion now to criticise the rule of the British on land in their imperial days, but prejudice apart, it is hard to find fault with what they did at sea. They conceived that sovereignty of the seas was a trust, and should not be exclusive or repressive – that at sea humanity came first, and the national flag it flew was less important. If Britain had not imagined the seas should be free, and commanded them long enough to ensure it, who knows what national rivalries might have divided them? Nations would surely have drawn jealous frontiers across them like the land. In centuries past, Spain had claimed the exclusive ownership of the Pacific, and Portugal of most of the south Atlantic. The British themselves before that had claimed the narrow seas. The same thing might very easily have happened all over the world in the age of steam.

But the opposite happened. Every yard of habitable land on earth has a national owner, but the seas beyond coastal waters belong to everyone now, and everyone has an equal right to sail across them in peace wherever he will. The rules and customs the British devised are observed because they were just; and it seems so natural that people forget it is not an ancient right of mankind; it is a freedom that needed one seafaring race with the wisdom to begin it a century and a half ago. No doubt there are other nations that would have done the same if they had had the power; but the British did it, and freedom is the best memorial to any age of supremacy.

Freedom of the seas even now should not be taken for granted. There are always new uses for the sea that threaten it. At present, off-shore oil-fields and intensive fishing are the greatest temptations to national claims of ownership, and no doubt there will be others in the next decades. No navy now can protect this kind of freedom; it can only be guarded against encroachment by international vigilance and wisdom.

Sea captains now can find their precise positions by radio, talk to the shore from anywhere, see their landfalls by radar and their depths by echo-sounder, and steer their ships with nobody at the helm. Sometimes it seems to make it all too easy. But the British are still to the fore in these maritime inventions, and it would be stupid to cherish the dangers they avert. When Francis Chichester sailed alone round the world and became a national hero, some people laughed at the British for living in the past: Russians and Americans were doing the same thing in spacecraft. And yet, while the seas are free, there will probably always be people, not only British, who are enchanted by them, however far other people may venture into space. Good seamanship can still be a pleasant art, although its crowning excitement is gone for ever: the solitude of sailing oceans unknown to man, and sighting uncharted shores.

ACKNOWLEDGEMENTS

The publisher is grateful to the copyright owners for permission to reproduce the following illustrations:
Jacket *by kind permission of the National Maritime Museum, London.*

BETWEEN PAGES 40-41
Curraghs, *photo Bord Failte Eireann;* Bayeux Tapestry, *Town of Bayeux, photo Giraudon;* Carved pew ends, *Victoria and Albert Museum, photo Crown Copyright;* Fifteenth Century navigation, *Society of Antiquaries, London, photo Eileen Tweedy.*

BETWEEN PAGES 88-89
English ships, *Trustees of the British Museum;* The Armada, *The Worshipful Society of Apothecaries of London, photo Eileen Tweedy;* Elizabeth I, *by courtesy of F. Tyrwhitt-Drake, photo R. B. Fleming & Co.*

BETWEEN PAGES 136-137
Drake, *National Portrait Gallery, London;* Howard of Effingham, *National Maritime Museum, (Greenwich Hosp. Coll.);* Sixteenth Century Galley, Shipwrights, *by courtesy of the Master and Fellows of Magdalene College, Cambridge.*

BETWEEN PAGES 184-185
Eskimos, *Trustees of the British Museum;* Sovereign of the Seas, *National Maritime Museum, London;* Charles II, *by kind permission of the Governors of Christ's Hospital.*

BETWEEN PAGES 216-217
Pett, *National Portrait Gallery, London;* Pepys, 'Royal Prince', The Royal Observatory, *National Maritime Museum, London.*

BETWEEN PAGES 248-249
Ships at Calcutta, *Foreign & Commonwealth Office, photo Eileen Tweedy;* The 'Resolution' and 'Adventure' (*on loan from Min. of Def., Navy*), Chronometers, *National Maritime Museum, London.*

BETWEEN PAGES 264-265
Nelson boarding (Greenwich Hosp. Coll.), The Bounty, Sailors Carousing, *National Maritime Museum, London.*

375

Acknowledgements

BETWEEN PAGES 280-281

Nelson, *National Maritime Museum, London;* Trafalgar, *by kind permission of The United Services & Royal Aero Club, photo Eileen Tweedy;* Naval Uniforms, *photo Eileen Tweedy.*

BETWEEN PAGES 312-313

Brunel, 'Great Eastern', *Brunel University Library;* River scene, *National Maritime Museum, London;* Gunboat, *The Parker Gallery, London.*

BETWEEN PAGES 328-329

'Great Eastern', *National Maritime Museum, London, photo Michael Holford Library;* 'Cutty Sark' & SS 'Britannia', *Royal Society of Marine Artists, photo Eileen Tweedy;* Spithead, *National Maritime Museum, London, photo Eileen Tweedy;* George V, by kind permission of *United Services and Royal Aero Club, photo Eileen Tweedy.*

BETWEEN PAGES 344-345

Fisher, (Greenwich Hosp. Coll.) *National Maritime Museum, London;* HMS *Dreadnought, Imperial War Museum;* Arctic Convoy, The *Bismarck, National Maritime Museum, London;* HMS *Ocean* and HMS *Prince of Wales, Imperial War Museum.*

BETWEEN PAGES 360-361

HMS *Superb*, Dunkirk, The Quick Turnround, *Imperial War Museum, photo Eileen Tweedy.*

Picture Research by Marian Berman.

INDEX

Index

Index

DAVID HOWARTH

David Howarth was born in London and lives in the South of England. After graduation from Cambridge University he joined the British Broadcasting Corporation. In the early part of World War II he was a radio war correspondent. Then he served in the Navy, in ranks from Seaman to Lieutenant Commander, and became involved with smuggling saboteurs and weapons into occupied Norway, an experience that provided the materials for his first two factual books, ACROSS TO NORWAY *(1952) and* WE DIE ALONE *(1955). His later books include* THE SLEDGE PATROL *(1957),* D DAY *(1959),* THE DESERT KING *(1964),* PANAMA *(1966),* WATERLOO: DAY OF BATTLE *(1968) and* TRAFALGAR: THE NELSON TOUCH *(1969). He keeps his own boat on the river Medway, where H.M.S.* Victory *was built and Nelson learned to sail.*

Places mentioned in the text